THE JAZZ
HANDBOOK

G.K. HALL
PERFORMING
ARTS
HANDBOOKS

THE JAZZ HANDBOOK

Barry McRae

G.K. Hall & Co.
Boston

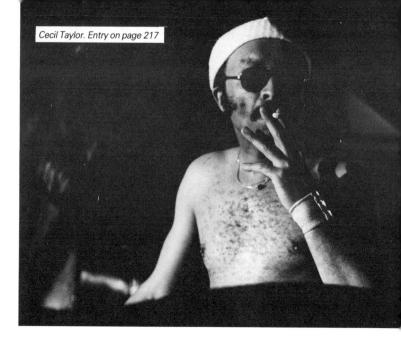

Cecil Taylor. Entry on page 217.

First published in 1987 by Longman Group UK Limited, Longman House, Burnt Mill, Harlow, Essex CM20 2JE, England and Associated Companies throughout the world.

Compiled and edited for and on behalf of Longman Group UK Limited by Red Herring Publishing Ltd., 83-84 Long Acre, London WC2E 9NG, England

Published in the United States by G.K. Hall & Co., 70 Lincoln St., Boston, Massachusetts, 02111.

10 9 8 7

Library of Congress Cataloging-in-Publication Data

McRae, Barry.
     The jazz handbook / Barry McRae.
       p. cm.—(G.K. Hall performing arts series)
     "First published in 1987 by Longman Group UK Limited"—T.p. verso.
     Includes bibliographical references and discographies.
     ISBN 0-8161-9096-8   ISBN 0-8161-1828-0 (pbk)
       1. Jazz music—Bio-bibliography. 2. Jazz musicians—Biography. 3. Jazz music—Discography. I. Title. II. Series.
     ML105.M455   1989
     781.65'092'2—dc20   89-77757
     [B]   CIP
                                                                                      MN
The paper used in this publication meets the minimum requirements of American National Standard for Information Sciences—Permanence of Paper for Printed Library Materials. ANSI Z39.48-1984.   ∞™
MANUFACTURED IN THE UNITED STATES OF AMERICA

CONTENTS

For my daughter, Fiona.

TO ALL of the musicians who spared time to answer questions, I would like to say a special thank you. I am also particularly pleased to have had David Redfern as the main photographer on the team, Tony Middleton as the indefatigable discographical expert and Ron Cunnington as the designer responsible for the 'shape' of the book.

Special mentions are due to CBS, Affinity and Island Records for the provision of vital recordings and to collector and friend Graham Fowler for the loan of other specialised items; to Doug Dobell for excusing my clutter in his famous record shop, and to stalwarts Brian Peerless and Leslie Fancourt for their knowledge and advice. For essential extra information, I also owe much to Alan Balfour, Nick Carnac, Reg Cooper, Charles Crump, Brian Davis, Dave Illingworth, Hazel Miller, Howard Rye, Ray Smith (Ray's Shop) and Neil Wyatt.

I was grateful to refer to *Down Beat, Jazz Journal International* and *Jazz Monthly*, and to such important books as Leonard Feather's *Encyclopedia Of Jazz*, Feather and Ira Gitler's *Encyclopedia Of Jazz In The Seventies*, Val Wilmer's *As Serious As Your Life* and John Chilton's *Who's Who Of Jazz*.

It was an advantage to have as sounding boards the intellect and straight jazz thinking of friends like Michael Bourne (*Down Beat*), Jim Dow, Charles Fox, Peter Gamble (*Jazz Journal International*), Lee Jeske (*Cash Box, New York Post*), Art Lange (*Down Beat*), Jack Massarik (*The Guardian*), Richard Palmer (*Jazz Journal International*) and Peter Symes.

Finally, I would like to say a special thanks to Philip Dodd of Longman for his support, to Peter Herring for his unstinting editorial assistance, and to my wife Sylvia who, with me, listened to hours of jazz, and who put the whole manuscript through our word processor and weighed in with invaluable suggestions.

Thanks also to Paul Acket, Juul Anthonissen, Silvana Benedetti, Heidi Boulton, Rex Finch, Lynn Hickerson, Nicolas le François, Alison McGowan, Mark Miller, Bo Scherman, Tony Williams.

Who needs another jazz book? Well, probably no one – unless that book can help you enjoy the real thing and encourage the reader to buy records and spend time in clubs listening to live music. Barry McRae and David Redfern (the main photographer in this book) have spent enough time in my club to have gained some idea about the music and, as a result, have produced a book with strong opinions and great photographs.

Had *The Jazz Handbook* been around when I first came on the jazz scene, it might well have helped in my own discovery of jazz. It would certainly have been lighter in terms of bodily wear and tear than travelling, as I did, across the Atlantic to hear the likes of Charlie Parker and Dizzy Gillespie in New York.

It's very gratifying to note the number of players in this book who have appeared at the club. We have played host to the vocal mastery of Sarah Vaughan, the dexterity of Oscar Peterson, the avant-garde of Ornette Coleman and Cecil Taylor, as well as the effortless grace of Zoot Sims. Few escaped our net, and then only for the best reasons. For instance, Freddie Keppard wouldn't play in public in case he was copied, Fats Waller didn't like the food and Benny Goodman objected to the P.A. Stan Getz didn't speak the same language, but came anyway, and the Woody Herman Orchestra performed even though it required them to sit on each other's heads.

There are no such reservations in this book and I can recommend its healthy attitude toward even the most prejudiced reader. It is divided into decades so that the purchaser can cut out the styles that most offend. For the tidy-minded, it is best balanced by believing that jazz either started or ended in 1949. That way you only have to cut the book in half.

Ronnie Scott

Jazz can often seem inaccessible, particularly to the newcomer, and it can be frustrating to try and develop an initial interest in the music. This is perhaps due to the fact that jazz has tended to receive less media exposure than many other forms of music, and as a result sampling the broad range of jazz styles in any coherent way becomes a long and erratic journey.

The Jazz Handbook is a practical guidebook designed to make that journey easier. Within a basic framework of 200 entries covering major musicians and groups, the Handbook suggests new directions to take and connections to make. Its job is to cut out much of the groundwork needed to build up an overview of jazz, but to allow you nonetheless to create a personal network of knowledge and taste. The possible routes are clearly signposted; you choose whether or not

to pursue them. And along the way, the Handbook provides a back-up of hard facts and information. *The Jazz Handbook* is meant to be used: it is an active reference book. We want you to act on the suggestions and recommendations it contains; go out and listen to the music.

The entries

At the core of the Handbook are the main entries, which have been selected to provide a wide spread of starting-points: the Handbook is not intended to be a comprehensive encyclopedia, but rather a stimulus and a springboard for further exploration.

All entries cross-refer to other main entries, and of course also refer to a much larger outer circle of names, so that the network ultimately reaches more than 1000 musicians, all indexed

TO USE THE JAZZ HANDBOOK

at the back of the book. Use the index to make the Handbook work for you: if Wayne Shorter's recordings with Miles Davis have sparked an interest, look up Shorter in the index – it will refer you to the main Weather Report entry plus all other entries in which he is mentioned.

The entries have been grouped into seven chapters covering the Pre-Twenties and then each decade through to the Seventies/Eighties. Clearly many musicians straddle decades, but we have placed each musician in the decade of their greatest initial impact. Three giants of jazz have two entries, such is the length and consistency of their career: Louis Armstrong, Count Basie and Duke Ellington. A double-page spread opens each chapter with a summary of the salient trends and features of the era.

Main entries contain the following elements:
1 A block of **biographical information**, which can include date and place of birth/death, instrument(s), recording career dates, and nickname where relevant.
2 The **main critique** sets the musician or group in context, identifying the significant aspects of their work, their impact on jazz, and what to listen for in their music. References to other main entries are picked out in **bold**, and references to tracks or albums in the Listening section (see 5 below) are indicated by an arrow symbol (>).
3 **Lineage**: the heart of the Handbook's network of connections, naming influences on the musicians, and who they in turn influenced.
4 The **Media** section gives pointers to other background material available on the musician or group: for example, books by or about their life and work (with original publication date where known) and film/TV appearances and composing.
5 **Listening**: a critical selection of representative recordings which relate back to the arrow symbols (>) in the main critique. Discographical information is provided throughout: because the Handbook is a practical guide, we have given the latest available versions. Some historically important albums may be deleted, but obtainable either through

secondhand record stores or the constant re-issuing of deleted albums.

All catalogue numbers given refer to the LP format of the recording. However, many jazz recordings are also available on pre-recorded cassette and a fast-increasing number of titles are appearing in the compact disc medium.

The Databank

Following the main chapters is a Databank of additional information, including:
○ The **record label** section introducing labels which have documented their era, helped shape jazz styles, or given the lead in recording techniques.
○ A **glossary** listing jazz-related terms in the Handbook which may require clarification.
○ **Jazz books**: includes those titles which will instruct the reader, and also provide an additional entrée to the jazz world.
○ A country-by-country listing of **information sources**: jazz magazines, or publications which regularly carry guides to current events or gigs. This is more effective than attempting to reflect the shifting schedules of individual clubs and venues. Major festivals with contact points and usual time of year are listed together with other resources (for example, jazz video companies).
○ **Index**: an A-Z of all people/groups named in the Handbook. This is where the journey begins.

The Jazz Handbook is the first title in a series of Longman Handbooks exploring the performing and visual arts. See the cover for further details.

Pictured top left, one of jazz's converts – Billy Cobham. See entry on page 233

THE PRE-TWENTIES

JAZZ history has been reasonably well documented by the gramophone. Although loaded in favour of certain geographical areas, there has been enough recorded evidence from the early twenties onwards to offer today's listeners a chance to get to know the music of an era and to trace the way in which it has evolved.

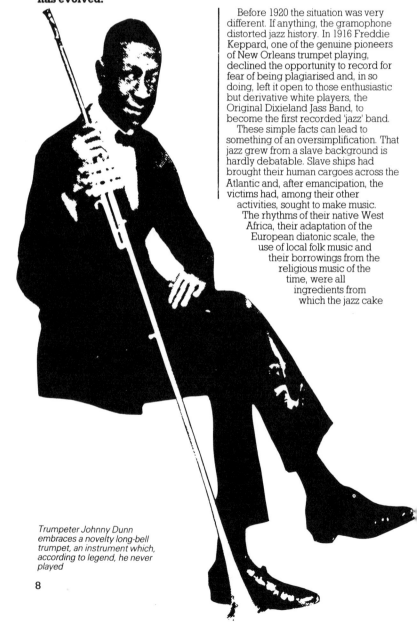

Before 1920 the situation was very different. If anything, the gramophone distorted jazz history. In 1916 Freddie Keppard, one of the genuine pioneers of New Orleans trumpet playing, declined the opportunity to record for fear of being plagiarised and, in so doing, left it open to those enthusiastic but derivative white players, the Original Dixieland Jass Band, to become the first recorded 'jazz' band.

These simple facts can lead to something of an oversimplification. That jazz grew from a slave background is hardly debatable. Slave ships had brought their human cargoes across the Atlantic and, after emancipation, the victims had, among their other activities, sought to make music. The rhythms of their native West Africa, their adaptation of the European diatonic scale, the use of local folk music and their borrowings from the religious music of the time, were all ingredients from which the jazz cake

Trumpeter Johnny Dunn embraces a novelty long-bell trumpet, an instrument which, according to legend, he never played

was cooked. West Indian music spiced it further and, at least in New Orleans, there was the influence of the French balladeer.

It was music without a name, without one true home but very much the property of everyone. Certainly, the music that would later be thought of as jazz was performed in the southern states of America some ten or twenty years before the turn of the century. With equal certainty, it can be said that it was not totally centred around New Orleans as has been often suggested. There is much evidence of improvised music in Texas, Mississippi, Florida and Tennessee as well as in urban districts like Baltimore, St Louis and Oklahoma City. At that stage, the music was still thought of as ragtime, whether it was played in pure piano form or featured by a parade or dance band.

New Orleans was perhaps the most important centre. Storyville, its red-light district, employed piano professors and appropriate bands but the whole town was alive with music. From colourful funerals to secret societies, music became a vital part of everyone's life. The prestige to be gained by the leading musicians was tremendous and all of them had their own following, the groupies of the day.

The outstanding trumpet players were especially feted and were crowned unofficial 'kings' of the town. Buddy Bolden was perhaps the first to be so acclaimed but he was rapidly superseded by Freddie Keppard, who in turn gave way to Joe 'King' Oliver. The extrovert musical style of the city was perhaps a contributory factor to the status they enjoyed, since the trumpeter was very much the leader of the collective playing of the band. The lead he played was powerful and straightforward and he left the musical decoration to the clarinettist and the punctuation to the trombone.

This was the basis of what became known as the New Orleans style, even if there were permutations of the formula. Two trumpets were sometimes used, and saxophones were introduced for added colour; but, in seeing the trumpet-trombone-clarinet front line as a perfect instrumental form, the pioneer critics had stumbled on a genuine truism. Later in jazz history, we were to hear the strict organisation of the swing

orchestra, the fine balance of the bebop quintet, the two saxophone free-form quartets and the powerful octets of the seventies. None equalled the formal perfection of the New Orleans ensemble style. It ensured its own rhythmic buoyancy, evidenced that its own creative processes could be applied to almost any material and, most importantly, gave a formula for collective jazz-playing that has never been equalled.

An area of parallel development, but one that also had important repercussions, was that of the ragtime piano. Known up to the end of the nineteenth century as 'jig piano' it blossomed in towns like Sedalia and St Louis in Missouri, and in the hands of men like Scott Joplin, Tom Turpin and James Scott became an art form in its own right. In performance it was not improvised, but brought to the jig bands a form of syncopation that advanced hand-in-hand with jazz.

Listening to the rigid and upright timing of men such as Johnny Dunn, Freddie Keppard and the like, it is easy to imagine how the ragtime bands of the pre-twenties sounded. The term jazz was not in use and in a way it was appropriate that it was not. Classic jazz and its sinuous rubato was just around the corner but the recorded evidence of these men, who stayed on in music into the recording times, bears out the strong influence that piano ragtime had on the bands of the time.

Storyville's shutdown as an area for legalised prostitution in 1917 saw the demise of New Orleans as the leading jazz city. It disseminated jazz skills even more and shifted the emphasis of the music to Chicago, Dallas, Memphis, Kansas City and New York. Jazz, however, was now ready for the gramophone, although it was ironic that the only band to record before 1920 should be the all-white Original Dixieland Jass Band.

Eubie Blake

Born: 7th February 1883/Baltimore, Maryland, USA
Died: 12th February 1983/New York City, NY, USA
Instrument: Piano, composer
Recording Career: 1917-1982

IT WAS in 1915 that James Hubert 'Eubie' Blake met Noble Sissle and in 1919 they formed the Dixie Duo, a vaudeville team that became famous throughout the world. Its connections with jazz were slight: Blake's sprightly piano never actually progressed beyond a personal adaptation of ragtime and Sissle sang in a theatrical manner with little sense of emotional involvement. *Broadway Blues* or *Doggone Struttin' Fool* >**1** are excellent examples of their natural rapport and of the joie de vivre that permeated their music in the early twenties. Jazz of a high order it was not and, throughout the twenties and thirties, Blake's main claim to fame was in his co-composing of several successful shows with Sissle.

They toured together entertaining the troops during the Second World War but in 1946 Blake virtually retired. Amazingly, he made a comeback in the New Orleans Festival of 1969 at the age of eighty-six and continued to make highly successful appearances at such events for the rest of his life. A remarkable feature of his playing now was the adoption of stronger jazz elements and, although his vaudeville ties remained the more obvious, works like *Charleston Rag* >**2** and the like showed that he had been listening to jazz development in his later years. He died one week after his 100th birthday.

Lineage

Blake emerged with little-known pianists like Big Eyes Wilber, One Leg Willie Joseph, Will Turk and Big Jimmy Green. In his way he paved the way for the stride giants and **James P. Johnson**, Luckey Roberts and Willie 'The Lion' Smith are reputed to have listened to him at length.

Media

Eubie, a show in his honour opened New York 1978. A book, *Reminiscing With Sissle And Blake* (1973) was written by Robert Kimball and William Bolcom.

Listening

1 Sissle And Blake
Noble Sissle & Eubie Blake/Stash ST 129
2 91 Years Young
Eubie Blake/RCA(F) FXM1 7157

Johnny Dunn

Born: 19th February 1897/Memphis, Tennessee, USA
Died: 20th August 1937/Paris, France
Instrument: Trumpet
Recording Career: 1920 (1919?)-1928

BEFORE **Louis Armstrong**'s 1924 arrival in New York, Johnny Dunn was the undisputed king of the Harlem trumpet players and may well have begun recording as early as 1919. Recordings from 1921, like *Birmingham Blues* >**1**, tell of a man strongly influenced by ragtime, even if his famous Jazz Hounds were a rather pedestrian band. Their timing relied firmly on the beat, but this somewhat stiff syncopation was normal at that time. On the credit side Dunn was a powerful player, who disguised the strangely military aspect of his style when working with the blues. Nevertheless, one could certainly be forgiven for thinking that a title like *Four O'Clock Blues* >**1**, a studio recording, had actually been made on the hoof as marching jazz.

Dunn spent many of his later years in Europe, mainly in Paris, Amsterdam and Rotterdam. He went there originally with the touring revue, *Blackbirds Of 1926*, liked the life and after spells back in the States, settled in Europe. As war clouds began to gather in 1937, he died in Paris.

Lineage

He originally worked with, and learnt his trade from violinist/bandleader (and opportunist publisher) W. C. Handy in Memphis. His clipped style, with its somewhat cliché-ridden solo line, attracted few imitators outside his

Eubie Blake

immediate circle, and it was fascinating to hear that later work with **Jelly Roll Morton >2** showed that he himself had been affected by the more modern phraseology of the **Louis Armstrong** school.

Listening

1 Original Jazz Hounds
Johnny Dunn/VJM VLP 11
2 Doc Cook & Johnny Dunn
VJM VLP 27

Scott Joplin

**Born: 24th November 1868/
Texarkana, Texas, USA
Died: 1st April 1917/New York City,
NY, USA
Instruments: Piano, composer
Recording Career: None except piano
rolls**

WHEN Marvin Hamlisch used *The Entertainer >1* as the background music for the film *The Sting* he was guilty of an anachronism. The film was set in the twenties while the rag he chose was published in 1902 and belonged very firmly to that era. It was written by Scott Joplin, unquestionably the most famous of all the ragtime composers and himself an accomplished pianist. He was also a man of much wider talents; he played cornet in Sedalia, Missouri in the 1890s and also worked in a vocal quartet.

Joplin was certainly not the mystical originator of ragtime, as legend has it, but he brought to the form greater compositional talents than anyone else. He sold his first composition in 1895 and also cut piano rolls to document his own performances. By their very construction, rolls allow more intricate parts to be added, but recordings made of Joplin >1-3 do give the impression of authenticity. The precise syncopations of his right hand lent a dandified air, while his left hand acted as a somewhat staid prop. In his performances, however, the strong melody lines were there to disarm the listener and camouflage the music's faintly pedantic, rhythmic stance.

Sadly, Joplin despised ragtime's sporting house (a euphemism for brothel) origins and sought to make the music respectable. He wrote his first

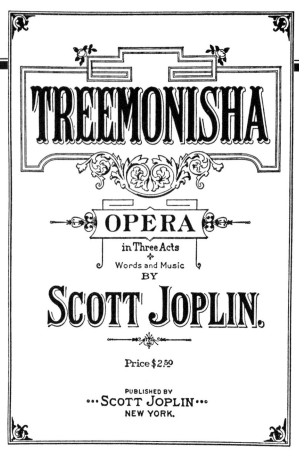

opera, *A Guest Of Honour* in 1903 and his second *Treemonisha* in 1911. Neither succeeded commercially and the failure of the latter is often cited as the reason for his personal decline. It was given only one performance in his lifetime, made little musical impact, and presaged a period of depression that finally led to the composer's insanity.

The mighty Joplin finished his life in an asylum, but had written rags such as *Original Rags, Maple Leaf Rag, The Cascades, Fig Leaf Rag* and *Euphonic Sounds* that became considered as classics of the genre. In the seventies, a reminder was given by Joshua Rifkin who recorded many Joplin compositions >**4** and played them, he claimed, as the master intended.

Lineage

Joplin followed ragtime pioneers such as Tom Turpin (rated by some the greatest of ragtime players), Louis Chauvin and James Scott but did as much as anyone to give ragtime a vernacular of its own. He was a tremendous influence not only on men like **Eubie Blake** and **Jelly Roll Morton** but also on the Harlem school of stride pianists (**James P. Johnson**, Willie 'The Lion' Smith, Abba Labba, **Fats Waller**) and more obscure but reputedly highly talented piano professors such as Jack The Bear, Fats Harris and The Beetle (Stephen Henderson).

Media

Joplin wrote an instruction book, *School Of Ragtime* in 1908; *They All Played Ragtime* (1966) by Rudi Blesh discusses his life and career at length. Music used in films *The Sting* (1973), *Pretty Baby* (1978).

Listening

1 The Entertainer
Scott Joplin/Biograph BLP 1013 Q
2 Ragtime
Scott Joplin/Biograph BLP 1010 Q

3 Scott Joplin Vol 2
Biograph BLP 1008 Q
4 Joshua Rifkin/Scott Joplin
Joshua Rifkin/EMI EMD 5534

Freddie Keppard

Born: 27th February 1890/New Orleans, Louisiana, USA
Died: 15th July 1933/Chicago, Illinois, USA
Instrument: Cornet
Recording Career: 1923-1928

LEGEND HAS IT that, as a member of the Original Creole Orchestra, Keppard could have been the first jazz cornettist on record. The facts are that the Creoles made a test pressing of *Tack 'Em Down* for Victor in December 1918, but whether they had turned down a similar opportunity in 1916, some months before the **Original Dixieland Jass Band**'s first date, is open to speculation.

Similar doubt surrounds the contention that Keppard was unofficially crowned 'King' of New Orleans horn men after the demise of Buddy Bolden and before the emergence of **King Oliver**. What is certain is that, in 1914, he became co-leader of the Original Creole Orchestra and played with the group throughout its five-year life.

In 1920 he worked briefly with King Oliver but, apart from spells with Ollie Powers and Erskine Tate, Keppard spent most of the twenties in Doc Cooke's band. His powerful lead on *Hot Tamale Man* >**1** and judicious breaks on *Brown Sugar* >**1** show him as the strong man in Cooke's powerful twelve-piece orchestra and, although his playing could be somewhat stiff, the solo on *Messing Around* >**2** displayed good improvisational skills. As a cornettist, Keppard was very much of the ragtime era. His tone was full, his timing metronomically on-beat and his lead playing genuinely assertive.

In the hurly-burly of discographical research, many indifferent, small group performances have been attributed to him. In fact, he made very few combo

recordings in Chicago, although the 1927 *It Must Be The Blues* >**2**, with Jasper Taylor, and the 1926 *Stockyard Strut* >**2**, with his own Jazz Cardinals, contain fine work. On the former, in particular, his blues-tinged tone supported a well-spaced solo and he capped a fine performance with a concise coda. His health began to fail in 1929 and, although there is evidence of him leading a group around that time with pianist Lil Hardin (later second wife to **Louis Armstrong**), he was soon to retire from music. After a lengthy battle with tuberculosis he died in Cook County Hospital, Chicago.

Lineage
Keppard was originally taught by trumpeter Adolphe Alexander but came under the spell of fellow New Orleans men like Buddy Bolden. His own, somewhat staccato, style probably had more influence on the young white Chicagoans than did the more advanced playing of **King Oliver** or **Louis Armstrong**.

Listening
1 Doc Cooke/Johnny Dunn
VJM VLP 27
2 Freddie Keppard
Herwin 101

Jelly Roll Morton

Born: 20th October 1890/New Orleans, Louisiana, USA
Died: 10th July 1941/Los Angeles, California, USA
Instrument: Piano, vocals, composer, arranger
Recording Career: 1923-1940

WHETHER Jelly Roll Morton was picking his way through the minefield of open space in *The Crave* >**1** or scuttling through the multi-noted runs of *Shreveport Stomp* >**2** he was an excellent pianist. This was a central point throughout his career, a career that led him to claim to be the 'creator of jazz' around the turn of the century. Indeed, it was Morton more than any other who transformed the rigidity of

13

ragtime and ushered in the rubato of jazz.

Born Ferdinand Le Menthe (or Lemott – doubt remains about his true surname) in New Orleans, Morton's personality mirrored his creole background. It was inevitably class conscious, and his parents typified that; as patrons of the French opera house, they were horrified to discover that their teenage son was playing piano in the red-light district of the city. In the early 1900s the sporting houses often employed piano 'professors' and Morton was a sought-after performer.

He was much more, however, and it is significant that he wrote *King Porter Stomp* and *New Orleans Blues* in 1902, *Jelly Roll Blues* in 1905 and *Frog-i-more Rag* in 1908. Nevertheless, music was not his only love; he had a taste for elegant ladies and he told Alan Lomax in the book, *Mister Jelly Roll*, that he aspired to be the world's greatest pool player! With this in mind, he spent the years up to 1909 using piano as a decoy occupation while he was hustling pool.

For the next dozen years Morton toured extensively, concentrating on the piano, and including gigs at the important music centres of St Louis, Kansas City, Detroit and Los Angeles. In 1923 he returned to Chicago and over the next five years put his immense stamp on jazz history. In June 1923, he made his recording debut with Paramount but, more significantly, went to the Gennett studios in Richmond one month later in the company of the **New Orleans Rhythm Kings**. The titles he recorded with them have a pleasing sense of organisation but it was his solo piano recordings that were more important.

There were bravura performances like *Grandpa's Spells* and *Wolverine Blues* >**2** which allayed any doubts about his instrumental skills. There were hints of Morton's much loved 'Spanish tinge' on titles such as *Mammamita* and *Tia Juana* >**2**; but, more importantly, the world was introduced to the man as a musical architect.

As the ensuing years were to show, tunes such as *Kansas City Stomps, King Porter Stomp* and *Jelly Roll Blues* were blueprints for later full band performances. Proof positive was given in 1926 when Morton began a series of recordings for Victor that were to become landmarks in jazz history. Here, Morton harnessed the freedom of New Orleans jazz to a highly personalised style and did so without restricting himself. *The Chant* >**3**, **4**, *Doctor Jazz* >**3** and *The Pearls* >**3** were masterpieces of formal organisation, while *Black Bottom Stomp* >**3**, *Grandpa's Spells* >**3**, **4** and *Cannon Ball Blues* >**3**, **4** suggested the wild freedom of New Orleans jazz, with latent power in hand.

Morton's group, appropriately dubbed the Red Hot Peppers, continued to turn out records of a remarkable standard up to 1928. The leader, however, had become conscious of the move away from New Orleans principles and toward bigger bands. His response was to increase the size of his own line-up, a move that did little to enhance his music. The élan of his best work was replaced by an uneasy affectation and the forward-looking idealist became a self-conscious copyist.

Returning to the smaller line-up still produced odd outstanding performances such as *Ponchatrian* >**4** or *Low Gravy* >**5** but the attitude had changed and Morton did not record between 1930 and 1938. Occasionally he led bands, but he had lost most of his money in a business venture.

In 1938 he returned to New York and over a period of three months took time out to tell his life story to musicologist Alan Lomax. They worked together in the Coolidge Auditorium of Washington's Library of Congress and the outcome was a remarkable document >**6**, filling many gaps in our knowledge of pre-recording jazz. The resulting recordings renewed interest in Morton and, in 1939 and 1940, he again fronted a band in the studio. Major figures such as **Sidney Bechet**, Albert Nicholas, **Henry Allen** and Sidney de Paris graced his bands >**7** and much of his old spirit was renewed.

Sadly, Morton's health was failing – a lengthy journey back to California late in 1940 did not help, and in the following year two spells in hospital failed to save

his life. It was left to those that remained to plead the case of a man who claimed to have 'invented jazz single-handed'.

Lineage
Morton was originally inspired by pianist Tony Jackson, but his own brilliant mixture of ragtime and New Orleans jazz affected few pianists as individuals.

Media
The excellent *Mister Jelly Roll* by Alan Lomax published 1950, followed by Laurie Wright's *Mr Jelly Lord* 1980. Played a track in the film *Pretty Baby* (1978). *Wolverine Blues* performed by The World's Greatest Jazz Band in *Interiors* (1978).

Listening
1 New Orleans Memories
  Jelly Roll Morton/Commodore 6 24062 AG
2 The Incomparable 1923/6
  Jelly Roll Morton/Classic Jazz Masters SFP 5507
3 The King Of New Orleans Jazz
  Jelly Roll Morton/RCA International NL 89015
4 The Complete JRM Vol 1/2
  Jelly Roll Morton/RCA Jazz Tribune PM 42405
5 The Complete JRM Vol 7/8
  Jelly Roll Morton/RCA Jazz Tribune PM 45372
6 Library Of Congress
  Jelly Roll Morton/Swaggie S1311-1318
7 The Last Dates
  Jelly Roll Morton/Commodore 6 24546 AG

King Oliver

Born: 11th May 1885/New Orleans, Louisiana, USA
Died: 8th April 1938/Savannah, Georgia, USA
Instrument: Cornet, composer
Recording Career: 1923-1931
Nickname: Bad Eye

IN 1923 Joseph 'King' Oliver led his Creole Jazz Band on some of the greatest New Orleans-style records of all time >**1**, **2**. Shortly before this, he had shocked the jazz world by inviting

come to terms with an alien style and their leader's efforts to make them sound more modern were largely abortive.

Lineage

Oliver studied with cornet player **Bunk Johnson**, one of New Orleans' foremost primitives, and developed an original style that made use of freak, muted effects. This made him the model for men like Tommy Ladnier, **Bubber Miley** and Sidney de Paris, although the true essence of his playing had more far-reaching effects.

Without claiming that he was a stylistic iconoclast to equal **Louis Armstrong**, he did point the brilliant youngster in the right direction and his own importance can be assessed by comparing his solo on *Workingman Blues* >**1**, **2** with Armstrong's on *Chimes Blues* >**2**.

Media

A fine analytical book *King Joe Oliver* (1955) by B. A. L. Rust and Walter C. Allen.

Listening

1 The Okeh Sessions
King Oliver EMI EG 26 0579 1
2 King Oliver And His Creole Jazz Band
VJM VLP 49
3 King Oliver And His Dixie Syncopators Vol 1
Swaggie 821

his protégé, and potentially his greatest rival, **Louis Armstrong**, to play alongside him in Chicago.

These two important facts tend to blur the issue regarding this remarkable player. His three smouldering choruses on *Dippermouth Blues* >**1**, **2** are known by most trumpet and cornet players, and played note-for-note by many. His unison interjections with Armstrong are still talked about in awe and his high octane breaks on *Sweet Lovin' Man* >**1** are jazz at its most spontaneous and most inspired.

This, however, does not put Oliver in his correct chronological position. He had worked with various New Orleans bands before 1912 and shaped up very favourably against all opposition. Obviously, there are no recordings to document this but, judging by his finest work at the age of thirty-eight, it can be assumed that, as a younger man, he was playing better. What does seem certain is that his style did not change radically. By the same token, we know what his contemporaries sounded like. Their stiff ragtime styles were put into sharp relief by his more modern timing and his fine rubato gifts opened the door to the more subtle trumpeters that were to follow.

Oliver's later bands, including the Savannah Syncopators >**3**, were not without merit but they struggled to

Original Dixieland Jass Band

Original Recorded Line-up:
Nick La Rocca (cornet)/Eddie Edwards (trombone)/Larry Shields (clarinet)/Henry Ragas (piano)/Tony Spargo (drums)
Recording Career: 1917-1924

IN JANUARY 1917, the Original Dixieland Jass Band (*sic*) became the first real jazzband to make a gramophone record >**1**. ODJB's original clarinettist, Alcide Nunez, had been replaced by Larry Shields before this date but the replacement proved to be the group's outstanding talent. The music they played was not typical of the best jazz of the day and was firmly based on the vertical rhythms of ragtime. Trumpeter 'Nick' La Rocca proffered a stiff but positive lead and trombonist Eddie Edwards played a form of tailgate trombone that owed much to the circus ring. Only Shields demonstrated a flair for melodic invention but even his sprightly figures on titles like *Jass Band Ball* >**1** and *Sensation Rag* >**1**, **2** were delivered with a cakewalker's gait rather than with the sinuous slide of the soft-shoe shuffler.

Despite their musical limitations, the men of the ODJB were important figures. They brought jazz to Britain and at least provided the world with a recorded model of New Orleans jazz, albeit in a somewhat diluted form. Six years later, the records made away from New Orleans by the major black musicians were destined to present the true picture, but these five young men had played their part in jazz history.

Lineage

La Rocca played with the legendary Papa Laine's Reliance bands in New Orleans, as did Eddie Edwards and the group's drummer Tony Spargo (born Antonio Sbarbaro). Although originally from New Orleans, Shields came to prominence with Tom Brown's Band in Chicago before joining the ODJB. Despite the band's historical position, it exerted little influence on the jazz that followed. Recreations of the group, with men like trumpeter **Wild Bill Davison** and trombonist Brad Gowans, strayed some distance from the original stylistic model.

Media

Appeared in film *The Good-for-nothing* (1917), possibly the first appearance of jazz performers in a fictional film.

Listening

1 Sensation
  ODJB/ASV Living Era AJA 5023
2 ODJB/Louisiana Five
  Fountain FJ 101

ODJB: Left to right, Edwards, Shields, Ragas La Rocca and Spargo

The decade of the twenties saw a greater change of musical direction and of artistic intent than any other in jazz history. It was rightly dubbed the 'jazz age' because, although the Original Dixieland Jass Band had presented the music's credentials to the world in 1917, it was the twenties that saw the flowering of the record industry and, therefore, the establishment of traditions based on fact rather than hearsay.

The First World War had affected the USA to a lesser extent than Europeans had imagined: life in homeland America carried on much as before, and jazz maintained its cosy links with ragtime, as well as continuing to reside in the dance hall, bordello and theatre. New Orleans remained its spiritual home. Although it has rightly been acknowledged that there were other jazz centres, it was players from N.O. that made up the avant-garde of the day and when King Oliver opened at the Lincoln Gardens in 1922, he introduced the *real* New Orleans jazz to a Chicago ready for the experience. Gradually jazz was to centre on Chicago, and on New York.

Bands in the northern cities had still been in the grip of ragtime, with its staccato phraseology and military band timing. New Orleans bands and individual reed men like Jimmie Noone and Sidney Bechet introduced those bands to a looser musical approach, to new dancing rhythms and to the rubato slurs of their local style.

Even more significantly, in 1924 New Orleans' greatest son, Louis Armstrong, joined the prestigious Fletcher Henderson band in New York. Although in a group of more academically-trained men, and unable to read music, Armstrong nevertheless updated the band's image and began to extend the collective concept of New Orleans jazz into a solo art. In so doing, he set jazz on an irreversible path away from the ensemble style of his native city and, by establishing new ground rules, pointed his contemporaries towards a jazz world dominated by soloists.

The New Orleans style, with its clearly-defined roles, perfected the collective band principles. Jazz was now changing rapidly and, although equipped with featured soloists, it had acquired a responsibility to a new generation of dancers and to the vaudeville theatre. There were also more general constraints which created a growing need for greater organisation. Each band faced the new circumstances in its own way but a misguided sense of propriety in some leaders led them toward the sleek ideals of the mundane society bands.

As a result, bands were increasing in size and the time was ripe for the jazz arranger. They came in many guises, but it was not long before Duke Ellington and Don Redman emerged with groups which showed just how

THE TWENTIES

Left: The Duke Ellington Orchestra
Below: An early Ma Rainey record label

well a detailed arrangement could showcase one or more soloist. Initially, this produced only a limited diminution in the importance of the New Orleans influence, and Armstrong's style in particular continued to seep into every fabric of the music and to inspire players on many different instruments.

Only the more obscure of bands were untouched by the man: leaders like Jesse Stone from Dallas (later Kansas), Alphonso Trent, also from Dallas, Zack Whyte from Cincinnati and Bennie Moten from Kansas had a fair stab at achieving the same buoyancy. However, it must be said that the presence of New Orleans men in the bands of Duke Ellington and Luis Russell was a crucial factor in their success. Russell was perhaps the most successful in capturing the spirit of Storyville in his well-organised ten-piece unit; he did so with no loss of vitality and with the quality of his soloists maintained at a very high level.

New York's Harlem, with its Savoy Ballroom and Cotton Club, became the home of such bands but there were parallel musical movements elsewhere. Chicago's South Side catered for listeners who were happy with the old New Orleans ideals and not prepared for more sophisticated ways and larger showbands.

There had also emerged an – at first – independent body of white musicians, thrilled with black jazz, whose attempts to emulate it led to a different and totally original style. Men like cornettist Bix Beiderbecke, saxophonists Frankie Trumbauer and Bud Freeman and drummer Gene Krupa had borrowed from black musicians and arrived at music that was idiosyncratic but still vital.

The Volstead Act, passed over President Wilson's veto, made America a dry nation on 16th January 1920. Prohibition ushered many Americans onto mini-cruises outside the 'three mile limit' and bred illicit 'speakeasies' where patrons could drink specialised 'coffee' and listen to jazz. To an extent, this aspect of the jazz age has been over-emphasised, but there is little doubt that the air of hazardous excitement did have an effect.

In ten years, 'jass' had become jazz: the prancing rhythms of ragtime had been tailored to the more sinuous requirements of a new musical ethic, and America had been presented with a brand of brilliant solo performer. Many of the arrangers who had arrived in the mid-twenties were producing a hybrid which lacked both the wit and the natural inventiveness of New Orleans jazz. Yet this was the route on which jazz would travel even if, at the end of the decade, interest was shared between the new modernists like Ellington and the casual 'good-time' element presented in aspic on Chicago's South Side.

Henry Allen

**Born: 7th January 1908/New Orleans, Louisiana, USA
Died: 17th April 1967/New York City, NY, USA
Instrument: Trumpet, vocals, composer
Recording Career: 1937-1967
Nickname: Red**

IT WAS in 1965 that modern trumpeter Don Ellis described Red Allen as 'the most creative and avant-garde trumpet player in New York'. It is not difficult to know what he meant. Many excellent players played with similar instrumental skill, creative flair and sense of swing. What placed Allen apart from all, perhaps including **Louis Armstrong**, was that he was arguably the most unpredictable player of his era.

The son of a brass band leader, Henry James Allen marched with his father's band when very young. It was not until he joined **King Oliver** in 1927 that his own career began to take off. Through this connection, he joined **Luis Russell** and thus came to play in one of the most influential bands of the twenties >**1, 2**. His brilliant solos

made him much sought-after by bandleaders and he had spells with Charlie Johnson (1932), **Fletcher Henderson** (1933-4) and the Mills Blue Rhythm (1934-6).

Throughout the thirties, a period that saw him playing superbly, he also made records under his own name, often in the company of his friend **Coleman Hawkins**. He had room to spread out, and his brassy tone burnt its way through the emotionless asbestos of such bland popular songs as *Red Sails In The Sunset* >**3**.

Allen played a secondary role in Armstrong's orchestra in the late thirties, but after 1949 began leading his own groups. He was for many years leader of a Dixieland band, above the heads of drinkers at New York's Metropole Club, and he toured Europe with **Kid Ory** in 1959. The latent power of his playing occasionally gave way to the raucously extrovert but even in his later years he took linear routes more in keeping with music of the sixties.

Lineage

Allen took lessons from his own father, and from Peter Bocage and Manuel Manetta, but there can be little doubt that he was greatly influenced by **Louis Armstrong**. Because of this, his position in jazz history is clearly established. Later, flamboyant trumpeters like **Roy Eldridge** and Charlie Shavers, devoted Armstrong disciples, had a lot of Allen in their souls. The line from Armstrong, though Allen, Eldridge and on to **Dizzy Gillespie** has been acknowledged by all concerned.

Media

Featured in the 1957 CBS film *The Sound Of Jazz*.

Listening

1 Luis Russell 1926-30
    VJM VLP 54
2 Luis Russell 1930-1934
    VJM VLP 57
3 Red Allen 1935-1936
    Henry Allen/Collector's Classics CC 46

Louis Armstrong

Born: 4th(?) July 1900/New Orleans, Louisiana, USA
Died: 6th July 1971/Corona, NY, USA
Instruments: Cornet, trumpet, vocals, composer
Recording Career: 1923-1970
Nickname: Satchmo, Pops

TO DESCRIBE one man as the greatest figure in jazz is a sweeping assertion. Yet Louis Daniel Armstrong is a man for whom such a claim might rightly be made – not only because of his trumpet playing and singing, but because he was the music's ultimate ambassador.

As a jazzman, he was without peer and, although his once unassailable trumpet technique has now been surpassed many times, no one has produced a fraction of the musical masterpieces attributable to him. Judged in the context of the early twenties, his supremacy was even greater. At that time horn players fell broadly into two groups, the relaxed but uncomplicated ensemble players from New Orleans or the staccato, military-style trumpeters like New York's **Johnny Dunn**. Only **King Oliver**, the young Armstrong's mentor, gave any hint of the more subtle

phrasing and more fragmented timing that was to reach fruition with Armstrong. Although Armstrong was only twenty-two, the records they made together in 1923 show a man with an already impressive talent. His solo on *Chimes Blues* >**1** or his great lead playing on *Froggie Moore* >**1** stamp him as more than just an original stylist.

Good as such works were, however, his progress in the next five years was staggering by any standards. Urged on by his wife Lil, he broadened his outlook and joined the **Fletcher Henderson** Orchestra in New York in 1924. In just over one year he transformed a rather turgid band into an outstanding jazz aggregation. His lead in *Everybody Loves My Baby* >**2** really carried the band, but it was dynamic solos like those on *How Come You Do Me* and *TNT* >**2** that stopped the jazz world in its tracks.

At the same time, he was recording with Clarence Williams' Blue Five and, while titles like *Livin' High* >**3** were beginning to display the bravura soloist in all his glory, there were others like *Texas Moaner* >**3** to show him as a feeling, almost tender player. It was this side of his personality that endeared him to many of the blues singers and he was captured on record giving superb support to Chippie Hill, Clara Smith, Maggie Jones and Hociel Thomas.

In a class of their own, however, were the records he made with **Bessie Smith**. There was the majesty of *St Louis Blues* >**4** with Armstrong effortlessly verbose, *Careless Love* >**5** with him at his most caring, and *Cold In Hand* >**4**, one of the most perfect marriages of voice and trumpet on record.

Even greater triumphs were to follow. In November 1925, Armstrong made the first recordings with his Hot Five, a studio group comprising clarinettist **Johnny Dodds**, trombonist **Kid Ory**, banjoist Johnny St Cyr, and wife Lil on piano. The records they made must be rated among the finest in jazz history and they show how completely Armstrong had freed himself from the New Orleans ensemble style. His bristling attack adorns *Come Back, Sweet Papa* >**6**, his virtuosity shouts from *Cornet Chop Suey* >**7**, while his control and sense of timing transforms the novelty number *Skid-Dat-De-Dat* >**7**.

*Louis Armstrong
during a radio broadcast*

Augmenting his group to septet proportions led to further glory: Armstrong's solos on *Wild Man Blues* and *Potato Head Blues* >**7** brought a previously unknown grandeur to the solo trumpet art and made him the model for players on almost all instruments.

In 1928 he returned to the big band arena with Carroll Dickerson but his taste for small group work remained. With a new six-piece Hot Five, he further developed the solo side of his style. The opening to *West End Blues* >**7** is possibly the most famous cadenza in jazz history and Armstrong, on hearing the playback, actually ran off with the acetate in excitement.

Armstrong was also becoming increasingly involved in the show business side of music and, as the thirties were ushered in, was recording more with big orchestras. The fortunate spin-off from this enterprise was that, while still allowing plenty of room for stupendous trumpet playing, the public began to hear more of Armstrong's singing.

His vocals were an obvious extension of his instrumental method but had their own individual quality. Though his range was limited and his voice dreadful by academic standards, his timing, melodic phrasing and infectious swing on titles like *Them There Eyes* or *Walkin' My Baby Back Home* >**8** set the standard for jazz singing and popular music from that date forward.

In 1933 he made his first visit to Europe, but lip trouble two years later forced him to take a short sabbatical. In 1935 he began fronting the **Luis Russell** band, demonstrating with *Mahogany Hall Stomp* and *Swing That Music* >**9** that he was playing as well as ever. The emphasis was on showcasing his trumpet skills and, as such, they offered excitement rather than the splendour of the Hot Five items. This was jazz of a very high order but an element of the histrionic somewhat diminished the pieces as works of art.

Not that this was his concern. He had become an internationally-famous entertainer and it was the changing face of jazz that made his theatre of operation the front of a large orchestra and his material the popular music of the day.

Armstrong, now a big band trumpeter of rare skill, continued to solo with distinction in the late thirties, although there was the occasional suspicion of a reduction in his powers. Increasingly, there was a noticeable economy of expression. His greatness, and the affection in which he was held, remained undiluted, however. The remainder of Armstrong's long and illustrious career is evaluated in the chapter on The Forties, page 102.

Lineage

Armstrong was strongly influenced by **King Oliver** but came to form the base of the pyramid from which all jazz trumpet styles evolved. His obvious immediate influence on **Red Allen**, **Roy Eldridge**, Cootie Williams, Jonah Jones, **Hot Lips Page**, Bill Coleman, **Bunny Berigan** and Nat Gonella should not disguise the fact that it was also an influence that permeated the instrument's entire history through to **Dizzy Gillespie**, **Miles Davis**, **Clifford Brown** and Lester Bowie. He also

inspired musicians on other instruments and men like **Earl Hines** (piano), Jimmy Harrison (trombone) and **Coleman Hawkins** (tenor saxophone) are amongst those that acknowledge his position.

Media

Armstrong wrote *Satchmo – My Life In New Orleans* (1954) and *Swing That Music* (1936). Excellent biographies include *Louis Armstrong* by Albert McCarthy, *Louis Armstrong* (1971) by Hughes Pannassié, Robert Goffin's *Horn Of Plenty* (1977) and *Louis – The Louis Armstrong Story 1900-71* by Max Jones and John Chilton (1971).

Thirties film appearances: *Pennies From Heaven* (1936); *Artists And Models* (1937).

Listening

1 King Oliver's Creole Jazz Band
VJM VLP 49
2 Study In Frustration
Fletcher Henderson/CBS 66423
3 Clarence Williams Blue Five
Armstrong/Bechet/CBS 63092
4 The Empress
Bessie Smith/Columbia CG 30818
5 Nobody's Blues But Mine
Bessie Smith/CBS 67232
6 The Louis Armstrong Legend 1925-1926
World Records SH 404
7 The Louis Armstrong Story 1925-1935
CBS 66427
8 Louis Armstrong & His Orchestra 1929-1931
Swaggie S 1402
9 Struttin' With Some Barbecue
Louis Armstrong/Affinity AFS 1024

Sidney Bechet

Born: 14th May 1897/New Orleans, Louisiana, USA
Died: 4th May 1959/Paris, France
Instruments: Soprano, alto and tenor saxophones, clarinet, drums, piano, bass, vocals, composer
Recording Career: 1923-1958
Nickname: Pops

SIDNEY JOSEPH BECHET was the first man to produce mature and durable

Above: Sidney Bechet. Far right: Bix Beiderbecke

jazz on the saxophone. As early as 1923, his soprano sax playing on record stamped him as a major soloist, an achievement made all the more impressive because it was over thirty years before **Steve Lacy** and **John Coltrane** provided the instrument with another truly new stylistic direction.

His 1923 recordings with the **Clarence Williams** Blue Five >**1** reveal a completely cohesive style when it would have been easier for him to imitate the clarinet's role in the popular New Orleans styles of the day. The two-trumpet bands as exemplified by **King Oliver** and **Louis Armstrong**, or Papa Celestin and 'Kid Shots' Madison were then in vogue. Bechet, by the sheer power of his playing and by his grasp of the implications of this trend, claimed for the soprano a status equal to the trumpet in the hierarchy of instruments.

Ironically, despite the impact of the Williams records, Bechet was only in the studios twice with Noble Sissle and on odd occasions with blues singers in the next eight years. After some time in Europe, his next significant recordings were not until 1932. By then he was the complete bravura soloist, dominating colleagues with his fiery music, and in the process creating brilliant jazz: a title such as *Shag* >**2** demonstrates virility, creative intensity and rhythmic projection.

In the thirties, Bechet sank into obscurity only to re-emerge as part of the renewed interest in New Orleans jazz in 1940. He featured to great effect with players like **Earl Hines**, Charlie Shavers and Sidney De Paris >**2**, **3**, and in 1945 began a series of records with Mezz Mezzrow that truly matched his earlier triumphs. Yet it was an uneasy partnership in many ways, teaming one of the music's most passionate individualists with a white negrophile of limited musical imagination. Nevertheless, both men had a natural feeling for the blues and titles like *Gone Away Blues* >**4** and *Out Of The Gallion* >**5** are typical of their unhurried, but emotion-filled performances.

Bechet had come to like Europe on his trips there, and in 1949 settled in Paris. His work with local French groups failed to reach his highest standards, but even Bechet's routine recordings are impressive and there were always odd sessions with visiting Americans to give inspirational help. He was notably captured on record with **Charlie Parker** >**6** but a mainstream style group led by Sammy Price in 1955 showed just how effectively Bechet could play in any company >**7**.

Lineage

Bechet came from a musical family. Although largely self-taught, he did study with New Orleans' master Lorenzo Tio as well as with Big Eye Louis Nelson and George Baquet. Despite his own musical stature, his influence was not as widespread as might have been expected. He greatly influenced **Johnny Hodges** and Tab Smith, but otherwise it was left to a legion of European revivalists to capture – to a greater or lesser degree – the wonderful throbbing vibrato of the master.

Media

In 1955 he appeared in the French film *Blues*. Autobiography *Treat It Gentle*, appeared 1969.

Listening

1 Clarence Williams Blue Five
Armstrong/Bechet/CBS 63092
2 The Complete Sidney Bechet Vols 1/2
Sidney Bechet/RCA NL 89760 (2)
3 Jazz Classics
Sidney Bechet/Blue Note BST 81202
4 The King Jazz Story
Mezzrow/Bechet/Storyville SLP 141
5 The King Jazz Story
Mezzrow/Bechet/Storyville SLP 153
6 Bird In Paris
Charlie Parker/Spotlite 118
7 With Sammy Price's Bluesicians
Sidney Bechet/Vogue 416033

Bix Beiderbecke

Born: 10th March 1903/Davenport, Iowa, USA
Died: 6th August 1931/Queens, NY, USA
Instruments: Cornet, piano, composer
Recording Career: 1924-1930

THE COMPLETE antithesis of the **Louis Armstrong** school of jazz trumpet was embodied in Leon 'Bix' Beiderbecke. Where the New Orleans trumpeter traded in passion, Beiderbecke dealt in understatement and lyricism – his bell-like tone was a joy, and he organised his elegant solos with a draughtsman's hand.

He was the single-handed inspiration of the Wolverines >**1** in 1923, and in the mid-twenties languished in the commercial band of Charlie Straight. It was a period of musical ferment, however, and he spent much of his spare time listening to negro giants like Armstrong, **King Oliver** and **Jimmie Noone**, all then playing in Chicago. In 1925 he joined the Jean Goldkette organisation and made the acquaintance of a young saxophonist, Frankie Trumbauer, who was leading a

band under the Goldkette banner. Both moved to the ill-fated Adrian Rollini Big Band and then in 1927 joined Paul Whiteman.

In the meantime they produced a series of records that reveal Trumbauer as a good jazz musician and Beiderbecke as a unique talent. Comparisons between different 'takes' confirm his total commitment to improvisation and titles like *I'm Coming Virginia* and *Jazz Me Blues* >**2** are masterpieces of the jazz-maker's art.

It was often claimed that the young cornettist joined bigger bands reluctantly but there seems little to support this theory. He personally claimed to like working with them and the quality of his brief solo interludes is adequate proof. It was true that their arrangements were not designed for jazz ears, but Beiderbecke's dancing, gently contoured solos emerged from the orchestral congestion to bring the performances to life >**3**.

Although Beiderbecke's later years were plagued by alcoholism, Whiteman was supportive and it was certainly not his fault that the horn man seemed unwilling to make an effort on his own behalf. Bix Beiderbecke was still only twenty-eight when he died of pneumonia.

Lineage

Beiderbecke always claimed to have

Above: Eddie Condon plays his four-string guitar, tuned to give the sound of a ukelele
Far right: Johnny Dodds

been inspired by a white trumpeter called Emmett Hardy, but also listened hard to black giants like **Louis Armstrong** and Joe Smith. He sired a school of excellent trumpeters including Bobby Hackett, Jimmy McPartland, Red Nichols, Andy Secrest, Leo McConville and, latterly, **Ruby Braff**. Perhaps with some justification his name has also been linked with **Miles Davis**.

Media

Subject of Dorothy Baker's novel *Young Man With A Horn;* Brigitte Berman's fine film, *Bix* (1981), contains footage of the man himself. An impressively large book, *Bix – Man And Legend* was written by Richard Sudhalter and Philip R. Evans, while a less exhaustive study, *Bix Beiderbecke* came from Burnett James.

Listening

1 The Complete Wolverines
   Bix Beiderbecke/Fountain FJ 114
2 The Young Man With The Horn
   Bix Beiderbecke/CBS 22179
3 The Indispensable Bix Beiderbecke (1924-30)
   RCA NL 89572 (2)

Eddie Condon

Born: 16th November 1905/Goodland, Indiana, USA
Died: 4th August 1973/New York City, NY, USA
Instruments: Guitar, banjo, vocals
Recording Career: 1927-1972

'THIS MAN needs a drink right now'. So wrote a military psychiatrist who deemed Albert Edwin Condon unfit for war service. In so doing he summed up the career of an unspectacular guitarist, club owner, author, irresistible raconteur and enthusiastic drinker. His considerable contributions to jazz may not have taxed his instrumental skills to any great extent. They did, however, achieve for him a position as father figure to Chicago-style Dixieland.

The Chicago Rhythm Kings >**1**, the Windy City Five >**2**, the Summa Cum Laude Orchestra >**2**, the Mound City Blue Blowers >**3** and the McKenzie/Condon Chicagoans >**1** all rang with the light strumming of this highly professional and rhythmically-minded guitarist. No rhythm section with Condon on board was ever pedestrian. He lent a buoyancy and vigour to them all.

His most important role, however, was as a promoter of jazz concerts and jam sessions. This began in 1939 and continued until the time of his death. He opened a nightclub of his own (called 'Eddie Condon's') in New York in 1946 and also had his own jazz series on American television. He was a regular contributor to the Newport Jazz Festival and often toured Europe.

Lineage

The cornet and piano playing of **Bix Beiderbecke** made a lasting impression on Condon but his own guitar style, for all its appeal, was somewhat anonymous.

Media

Hilarious autobiography *We Called It Music* (1947) co-written with Thomas Sugrue then *Treasury Of Jazz* with Richard Gehman and finally *Scrapbook Of Jazz* (1973) with Hank O'Neal. He also made an important film for Time Life and one for Goodyear entitled *Eddie Condon* (1961) with **Wild Bill Davison** and Cutty Cutshall.

Listening

1 Chicago Style
Eddie Condon/VJM VLP 55
2 Chicago Styled
Bud Freeman/Swaggie S 1216
3 The Indispensable J.T.
Jack Teagarden/RCA PM 45695

Johnny Dodds

Born: 12th April 1892/New Orleans, Louisiana, USA
Died: 8th August 1940/Chicago, Illinois, USA
Instruments: Clarinet, alto saxophone
Recording Career: 1923-1940

THE CLARINET was the instrument most faithfully reproduced by the primitive recording equipment used by the Gennett label for the **King Oliver** Creole Jazzband in 1923 >**1**. The player was Johnny Dodds and these recordings represent the high spot of a

distinguished career. His strong, sometimes piercing tone was able to cut through the brass-dominated ensemble and he compensated for any partial loss of balance by playing quite superbly. His beautiful chalumeau work on *Sobbin' Blues* >**1** typified this.

Dodds, however, was one of the more individual of clarinettists. Within the New Orleans ensembles this instrument had been established as the buoyant and decorative part of the three-voice counterpoint. Dodds perhaps lacked the fluency exhibited by the finest of his peers but he fashioned a style that allowed for his comparative limitations. It was a process that concentrated his attention on the blues and made him one of the greatest of all blues players.

Perhaps almost inevitably he was alone amongst clarinettists in being able to capture something of **Louis Armstrong**'s sense of timing. They worked together in the trumpeter's Hot Five >**2** and Hot Seven >**3** pick-up groups and Dodds' style became more angular on titles like *Potato Head Blues* >**2** as he sought to emulate his leader's declamatory style.

He was at home in less daunting company and a series of records with the New Orleans Wanderers produced titles such as *Perdido Street Blues* and *Gatemouth* >**4** which took him near to the quality of his records with King Oliver. Of similar value were the trio and full group records with **Jelly Roll Morton** >**5**, where that gifted organiser made Dodds sound very much at ease. Even more relaxed were the records made in Chicago in the late twenties with the Dixieland Thumpers >**6**, Lovie Austin >**6**, and the Chicago Feetwarmers >**4** and their skiffle atmosphere is a good introduction to his work.

Sadly, Dodds did not record after 1929, save for an inappropriate date with swingsters in 1938 and an unhappy revivalist effort in 1940. But, at his best, Dodds had been one of the most emotionally involved of all reed players.

Lineage

Although stylistically distant from his contemporaries, Dodds also received tuition from the legendary clarinet teacher, Lorenzo Tio. He had little influence on the generation that followed him but curiously became an almost god-like figure to European revivalists of the late forties such as Claude Luter, Wally Fawkes and Cy Laurie.

Media

In 1961 G. E. Lambert made him number ten in the *Kings Of Jazz* book series.

Listening

1 King Oliver's Jazz Band 1923
  King Oliver/Swaggie S 1257
2 VSOP Vols 1/2
  Louis Armstrong/CBS 88001
3 VSOP Vols 3/4
  Louis Armstrong/CBS 88002
4 The Immortal
  Johnny Dodds/VJM VLP 48
5 The Complete Jelly Roll Morton Vols 1/2
  RCA Jazz Tribune PM 42405
6 Johnny Dodds & Tommy Ladnier 1923/28
  Biograph BLP 12024

Duke Ellington

Born: 29th April 1899/Washington DC, USA
Died: 24th May 1974/New York City, NY, USA
Instrument: Piano, composer, arranger
Recording Career: 1923-1974

THE MUSIC of Edward Kennedy Ellington has been analysed and dissected in every book or magazine that boasts even the most tenuous connection with American music. His stature as a composer and band leader is incomparable and it would be pointless to give exhaustive details of his background in the limited space available in this Handbook.

His prime talent was as a songwriter, but this must be coupled with his skill as an arranger. His intuitive ability in creating excellent themes would alone be enough to stamp him as a great figure. The fact that he then arranged them to make the maximum use of the instrumental voices at his disposal enhanced those themes even further. He also devised some of the most

Above: Duke Ellington (right) with Django Reinhardt

beautiful unison voicings and brought together instruments that had previously been considered incompatible.

His first great unit was dubbed the 'Jungle Band' and, despite the New Orleans influence of clarinettist Barney Bigard, it was the brass that dominated the late twenties. The vocalised tones of trumpeter **Bubber Miley** and trombonist **Tricky Sam Nanton** brought an almost surealistic drama to titles like *Creole Love Call* >**1**, *Jubilee Stomp* >**2**, *Black And Tan Fantasy* and *Hot And Bothered* >**3**.

In 1932, the smooth sound of Lawrence Brown's trombone was added to the band and there was some emphasis placed on the trombones in the middle thirties, with items like *Slippery Horn* >**4** devised to showcase that particular three-man department. Generally it was a period of entrenchment; the mood of America was one of caution and Ellington was aware that sentimentality was a very saleable commodity. In this climate the reeds, with **Johnny Hodges** and Harry Carney prominent, came into their own and the whole emphasis was switched. Duke wrote beautiful ballads like *Solitude* and *In A Sentimental Mood* and had the men available to do them justice.

Towards the end of 1939, Duke was joined by bassist **Jimmy Blanton** and early the following year by tenor saxophonist **Ben Webster**. With their arrival the band was 'complete' and, although there were masterpieces both before and after this date, for some three years this was the finest orchestra in jazz history. **Billy Strayhorn** was added as an extra composer/arranger and a stream of great performances were inspired by their 'pens'. *Concerto For Cootie* >**5** was devised to showcase the mature talents of trumpeter Cootie Williams, *Just A-Sittin' And A-Rockin'* >**6** was a yarn-spinning exercise for Webster, while *Warm Valley* switched the spotlight to Johnny Hodges' sensuously lyrical romanticism. Strayhorn's *A Train* >**6** became the band's lifelong signature tune, while *Harlem Air Shaft* >**5** escorted us into life in a New York tenement building, and *Main Stem* >**6** proved that the spirit of the jam session lived on.

With Blanton in the bass chair, the rhythm section achieved a greater fluency, an aspect of the band's work that Ellington never surrendered. Changes in personnel during the forties

Right: Bud Freeman

reduced the potency of the band, but none more than the loss of Hodges in 1951. Without him the entire sound was different, and it was not surprising that it took his return in 1955 to revitalise the band.

The pianistic skills of the leader graced all his bands as well as all of the Ellington periods, but he never lost his love of the stride tradition and was never happier than announcing the band's piano player in the *Kinda Dukish* opening to *Rockin' In Rhythm*. He experienced great public acclaim but by the middle fifties had fallen on poor times artistically.

Many concluded that Ellington had reached the end of the road: how wrong they were (see The Fifties, page 148).

Lineage

Ellington was greatly impressed by New York's stride pianists – both the famous, Willie 'The Lion' Smith and **James P. Johnson** among them, and the almost-infamous, like Abba Labba and The Beetle. His effect on pianists was slight, although the likes of **Thelonious Monk** have declared their loyalty. As a writer, leader and arranger, however, his influence has been inestimable, not only on all other jazz orchestras, but also on the new-commercial bands of Charlie Barnet, **Tommy Dorsey** and Glenn Miller.

Media

The Ellington Band has appeared in films such as *Check And Double Check* (1930), *Dancers In The Dark* (1932), *Belle Of The Nineties* (1934) and *Cabin In The Sky* (1943) (see also Fifties entry).

Listening

1 Duke Ellington Mar-Dec 1927
VJM VLP 72

2 The Essential Duke Ellington 1927-28
VJM VLP 73

3 Hot From The Cotton Club
Duke Ellington/EMI EG 26 0567 1

4 The Complete Duke Ellington Vol 5
CBS 88052 (2)

5 The Indispensable Duke Ellington Vol 5/6
RCA PM 45352

6 The Indispensable Duke Ellington Vol 7/8
RCA NL 89274

Bud Freeman

Born: 13th April 1906/Chicago, Illinois, USA
Instruments: Tenor saxophone, clarinet, composer
Recording Career: 1927-

WHEN the early history of the tenor saxophone in jazz is recounted, **Coleman Hawkins** is rightly pre-eminent. Nevertheless, a parallel development did flourish in the late twenties in the person of Lawrence 'Bud' Freeman. He was one of the Austin High School Gang, a college band that aped the great black Chicago players but without any appreciable success.

From their comparative failure grew a style of their own which fostered the eccentric skills of clarinettist Frank Teschemacher and the prodigal drumming of the young Gene Krupa >1. Many consider it the source of the white Chicago school that finally came to reside at **Eddie Condon**'s club in New York, the shrine of this music from the forties onwards.

Freeman's embryonic style was largely born of playing in a group that aspired to New Orleans music yet lacked a trombonist. Freeman filled the ensemble gaps of William 'Red' McKenzie and Eddie Condon's

Chicagoans with a busy, rambling style and his playing matured along these lines. The contours of his solo lines were gently tapered, the tone was light, and he nursed his melody lines with a certain loving care. A title like *The Eel* >**1** has been called a blueprint for all of his solos, but one has only to listen to the changing face of his music through sixty years in the business to discount such a jibe.

In the thirties, he fitted effortlessly into the big bands of Roger Wolfe Kahn, Ray Noble, **Tommy Dorsey** and **Benny Goodman**. However, his heart was always in the smaller units, and apart from his association with leader Eddie Condon >**2**, he was also, in more recent years, a stalwart of the World's Greatest Jazz Band >**3**, **4**.

Even into the eighties, he continued to play impressively and for many *The Real Bud Freeman 1984* >**5** can be ranked among his finest performances.

Lineage

He started on C-melody saxophone at seventeen and studied with Duke Real as well as Jimmy McPartland's father. On his final choice, tenor saxophone, he became an important influence and was often cited, along with Frankie Trumbauer, as **Lester Young**'s mentor.

Media

Two autobiographical books, *You Don't Look Like A Musician* (1974) and *If You Know A Better Life* (1976).

Listening

1 **Eddie Condon Chicago Style**
  Eddie Condon/VJM VLP 55
2 **That Toddlin' Town**
  Eddie Condon/Atlantic 90461-1
3 **WGJB Of Lawson & Haggart**
  World's Greatest Jazz Band/Project 3 PR 5039
4 **WGJB At The Plaza**
  World's Greatest Jazz Band/World Jazz WJLP 5
5 **The Real Bud Freeman 1984**
  Bud Freeman/Principally Jazz Productions PJP 01

Fletcher Henderson

Born: 18th December 1897/Cuthbert, Georgia, USA
Died: 28th December 1952/New York City, NY, USA
Instrument: Piano, arranger, composer
Recording Career: 1921-1950
Nickname: Smack

FLETCHER HAMILTON HENDERSON was too pleasant a man to be a completely successful bandleader, and too educated a man to be a barrelhouse

Below: The Fletcher Henderson Band

pianist. In truth, he frequently got very near to becoming the former, and was perhaps a better stride piano player than is sometimes admitted.

He began playing at the age of six, but a degree in chemistry, obtained at Morehouse College in 1916, threatened to rule out any musical career. Against his better judgement, Henderson became a song demonstrator, which led to a post of recording manager for the Black Swan Recording Company. Almost accidentally, he then began leading a band at New York's Roseland Ballroom: a 'temporary' booking that lasted for ten years!

Dicty Blues >**1** by Henderson's earliest band was merely foppish, but the arrival of **Louis Armstrong** late in 1924 began an upward turn in their fortunes (witness *Go Long Mule* >**1**). The following years saw the blossoming of Don Redman's arranging talents for the band >**1**, and the emergence of a dazzling array of outstanding solo talents. There was the dominating artistry of **Coleman Hawkins** bringing the phrase-shapes of Armstrong to the tenor; additionally there were the darting, rapier-like skills of clarinettist Buster Bailey and the superbly lyrical beauty of trumpeter Joe Smith >**1**.

However, it was perhaps for the great trombonists that the band was justly famed. Jimmy Harrison with Miff Mole and Thamon Hayes, led the instrument's avant-garde. The underpraised Charlie Green was a moving blues player, but equally an articulate big-band soloist, and the young Benny Morton was strong of voice and rock-steady of comment.

Benny Carter's arrangements ushered the band into the thirties >**1**, and by 1936 the band was changed beyond recognition. Newcomers included trumpeter **Roy Eldridge** and gifted tenor saxophonist Chew Berry, a superb replacement for the departed Hawkins >**1**. Henderson had always been a casual leader, however, and this never changed. As the thirties came to an end, morale dropped too low to be tolerated and the band folded.

Henderson joined **Benny Goodman** as an arranger and featured soloist in the sextet but the Smack legend was over. He made abortive attempts to reform a band after the Second World War but his time had passed and, after

suffering a stroke in 1949, he was never able to play again.

Lineage

As a pianist, Henderson was influenced by **James P. Johnson** and all of the New York stride pianists. He turned to arranging late in his career but soon had quite a following. His arrangements for **Benny Goodman** set a pattern that was followed by most big swing bands of the thirties.

Media

The magnificent *Hendersonia*, by Walter C. Allen published 1973.

Listening

1 A Study in Frustration Vols 1-4
Fletcher Henderson/CBS 66423

Earl Hines

Born: 28th December 1903/Pittsburgh, Pennsylvania, USA
Died: 22nd April 1983/Oakland, California, USA
Instrument: Piano, vocals, composer
Recording Career: 1923-1982
Nickname: Fatha

HAVING MAJORED in music, Earl Kenneth Hines began his professional career as pianist with Lois B. Deppe's Serenaders while still a teenager. He later worked with Carroll Dickerson and Erskine Tate, and in 1927 was appointed **Louis Armstrong**'s musical director at the Sunset Café in Chicago. Later that year he joined **Jimmie Noone** at the Apex Club and with him produced a magnificent set of records. Hines' brilliantly fragmented solos on titles such as *Apex Blues* and *My Monday Date* >**1** demonstrate his 'trumpet' style to perfection and they contrast well with Noone's flowing clarinet.

In the same year, he recorded with Armstrong's second Hot Five and on *Fireworks* and *Skip The Gutter* >**2** shamed the other sidemen in their efforts to match the trumpeter. His diverse changes of rhythm at times

suggested that he might have lost his way but, despite this audacity, Hines was always in control and aware of his position within the solo.

Also in 1928, he formed his own band which he led at Chicago's Grand Terrace for much of the thirties. With sidemen like Darnell Howard, Omer Simeon and George Dixon, the initial emphasis was on traditional material >**3** but, as the decade progressed, the band became increasingly sophisticated >**4**. By the forties, it had embraced the language of bop and at various times Hines' bands included **Charlie Parker**, Willie Cook, Bennie Green, **Wardell Gray** and **Sarah Vaughan**.

From 1947 to 1951 Hines toured with Louis Armstrong's All Stars but seemed less affected than most by the repetitive material. During most of the fifties and sixties he played on the West Coast, but a revitalised Hines emerged in the sixties and seventies. Recording alone, with a trio, or as part of an all-star line-up, Hines' brilliance was readily evident and an exceptional album >**5** documents his undiminished skills.

Right up to the time of his death he had a life contract to play at San Francisco's Cannery Club whenever he chose.

Lineage

It was the work of trumpeter **Louis Armstrong** rather than of any pianist that most affected Hines' approach to the piano. He was a master of angular playing that was aptly described as 'trumpet' style. His influence was widespread and included such pianists as **Art Tatum**, Zinky Cohn, Billy Kyle, **Nat King Cole** and **Mary Lou Williams**.

Listening

1 Apex Club Blues
Jimmie Noone/Affinity AFS 1023
2 The Louis Armstrong Legend
Louis Armstrong/EMI World Records SH 406
3 Deep Forest
Earl Hines/HEP 1003
4 The Indispensable (1939/45) Vols 3/4
Earl Hines/RCA PM 43266
5 The Indispensable (1944/66) Vols 5/6
Earl Hines/RCA PM 45358

Rising High Water >3 told of natural disasters; and Baker Shop Blues >3 graphically portrayed the horrors of constant hunger. Whatever the material, Jefferson sang with an overwhelming expressiveness, and possessed a rhythmic awareness that placed even the most inappropriate phrase perfectly in position.

Hot Dogs >1 showed that he could play dance reels although, as a guitarist, he could be erratic. In support of his own voice, however, he was perfect. It did not matter that he played thirteen-bar blues – he was an original and cared nothing for musical niceties.

Blind Lemon Jefferson died in Chicago, in 1930, reputedly at the height of a snowstorm.

Blind Lemon Jefferson

Born: c.1897/Coachman, near Wortham, Texas, USA
Died: 1930/Chicago, Illinois, USA
Instrument: Guitar, vocals, composer
Recording Career: 1925-1929
Nickname: Deacon L. J. Bates

ONE OF the major figures in blues history, Blind Lemon Jefferson was born sightless and quickly realised that music was his best chance of making a living. While still a teenager he played at local dances, but at seventeen he moved to Dallas – where he improved his income by working as a wrestler! He also earned a good living playing, at one time, in that city's red-light district.

In 1925, he began recording and was an immediate success. His records sold prolifically on the Race market and, he recorded some one hundred titles. Most were his own compositions, the lyrics proving him to be something of a folk poet. They told of bad women and sexual excesses and some were descriptive to the extent of throwing doubt on his sightlessness. All were delivered with a tough, untutored voice that evoked feelings of desperate desolation and titles such as Shuckin' Sugar, Bad Luck Blues >1 and Tin Cup Blues >2 have an almost unbearable sadness. Jack O'Diamonds >3 was a gambling song built on work song lines;

Lineage
Jefferson was a true original, but influenced a whole generation of blues singers, most notably Huddie Ledbetter and Josh White, who both worked with him; Isaiah Nettles most successfully copied him; and Hobart Smith was unique in being a white copyist.

Media
Samuel Charters, in The Country Blues (1959), described him as 'fat, dirty and dissolute', but nevertheless found him the most exciting country blues singer of the 1920s.

Listening
1 King Of The Country Blues
   Blind Lemon Jefferson/Yazoo 1069
2 Blind Lemon Jefferson Vol 3
   Roots RL 331
3 Blind Lemon Jefferson
   Milestone M 47022

James P. Johnson

Born: 1st February 1894/New Brunswick, New Jersey, USA
Died: 17th November 1955/New York City, NY, USA
Instrument: Piano, arranger, composer
Recording Career: 1921-1949

THE STRIDE PIANO style, in which the left hand plays such an important part,

was born in New York and was an adaptation of the more universal ragtime style. To describe it as alternating a chord on the weak beats with a bass note on the strong beats is to simplify the process somewhat. Yet this is exactly what it entailed, and James Price Johnson was the father of that style.

His career took off after his family moved to New York. Only fourteen, it was not long before he began to work in Harlem cabarets. He also wrote stage shows and was often featured in them: so much so, that when he first recorded in 1921, he was already a mature soloist.

Johnson brought to stride piano a fullness of style that completely transcended its ragtime roots, playing with tremendous power and infectious élan. His legendary *Carolina Shout* >**1** tells the whole story: it is a virtuoso piano exercise, but with an ineluctable swing and masterly improvisational skills.

During the thirties he devoted a great deal of his time to composition but, by 1938, had become disenchanted and re-appeared on the New York scene as a pianist. He took part in the *Spirituals To Swing* concerts of 1938 and worked with **Eddie Condon** on and off through the forties despite two strokes. However, a third made him a virtual invalid after 1951 and arguably the least appreciated of all jazz pianists could not play for the last four years of his life.

Lineage

Johnson had a thorough musical training, but he fashioned a style in the manner of Luckey Roberts and Abba Labba, men he admired greatly. Regarded as the father of the stride piano school, he had an impressive band of followers that included **Fats Waller**, **Duke Ellington**, **Count Basie**, Willie 'The Lion' Smith, Cliff Jackson and **Art Tatum**.

Media

Appeared in Bessie Smith's 1929 film *St Louis Blues* and in 1940 was musical director of *Pinkard's Fantasies*. In 1949 wrote the show *Sugar Hill*.

Listening

1 From Ragtime To Jazz: The Complete Piano Solos (1921-1939)
James P. Johnson/CBS 85387

Lonnie Johnson

**Born: 8th February 1899 (?)/New
Orleans, Louisiana, USA
Died: 16th June 1970/Toronto, Canada
Instrument: Guitar, vocals
Recording Career: 1924-1965**

ALLOWING THAT **Eddie Lang** was the
first guitarist to earn an international
reputation, Alonzo 'Lonnie' Johnson was
nevertheless the first true soloist of the
jazz guitar. He began as a violinist, later
switching to guitar, and played in his
hometown for several years. In 1922 he
moved to St Louis where he worked
with Charlie Creath and Fate Marable,
but it was 1925, when he won a Okeh
Record Company talent competition,
before his career took off.

In 1927 Johnson joined **Louis
Armstrong**'s Hot Five, who were
recording for Okeh, and took a relaxed,
but stunning solo on *Savoy Blues* >**1**.
1928 titles like *Move Over* >**2** show how
his effortlessly swinging and creatively
delivered guitar could feature in the
Duke Ellington set up, while his
masterful solo on *Stardust* >**3**
illuminated the **McKinney's Cotton**
Pickers performance of that standard in
the same year.

It was, however, magnificant duets
with Eddie Lang that marked his true
stature. *Two Tone Stomp, Bull Frog
Moan* >**4** and *Blue Guitars* >**5**
demonstrate his superiority over the
more feted Lang. Doubters should
sample the latter, where Lang's clipped
and edgy solo is followed by Johnson's,
full of melismatic magic and rhythmic
strength.

This was Johnson at his best, playing
in a style that was uniquely his own. It
was as a blues singer, however, that he
really made his name. From 1925 until
1932 he recorded prolifically for the
Okeh company, his blues a strange
mixture of New Orleans charm, folk
poetry and jazz know-how >**6,7**. His
guitar was beautifully showcased and
his vocals compensated for their
occasional lack of depth by being timed
to perfection.

Later, in the thirties, Johnson teamed
up with Putney Dandridge and **Johnny
Dodds**, and visited England in 1952. He
worked for Duke Ellington again as late
as 1963. From then until the time of his
death, he operated out of Toronto,
Canada and made what proved to be
his final important appearance at a
Toronto Blues Concert in 1970.

Lineage

Johnson was mainly self-taught, but his style influenced not only jazz guitarists like Teddy Burn and **Charlie Christian**, but also certain of the more expressive blues guitarists like Scrapper Blackwell and Blind Boy Fuller.

Listening

1 The Legend
Louis Armstrong/World Records SH 406

2 The Complete Duke Ellington Vol 1
CBS 67264

3 The Chocolate Dandies
Swaggie S1249

4 Eddie Lang/Joe Venuti
Swinging The Blues/CBS 88142

5 Jazz Guitar Virtuoso
Eddie Lang/Yazoo 1059

6 Lonnie Johnson Vol 1 1926-28
Matchbox MSE 1006

7 Lonnie Johnson – Vocals & Instrumentals 1927-32
Origin OJL 23

Robert Johnson

Born: c.1913/Clarksdale, Mississippi, USA
Died: 1938/San Antonio, Texas, USA
Recording Career: 1936-1937
Instrument: Vocals, guitar

ONE OF THE FINEST of all blues singers, Robert Johnson came from the Mississippi Delta country that also produced Charlie Patton, Son House and Bukka White. He had made less than thirty record sides when murdered at twenty-five by a jealous girlfriend. His first 'studio' experience was in a converted hotel room in San Antonio, and his second at the back of a Dallas office block! In these unlikely surroundings, Johnson made recordings of amazing intensity. *Hellbound On My Trail* and *Stones In My Passway* >**1** suggest inner turmoil and make use of a savage imagery that perhaps reflects his alcoholic excesses. As his voice wrings every emotion from the lyric, excursions into the falsetto range take his performances into the realms of the 'wounded animal'.

Johnson's guitar playing was an ideal adjunct to his voice and titles such as *Rambling On My Mind* and *Preachin' Blues* >**2** demonstrate his skill with bottleneck (slide guitar) techniques. To complete the package, he occasionally ventured into the world of guitar rags, *They're Red Hot* >**2** being a prime example.

Lineage

Although he did not record until 1936, he was a primitive, reflecting something of the free spirit of Charlie Patton and Bukka White. His influence, however, was widespread: **Muddy Waters** listened constructively, and pianist Sunnyland Slim translated his ideas to the piano, as did Little Brother Montgomery. Beyond this, his influence went to a far wider audience through rhythm and blues: the Rolling Stones recorded a Johnson tune, *Love In Vain* >**2**, while *Rambling On My Mind* and *Crossroads* have featured in Eric Clapton's repertoire.

Listening

1 King Of The Delta Blues Singers Vol 1
Robert Johnson/CBS 62456*

2 King Of The Delta Blues Singers Vol 2
Robert Johnson/CBS 64102*

(*available together on two-record set CBS 22190)

Eddie Lang

Born: 25th October 1902/ Philadelphia, Pennsylvania, USA
Died: 26th March 1933/New York City, NY, USA
Instruments: Guitar, banjo
Recording Career: 1924-1933

IT COULD BE ARGUED that Salvatore Massaro (Lang's real name) was the first solo guitarist to acquire an international reputation. With the Mound City Blues Blowers, a group built around the slender talents of comb-and-paper blower Red McKenzie, he toured extensively in the US and played the Piccadilly Hotel in London. Lang had spent eleven years studying the violin, even playing in his school orchestra

with fellow-fiddler, **Joe Venuti**, before turning to the guitar.

The association with Venuti was one that was to yield an especially rich musical crop, and Lang's dapper guitar was welcome in fields outside jazz. He played with several of the chintzy dance bands of the day, but it was his creative work with jazz masters such as **Bix Beiderbecke** that endeared him to the jazz public. His break on *Singin' The Blues* >**1** became something of a test piece for guitarists, yet his lightly rhythmic style remained a perfect complement to the playing of cornettist Beiderbecke.

He was not quite so happy in earthier surroundings; comparing the three titles recorded in 1928 with blues singer **Bessie Smith** >**2** with the Beiderbecke sessions gives the listener a true insight into the man. In the clean-cut atmosphere engendered by Beiderbecke's music, Lang's beautifully articulated solo lines are ideal but, alongside Smith's slurred timing and gut-wrenching intensity, he sounds diffident and out-of-place. On the other hand, he recorded many charming jazz pieces in association with Venuti >**3** and was on a number of record dates with Red Nichols, Paul Whiteman and

Roger Wolfe Kahn. He accompanied singer Bing Crosby for two years but it was the outstanding duets recorded in 1928/9 with guitarist **Lonnie Johnson >4** that mark the high point of Lang's career. It is here that his sensitive chord patterns and meticulous single string work are shown to best advantage.

His death came as a tremendous shock to the jazz fraternity: otherwise in good health, he died from complications that occurred during a tonsillectomy operation.

Lineage

Something of an original, Lang was held in remarkably high esteem in the thirties and became the model for fine players such as Dick McDonough, Carl Kress >**5** and Nappy Lamare.

Media

Lang took part in the films *King Of Jazz* (1930) and *The Big Broadcast* (1932). His recordings were used on the soundtrack of *The Fortune* (1974).

Listening

1 Young Man with The Horn
   Bix Beiderbecke/CBS 88030
2 Any Woman's Blues
   Bessie Smith/CBS 66262
3 Joe Venuti And Eddie Lang 1927-29
   Swaggie S 1276
4 Eddie Lang And Lonnie Johnson Vols 1/2
   Swaggie S1229/S1276
5 Jazz Guitar Virtuosos
   Lang/Kress/Johnson/Yazoo 1059

Meade Lux Lewis

Born: 4th September 1905/Chicago, Illinois, USA
Died: 7th June 1964/Minneapolis, Minnesota, USA
Instrument: Piano, composer
Recording Career: 1923-1962
Nickname: Lux (Duke of Luxembourg)

FOR THE FIRST thirty years of his life Meade Anderson 'Lux' Lewis only worked on his music sporadically. After various jobs taken to augment his earnings, he was discovered by John Hammond while working in a car wash.

The New York musicologist persuaded him to re-record his classic 1927 recording, *Honky Tonk Train Blues >***1** and it presaged a return to boogie woogie, the blues style with its insistent eight-to-the-bar left-hand figures and descriptive treble melodies. In the America of the late thirties, interest in this music took on almost epidemic proportions and Lewis became a central figure.

After moving to New York, he joined forces with two other exponents of the art, Albert Ammons and Pete Johnson, and their Boogie Woogie Trio was a sensation. Ammons and Johnson had stronger affinities with the jazz mainstream but, while together, they stayed loyal to boogie >**2**, **3**. Lewis was the more subtle, his trains loping between stations, flowing over the rhythmic points effortlessly and emerging unflustered from even the longest improvisational tunnel.

It is sometimes instructive to acknowledge failures, and it has to be conceded that on a frenetic JATP live recording, Lewis abandoned almost all of the qualities above to create false excitement. To counter this, he can be heard as **Sidney Bechet**'s superb accompanist on *Summertime >***4**, and on most of his known recordings he showed himself to be a master of the boogie art.

Lineage

Lewis was first inspired by Jimmy Yancey in Chicago, and actually recorded before the legendary Pine Top Smith. He was undoubtedly a seminal influence on the whole boogie field. Not only did he direct major figures who were his peers, but his presence can even be felt in the novelty boogie players of the fifties, such as Winifred Attwell.

Media

Appeared in film *New Orleans* (1947).

Listening

1 Paramount Volume 2
   The Piano Blues/Magpie PY 4417
2 Boogie Woogie Trio
   Storyville SLP 184
3 Unissued Boogie 1938/45
   The Piano Blues/Magpie PY 4421
4 Jazz Classics Volume 1
   Sidney Bechet/Blue Note BST 81201

McKinney's Cotton Pickers

(William McKinney – Born 17th September 1894/Cynthiana, Kentucky, USA; died 14th October 1969/Cynthiana, Kentucky, USA)
Original Line-up:
John Nesbitt (trumpet)/Langston Curl (trumpet)/Claude Jones (trombone)/ Don Redman (clarinet, alto saxophone, baritone saxophone, arranger)/Milton Senior (clarinet, alto saxophone)/George Thomas (clarinet, trombone)/Prince Robinson (clarinet, trombone)/Todd Rhodes (piano)/Dave Wilborn (banjo, guitar)/Ralph Escudero (tuba)/Cuba Austin (drums) Recording Career: 1928-1931

SHORTLY AFTER the First World War, William McKinney formed a band in Springfield, Ohio called the Synco Septet (not to be confused with the Synco Jazz Band, an unadventurous New York band of the time) which concentrated its efforts in that locality. In 1923, McKinney turned the drum stool over to Cuba Austin and elected himself business manager. Increasingly popular, the group adopted the McKinney's Cotton Pickers tag for the first time in 1926. In the following year they took up a residency at the Greystone Ballroom in Detroit but, more importantly, employed Don Redman as the band's musical director. Fresh from **Fletcher Henderson**, Redman was an avant-garde arranger to rival **Duke Ellington**.

The band began recording in 1928 and immediately established itself as one of the outstanding Negro bands of the day. Redman's charts were a joy, and stomping performances such as *Milenburg Joys* and *Stop Kidding* >**1** were models of their kind, showing that the arranger had already freed himself from the restrictions of section harmonies. The soloists were not the band's strongest point, but trombonist Claude Jones, trumpeter John Nesbitt and reed specialist Redman himself contributed impressively.

Perhaps due to the Greystone connections, the Cotton Pickers' activities overlapped with the white Jean Goldkette Orchestra. Recording dates were shared and the bands' members interchanged so that some issues could go out under the more commercially successful Goldkette banner. *My Blackbirds Are Bluebirds Now* and *Don't Be Like That* >**1** are obvious examples but Redman was not averse to shuffling his own deck of talents. For dates in 1929 and 1930 he introduced former Henderson colleagues like Joe Smith, **Benny Carter**, **Coleman Hawkins** and the ubiquitous **Fats Waller** for sessions that produced outstanding performances like *Miss Hannah* >**1** and *Wherever There's A Will* >**1**.

Bubber Miley

Born: 3rd April 1903/Aiken, South Carolina, USA
Died: 20th May 1932/Welfare Island, NY, USA
Instrument: Trumpet, composer
Recording Career: 1923 (1921?)-1931

HEARING the early **Duke Ellington** Orchestra for the first time can be a shattering experience for the jazz newcomer. Initially, the biggest barrier is the ferocity of the growling brass, a style that was adopted as being compatible with Ellington's musical policy at the Cotton Club. It was a feature of the band's music right up to the time of its leader's demise yet its origins can be traced almost uniquely to the work of one musician in the band: James Wesley 'Bubber' Miley.

After serving in the US Navy, Miley decided on a musical career in 1919 and before long was touring with Mamie Smith. He joined the Washingtonians in 1923 and remained with them when Ellington assumed the leadership in the following year. Once within the band he perfected the art of 'freak' trumpet playing: his growling 'wa-wa' style was achieved by the use of the rubber plunger mute. Using this kitchen utensil, he was able to produce the most amazing range of sounds, at times preaching like a human voice and at others roaring in a completely animated manner. *Creole Love Call*, *Black And Tan Fantasy* and *East St Louis Toodle-oo* >**1** are masterful examples and they make clear why the Ellington band was said to play in the 'jungle' style at the time.

Miley left Ellington in 1929 and came to Europe with Noble Sissle. Back home the following year he played with the white band of Leo Reisman and then worked in several reviews. He was already suffering from tuberculosis, however, and he died still short of his thirtieth birthday.

Despite his early death, in a period of less than five years he put his stamp on the greatest of all jazz orchestras. It was a stamp that was never eradicated.

Lineage
His style, judged with or without growl

The band's last recording was in September 1931 but sidemen had already begun to complain of poor working conditions, bad pay and disorganised tours. Although McKinney, with the aid of Benny Carter, tried to revive its fortunes, the Cotton Pickers ceased to exist in 1933. However, in its lifetime the band left a body of recorded work that marked it out as one of the best of the era. Quaint Redman vocals on titles like *Gee Baby Ain't I Good To You* >**1** and *Rocky Road* >**2** were trademarks, but it is as an excellent shouting band that the Cotton Pickers will always be remembered.

Lineage
The Cotton Pickers would have been just another territory band had not Don Redman transformed them. They had used mainly stock arrangements and had modelled themselves on other hot dance bands of the era, but Redman's arrangments turned them into a highly original and potent jazz unit. However, by the time of their demise, most big bands had progressed along wholly different lines.

Listening
1 The Complete McKinney's Cotton Pickers (1928-29) Vols 1/2
RCA PM 42407
2 The Complete McKinney's Cotton Pickers Vols 3/4
RCA PM 43258

effects, might be considered as from the **King Oliver** school. Certainly titles like *Got Everything But You* and *Flaming Youth* >**2** employed the same delays within his line and the same contrasts between legato blues phrases and staccato flurries. Miley's own influence is discernible in all growl specialists, with Cootie Williams and Sidney De Paris the most obvious candidates. Through **Tricky Sam Nanton**, he also influenced 'plunger' users on the trombone including Tyree Glenn, Quentin Jackson, Booty Wood and even, latterly, Lawrence Brown.

More recently, an affectionate version of *East St Louis Toodle-oo* was used by Steely Dan on their album *Pretzel Logic* (1974).

Media

Black And Tan Fantasy >**1** features on the sound track of *Adalen 31* (1969).

Listening

1 Cotton Club Days
  Duke Ellington/RCA CL 89801
2 Indispensable Duke
  Duke Ellington/RCA PM 43687

Bennie Moten

Born: 13th November 1894/Kansas City, Missouri, USA
Died: 2nd April 1935/Kansas City, Missouri, USA
Instrument: Piano, leader, composer
Recording Career: 1923-1932

BENNIE MOTEN represents yet another stumbling block to the 'jazz up the river from New Orleans' theory. By the early twenties, he had an uncompromising band of his own in Kansas City and by 1923 was recording a very personal brand of jazz >**1**. Trumpeter Lammar Wright, and trombonist Thamon Hayes were prominent and impressive soloists in the band but as the sextet of 1923 became larger, Moten began to establish his own, very significant traditions.

Certainly, by 1926 his band compared favourably with the

contemporary **Duke Ellington** and **Fletcher Henderson** bands. At that time, it retained something of its rural identity, with a hint of the banjo-picker and chicken-reel but, as the thirties arrived, more sophisticated players joined the group. Pianist **Count Basie** and multi-instrumentalist Eddie Durham enlisted in 1929, followed in 1930 by trumpeter **Hot Lips Page**. Showcase items such as *Small Black* >**2**, for Basie, or *Lafayette* >**3**, for Page showed their true quality as soloists but also how the band had changed to accommodate them.

The Moten band did not record after 1932, however, and after some personnel juggling, Basie took over the nucleus of the band when Moten died, still only forty, as the unfortunate consequence of a tonsillectomy.

Lineage

His mother was a pianist, but Moten also played baritone horn as a youth. Despite his importance in the history of Kansas City jazz, he had no discernible imitators.

Listening

1 Kansas City Orchestra 1923-1929
  Bennie Moten/Historical Records 9
2 The Complete Moten Vols 3/4
  Bennie Moten/RCA PM 43693
3 The Complete Moten Vols 5/6
  Bennie Moten/RCA PM 45688

Tricky Sam Nanton

Born: 1st February 1904/New York City, NY, USA
Died: 20th July 1946/San Francisco, California, USA
Instrument: Trombone
Recording Career: 1925-1946

JOSEPH NANTON'S first professional job was with pianist Cliff Jackson. Then came spells with Earl Frazier and Jackson again, before he joined the Washingtonians under Elmer Snowden in 1925. **Duke Ellington** took over the band in the following year, and the trombonist remained with him until his death twenty years later.

Nanton was one of jazz's truly unique artists. He was fascinated by **Bubber Miley**'s use of the 'wa-wa' mute and worked tirelessly, both in solitary practice sessions and within the band, to incorporate it into his own style. The extent of his success leaps out from countless recordings of the era. It is only necessary to listen to the 1930 *Jungle Night In Harlem* >**1** to appreciate the intensity of his work, to the 1927 *Black And Tan Fantasy* >**2** for the poignancy, and to the 1930 *Old Man Blues* >**1** for the sheer swing. His playing was never without a sense of humour and, as *Stevedore Stomp* >**3** shows, he could also be a dashing player without the mute.

Nanton's was an ageless style that fitted the sleek 1940/41 band just as well as the earlier units. Whether sharing *Just A Sittin'* >**4** effortlessly with **Ben Webster** or jousting with fellow trombonist Juan Tizol on *Flaming Sword* >**5**, it still sounded just right. Nanton's death affected his leader to the same extent as did the leaving of Miley, Barney Bigard, Sonny Greer and – somewhat later – **Johnny Hodges**.

Lineage

His playing with the 1925 Get Happy Band >**6** suggests a good but unspectacular traditionalist. In that year, however, he joined the Washingtonians and came under the spell of 'wa-wa' specialist **Bubber Miley**. Nanton learnt quickly and did for the trombone what Miley had done for the trumpet. He set the pattern for a generation of swing era trombonists, among them Tyree Glenn, Quentin Jackson, Booty Wood and Lawrence Brown.

Listening

1 The Indispensable Vols 3/4
 Duke Ellington/RCA PM 43697
2 Cotton Club Days
 Duke Ellington/RCA CL 89801
3 Jazz Cocktail
 Duke Ellington/Living Era AJA 5024
4 The Indispensable Vols 7/8
 Duke Ellington/RCA NL 89274
5 In A Mellotone
 Duke Ellington/RCA RD 27134
6 Sam Morgan/Get Happy Band
 VJM VLP 32

New Orleans Rhythm Kings

Original Line-up:
Paul Mares (cornet)/George Brunis (trombone)/Leon Roppolo (clarinet)/ Jack Pettis (saxophone)/Lou Black (banjo)/Steve Brown (bass)/Frank Snyder (drums)
Recording Career: 1922-1925 (1934)

THE FIRST ensemble comprising all white musicians to successfully capture the style and spirit of the black New Orleans bands was the New Orleans Rhythm Kings. They came together in 1921, and were originally called the Friars' Inn Society Orchestra. They disbanded in 1924 but, in that brief time, put their stamp on jazz with little more than twenty recorded titles.

The band's trumpeter, Paul Mares, modelled himself on **King Oliver** and he made a particularly good job of simulating that great player's 'preaching' style. On *Maple Leaf Rag* >**1**, he produces a smouldering solo that has all the latent power of his mentor. At the heart of the ensemble was the rustic trombone of George Brunis (original name George Brunies), but it was the silky sound of clarinettist Leon Roppolo that gave the band its distinctive trademark. On up-tempo material such as *That's A Plenty* >**2**, his playing was an amalgam of the Lorenzo Tio school and the spiky Larry Shields' **ODJB** (Original Dixieland Jass Band) style. On slows like *Tin Roof Blues* >**1**, more of the Creole language came through as the young Roppolo painted his blues in pastel shades. Not for him the passion of **Sidney Bechet** or **Johnny Dodds**; his brush was always just less than fully-charged, and he applied his gentle washes to a musical canvas ideally suited to receive them.

A revivalist session was organised in 1925, and *Golden Leaf Strut* >**3** was evidence of its success. More were attempted in 1934 and 1935, but only Brunis remained of the original band and the results, although pleasing in their own right, bore little resemblance to the fine music of the early twenties.

Lineage

NORK took their inspiration from the early **King Oliver** bands but, ironically, were not as influential as the later, and less musically equipped, Austin High School Gang.

Listening

1 New Orleans Rhythm Kings Vol 2
Swaggie 830
2 New Orleans Rhythm Kings Vol 1
Swaggie 829
3 Golden Leaf Strut
NORK/Parlophone R3254 (78rpm single)

Jimmie Noone

**Born: 23rd April 1895/Cut-Off,
Louisiana, USA
Died: 19th April 1944/Los Angeles,
California, USA
Instruments: Clarinet, soprano and
alto saxophones
Recording Career: 1923-1943**

OF ALL the great New Orleans clarinettists, Jimmy Noone was technically the best equipped. It is reputed that the French composer, Maurice Ravel, once notated a solo by him, only to be told subsequently by the first clarinet in a symphony orchestra that parts of it were impossible to play. Certainly, his virtuosity was daunting, the tone was full, the vibrato fast and his ability as an ensemble player beyond comparison.

His solos were usually a showcase for his brilliant, instrument skills. Well-practised runs which became favourite clichés were there to impress his peers,

but these were used sparingly and rarely impaired Noone's genuine, creative flow. *Play That Thing* >**1** with Ollie Powers, and a series of records with **King Oliver** >**2** showed him as a brilliant soloist and an impeccable band clarinettist.

Noone began by playing guitar, but by the age of fifteen had taken to the clarinet, with a professional debut at eighteen. Within a year, he was co-leading his own band with Buddy Petit. He was with **Freddie Keppard** in the Original Creole Band before periods with King Oliver and Doc Cooke. From 1926, he led the resident band at the Apex Club in Chicago and, in the company of men like altoist Joe Poston and piano wizard **Earl Hines**, made some of the most thrilling recordings of the period >**3**. Noone had moved into the swing era almost ten years early: his instrument sang like a New Orleans bird, and he swung in a way that pointed the way for his successors.

During the thirties he vacillated between Chicago and New York, and in 1939 actually led a large broadcasting orchestra. In the forties, he moved to California and, just as it looked as though he would join **Kid Ory** as a major figure in the New Orleans Revival, died of a heart attack.

Lineage

Noone studied the method of great teacher Lorenzo Tio secondhand by taking lessons from **Sidney Bechet**. His own stature was immense and he came to influence clarinettists Albert Nicholas, Barney Bigard and Omer Simeon among his New Orleans contemporaries. **Benny Goodman** made no secret of the fact that Noone was his prime influence as did **Woody Herman** and Ed Hall, who, like Noone, worked with trumpeter Buddy Petit in pre-recording days.

Media

Noone appeared in 1944 film *The Blockbusters.*

Listening

1 New York To Chicago 1923/8
Biograph BLP 12007
2 New Orleans Stomp
King Oliver/VJM VLP 35
3 Apex Club Blues
Jimmie Noone/Affinity AFS 1023

Ma Rainey

**Born: 26th April 1886/Columbus,
Georgia, USA
Died: 22nd December 1939/Columbus,
Georgia, USA
Instrument: Vocals
Recording Career: 1923-1928
Nicknames: Ma, The Black
Nightingale, The Paramount Wildcat**

UNQUESTIONABLY, Ma Rainey was
the mother of the blues. Artists such as
Trixie Smith and **Bessie Smith** may
have recorded before her, but she was
the doyenne of the female blues
singers.

Gertrude Malissa Nix Pridgett (her
real name) made her first public
appearance at the age of twelve in the
Bunch Of Blackberries show in
Columbus, Georgia. Three years later
she was a married 'woman' and from
then on performed in various Negro
vaudeville shows throughout the South.
she worked the TOBA (Theatre Owners
and Bookers Association) circuit famed
as the only source of entertainment for
many black southern towns, but was
given reason to believe those initials
could also mean 'Tough On Black
Artists'.

She travelled north in 1923 for
recording purposes, working only for
the Paramount Company. Although the
technical quality of these records was
generally poor, they brought Ma Rainey
widespread success and enabled her to
front her own shows. Her Georgia Jazz
Band became a permanent
accompaniment and her theatre and
tent-show tours of the twenties were
consistently successful. Rural audiences
loved the melancholia of her marvellous
voice, just as they thrilled to the way in
which the majesty of the delivery was
supported by a propulsively rhythmic
undertow. She left nothing to chance,
singing simply but with drama, and
gauging audience reaction with a skill
given only to great vaudeville artists.

Ma Rainey's records are among the
finest of the genre. The magnificent
Countin' The Blues >**1** matched the
inner sadness of her voice with the
plaintive lilt of **Louis Armstrong**'s cornet.
The series of records she made with

Lovie Austin's Blues Serenaders >**2** were models of shape and balance, while her folk origins were evoked with guitarists like Tampa Red and pianist Georgia Tom Dorsey in more primitive performances such as *Leaving This Morning* >**3** or *Blame It On The Blues* >**2**.

In the five years from 1923 to 1928, she recorded close on one hundred titles, mostly with the Georgia Jazz Band >**1**, **4** but retired from music in 1933 to live for the rest of her life back in her beloved Georgia.

Lineage

Originally trained as a singer and dancer, Rainey toured and learnt her craft as part of the famous Rabbit Foot Minstrels. Her own legacy was considerable. **Bessie Smith** was a 'student' at her court and her influence extended through the likes of Clara Smith, Ida Cox and Mamie Smith and on to male heavyweights such as Walter Brown, **T-Bone Walker**, and **Joe Turner**.

Media

Play *Ma Rainey's Black Bottom* by August Wilson, major success on Broadway, opened 1984.

Listening

1 Oh My Babe Blues
  Ma Rainey/Biograph BLP 12011
2 Queen Of The Blues
  Ma Rainey/Biograph BLP 12032
3 First Of The Great Blues Singers
  Ma Rainey/London AL 3502
4 Blues The World Forgot
  Ma Rainey/Biograph BLP 12001

Luis Russell

Born: 6th August 1902/Careening Clay, near Bocas Del Toro, Panama
Died: 11th December 1963/New York City, NY, USA
Instrument: Piano, arranger
Recording Career: 1926-1946

OBVIOUS CONFUSION had arisen in the world of jazz history when a picture of Luis Carl Russell accompanied by Albert Nicholas in Tom Anderson's Cabaret was listed in the *Pictorial History Of Jazz* as being taken in 1912. In fact, it was not until 1919 that Russell left his native Panama for New Orleans, and not until 1923 that he played with Nicholas at Anderson's. After his emigration, however, he had a hectic musical life. He worked with Doc Cooke and **King Oliver** in Chicago before joining George Howe's band in New York in 1927. Later that year he was appointed leader and for the next few years fronted one of the most successful bands of the era.

As a pianist he was a modest performer, stylistically touched by the players of New York but not himself a fully committed 'stride' pianist. It was his *band* that was important. Apart from the mammoth talent of **Duke Ellington**, no other leader successfully made the difficult transition from New Orleans style to swing formula, but this is just what Russell achieved.

The Luis Russell Band, with the leader at the piano

In just two years from January 1929, Russell's nine- or ten-piece band made records that progressed the New Orleans ideal into the swing era. Their jazz was uncomplicatedly inventive and it had in **Henry Allen** a superb trumpeter and in Nicholas a clarinettist who was already a master of collective playing. Trombonist Jay C. Higginbotham was a modern thinker of his time and his explosive solos make titles like *Doctor Blues* >**1**, *Panama* >**2** and *Swing Out* >**3** models of the type, while altoist Charlie Holmes proved himself to be both an impressive soloist, comparable to **Johnny Hodges** at the time, and also a selfless bandsman. Driving the whole band was George 'Pops' Foster, the most important string bassist of the twenties, and the man who made the band 'sit up and beg' on powerhouse performances such as *It Should Be You* >**3** and *Sugar Hill Function* >**4**.

Russell spent much of the thirties as a sideman for **Louis Armstrong**, finally leaving music as a full-time profession in 1948. In 1959 he gave classical piano recitals back in Panama but up until the time of his death worked mainly as a chauffeur and part-time piano teacher.

Lineage
Russell originally studied piano with his father and was impressed by pianists such as **James P. Johnson**, The Beetle and Abba Labba while in New York. However, he has had no discernible influence on other players.

Listening
1 Luis Russell 1926-1930
  VJM VLP 54
2 Luis Russell 1930-1934
  VJM VLP 57
3 Henry Red Allen And His New York Orchestra Vol 1
  RCA (F) FXM1 7060
4 Henry Red Allen With Luis Russell (1930/1)
  RCA (F) FXM1 7192

Bessie Smith

**Born: 15th April 1895/Chattanooga,
Tennessee, USA**
**Died: 26th September 1937/
Clarksdale, Mississippi, USA**
Instrument: Vocals
Recording Career: 1923-1933
Nickname: Empress of the Blues

THE MASSIVE talent of Bessie Smith
transcended both the blues and the jazz
world. Her earliest records >**1**
maintained some links with the folk-
blues tradition, but the intuitive way in
which she placed her notes to
accommodate the natural cadence of
her negro speech and her aptitude for
the rhythmically dramatic made her a
unique artist. She was an idol of the
music-halls and, at the height of her
fame, earned up to $2000 a week.

Smith's musical stature ensured that,
as her career progressed, she enjoyed
the best of accompanists. With **Louis
Armstrong** she made the timeless
Cold In Hand and the stately *St Louis*
Blues >**2**. With Joe Smith she wrang
every emotion from *Baby Doll* >**3**,
while with Tommy Ladnier on *Dyin' By*
The Hour >**2**, she captured an intensity
of grief seemingly beyond musical
expression.

She proved to be a master of the
double entendre and, on *Them's*
Graveyard Words >**2** and *Yes Indeed*
He Do >**4**, an 'actress' happy with
cynicism. Every inflexion had meaning
and the grandeur of her voice added a
poignancy even to less intense subjects.
Her first record in 1923 was a
tremendous hit and, despite a falling off
of interest in the blues, she remained a
bill-topper until the early thirties.

In 1933, jazz critic John Hammond
invited her to record with some of the
new generation of jazzmen. With Chew
Berry, **Jack Teagarden** and **Benny**
Goodman she recorded only four
sides >**1**, but these were enough to show
that her rhythmic power, natural
improvisational skill and marvellous
sense of swing had taken her into the
field of pure jazz. Tragically, in 1937, just
as Bessie Smith was poised to re-
emerge as a major voice, she was killed
in a road accident in Mississippi.

Lineage

While a teenager she toured with **Ma Rainey** and was considerably influenced by her. She in turn influenced a whole generation of female blues and jazz singers: some talented but slavish copyists such as Cleo Gibson; others more independently-inspired women – Cara Smith, **Dinah Washington**, Lavern Baker and Juanita Hall. She even had some influence on **Billie Holiday**, and certainly on male singers such as **Jimmy Rushing**, **Joe Turner** and **Jimmy Witherspoon**.

Media

In 1929 made a short film entitled *St Louis Blues* with Johnny Lee, and was the subject of a dramatic, but somewhat falacious play called *The Death of Bessie Smith* >**5**. An excellent biography, *Bessie* (1972) written by Chris Albertsen, and a fine assessment of Smith's singing style *Empress Of The Blues* (1957) put together by Albertsen and Gunther Schuller.

Listening

1 The World's Greatest Blues Singer
  Bessie Smith/CBS 66258
2 The Empress
  Bessie Smith/Columbia GC30818*
3 Nobody's Blues But Mine
  Bessie Smith/CBS 67232
4 Empty Bed Blues
  Bessie Smith/CBS 66273
5 The Death Of Bessie Smith Soundtrack
  Bessie Smith/CICALA BLJ8025
6 Any Woman's Blues
  Bessie Smith/CBS 66262

*Only available in the USA

Jabbo Smith

Born: 24th December 1908/Pembroke, Georgia, USA
Instruments: Trumpet, trombone, vocals
Recording Career: 1926-

THE SUCCESS of **Louis Armstrong**'s records in the late twenties made rival record companies desperate to find a comparable artist. Brunswick came closest when, in 1929, they launched a series of records by Cladys 'Jabbo' Smith and His Rhythm Aces. Smith had already recorded with **Duke Ellington**, the Georgia Strutters (Perry Bradford), **James P. Johnson**, **Fats Waller**, Thomas Morris and **Clarence Williams**, but these recordings gave no hint of the type of music that the explosive Rhythm Aces would offer. The contrast was such it was once assumed that there were two Jabbo Smiths! Ellington and Johnson's 'version', in particular, portrayed a lyrical, almost restrained player, whose solos unfolded with grace.

In contrast, the trumpet on titles such as *Jazz Battle* >**1**, **2** and *Boston Skuffle* >**3** seemed to explode from the record. Notes were almost spat out with apoplectic venom. On *Croonin' The Blues* >**1** Smith even essayed an opening cadenza to rival Armstrong's famous *West End Blues* statement. In fairness, there were also easy flowing moments on numbers like *Little Willy Blues* >**1**, **2** and sweeter ones on *Moanful Blues* >**3** but the series of recordings did not enjoy its deserved success.

Smith was justifiably disappointed and, although he remained active in music, frequently working in Milwaukee during the thirites, he made no records to equal the superb Aces items. He worked with **Sidney Bechet** in New York during the Second World War, but was in and out of the music world in Milwaukee through the fifties and sixties, making several comeback attempts.

Lineage

Smith was taught trumpet and trombone at an orphanage in Charleston, South Carolina. Later the tremendous influence of **Louis Armstrong** entered his world although there was sufficient that was special to Smith to make him unique. He was also a proficient pianist, but there is no evidence of disciples on any of his instruments.

Listening

1 Trumpet Ace Of The Twenties Vol 1
  Jabbo Smith/Melodeon MLP 7326
2 Sweet 'n' Low Down
  Jabbo Smith/Affinity AFS 1029
3 Trumpet Ace Of The Twenties Vol 2
  Jabbo Smith/Melodeon MLP 7327

Muggsy Spanier

**Born: 9th November 1906/Chicago,
Illinois, USA
Died: 12th February 1967/Sausalito,
California, USA
Instrument: Cornet
Recording Career: 1924-1964**

BORN FRANCIS JOSEPH, Spanier will
probably be mostly remembered as the
trumpeter who avoided all high-note
pyrotechnics. He made his professional
debut at sixteen and in the following
year made recordings with the
Bucktown Five where he demonstrated
remarkable maturity. His lead, and his
use of breaks on *Buddy's Habits* >**1** was
distinctly **King Oliver**-ish and his
preaching, muted solo on *Steady Roll
Blues* >**1** exhibited tremendous verve.
   In the late twenties he was with Floyd
Town, and from 1929 until 1936 with Ted
Lewis. He also worked on and off with
Ray Miller, the **Dorsey** Brothers and
other commercial bands of the era. In
1930, however, he formed a band that
greatly influenced the course of jazz
history. At a time when traditional jazz
was wholly out of favour, his Ragtimers
band with trombonist George Brunis,
clarinettist Rod Cless and pianists
George Zack and Joe Buskin, made a
series of records for Victor that truly
captured the spirit of the pioneer
musicians. *Relaxin' At The Touro* >**2**
showed the leader's mastery of the
blues, *Livery Stable Blues* >**2** the
group's superbly integrated ensemble
playing, and *Big Butter And Egg
Man* >**2** the sheer élan of their delivery.
It was not difficult to see why so many
traditional bands took their inspiration
from the Ragtimers.
   Spanier led a big band during the
Second World War but, although he
played good, attacking trumpet on titles
like *Little David, Play On Your Harp*
and *Chicago* >**3**, it was an uneasy
mixture of styles. After a period back
with Ted Lewis, Spanier remained
mainly on the West Coast, playing in a
more traditional manner but never
finding that special quality that
distinguished the Ragtimers.

Lineage
Influenced by **King Oliver** and **Louis
Armstrong**, Spanier favoured the more
conservative side of their personalities.
Apart from revivalist bands, his own
influence has been negligible.

Media
Spanier played with the **Bob Crosby**
Band in a film entitled *Sis Hopkins*
(1941). Also featured in *Is Everybody
Happy?* (1929) and *Here Comes The
Band* (1935).

Listening
1 The Bucktown Five
   Bix Beiderbecke and Muggsy Spanier/
   Milestone M 47019
2 Spanier's Ragtime Band Vol 1
   Muggsy Spanier/Joker SM 3574
3 Muggsy Spanier
   Coral CP 101

Jack Teagarden

**Born: 29th August 1895/Vernon,
Texas, USA
Died: 15th January 1964/New
Orleans, Louisiana, USA
Instrument: Trombone, vocals
Recording Career: 1927-1963
Nicknames: Big T, Tea**

THE SAD-EYED MOOD of Jack
Teagarden's trombone was a natural
tearjerker. His relaxed, almost lazy
delivery made his jazz melancholy but
never maudlin, and he was probably
the first of the 'blue-eyed, blues-singers'
almost forty years before what is
generally assumed to be a pop music
phenomenon.
   Weldon Leo Teagarden came from a
musical family: his father toyed with the
trumpet, brothers Charles and Clois
became excellent professionals on
trumpet and drums respectively and
sister Norma was a well-considered
pianist. For two years, Jack played
trombone with Peck Kelley's Bad Boys,
but it was his 1927 arrival in New York,
still a gauche country boy, that turned

the jazz world on its ear >**1**.

He was already a superb instrumentalist, his style was established, and was to show no appreciable change for his entire career. In his solos Teagarden juxtaposed fluttering arpeggios and long drawn legato phrases, straight from his native Texas speech, and a title like *Basin Street Blues* >**2** showed that his blues displayed mournful acceptance rather than angry protest.

From 1928 to 1933, he worked with Ben Pollack >**1**, **3**, from 1934 to 1938 with Paul Whiteman >**3**, and from 1939 until 1946 he led his own bands. In 1947, Teagarden joined the **Louis Armstrong** All Stars and began a four-year stint that introduced his

playing to audiences that went wider than the jazz world. It was an unlikely but fruitful partnership. Neither player was interested in the pure New Orleans ensemble style, and both had room to solo. Titles such as *Rockin' Chair* >**4** set a pattern for their performances, and virtuoso pieces like *Stardust* >**5** show the trombonist's skills undiminshed.

Teagarden remained an 'All Star' in his own right after leaving Armstrong, and he led (or co-led) quality groups until the time of his death from bronchial pneumonia. He had played at the Dream Room in New Orleans only one day before his death.

Lineage

Unlike his contemporary trombonists,

Above: Joe Venuti

Jimmy Harrison and J. C. Higginbotham, he was not influenced by **Louis Armstrong.** He claimed that it was the playing of pianist Peck Kelley that had most effect upon him. His own influence on the Dixieland and Chicago players was considerable. Trombonists like Cutty Cutshall, Lou McGarity and Abe Lincoln were all strongly influenced, as indeed were seventies revivalists including Tom Artin and Roy Williams.

Media

Career summarised in Howard J. Walters Jnr's excellent *Jack Teagarden's Music*, and Walter C. Allen's *Jazz Monograph* series (both 1960); fine biography, *Jack Teagarden* (1960) by Jay D. Smith and Len Gutteridge. Teagarden appeared in the film *Jazz On A Summer's Day* (1960).

Listening

1 King Of The Blues
Jack Teagarden/Epic JSN 6044
2 Trombone T From Texas
Jack Teagarden/Affinity AFS 1015
3 The Indispensable 1928-57
Jack Teagarden/RCA PM 45675
4 At Town Hall
Louis Armstrong/RCA NL 89746 (2)
5 At Pasadena
Louis Armstrong/Coral CP 50

Joe Venuti

Born: 16th September 1903(?)/South Philadelphia, Pennsylvania, USA(?)
Died: 14th August 1978/Seattle, Washington, USA
Instrument: Violin
Recording Career: 1925-1977

ONE OF THE really outstanding jazz violinists, Giuseppe (Joe) Venuti was a complete original. He worked in the prestigious orchestras of Jean Goldkette, Roger Wolfe Kahn and Paul Whiteman, but it was the small group records that he made with **Eddie Lang**, Arthur Schutt and Adrian Rollini in 1927 which established him internationally. Cuts like *Cheese And Crackers* and *Beatin' The Dog* >**1** demonstrate the loose-jointed swing of the Blue Four, as they called themselves, and the ensemble was to set the stage for the chamber jazz groups of the thirties.

Venuti's own playing was unashamedly romantic. He rebuilt his melodies with gentle care and played everything with an infectious swing.

Against the lugubrious insistence of Rollini's bass sax, his solo lines danced with great buoyancy and gave the group its distinctive character. In the thirties, his recording group grew in size, but there was no consequent loss of creativity or spontaneity. *Raggin' The Scale* >**2** (1933) with Jimmy Dorsey (who made it the Blue Five) was as free as the Blue Four piece had been, although if anything the players had become more sophisticated.

From the forties through to the sixties, Venuti did a great deal of studio work, mainly on the West Coast, but a hugely successful set at the 1968 Newport Jazz Festival encouraged him to set out his stall as a globe-trotting solo attraction. He began to appear at festivals throughout the world, with a resulting renewal of interest in his records. Unexpected partners fired his imagination: he recorded brilliantly with **Zoot Sims**, but perhaps one of the most surprising sessions was that with bebop maverick, Joe Albany. The latter's mixed piano style, full of swing era logic and bop angularity challenged Venuti, but *Blue Heaven* and *Sheik Of Araby* >**3** show just how well the septuagenarian fiddler could adapt.

Venuti survived serious illness in 1970 and seemed to have regained full health until his sudden death towards the end of the decade.

Lineage
At the outset, Venuti worked with guitarist **Eddie Lang**, although he was later influenced by Eddie South. His own style remained highly personal and he had no major disciples.

Media
Appeared in many films, most prominently in *Garden Of The Moon* (1938), *Two Guys From Texas* (1948), *Riding High* (1949) and *The Five Pennies* (1959). Performed on the soundtracks of *The Fortune* (1974) and *Inserts* (1975).

Listening
1 Stringing The Blues
  Eddie Lang/CBS 88142
2 Jazz In The Thirties
  Various/World Records SHB 39
3 Joe Venuti/Joe Albany
  Horo HDP 41-42

Clarence Williams

Born: 8th October 1898/Plaquemine Delta, Louisiana, USA
Died: 6th November 1965/Queens, NY, USA
Instrument: Piano, vocals, arranger, composer, leader
Recording Career: 1921-1947

ALTHOUGH a limited pianist, Clarence Williams held an important position in jazz: he was on **Bessie Smith**'s first issued recording >**1**. From 1923 to 1925, he recorded with his superb ensemble, Blue Five >**2**, which featured no less than **Louis Armstrong** and **Sidney Bechet**. He then led fine hokum bands >**3** with tuba specialist Cyrus St Clair and washboard wizard Floyd Casey, before later attempting to front somewhat unwieldy larger groups >**4**.

Williams began his musical life as a sporting-house pianist in Storyville. He worked with minstrel shows and also backed singers like Eva Taylor (his wife), Sara Martin, Sippie Wallace, Alberta Hunter, Maggie Jones and, of course, Bessie Smith. As early as 1913 he was active as songwriter and publisher, and in the thirties ran his own publishing house on Broadway. In his last years Williams ran a hobby shop in New York's Harlem.

Lineage
Originally he listened to men like Tony Jackson and **Jelly Roll Morton** and learned to play by ear. Morton was his idol but, in truth, few players could be said to have been influenced by Williams himself.

Media
Excellent book *Clarence Williams* (1976) by Tom Lord.

Listening
1 The World's Greatest Blues Singer
  Bessie Smith/CBS 66258
2 Clarence Williams Blue Five
  Armstrong/Bechet/CBS 63092
3 Jug Bands 1929-1934
  Various/Swaggie 877
4 New York Columbia Recordings 1929-31
  Clarence Williams/VJM VLP 47

THE jazz of the early thirties maintained strong links with the preceding decade. Big bands such as those led by Fletcher Henderson, Luis Russell and the waning King Oliver still reflected the influence of New Orleans instrumental giants like Louis Armstrong and even of arrangers like Jelly Roll Morton. Despite this, the move was emotionally away from the formula of Crescent City music, a style thought to be passé. The alternative was no improvement, however, and the augmented small groups of the era produced jazz that became dated almost overnight. The combos of the early thirties had no stylistic yardstick to match the near perfection of form achieved by the New Orleans ensemble and merely tried to replace it by greater, and as it turned out, musically stultifying organisation.

There is no doubt that the economic and political climate played an important part in these musical attitudes and jazz found some parallels in the field of popular music. The depression in America encouraged a mood of entrenchment. Romanticism replaced the strident optimism of twenties jazz

The Louis Jordan Band

and effusive instrumental styles emerged around figures such as tenor saxophonist Coleman Hawkins and pianist Earl Hines.

As the decade progressed, jazzmen were increasingly forced to earn their livings in big bands, with solo opportunities restricted to a minimum. The white big bands began to enjoy a disproportionate amount of exposure and the 'swing era' was ushered in. The mighty presence of Duke Ellington tended to offset this imbalance and, although his band softened its approach from the wilder 'jungle band' style, it did give its superb roster of soloists breathing space.

For some time jazz remained polarised around New York and Chicago, but the arrival of the Count Basie Orchestra from Kansas City signalled a turn-about in attitudes that had a far-reaching effect. It introduced a jazz world to the considerable talents of tenor saxophonist Lester Young and trombonist Dicky Wells and returned the music to the extrovert qualities of earlier times.

From the middle thirties, jazz at least maintained its voice through records and pianist Teddy Wilson, singer Billie Holiday and clarinettist Benny Goodman were amongst those who provided small group performances to keep the torch burning. Fats Waller successfully crossed the barrier into jazz-inspired popular music and generally the state of jazz was healthier as the Second World War approached.

Count Basie

**Born: 21st August 1904/Red Bank,
New Jersey, USA
Died: 26th April 1984/Hollywood,
Florida, USA
Instruments: Piano, organ
Recording Career: 1930–1983**

THE PIANO is an instrument which, by
its very nature, encourages a show of
technique, often tempting its
practitioners to fill every available
space. Names such as **Art Tatum**,
Oscar Peterson and **Cecil Taylor**
come readily to mind and there are few
pianists who can deny themselves the
luxury of frequent and extravagant
flourishes. One of the most notable
exceptions was William (Count) Basie
who, although capable of busy solo
work, was normally economical to the
degree of musical meanness. Basie's
introduction to jazz took place in the

theatre as an accompanist to vaudeville
acts. Following the break-up of a
touring group in 1928, he was stranded
in Kansas City and ended up joining
Walter Page's Blue Devils. His stay with
that colourful band lasted until they
disbanded almost a year later when,
together with several other members of
the group, he joined the **Bennie Moten**
Orchestra. Titles like *Small Black* >**1**
and *Toby* >**2** attest to Basie's ability to
play busy solos, in a style that was a
personal adaptation of New York stride.

Basie remained with Moten until 1934
when he left to form his own band in
Little Rock. In the following year Moten
died and Basie returned to work briefly,
under Buster Moten's leadership, but it
was not long before the pianist was
back in Kansas City. Once there, he
landed a residency for his Barons Of
Rhythm at the Reno Club and also
secured a radio spot.

He was now 'Count' rather than Bill
Basie and, through the broadcasts,
came to the notice of critic John

Hammond. The young writer was tremendously impressed and initiated the band's national tour, taking them to Chicago, Buffalo and, finally, on to New York. They were a pretty ragged band, using mainly 'head' arrangements, and did not showcase their soloists to the best advantage. With encouragement from Hammond, however, Basie strengthened his line-up and when the band made its New York recording debut in the following year it boasted such luminaries as trumpeter **Buck Clayton**, saxophonists **Lester Young** and Herschel Evans, vocalist **Jimmy Rushing** and a rhythm team that included Walter Page and Jo Jones. Almost at once Freddie Green completed what became known as the All-American Rhythm Section.

This gave the band its unmistakable trademark: four even beats to the bar, all delivered with a unique lightness of touch. At the heart of it was Basie the economical, playing beautiful fill-ins, never obstructing, but lifting his soloists masterfully. So began a series of outstanding performances that rank with anything in big band history. The great Lester Young turned *If I Didn't Care*, *Taxi War Dance* >**3** and *Honeysuckle Rose* >**4** into pure magic, Evans made *Blue And Sentimental* >**5** a rhapsodic gem, Clayton added his special talents to *Topsy* >**5** and *Good Morning Blues* >**6**; the list is endless. The gifted **Dicky Wells** joined in 1938 and made his mark with *Panasie Stomp* and *Texas Shuffle* >**5**, while later that year trumpeter Harry Edison strengthened it further, putting his stamp on *Every Tub* >**5** and *Broadway* >**7**.

Despite changes of personnel in the forties, Basie continued to lead a superb band with an emphasis on tenor saxophonists. Outstanding players like Buddy Tate, **Don Byas**, Lucky Thompson and Paul Gonsalves passed through the ranks and contributed to high musical standards. For a brief period Basie used an octet but, in 1951, he returned to the big band format (see second entry in The Fifties, page 132).

Lineage

Basie was inspired by the New York stride pianists but was personally helped by **Fats Waller** and Willie 'The Lion' Smith. Countless pianists adopted Basie's own mannerisms but none could be said to have been truly influenced by him.

Media

Books: *Count Basie And His Orchestra* (1957) by Raymond Horricks and *The World Of Count Basie* (1980) by Stanley Dance. He made several short films, including a particularly successful one with Billie Holiday in 1950 entitled *Sugar Chile Robinson, Billie Holiday, Count Basie And His Sextet*. He took a prominent part in the CBS film *Sound Of Jazz* (1957) and was a frequent TV performer. Other cinema appearances in the period covered by this entry were *Crazyhouse/Funzapoppin*, (1943), *Hit Parade Of 1943* and *Top Man* (1943). Posthumous autobiography *Good Morning Blues* (as told to Albert Murray) appeared in 1985, also *Count Basie A Biodiscography* by Chris Sheridan (1986).

Listening

1 The Complete Bennie Moten Vols 3/4 (1928-30)
RCA PM 43693

2 The Complete Bennie Moten Vols 5/6 (1930-32)
RCA PM 45688

3 Count Basie And His Orchestra 1936-39
CBS 88667

4 Swingin' At The Daisy Chain
Count Basie/Affinity AFS 1019

5 Swingin' The Blues
Count Basie/Affinity AFS 1010

6 Good Mornin' Blues
Jimmy Rushing/Affinity AFS 1002

7 Count Basie And His Orchestra Vol 3 1940-41
CBS 88672

Bunny Berigan

Born: 2nd November 1908/Hilbert, Calumet, Wisconsin, USA
Died: 2nd June 1942/New York City, NY, USA
Instrument: Trumpet, vocals
Recording Career: 1928-1942

THE SIMILARITY between Berigan's career and that of **Bix Beiderbecke** is remarkable. Both were white men who played black music, both had unique styles, both made commercial compromises, took to drink and set themselves onto a course of self-destruction. Why Berigan is a little-known figure and Beiderbecke a folk legend, we will never know.

Roland Bernart Berigan sat in with the **New Orleans Rhythm Kings** while still a teenager, but until joining Hal Kemp in 1930 was associated only with minor bands. He later played on a Dorsey Brothers show and linked up with Paul Whiteman for a year. In 1935 he joined **Benny Goodman** but did not remain with the King for long and formed his own big band in 1937. He was not a natural leader, exerting little in the way of discipline but, musically, he led a good band.

In 1936 Berigan had recorded *I Can't Get Started* with a pick-up group but his 1937 version >**1**, originally issued on a twelve-inch 78rpm disc, was justly his greatest hit. The leader's vocal is not without charm, but it is his masterful trumpet with its sweet and sour tone, rumbling rhythmic thrust and utter sincerity that communicates. Until the band folded, there were many such gems, some with an alcohol-induced fumble, but all possessed of the true spirit of jazz.

Changes Made >**1** was a terse lesson in the use of space, *Russian Lullaby* >**2** a swing style showcase and *Sobbin' Blues* >**1** a remarkable piece of understatement. He was to lead another big band in 1941 but finally the battle with alcohol was lost and, at the age of thirty-three, he was dead.

Lineage

Berigan began playing violin in a musical family but, although he switched to trumpet quite early, continued to double on both until 1927.

It was about this time that he began, according to band leader John Scott Trotter, to worship **Louis Armstrong** and titles such as *Mahogany Hall Stomp* >**1** show how near he got to his idol.

Media

Recorded soundtrack for the 1942 film *Syncopation*.

Listening

1 **The Indispensable 1937-1939**
Bunny Berigan/RCA NL 89744 (2)
2 **The Indispensable Bunny Berigan**
RCA (F) PM 43689

Jimmy Blanton

Born: October 1918/Chattanooga, Tennessee, USA
Died: 30th July 1942/Los Angeles, California, USA
Instrument: String bass
Recording Career: 1939-1942

IN COMPARISON to other instruments, the emancipation of the string bass was very slow. Even by the middle thirties it remained under the spell of violent New Orleans exponents such as Pops Foster and Wellman Braud. Although the end of the decade saw a refinement of its function by men like **John Kirby**, Hayes Alvis and Billy Taylor, it was not until the emergence of Jimmy Blanton in 1939 that its mature role was truly established.

Blanton's talent blossomed early. While still at college he provided entertainment on the riverboats with Fate Marable but, on abandoning his education in the third year, moved to St Louis and joined the Jeter-Pillars Band. News about his brilliantly expressive style spread quickly and, while doing a summer season with Marable, he was persuaded to join the **Duke Ellington** Orchestra.

Here he was given room to display his instrumental virtuosity. His new leader's piano work was beginning to show greater economy at this period (around 1940), and Blanton immediately grasped how he could complement the style by enlarging on the basic piano harmonies. In so doing, he unconsciously became the precursor of a style that found a parallel with the bop pianists, embellishing the bassist's traditional calibrations with dazzling treble runs. This was never more brilliantly illustrated than on band performances like *Sepia Panorama* >**1** or on duet masterpieces like *Pitter Panther Patter* >**1**. Blanton recorded six of these delightful duets >**1**, but it was his role in the Ellington band that established his true position. The rapid sixteen-note runs that flashed behind soloists would attract attention even today; in 1940 they were unheard of.

Blanton was the complete bassist. He combined the ability to lift the large orchestra rhythmically with a musical intelligence that made him an infallible supporter for individual soloists. He died at the age of twenty-three and yet, in his all too brief life, he re-wrote the ground rules for jazz bass playing.

Lineage

He began on violin, studied with an uncle involved in the 'mathematical' implications of music, and then switched to bass while at Tennessee State College. He was the great original on his instrument and influenced bassists in many different later styles. Oscar Pettiford, **Charles Mingus**, Eddie Safranski, Curley Russell, Ray Brown, Junior Raglin and Jimmy Woode were very directly influenced, but an endless number of bassists acknowledge his pre-eminence in broadening the instrument's potential.

Listening

1 The Indispensable Vols 5/6
Duke Ellington/RCA NL89750(2)

Teddy Bunn

Born: 1909/Freeport, Long Island, NY, USA
Died: 20th July 1978/Lancaster, California, USA
Instrument: Guitar, vocals
Recording Career: 1929-1968

THE UBIQUITOUS Theodore Leroy Bunn graced some of the most unlikely recording sessions, but this was hardly surprising. Apart from **Lonnie Johnson**, there was no player at the time so readily equipped to play mature, well-conceived guitar solos within the band context. It was inevitable that **Duke Ellington**, always on the lookout for an interesting soloist or a change in

his orchestral texture, should choose to use Bunn.

Bunn had begun his musical life as a calypso singer, but solos like those on the 1929 *Haunted Nights* >**1** and *Oklahoma Stomp* >**2** show how well he could match Ellington's star soloists. He was a part of the band for a brief period only, and it was his playing with the Spirits of Rhythm throughout the thirties which made his name. They first came to the recording studio in 1933 but, considering their popularity, made remarkably few records. Bunn, on the other hand, was a prolific freelance recording artist. He featured on the famous **Johnny Dodds** and **Jimmie Noone** >**3** revivalist sessions in 1940, and was on hand to help revive the careers of Trixie Smith and Rosetta Crawford. Typical of his laconic blues style was the moving solo on *Blues For Tommy Ladnier* >**4**, and his singing and playing was showcased on *If You See Me Comin'* >**5** to the extent that it deflected the limelight from principals **Sidney Bechet**, Frankie Newton and J. C. Higginbotham.

Throughout the forties the Spirits were forever breaking up only to reform again. They were now based on the West Coast and when the group finally disbanded, Bunn had periods working wtih Edgar Hayes, Jack McVea and even, in 1959, with **Louis Jordan**. During the sixties health problems restricted his music-making, but towards the end of the decade he was still performing as well as ever in Hawaii.

Lineage
Bunn came from a musical family and was largely self-taught. His influence has been discerned in the work of Al Casey and Freddie Green, but this is not confirmed by either of these players.

Listening
1 The Indispensable Duke Ellington Vols 1/2
RCA PM 43687
2 Cotton Club Days
Duke Ellington/Ace Of Hearts AH 89
3 Apex Club Blues
Jimmie Noone/Affinity AFS 1023
4 Blues Classics
Sidney Bechet/Blue Note BST 81202
5 The Complete Sidney Bechet Vol 5
RCA NL 89751 (2)

Cab Calloway

Born: 25th December 1907/Rochester, NY, USA
Instrument: Vocals
Recording Career: 1925-

DESPITE occasional jobs as relief drummer and as stand-in altoist, Cabell Calloway Jnr was no musician. He was also something of an unlovely singer and his position in jazz is based very much on his personality and on the band that he fronted.

Calloway gained quite a reputation as a master of ceremonies during the twenties and acted in this capacity for the Alabamians in Chicago in 1929. A year later he moved on to join the Missourians, a superb band whose version of *Tiger Rag – Market Street Stomp* >**1** had enjoyed considerable commercial success. The billing was changed to Cab Calloway and His Orchestra and by 1931 it had followed **Duke Ellington** into the Cotton Club. It was there that Calloway developed his unique style of scat singing: titles like *St Louis Blues* and *Minnie The Moocher* >**2** were devised to show it off, a gimmick-laden mixture of sweet singing and the famed Hi-de-Ho shout,

which became a national catch-phrase throughout the United States. Weighed against this there were good solos from Harry White (trombone), Walter Thomas (tenor) and William Blue (clarinet) to make the early thirties band attractive to jazz followers.

Calloway continued to lead big bands of good pedigree and to attract talented sidemen throughout the thirties: the 1940 line-up was a particularly star-studded one. Superb arrangements like *Callin' All Bars* >**3** by **Benny Carter** were embellished by rhapsodic solo performances like *Ghost Of A Chance* >**4** by Chew Berry, fiery offerings such as *Bye Bye Blues* >**3** by **Dizzy Gillespie** and vibist Tyree Glenn, and the Jonah Jones showcase, *Jonah Joins The Cab* >**3**. These put the stamp of class on the band.

Calloway disbanded the outfit in 1948 and, apart from special engagements during the ensuing two years or so, did not lead a big band again. He still remains one of the great characters on jazz's fringe, but will be remembered with most affection as the leader of some of the finest bands to have graced the period from 1930 to 1962.

Lineage

Brother of singer Blanche, Cab Calloway was largely a self-taught vocalist.

Media

Played the role of Sportin' Life in a production of *Porgy And Bess* (1952) and acted with Pearl Bailey in *Hello Dolly* during the sixties. Also appeared in numerous films: *Big Broadcast* (1932), *International House* (1933), *The Manhattan Merry-go-round* (1937), *The Singing Kid* (1936), *Stormy Weather* (1943), *Sensations Of 1945* (1944), *St Louis Blues* (1958), *The Cincinatti Kid* (1965), *The Blues Brothers* (1980), plus several 'shorts'.

Listening

1 The Missourians And Cab Calloway
VJM VLP 58
2 King Of Hi-De-Ho
Cab Calloway/Ace Of Hearts AH 106
3 Penguin Swing
Cab Calloway/Jazz Archives JA 8
4 Chew Berry And His Stomping Stevedores
Epic JE 22007

Benny Carter

Born: 8th August 1907, New York City, NY, USA
Instruments: Alto and tenor saxophones, trumpet, clarinet, trombone and piano, arranger, composer
Recording Career: 1923-
Nickname: The King

A BRILLIANT instrumentalist on alto, clarinet and trumpet, Bennett Lester Carter remains a skilled arranger/composer who has led some outstanding bands. His position as a major jazz figure would have been assured had he been judged in any one of these roles.

In the twenties he worked and arranged for June Clark, Horace Henderson, **Fletcher Henderson**, Charlie Johnson and even briefly for **Duke Ellington**. He excelled as musical director of **McKinney's Cotton Pickers** in 1931 and, in the thirties, **Chick Webb**, Mills Blue Rhythm, Teddy Hill and **Benny Goodman** joined the list of those using his arrangements.

In 1933-4 Carter led his own band and, during this period, loaned it to English musicologist Spike Hughes for his all-American recording project. The band's brilliant reed voicing did justice to the likes of *Arabesque* >**1**, and guest soloists, among them **Henry Allen** and **Coleman Hawkins**, gave memorable performances such as *Sweet Sorrow Blues* >**1**.

In 1936 he was appointed musical director of Henry Hall's orchestra in London. This began a fruitful period in Europe where masterful solo work distinguished his musical output. In the company of **Django Reinhardt** and **Coleman Hawkins**, titles like *Farewell Blues* (second solo), and *I'm Coming Virginia* >**2** exemplified Carter's superb alto technique, a sample of his effortless lyricism, peerless tone and broad scope of melodic invention.

Back in America in the early forties he led his own band, and the mastery of his arranging for reeds is nowhere better heard than on *All Of Me* >**3**; similarly the interaction between brass and reeds on *My Favourite Blues* >**3**.

In 1941, with **Dizzy Gillespie** as a sideman, Carter became intrigued with bebop. On the West Coast in 1943, he employed **Max Roach** and **J. J. Johnson** and became a proficient performer in the new style. A new career was beckoning, however, and during much of the fifties and sixties Carter was working in studios both for films and TV. In the seventies he devoted himself increasingly to jazz tuition and general musical education, although there were always concerts, club dates and records to remind us that 'The King', as his peers called him, was still very much alive and active.

Amazingly, no matter how long his lay-offs, he always seemed in shape for the job. He would joke about 'being out of practice' and then give a faultless recital. From time to time he cut and thrust on the JATP circuit >**4**, traded his silky smoothness against **Art Tatum**'s rhetoric >**5**, or joined arms with old comrades **Ben Webster** and Barney Bigard for a lesson in relaxation on *Lula* >**6** and his own *When Lights Are Low* >**6**. Carter clearly demonstrated that he had lost none of his arranging skills in *Further Definitions* >**7** from 1961, a brilliant album that teamed him with Hawkins, Charlie Rouse and Phil Woods.

He still plays immaculately and, in the eighties, is still taking over the Sweet Basil club in New York and introducing another generation of listeners to his effortless grace.

Lineage

Carter began on piano in a musical family, was inspired to play trumpet by **Bubber Miley** but swopped it for a C-melody saxophone. His progress to alto and clarinet followed and on these he was largely self-taught. **Louis Armstrong** influenced his further trumpet studies around 1930, and by the early thirties he was the complete multi-instrumentalist. He, in turn, influenced Pete Brown, Fletcher Allen and countless swing-era altoists, and many quality dance-band players throughout the world.

Media

Carter arranged and composed music for many successful films, as well as playing in *As Thousands Cheer* (1943), *Stormy Weather* (1943), *Clash By Night* (1952), *The Snows of Kilimanjaro* (1952), *A View From Pompey's Head* (1955). Also wrote scores for TV shows, among them *M Squad* (1957-60), *Ironside* (1967-74) and *Banyon* (1972).

Listening

1 **The All American Orchestra**
   Spike Hughes/Jasmine JASM 2012
2 **Django Swing 1937-1939**
   Django Reinhardt/Swaggie S 1252
3 **Benny Carter 1928-1952**
   RCA PM 42406
4 **One O'Clock Jump 1953**
   JATP/Verve VRV 1
5 **The Tatum Group Masterpieces**
   Art Tatum/Pablo 2625-706 (8)
6 **Opening Blues**
   Carter/Webster/Bigard/Prestige HBS 6148
7 **Further Definitions**
   Benny Carter/Jasmine JAS 14

Charlie Christian

Born: 29th July 1916/Dallas, Texas, USA
Died: 2nd March 1942/New York City, NY, USA
Instrument: Guitar
Recording Career: 1939-1941

FOR AN INNOVATION to have validity it must be compatible with the musical climate that gives birth to it. In the late thirties, rhythm section roles were changing and various cymbal techniques were beginning to replace the rich pulse of the guitar. If the guitar was to survive, its position would unquestionably have to be that of a solo instrument. The normal acoustic guitarist always experienced trouble making himself heard in the jazz ensemble, and players such as Floyd Smith (with Andy Kirk) and Eddie Durham (with **Count Basie**) began experimenting with amplification.

Charles Christian came from the blues country of Texas and actually played trumpet before settling for the guitar at the age of twelve. During the thirties he played with his brother's band, with Anna Mae Winburn and as joint leader of a band with James Simpson. He was in Alphonso Trent's territory band in 1938 but, in the following year, John Hammond, captivated by his innovatory skills on the amplified instrument, recommended him to **Benny Goodman**.

The clarinettist took him on and Christian's impact was immediate. He played in both the sextet and the big band, although it was in the smaller unit that he shone. His finely wrought eighth-note phrases took him into areas that extended his harmonic vision and he played everything with effortless facility. He could swing at all tempos and his thinly-veiled blues readings were masterful. The blues song *My Daddy Rocks Me* redressed as *Six Appeal* >**1** showed how well he played near to a theme while still re-shaping. *Seven Come Eleven* >**1**, by contrast, was treated to some startling improvisations, and *Breakfast Feud* >**1** had a drive that took us back to those territory bands.

While employed by Goodman, Christian began to join after-hours jam sessions at Minton's Playhouse, the club that fostered the emerging jazz style known as bebop. His involvement was highly successful >**2**, and he is widely regarded as a pioneer of that style. In fact, he remained a swing era stylist, whose solos were based on riff patterns and whose use of unusual intervals had more in common with **Art Tatum** than with 'modernists' like **Thelonious Monk**.

Unfortunately, Christian had a history of tuberculosis and the necessarily late-night lifestyle of a jazz musician further undermined his health. He was admitted to a sanitorium on Staten Island in 1941 and died before he could fully explore the potential of his new music.

Lineage

Christian's father originally taught him guitar but his personal experiments with amplification made him an original stylist on what was, effectively, a new jazz instrument. His influence on successors was nigh-on all-pervading, with Barney Kessel, Herb Ellis, Billy Bauer, Jimmy Raney, Chuck Wayne and Charlie Byrd prominent amongst those who acknowledge his impact. Even an original such as **Wes Montgomery** was affected by his style and not until the emergence of the European school and the merger with rock elements was his style supplanted as a yardstick for jazz guitar.

Listening

1 Benny Goodman/Charlie Christian
American Columbia CG 30779
2 Charlie Christian Live 1939/41
Various/Festival ALB 377

Nat King Cole

Born: 17th March 1917/Birmingham, Alabama, USA
Died: 15th February 1965/Santa Monica, California, USA
Instrument: Piano, vocals
Recording Career: 1936-1964

EXTREMELY SUCCESSFUL as a singer of popular songs, the deep, jazz-tinged voice of Nathaniel Adams Cole was unmistakeable and persuasive enough to overcome the sometimes shallow content and maudlin sentimentality of many of the lyrics he chose. Even when he failed, he still brought a professionalism of performance to dross like *Mona Lisa* and *Too Young* >**1**, at least to the extent of attenuating their worst excesses.

He was raised in Chicago in a musical family and settled in Los Angeles when a revue in which he was featured broke up. He worked briefly as a soloist, then in 1939 formed the King Cole Trio with

guitarist Oscar Moore and bassist Wesley Prince. This was an impressively tight-knit unit and strongly featured Cole's flowing piano style, with jaunty performances such as *Honeysuckle Rose* >**2** couched in the crisp, cleanly articulated style of the day. *Early Morning Blues* >**2** hinted at his familiarity with more modern developments, while *Slow Down* >**2** showed just what a superb accompanist to his own voice he could be.

His loss to the field of popular music was never total. He continued to make occasional appearances as a pianist but the popularity of his dark-brown voice had sealed his financial fate – and very favourably so.

Lineage
Original influenced by **Earl Hines**, Cole's piano style strayed nearer to **Teddy Wilson** and Billy Kyle as he moved into the sophisticated club business.

Media
Appeared as W. C. Handy in the 1958 film, *St Louis Blues*. Singing roles in others such as *Small Town Girl* (1953), *Blue Gardenia* (1953), and *The Nat King Cole Story* (1955). His recording was used as the title track for the film *Mona Lisa* (1986).

Listening
1 **The Nat King Cole Collection**
  Dèja Vu DV LP2012
2 **Trio Days**
  Nat King Cole/Affinity AFS 1001

Bob Crosby

Born: 23rd August 1913/Spokane, Washington, USA
Instrument: Vocals, leader
Recording Career: 1934-

FOLLOWING IN the steps of his elder brother, Bing, George Robert Crosby started out as a singer. He joined the

Dorsey Brothers in 1935 and then took over the remnants of the Ben Pollack orchestra from Gil Rodin. For the next seven years, Crosby led a big swing band – but one with a difference: instead of the normal swing era style, he devised a form of strictly orchestrated Dixieland. It had the advantage of outstanding soloists: trumpeters Yank Lawson and Billy Butterfield, tenor saxophonist Eddie Miller, clarinettists Matty Matlock and Irving Fazola, and pianists Bob Zurke, Joe Sullivan and Jess Stacy were prime examples. His 'band-within-a-band', called the Bobcats, carried on the tradition of the parent orchestra but in a smaller, more informal way.

South Rampart Street >**1** became a favourite with the band's followers; it typified the way in which a well-organised thirteen-piece group could sound like a septet. Joie de vivre was always their trademark and even on *Gin Mill Blues* >**1** or similar slow items, there was no hint of the ponderous. Despite rubbing stylistic shoulders with their contemporaries, the **Muggsy Spanier** Ragtimers, titles such as *Who's Sorry Now* >**1** and *Big Foot Jump* >**2** showed that the scope of their music was wider.

When the band broke up in 1942, Crosby served in the US marines and after demob enjoyed a successful career in radio and television, mainly as a solo performer.

His orchestra, however, was not dead and when former Bobcats, Yank Lawson and bassist Bob Haggart formed the World's Greatest Jazz Band (sic) in 1968, it was a brave man that would question the claim on the strength of its roots. *Five Point Blues*, *Royal Garden Blues* >**3** and *Winter Wonderland* >**4** certainly resurrect the spirit and musical standards of the Bobcats.

Lineage
The Crosby band adapted the sound of Dixieland jazz to a more ambitious line-up. Traces of its influence can be found in The World's Greatest Jazz Band.

Media
Crosby, oddly, had a non-singing role in the film *The Singing Sheriff* (1944), but the Bob Crosby band featured in *Sis Hopkins* (1941), *Presenting Lily Mars* (1943) and *As Thousands Cheer* (1943). Also recorded the soundtrack for *Holiday Inn* (1942). Excellent book *Stomp Off, Lets Go!* (1983) written about Crosby by John Chilton.

Listening
1 Mournin' Blues
  Bob Crosby/Affinity AFS 1014
2 Stomp Off, Lets Go
  Bob Crosby/Ace of Hearts AH 29
3 Live At The Roosevelt Grill
  World's Greatest Jazz Band/Atlantic SD 1570
4 Hark The Herald Angels Swing
  World's Greatest Jazz Band/World Jazz WJLP 5-2

Bob Crosby

Tommy Dorsey

**Born: 19th November 1905/
Shenandoah, Pennsylvania, USA
Died: 26th November 1956/
Greenwich, Connecticut, USA
Instruments: Trombone, trumpet,
clarinet
Recording Career: 1924-1956**

ALTHOUGH HE BEGAN by studying trumpet with his father, it was not long

During a stint as disc jockey, Tommy Dorsey interviews singer Beryl Davis

before Thomas Dorsey switched to trombone. He rapidly mastered the slide instrument and, while still a teenager, co-led a band with his brother Jimmy. In 1924, he joined the Jean Goldkette band where, although still something of a mechanical player, he began to earn a reputation as a soloist.

In the late twenties, he heard Jimmy Harrison for the first time and from that time on exhibited greater fluency in his playing. The 1928 *My Angeline* >**1** with the Mississippi Maulers had distinctly Harrison-esque phraseology and his eight telling bars on Hoagy Carmichael's *Rockin' Chair* >**2** told an interesting story in a very short space of time. He continued to play trumpet on certain occasions and *It's Right Here For You* >**3** with his Novelty Orchestra reveals a more than passing knowledge of **Louis Armstrong**'s language. *Blue Prelude* >**4** indicates Dorsey's return to more formal climes and in 1934, after forming a big band with his brother on a permanent basis, he increasingly concentrated on sweet-toned trombone solos. It is on these that his reputation is now mainly based and the band became a showcase for these solos when he split with his brother and led the band alone.

Occasionally, sessions away from the band stirred his jazz blood, but it was faultless masterpieces of trombone dexterity like *Song Of India*, *I'm Getting Sentimental*, and *Marie* >**5** that won him an international following, but alienated jazz followers. Nevertheless, success in magazine polls did push him into all-star jam sessions in the forties, although his heart never seemed to be in the resulting recording dates. From 1953 until his death, he resumed the partnership with his brother but the age of the big band was waning and they had to accept arduous tours to keep working.

Lineage

Originally influenced by Miff Mole, he later came under the spell of **Louis Armstrong** and Jimmy Harrison. His own influence was most readily noticeable in the dance band world.

Media

Joined brother Jimmy in film *The Fabulous Dorseys* (1947); also appeared in *Las Vegas Nights* (1941), *Ship Ahoy!* (1942), *Girl Crazy* (1943), *I Dood It* (1943), *Broadway Rhythm* (1944), *Thrill Of A Romance* (1945) and *A Song Is Born* (1948). Performed on the soundtracks of *Road To Zanzibar* (1941), *Du Barry Was A Lady* (1943) and music

used in *Annie Hall* (1977). Biography, *Tommy And Jimmy – The Dorsey Years* by Herb Sandford appeared 1972.

Listening

1 New York Jazz 1927/30
Mississippi Maulers/VJM VLP 41
2 Hoagy Carmichael
RCA NL 89096
3 Stringing The Blues
Lang/Venuti/CBS 88142
4 Jazz Of The Thirties
Various/World Records SHB 39
5 The Indispensable Tommy Dorsey Vols 1/2
RCA NL 89752(2)

Roy Eldridge

Born: 30th January 1911/Pittsburgh, Pennsylvania, USA
Instruments: Trumpet, flugelhorn, piano, drums, vocals, composer
Recording Career: 1935-
Nickname: Little Jazz

ALTHOUGH OFTEN DESCRIBED in jazz history as the link between **Louis Armstrong** and **Dizzy Gillespie**, this is a singularly simplistic analysis of a trumpeter who was not only one of the greats on his instrument, but also an original in every sense of the word. David Roy Eldridge began on violin and alto sax but switched to trumpet, playing with the quality bands of Horace Henderson, Zack Whyte and Speed Webb. He moved to New York in 1930 and played with Elmer Snowden, Charlie Johnson and the ailing **McKinney's Cotton Pickers**. Then in 1935 he joined Teddy Hill, locking himself in battle with the formidable tenor of Chew Berry.

Together they moved over to the prestigious **Fletcher Henderson** band in the following year, and titles such as *Blue Lou* and *Christopher Columbus* >**1** gave notice that both were major soloists. In his own studio band, Eldridge also recorded titles like *Hecklers' Hop* and *Wabash Stomp* >**2** that laid out all his wares. Here was the avant-garde trumpeter of the day, technically well in advance of his peers and gifted with a previously unknown instrumental control. He moved effortlessly in the high register but, once there, hit notes with the clarity of an angelus.

Eldridge could also play with great sensitivity and excelled on record with **Benny Goodman**, **Coleman Hawkins** and, most especially, **Billie Holiday**: titles like *Sugar* and *Falling In Love* >**3** have relaxed solos that perfectly match the singer's own work.

After the Second World War, he embraced the boppers and, although he never adjusted his style to any great extent, records like *I Can't Get Started* >**4** with Dizzy Gillespie show Eldridge as astylistic. This was an asset when joining the Norman Granz stable and for many years he was a fixture of JATP. Although rabble-rousing exploits of the show often brought out the worst in him, Eldridge usually managed to fit in a ballad to remind the audiences of his real stature.

He was perhaps at his best on record, and albums with the likes of **Ben Webster**, **Lester Young** and **Johnny Hodges** tell of undiminished skills. In 1980, he suffered a heart attack and although no longer able to play trumpet, he still sings for his supper at most American festivals.

Lineage

Eldridge was originally influenced by **Louis Armstrong** but absorbed something of **Benny Carter** and **Coleman Hawkins'** method of delivery. He inspired most of the boppers but, most especially, **Dizzy Gillespie**, **Howard McGhee** and **Fats Navarro**.

Listening

1 A Study In Frustration
Fletcher Henderson/CBS (F) 66423

2 Roy Eldridge – The Early Years
CBS 88585

3 The Billie Holiday Story Vol 3
CBS 68230

4 Diz And Roy
Dizzy Gillespie/Roy Eldridge/Verve 2-2524

Benny Goodman

Born: 30th May 1909/Chicago, Illinois, USA
Died: 13th June 1986/New York City, NY, USA
Instruments: Clarinet, alto saxophone
Recording Career: 1926-1986
Nickname: King Of Swing

AS A MUSICIAN Goodman has borne the extremes of critical judgement: in the late thirties he was praised even beyond his admittedly considerable talents, while during the New Orleans revival he was unconditionally condemned. Although it is the oldest of critical platitudes, the truth does indeed lie somewhere in between.

Benjamin David Goodman's first real experience with a name band was with Ben Pollack in the late twenties. Here, Goodman had the opportunity to lead on recording dates and he proved to be an impressive soloist. His tone was a mite more reedy, his timing a shade more spiky than it later became, but he put his individual stamp on the likes of *Clarinetitis* and *Shirt Tail Stomp* >**1** with solos that showed his superb sense of construction.

His total professionalism made him welcome as a studio freelance in the early thirties until he formed his big band in 1934. Some concessions were made to commercialism, but essentially this marked the beginning of the swing era. Goodman became the 'King of Swing' and with the aid of arrangers like **Fletcher Henderson**, **Benny Carter** and Edgar Sampson, enjoyed more fame than rather better coloured bands of the era. His 1938 Carnegie Hall concert >**2** was something of a jazz landmark but what really distinguished Goodman's jazz career were the superb small group recordings building from a trio to the most outstanding of them all – the sextet. With pianist **Teddy Wilson**, vibist **Lionel Hampton** and drummer Gene Krupa, the quartet made even trite material like *My Melancholy Baby* and *Ding Dong Daddy* >**3** into pure chamber music. The sextet, with its more cosmopolitan sound, scaled even greater heights: *Seven Come Eleven* >**4** with guitarist **Charlie Christian** flowing, *Breakfast Feud* >**4** with trumpeter Cootie Williams preaching, or *Wholly Cats* >**4** with **Count Basie** picking his way around like a rhythmic fakir are all masterpieces – and Goodman has something pertinent to say on each.

Goodman's brief flirtation with bebop was unsuccessful but, during the fifties, he undertook several State Department-sponsored tours that did much to foster interest in jazz worldwide. He was often found at the Rainbow Grill in the sixties, and in 1968 celebrated the Carnegie Hall's thirtieth anniversary. A frequent visitor to Europe in the seventies, he remained an immaculate performer right up to his death in June 1986.

From 1938, Goodman also enjoyed a concurrent career as a classical clarinettist. He recorded with the Budapest String Quartet, worked with the Hungarian-born composer Béla Bartók on *Contrasts*, made guest appearances with the Chicago Symphony Orchestra and commissioned concertos from leading contemporary composers – America's Aaron Copland and Germany's Paul Hindemith.

Lineage

Goodman was originally influenced by Frank Teschemacher, **Jimmie Noone** and Leon Roppolo of **NORK**, but as a novelty did Ted Lewis imitations. The impact of his own playing is apparent in the work of Irving Fazola, Matty

Matlock, Ed Hall and a whole army of swing era aspirants. In post-war years, the torch has been carried by revivalists such as Britain's Dave Shepherd.

Media

The Kingdom Of Swing, co-written by Irving Kolodin and Goodman, was published in 1939 and a bio-discography *BG Off The Record* by Donald Russell Connor appeared in 1958, and was up-dated with Warren W. Hicks as *BG On The Record* (1969). Goodman appeared as actor and musician in the film *A Song Is Born* (1948), and was featured with the orchestra in *Hollywood Hotel* (1937),

The Big Broadcast Of 1937, Stage Door Canteen (1943), and *Sweet And Lowdown* (1944). *The Benny Goodman Story* (1955) was Hollywood's version of his life story but, despite featuring the playing of the subject himself, paid scant attention to the facts.

Listening

1 **Clarinetitis**
   Benny Goodman/Affinity AFS 1018
2 **1938 Carnegie Hall Concert**
   Benny Goodman/CBS 66202
3 **The Complete Small Combinations Vols 3/4**
   Benny Goodman/RCA PM 43684
4 **Charlie Christian With The Sextet**
   Columbia CG 30779

Stephane Grappelli

Born: 26th January 1908/Paris, France
Instruments: Violin, piano
Recording Career: 1934-

PARTNERED BY **Django Reinhardt**, Grappelli (then spelt Grappelly) made a tremendous impact with the Quintet Of The Hot Club Of France when they first recorded in 1934. He had become involved in music at an early age and the violin was only one of the instruments on which he became proficient in his early teens.

By a strange quirk of fate, the Quintet were in Britain at the outbreak of the Second World War and, although the remainder of the group returned to France, Grappelli stayed on. He became a sought-after sessionaire in London during the hostilities but, on returning to his homeland after the armistice, found that much of the magic that had existed between himself and the gypsy guitarist had died.

Since then, however, he has operated mainly as a solo artist. He has appeared at just about every European jazz festival and built up a popularity to rival that of the halcyon days in Paris. In one respect, he is the exception to the rule that jazzmen rarely improve with age. An early classical training tended to place a restraining hand on his shoulders during the thirties, but this has since been eschewed, giving way to more attack, more overtly surging power and an unexpected feeling for the blues.

Special recording projects have shown the world a many-sided Grappelli. In 1966, *Violin Summit* >**1** exposed him to the fury of **Stuff Smith** and the more modern predilections of **Jean-Luc Ponty** and Svend Asmussen: Grappelli emerged with very little

be heard on the soundtracks of *Eins* (1971), *Liza* (1972), *Lacombe Lucien* (1974), *Les Valseuses* (1974), *King Of The Gypsies* (1978) and *L'Adolescente* (1978). *Stephane Grappelli: A Biography*, by Geoffrey Smith (1987).

Listening

1 Violin Summit
Stephane Grappelli/MPS 821 303.1
2 Paris Encounter
Grappelli/Burton/Atlantic SD 1597
3 Stephane Grappelli/Bill Coleman
Classic Jazz CJ 24
4 Grappelli Meets The Rhythm Section
Stephane Grappelli/Black Lion BLP 30183
5 Violinspiration
Stephane Grappelli/Memoir MOIR 110
6 Stephane Grappelli/Yehudi Menuhin
EMI EMD 5503

Lionel Hampton

Born: 12th April 1909/Louisville, Kentucky, USA
Instruments: Vibes, drums, piano, vocals
Recording Career: 1924-
Nickname: Hamp

ALTHOUGH Hampton is the doyen of jazz vibraphonists, he first came to prominence as a drummer. He was hardly a subtle exponent of the art, but he played with a prodigious swing and an inherent feeling for the needs of the showbands in which he worked. This vaudeville aspect of his work was very important, and ever since he has shown an awareness of the audience and a desire to sell himself as an entertainer. Perhaps because of this, one of his earliest jobs was as permanently featured artist at Frank Sebastian's Little Cotton Club in Culver City, first as a member of Paul Howard's Quality Serenaders and, later, with the Les Hite Orchestra.

While **Louis Armstrong** was fronting the Hite band it was the swinging, if uncomplicated drumming on titles like *Ding Dong Daddy* >**1** that brought Hampton to general notice. It was also then that the drummer began to experiment with the vibraphone, and

damage done! Highly successful were his duels with vibraphonist **Gary Burton** >**2**, trumpeter Bill Coleman >**3** and pianist Roland Hanna >**4**, and listening to him on titles like *Shine* and *Lover Man* >**5** evidences how authoritative he has become. He has recorded with the great classical violinist Yehudi Menuhin >**6** and the sessions prompted the latter to comment: 'Stephane Grappelli is a colleague who I admire and would love to emulate'.

Lineage

Grappelli was originally inspired by **Louis Armstrong** and Eddie South, but has had scant influence on younger violinists as they have moved toward the saxophone styles of **John Coltrane** and **Ornette Coleman**.

Media

Grappelli has appeared in films *Time Flies* (1944), *The Lisbon Story* (1945), and *The Flamingo Affair* (1948). He can

he made his debut on the instrument on *Memories Of You* >**1** in 1930.

In 1932 Hampton formed the first of his big bands to play another of Sebastian's 'Cotton Clubs', this time in Los Angeles. He was heard by **Benny Goodman** who used him to augment Goodman's new and popular trio with **Teddy Wilson** and Gene Krupa, for a record date.

The impact was immediate: the swing he had produced on the drums was translated to the vibes, and this was matched by brilliant improvisational skill. His natural flair for the blues came out in *Blues In My Flat* >**2** and *Vibraphone Blues* >**3** and Goodman, highly impressed, persuaded him to give up his own band.

Hampton was a Goodman sideman until 1940 and played a prominent role in the big band, as well as in the chamber combos. The Victor record company were quick to recognise this personal contribution and gave him a free hand to select sidemen for a series of records under his own name. The results were highly successful. Using sidemen such as **Johnny Hodges**, Lawrence Brown, Chew Berry, Cootie Williams and Herschel Evans, Hampton produced brilliant jazz in circumstances of the utmost informality >**4**, **5**.

After leaving Goodman in 1940, Hampton returned to the arduous task of leading his own big band. His enterprise was given a tremendous fillip in 1942 when his first big band version of *Flying Home* became a hit and for the remainder of the decade the band's trademark was swing and excitement. Creative players such as Illinois Jacquet, **Dexter Gordon** and Milt Buckner were prominent but, as the fifties were ushered in, Hamp began to undersell the creative element and to push the theatrical. His 'trigger finger' piano style got more

gig when, faced with a power failure, he led his band through a lengthy acoustic session.

Though renowned as a big band leader, Hamp's greatest moments on record have come in small group contexts. No man matched **Art Tatum** quite so superbly as Hampton. The majestic *I'll Never Be The Same* >**6** almost became a conversation between piano and vibes while *Makin' Whoopee* >**6** had a kind of momentum that lesser players could only envy. His association with **Oscar Peterson** was equally dazzling and *Love For Sale*, *Star Dust* and *Indiana* >**7** showed how different material brought out contrasting, but compatible talents.

For many observers, Lionel Hampton, with his powers of improvisation, his peerless ability to swing and his own natural charm, is the player who most epitomises the spirit of jazz today.

Lineage

At various times Hampton studied drums with Snags Jones, xylophone with Jimmy Bertrand and piano with Teddy Weatherford and his phrase-shapes suggest an awareness of **Louis Armstrong**. He was the first great vibraphonist and his influence is all pervading, but players such as **Red Norvo**, Terry Gibbs, Milt Jackson, **Gary Burton** and **Bobby Hutcherson** have all built on his stylistic foundations.

Media

Appeared with Louis Armstrong in *Pennies From Heaven* (1936). Minor roles in *Hollywood Hotel* (1937), *A Song Is Born* (1948), and featured in *The Benny Goodman Story* (1955).

Listening

1 **Louis In Los Angeles 1930**
  Louis Armstrong/Swaggie S 1265
2 **The Complete B.G. Vols 3/4**
  Benny Goodman/RCA PM 43684
3 **Small Combinations Vols 1/2**
  Benny Goodman/RCA PM 43176
4 **Historical Sessions 1939/41**
  Lionel Hampton/RCA PM42417
5 **Historical Sessions 1937/9**
  Lionel Hampton/RCA PM 42393
6 **Tatum Group Masterpieces**
  Art Tatum/Pablo 2625-706
7 **The Complete Quartet 1953/5**
  Lionel Hampton/Verve 813901-1

exposure, and the visual side of the act became more important.

Finally the big band business became so poor that he took his own off the road. However, in 1955 a part in the film *The Benny Goodman Story* revived his fortunes, and in 1956 he reformed the band and toured worldwide for the next ten years. He continued to process many outstanding youngsters through his band but, in the middle sixties, was forced to settle for a smaller group. Jazz Inner Circle, as it was called, set the pattern for his small group work for some years but, during the seventies, Hampton's big bands roared back.

Since that time, he has been omnipresent at jazz festivals across four continents. He has remained the most outstanding soloist in his own bands and – prominent until the early eighties – had bands chock-full of well-known jazzmen. He certainly won many friends during a London Capital Jazz Festival

Coleman Hawkins

Born: 21st November 1901/St Joseph, Missouri, USA
Died: 19th May 1969/New York City, NY, USA
Instruments: Tenor and bass saxophones, clarinet
Recording Career: 1922-1969
Nickname: Bean

ONCE A JAZZMAN has established a coherent style, it is very rare for him to attempt a change. He may continue to make a valid contribution to jazz but will normally restrict himself to the confines of the method he has established for himself. There are very few exceptions to this rule: **Benny Carter**, **Jackie McLean** and **Sonny Rollins** come to mind because they are among the rare figures who did succeed in breaking out.

The name missing from that list is Coleman Randolf Hawkins and, of them, he was the most important. Hawkins distilled the art of jazz playing to such a degree that he was at home in any company. More significantly, the decades proved that his original, mature style had a 'timeless' quality that enabled it to sustain two major stylistic changes.

Hawkins started piano lessons at five, later trying the 'cello, but by the age of nine was playing tenor saxophone. He studied music at Washburn College, Topeka, and at sixteen, Hawkins was playing professionally in the Kansas area, and within a year had been asked to join Mamie Smith's Jazz Hounds, with whom he toured until 1923. Less than twelve months later, he joined the prestigious **Fletcher Henderson** Orchestra. At first his playing with the band was unimpressive: he made copious use of the then popular 'slapped tongue' technique and his approach to solo building was still crude. However, *Tozo* >**1** from 1927 and 1928's *I'm Feeling Devilish* >**1** begin to show a growing authority although, oddly, it was not the Henderson band, but a 1929 pick-up group, the Mound City Blue Blowers, that perhaps presented to the world the first example of Hawkins the master. *Hello Lola* >**2**, a perambulatory,

medium-tempo romp, had the tenor preaching through a solo of unsophisticated splendour, while *One Hour* >**2** gave us the first real hint of the effusive romantic.

Now the die was cast and almost immediately his playing with Henderson began to grow in stature. The leader realised what a hot property Hawkins was and titles such as *Talk Of The Town* and *I've Got To Sing A Torch Song* >**3** became masterful showcases for his brilliant tenor saxophonist.

Hawkins now had a world-wide reputation and in 1934 left Henderson to try his luck in Europe. During a five-year stay, he played and recorded with the likes of the Ramblers (The Netherlands), **Django Reinhardt**, Stanley Black and Jack Hylton. Returning to the United States in 1939, he put together a nine-piece band and on a notable day in October recorded *Body And Soul* >**2**. It was a triumph of romantic and creative tenor playing, which rightly became his greatest hit.

Many players would have sat back on such a successful and well-tested formula, but Hawkins did not. He had become interested in the experimental music of the boppers and put his talent on the block with them. His tone adopted a gruffer aspect as he embraced the more angular phrase-shapes of the style and, as early as 1944, he was giving a lesson in bop timing to a fumbling **Ben Webster** on *Salt Peanuts* >**4**. In the following year, he stood shoulder-to-shoulder with experienced bop practioners like **Howard McGhee** on *Mop Mop* >**5** and with **Miles Davis** on *Bean A Re-Bop* >**4**.

In fact, Hawkins' fame was of considerable advantage to the new movement and some of the earliest recordings in the bop idiom were made under his name. Harmonically sophisticated, Hawkins accommodated the new language easily, beginning to play more freely and to build his solos on the harmonic foundation rather than being an organic part of it.

In 1946, he took part in the first national 'Jazz at the Philharmonic' and found its competitive jam session atmosphere very much to his liking. He had reason to be grateful for his involvement in this travelling 'circus' devised by Norman Granz because, in the early fifties, there was a shift in musical emphasis that did not serve him well: the jazz centre of the world briefly moved to the West Coast, the cool sound was in, and Hawkins' huge tone was regarded in some circles as passé. It was an attitude that certainly restricted his recording opportunities but throughout a difficult period he continued to be featured in all American jazz festivals.

Fortunately, this situation did not last long and as **Sonny Rollins** and **John Coltrane** emerged in the mid-fifties, Hawkins' star regained its ascendency. Almost as if to confirm his position, his playing began to adopt a more aggressive stance. He began to look a little harder at the blues, and in 1958 produced the earth-moving *Bird Of Prey Blues* >**6** considered by some to be his finest ever recording. The playing was more 'hard Hawkins' than hard bop, but his work with JATP, the Prestige Blues Singers, and all of his freelance recording dates did exhibit this very uncompromising sound. Although the tone was different, it was not until the sixties that he made his second, and perhaps most radical, change.

Hawkins had never been rhythmically dull but had always been somewhat metronomic in his approach to timing. In the sixties he became aware of free form and, although he never attempted this style, there are those who would say his unaccompanied *Picasso* >**7** hints at such thoughts. The playing here evidenced a greater flexibility and he matched Rollins' use of audacious and unpredictable note placements on *Yesterdays* and *Loverman* >**8** in a special star-meets-star recording project.

This aspect became increasingly apparent and, as late as 1966, Hawkins was cited as the touring JATP's outstanding player. Sadly his decline in health came quickly after this accolade, impairing his playing, although he performed only weeks before his death.

His role in the evolution of the saxophone family is unparalled. No jazzman maintained such a level of excellence in recordings over more than forty years and Hawkins can justly be regarded as the father figure of the tenor saxophone.

Lineage

Hawkins came under the all-pervading influence of **Louis Armstrong** and, as a reaction to him, devised a personal style that came to dominate the tenor saxophone. The line to **Ben Webster**, **Don Byas**, Buddy Tate, Herschel Evans, Illinois Jacquet, Arnett Cobb and Dick Wilson is obvious, but Hawkins also influenced players on other instruments, and modernists such as **Sonny Rollins**, **Archie Shepp** and **David Murray**.

Media

Featured in CBS film, *Sound Of Jazz* (1957), and took roles in *The Crimson Canary* (1945) and in an episode of *Route 66*. There is a biography (1984) by David Burnett James entitled *Coleman Hawkins*.

Listening

1 A Study In Frustration Vols 1-4
Fletcher Henderson/CBS 66423

2 The Indispensable Coleman Hawkins 1927-1956
RCA NL 89277 (2)

3 Ridin' In Rhythm
Various/World Records SHB 42

4 Bean A Re-Bop
Coleman Hawkins/Queen Q 038

5 Coleman Hawkins/Lester Young
Spotlite SPJ 119

6 The High & Mighty Hawk
Coleman Hawkins/Affinity AFF 163

7 The Essential Coleman Hawkins
Verve 2304 537

8 The Bridge/Sonny Meets Hawk
Sonny Rollins/RCA 741074/5

Johnny Hodges

**Born: 25th July 1907/Cambridge,
Massachusetts, USA
Died: 11th May 1970/New York City,
NY, USA
Instruments: Alto and soprano
saxophones, composer
Recording Career: 1927-1970
Nickname: Rabbit**

THERE ARE TWO **Duke Ellington**
Orchestras – one with Johnny Hodges in
the reed section, the other without.
Despite even the Ducal proclamations,
the band without **Bubber Miley**, Cootie
Williams, Barney Bigard and Sonny
Greer still managed to sound
unmistakably Ellington. Without the
small man, however, the sound
changed drastically.

John Cornelius Hodges began on
drums and piano, but by the age of
fourteen had turned to the saxophone.
He played with **Sidney Bechet** in 1925
and in the later twenties worked with
Lloyd Scott, Luckey Roberts and **Chick
Webb**. In May 1928, Hodges joined
Ellington and remained with him until
1951. Over that period his style
changed dramatically. In the earlier,
brass-dominated band, his playing put
the emphasis on rhythmic thrust and on
up-tempo items such as *Cotton Club
Stomp* and *Hot Feet* >**1** he was at his
best.

As the musical climate, along with the
economic and social one, changed in
the thirties, Hodges' music became
more romantic. *Dear Old Southland*
(1933) on soprano sax >**2**, *Bundle of
Blues* (1933) >**3** and *I Let A Song Go
Out Of My Heart* (1938) >**4** showed a
softer edge, but it was the arrival of
Billy Strayhorn as co-composer/
arranger in 1939 that saw Hodges
become the ultimate balladeer. Duke's
Don't Get Around Much >**5** and *Warm
Valley* >**6**, and Strayhorn's *After All* >**7**
and, for the small groups, *Day Dream*
and *Passion Flower* >**8** became the
jewels in Hodges' crown.

From 1951, the saxophonist led his
own bands until he rejoined the
Ellington orchestra in 1955 and, but for
brief spells away, remained there until
his death. He was now internationally
famous and recorded successfully with
unlikely modernists like **Gerry
Mulligan** and swing giants like **Roy
Eldridge** and **Earl Hines**. But it was
with the parent band that the greatest
triumphs came. He could still stomp it
out with the best, though it was on
ballads like *Star Crossed Lovers* >**9**,
Isfahan >**10**, *Black Butterfly* >**11**, and
Blood Count >**12** that we heard the
nonpareil romantic of the alto
saxophone.

Lineage

Originally self-taught, Hodges later took
lessons from **Sidney Bechet**, his great
idol. Hodges is a 'one-off', although he
has influenced players such as Tab
Smith and Willie Smith, as well as
revivalists like Bruce Turner.

Listening

1 **The Indispensable Duke Ellington
Vols 1/2**
RCA PM 43687
2 **The Indispensable Duke Ellington
Vols 3/4**
RCA PM 43697
3 **The Complete Duke Ellington Vol 5**
CBS 88082
4 **The Complete Duke Ellington Vol 10**
CBS 88220

Above: Billie Holiday

Billie Holiday

**Born: 7th April 1915/Baltimore,
Maryland, USA
Died: 17th July 1959/New York City,
NY, USA
Instrument: Vocals, composer
Recording Career: 1933-1959
Nickname: Lady Day**

THAT Billie Holiday never won a Down
Beat poll in her lifetime is perhaps
predictable. She was the greatest of all
pure jazz singers, a superb artist whose
career was inexplicably tainted by the
word 'loser'. Her greatest gifts were a
unique and intuitive sense of timing and
her ability to lend credibility to even
the most banal Tin Pan Alley tune.

Born Eleanor Gough McKay, her life
was a mixture of dire tragedy, artistic
acclaim, financial success and racial
problems. She was raped at the age of
ten, and had experience as a teenage
prostitute. When first heard by critic
John Hammond in New York in 1933 the
eighteen-year-old voice already had a
lifetime of experience built into it.
Hammond organised her first recording
date with **Benny Goodman** and so
launched a career of exceptional
brilliance. She worked with Louis
Metcalfe in Canada, did theatre dates
with **Jimmie Lunceford** and joined
Count Basie in 1937. A year later she

left and had a troubled nine months in
the white band of **Artie Shaw**.

More importantly, she had embarked
on a series of recordings that put her on
the pinnacle of success. Pianist **Teddy
Wilson** became her A & R man,
surrounding her with magnificent
players such as **Lester Young**, **Roy
Eldridge**, **Buck Clayton**, **Johnny
Hodges**, **Ben Webster**, **Hot Lips Page**
and **Count Basie**. Up to the Second
World War, Billie Holiday basked in
their support and turned *The Way You
Look Tonight*, *I'll Never Be the Same*,
Without Your Love, *On The Sentimental
Side* >**1**, *Mean To Me*, *He's Funny That
Way*, *More Than You Know* >**2** and
countless other numbers into pure gold.

This was a process that continued for
the remainder of her career. By the
mid-forties, a move to Decca found her
in the company of strings in an effort to
bring her records to the attention of a
wider audience. Such 'popularisation'
made no difference: she continued to
make everything sound totally realistic
and it was not until the turn of the
decade that her lifestyle and the
demands of constant touring began to
take their toll.

Billie Holiday had always had to
come to terms with racial prejudice, but
she was beginning to tire from the
effort. She sought escape in alcohol,
marijuana and, finally, heroin and her
health suffered accordingly. The quality
of her work during this period varied
tremendously, though in good
company, and in the right mood, she
was almost as good as ever. Her
mannerisms had become noticeably
exaggerated, but titles like *Foggy Day*
and *Say It Isn't So* >**3** from 1957 were
outstanding. The other side was to be
heard in sad performances like *Sleepy
Time Down South* and *Sometimes I'm
Happy* >**4** from 1959, where she was a
tragically pale shadow of her former
self. Within the year she was dead and
jazz had lost one of its most sensitive
performers.

Lineage
While acknowledging a great liking for
both **Bessie Smith** and **Louis
Armstrong**, her own singing reflected
very little of their styles. Rather, her
voice walked the shadows, as her
smokey-voiced lyricism adopted the
melodic grace of tenor saxophonist

77

Lester Young. Many singers have sought to imitate the Lady Day method but almost all have ended with a travesty of the masterful original.

Media

Subject of a film, *Lady Sings The Blues* starring Diana Ross in 1972. Excellent BBC TV film *The Long Night Of Lady Day* (1984) and equally fine CBS TV production, *Billie Holiday*, made in 1985, and appeared herself in *Symphony In Black* (1935) and *New Orleans* (1947). Wrote, in collaboration with William Dufty, the book *Lady Sings The Blues* (1956); definitive biography, *Billie's Blues*, written by John Chilton in 1975.

Listening

1 **Billie Holiday Story Vol 1**
  Billie Holiday/CBS 68228
2 **Billie Holiday Story Vol 3**
  Billie Holiday/CBS 68230
3 **Songs For Distingué Lovers**
  Billie Holiday/Verve 2304 243

4 **Last Recordings**
  Billie Holiday/Verve 817 802-1

Harry James

Born: 15th March 1916/Albany, Georgia, USA
Died: 5th July 1983/Las Vegas, Nevada, USA
Instruments: Trumpet, drums
Recording Career: 1936-1983

AT THE AGE of just seven, Harry Haag James began playing drums in his parents' travelling circus, taking trumpet lessons from his father three years later. During his teens he played with various leaders in Texas, where the family had made its home, and in 1935 joined Ben Pollack. He remained with that band for some two years and, by the time he joined **Benny Goodman**

in January 1937, was an undeniably impressive player.

Goodman's was very much an all-star band but James was vying almost immediately with the leader, and with drummer Gene Krupa, for the status of main attraction. His flamboyant style was well-suited to the band, his brassy tone serving a brilliant technique and, as his star-clipping phrases soared through the air, it was only the perceptive who realised that the grandeur brought by **Louis Armstrong** was absent. In fact, the likes of *Boo Woo* and *Woo Woo* >**1** with James' boogie woogie trio show a more restrained jazz style, and his outstanding playing at the Carnegie Hall Concerts >**2** demonstrated that, even in the presence of his peers, he was still a jazzman of some stature.

There remained, however, traces of the circus ringmaster in his personality and, after leaving Goodman to front his own band, James began to concentrate his energies into recording trumpet showcases. Shallow items such as *The*

Flight Of The Bumble Bee, *Ciribiribin* and *Trumpet Blues* >**3** brought him popular and international acclaim but deflected attention from his jazz talents. Fortunately, there were sessions with **Teddy Wilson** >**4** and **Lionel Hampton** >**5** to keep his jazz 'chops' in shape, a conscious policy on James' part.

Certainly he enjoyed a loyal following with the general public and continued to tour well into the fifties. He then took a lengthy sabbatical before reforming a big band towards the end of that decade, and one that delighted jazz followers. Arrangers Ernie Wilkins and Neal Hefti contributed to the book >**6**, and James remained with this **Count Basie**-influenced style for the rest of his playing career.

Lineage

James' own favourite horn men were **Muggsy Spanier** and **Louis Armstrong**, but his own followers like show-trumpeter Eddie Calvert have tended to come from outside the jazz field.

Media

Played on the soundtracks for *Young Man With A Horn* (1949) and *Yanks* (1979). Also appeared in many films, including *Springtime In The Rockies* (1942), *Private Buckaroo* (1942), *Two Girls And A Sailor* (1944), *Bathing Beauty* (1944), *Do You Love Me?* (1946), *If I'm Lucky* (1946), *Carnegie Hall* (1947), *I'll Get By* (1950), *The Opposite Sex* (1956), and *The Ladies' Man* (1961).

Listening

1 The Young Harry James 1936
CBS (F) 88499
2 Benny Goodman's Carnegie Hall Concert 1938
CBS 66202
3 Harry James Classics
CBS 88145
4 Teddy Wilson
CBS 66274
5 The Complete Lionel Hampton Vols 1/2 (1937/8)
RCA NL 89583 (2)
6 Harry James Plays Neal Hefti
MGM C 881

Left: Harry James leads his band

79

Louis Jordan

Born: 8th July 1908/Brinkley, Arkansas, USA
Died: 4th February 1975/Los Angeles, California, USA
Instruments: Alto, tenor and baritone saxophones, clarinet, vocals
Recording Career: 1929-1974

AFTER GAINING early experience with the Charlie Gaines band, Louis Jordan began a two-year stay with **Chick Webb** in the summer of 1936. In 1938 he began leading his own band in New York and before long it had adopted the name Tympany Five.

At first its progress was slow, the leader's wailing alto and idiosyncratic vocal style not perhaps in tune with war-time tensions. *Choo Choo Ch'Boogie* >**1**, made in 1946, changed all that. It sold a million copies and ushered in a series of records that enjoyed prolific sales for the next five years.

The five (despite the name, made up of anything from seven to nine players) still managed to sound like a big band. Jordan's marvellously sardonic voice tested the nursery rhymes in *School Days* >**1**, was unimpressed with the police action in *Saturday Night Fish Fry* >**1**, and on *Beware* >**1** warned the unwary male of female wiles. His reedy

alto sprang out of every arrangement, with the result that the whole style became dubbed as 'jump music'.

Jordan also recorded with **Louis Armstrong**, Bing Crosby and **Ella Fitzgerald** and, in 1950, organised a short-lived big band. After illness, the mid-fifties saw the Tympany Five back together with remakes of *Fish Fry* >**2** and new arrangements in the repertoire like *The Slop* and *The Jamf* >**2** to show that its verve was intact.

He toured Britain with Chris Barber in 1962, had tours of Asia in 1967 and 1968 and did some work with the Johnny Otis Show in the early seventies. His last recording was made in 1974, less than a year before he died.

Lineage
Jordan's father was a bandleader and he began on clarinet at the age of seven. No single figure influenced him, although he was fascinated by the music of **T-Bone Walker**. Surprisingly, **Sonny Rollins** told a BBC interviewer that Jordan was one of his earliest inspirations. More obvious is the influence that Jordan had on men like Sam 'The Man' Taylor.

Media
Played in the 1944 film *Follow The Boys*.

Listening
1 **Louis Jordan**
  MCA MCM 5005
2 **Rockin' & Jivin' 1956-58 Vol 2**
  Louis Jordan/Bear Family BFX 15207

John Kirby

Born: 31st December 1908/Baltimore, Maryland, USA
Died: 14th June 1952/Hollywood, California, USA
Instruments: String bass, tuba, arranger
Recording Career: 1929-1946

AFTER JOINING **Fletcher Henderson** as a tuba player at the age of twenty,

John Kirby switched to string bass, playing throughout the thirties with Henderson, **Chick Webb** and Lucky Millinder. In 1937 he took over as leader of the combo of the Onyx Club, originally with Frankie Newton on trumpet and Pete Brown on alto. They were soon to be replaced by Charlie Shavers and Russell Procope respectively and, together with clarinettist Buster Bailey, pianist Billy Kyle and drummer O'Neil Spencer, this line-up was known as the 'Biggest Little Band In The Land'. The personnel remained unchanged until 1942 and in that five-year period they established an enviable reputation with a unique brand of light, superbly arranged, small group music.

Kirby's own light touch on the bass gave the rhythm section genuine buoyancy and, with such impressive soloists, the front line was never short of ideas. With the fine singing of Kirby's wife Maxine Sullivan plus excellent compositions like *Pastel Blue* and *Undecided* by Charlie Shavers, the formula was exactly right. The group also made a speciality of working out swing arrangements of classical pieces and titles like Grieg's *Anitra's Dance* (from Peer Gynt), *Serenade*, *Humoresque*, and the sextet from Donizetti's *Lucia Di Lammermoor* >1 show just how imaginative they could be.

After 1942, changes in personnel had their effect on the group and its popularity waned. A brief revival in 1946, with **Sarah Vaughan** as vocalist and Bailey, Procope and Kyle reinstated, enjoyed little success. Kirby was disillusioned and spent his last years in California still trying to form a sextet and to recapture the magic of earlier times.

Lineage

Kirby began as a trombonist, but later took lessons in bass playing from no lesser exponents than Pops Foster and Wellman Braud. He himself brought a lighter touch to the instrument and has sometimes been suggested as an influence on Oscar Pettiford.

Listening

1 Flow Gently Sweet Rhythm
John Kirby/TAX M 8016

Jimmie Lunceford

Born: 6th June 1902/Fulton, Missouri, USA
Died: 12th July 1947/Seaside, Oregon, USA
Instruments: Multi-instrumentalist, leader, arranger
Recording Career: 1920-1947

THOSE JEALOUS of the success of the Lunceford Orchestra dubbed them 'trained seals', although rumour has it that the leader found that insult almost acceptable. He was something of a perfectionist and had studied with Paul Whiteman's father before getting a BMus degree at Fisk. During his college vacation, he worked as a saxophonist with Wilbur Sweatman and Elmer Snowden but after qualifying became a music teacher in his own right. Among his students were Edwin Wilcox, Willie Smith and Henry Wells, who all stayed with him when he formed a professional band in 1929.

The Lunceford band moved to New York in 1933 and in the following year succeeded **Cab Calloway** at the Cotton Club. The band was very much unique. Unlike **Duke Ellington** and **Count Basie**, their rhythm section put strong emphasis on the after beat and because of their exemplary discipline, there was a dashing interplay between trombone section, trumpet section and reeds. In Sy Oliver the band had a brilliant arranger and it was he who suggested

that these factors meant that he had updated the New Orleans style to the needs of the swing era.

In theory this was true, but there was no hint of the big band Dixieland feeling associated with **Bob Crosby**. Titles like *Stomp It Off* >**1** and *For Dancers Only* >**2** were far removed from the Crescent City but were object lessons in section interplay and balance. The rhythm section's objectives are clearly defined on *Swanee River* >**3** and the famous Lunceford dance tempo was never more explicit than on *Pigeon Walk* >**3**. The band was also visually precise, although the brilliant interpretation of the reed score of *Sleepy Time Gal* >**1** shows that the sidemen had more to think about than merely standing and swaying in unison.

Altoist Willie Smith was perhaps the star soloist – his work appears on nearly every recording made by the band – but there were also impressive individual contributions from Eddie Tomkins, Eddie Durham (on guitar) and Trummy Young, the latter with some strangely *sotto voce* vocals.

Sadly, Lunceford was not a generous man and the band's disintegration in the mid-forties was mainly due to his rates of pay. He did reform after the Second World War but the magic had gone and the music was no longer right for a band of which Count Basie said: 'They'd just rock all night long'.

Lineage

Lunceford was a useful multi-instrumentalist, but it was not until late in the band's life that he played much. The band grew in force thanks to arrangements by the likes of Sy Oliver, Ed Wilcox, Willie Smith and Eddie Durham, and its internal balance and instrumental precision were the envy of all bandleaders. However, its real influence was on **Tommy Dorsey**, who wooed Oliver to his ranks, and on **Stan Kenton**, who in the mid-forties sought to be a white Lunceford.

Media

The Lunceford band appeared in *Blues In The Night* (1941) as well as making several short films.

Listening

1 **Rhythm Is Our Business**
Jimmie Lunceford/MCA 1302
2 **Jimmie Lunceford & His Orchestra**
Jasmine JASM 1023
3 **Strictly Lunceford**
Jimmie Lunceford/Affinity AFS 1003

Jay McShann

Angeles. Brown had parted company with the band but McShann was fortunate to enlist the help of **Jimmy Witherspoon** and with a sextet or septet, he showcased the newcomer on classics like *Skidrow Blues* and *Money's Getting Cheaper* >**3**.

For most of the fifties and sixties McShann worked in Kansas. He appeared as a soloist at London's 1969 Jazz Expo, however, and this began a period of touring. Europe was often on his itinerary and in the early eighties he was a well-known figure along with drummer Paul Gunter >**4** at clubs and festivals across the continent.

Lineage

McShann studied piano from the age of twelve, and in his youth listened constructively to men like **Benny Moten** and **Count Basie**.

Media

US TV documentary on Jay McShann *Hootie's Blues* (1978).

Listening

1 Early Bird
Jay McShann/Spotlite 120
2 With Charlie Parker
Jay McShann/Affinity AFS 1006
3 Spoon Calls Hootie
Jimmy Witherspoon/Polydor 545 105
4 The Man From Muskojee
Jay McShann/Affinity AFF 147

Jay McShann

Born: 12th January 1909/Muskogee, Oklahoma, USA
Instrument: Piano, vocals
Recording Career: 1940-
Nickname: Hootie

A BANDLEADER in Arkansas even before he finished college, James Columbus McShann spent the middle thirties onward as sideman but also ran his own bands in Kansas City. This was a city that had just lost a lot of prominent players to New York; although it was still jumping, it was under the dubious control of Tom Pendergast, high priest of the local gangster world.

McShann's band was representative of the Kansas style, a natural for playing dances and very strong on the *Blues* >**1**. It was also blessed with one of the great blues shouters in Walter Brown and, from 1937 to 1941 frequently had **Charlie Parker** as a sideman. This player's early style was captured on the 1941 *Hootie Blues* >**2**, a performance typical of the band in the period up to McShann's call-up in 1944.

On his release a year later, he played in New York and then moved on to Los

Red Norvo

Born: 31st March 1908/Beardstown, Illinois, USA
Instruments: Vibraphone, xylophone, marimba, piano
Recording Career: 1933-

ALTHOUGH CONVERSANT with the vibraphone from an early age, Kenneth Norville became for many years the undisputed king of the xylophone. It is true that he had few rivals on the latter, but it was an instrument that suited his early style of playing rather better than its amplified brother.

Initially, Norvo took piano lessons but

Above: Hot Lips Page

turned to the xylophone while at school.
At the age of seventeen, he was leading
a marimba band in the mid-West and
later joined the Paul Ash Orchestra.
While working with Paul Whiteman in
the early thirties, Norvo married the
band's singer, Mildred Bailey. As 'Mr
and Mrs Swing' they led a band jointly
for some years, Norvo's chamber-
rooted and understated style a beautiful
foil for the light and highly rhythmic
singing of his wife >**1**.

Throughout the Second World War
he led bands of various sizes before
finally switching to vibes in 1943. He
effectively took the **Lionel Hampton**
role with the **Benny Goodman** sextet in
1945 and showed that his style was very
different from that of 'Hamp'. On an up
tempo 'tester' such as *I Got Rhythm* >**2**
his hard-driving, almost vibrato-less
style came as quite a shock, but his
swing and instrumental virtuosity were

more than evident.

Norvo spent a year with the **Woody
Herman** band, fitting in amazingly well
in that powerhouse unit. He led small
groups on both the East and West Coast
and made some particularly impressive
trio records with guitarist Tal Farlow
and bassist **Charles Mingus** >**3**. An
overdue European debut came in 1954,
to be followed by spells with Goodman
in 1959 and 1961. Tragically, he was
threatened with deafness in the sixties,
and on one British tour had become
very depressed by the prospect.
Fortunately, an operation in 1968 sorted
out the problem and in Paris the
following year there was no diminution
of Norvo's verve: as items like the
crackling *Sunday* >**4** and immaculately
strolled *Confessin'* >**4** confirmed, the
recovery was complete.

Norvo is still an active musician, often
touring with his old colleague Farlow,
and has played a prominent part in
several New York Jazz Festivals in the
eighties.

Lineage

Norvo cites nobody as an influence and, indeed, influenced few players himself.

Media

Wrote incidental music for films *Two Tickets To Broadway* (1951), *Kings Go Forth* (1958) (in which he also appeared) and *Screaming Mimi* (1958).

Listening

1 Her Greatest Performances
Mildred Bailey/Columbia JC 3L 22 (3)
2 The Alternate Goodman Vol XI
Benny Goodman/Phontastic NOST 7652
3 Trio With Tal Farlow & Charles Mingus
Red Norvo/Savoy WL 70540 (2)
4 Swing That Music
Various/Affinity AFF 45

Hot Lips Page

Born: 27th January 1908/Dallas, Texas, USA
Died: 5th November 1954/New York City, NY, USA
Instruments: Trumpet, mellophone, vocals
Recording Career: 1930-1953

PERHAPS the most enigmatic of jazzmen, Oran Thaddeus Page was one of the greatest of blues trumpeters, a man who had accompanied **Bessie Smith**, **Ma Rainey** and Ida Cox, yet adapted to the pre-bop jam sessions at Minton's more easily than any other swing era stylist.

His earliest childhood lessons on reed instruments proved to be abortive but, after switching to trumpet aged twelve, he progressed rapidly. It was on the TOBA that he worked with the aforementioned blues singers, but in 1928 he joined Walter Page and The Blue Devils. With this famous band his talents blossomed and within two years he had been invited to join **Bennie Moten** in Kansas City.

Recording frequently with this band, he immediately attracted attention with his broad tone, fiery delivery and superb control of growl effects. His fierce assault on *Toby* >**1**, the Armstrong-esque logic of the solo on *Moten Swing* >**1** and the poignancy of his playing on *New Orleans* >**1** give some idea of the man's breadth of style, a style which made him the band's star attraction up to the time of Moten's death in 1935.

Page worked briefly as a speciality act with **Count Basie**, then in the following year moved to New York. In 1937 he formed his own big band and signed for booking agent Joe Glaser – a less than desirable arrangement since Glaser was already handling **Louis Armstrong** and was somewhat jealous of any suggested rivalry. Nevertheless, *Feelin' High And Happy* and *I Let A Song Go Out Of My Heart* >**2** gave evidence that this was a good band and that Lips' Armstrong-style trumpet was well showcased.

In 1938, Page was re-united with his old Moten colleague, Count Basie, as part of the 'Spirituals To Swing' concert at New York's Carnegie Hall, and gave an object lesson in riff-based, up-tempo blues trumpet, including a masterly *Blues With Lips* >**3**. He endured a brief period with a sympathetic **Artie Shaw**: though musically satisfying, it exposed him to the worst aspects of the 'Jim Crow' syndrome as the one black man in a white band. His appearances at Minton's always attracted the young moderns, but titles like *Blood on the Moon* >**4** in the Mezzrow/**Sidney Bechet** King Jazz Series reminded the world that here was a blues master.

In 1949, Page made his first trip to Europe and became a regular visitor up to the time of his death.

Lineage

Page was influenced by **Louis Armstrong**, both as trumpeter and as singer, although he brought an earthier dimension to both. As one of the great primitives, it was inevitable that his own influence on the moderns was slight.

Listening

1 The Complete Bennie Moten Vols 5/6
Bennie Moten/RCA PM 45688
2 Feelin' High And Happy
Hot Lips Page/RCA LPV 576
3 Spirituals To Swing
Various/Vanguard VSD 47/48
4 The King Jazz Story
Mezzrow/Bechet/Storyville SLP 136

Django Reinhardt

Born: 23rd January 1910/Liverchies, Belgium
Died: 16th May 1953/Fontainebleau, Paris, France
Instruments: Violin, guitar
Recording Career: 1926-1953

THE EARLIEST musical experience of Jean Baptiste Reinhardt was as a gypsy guitarist, but at the age of eighteen he was seriously burned in a caravan fire. Tragically, he lost the use of two fingers on his left hand and had to change his fingering technique completely to accommodate this deficiency. Amazingly, though, he still fashioned a virtuoso style, and by the time he joined André Ekyan's band three years later had already become a master musician.

In 1934, Reinhardt formed the Quintet Of The Hot Club Of France with **Stephane Grappelli** and together they stormed the jazz world with the originality of their conception and the quality of their solo work. Titles such as *Dinah, Lady Be Good* and *Djangology* >**1** were immediate successes, displaying technical skill, inventive flair and superb tone. Unfortunately, they also revealed Reinhardt's less convincing credentials: the slightly folkish element of his phrase shapes, the fairground feeling in his timing, and the occasional almost cloying romanticism.

The highlights of his recording career, however, came in the later thirties when he made a series of recordings with visting Americans. He fitted into the reed–dominated **Coleman Hawkins** All Star Band effortlessly and his partnerships with violinist Eddie South >**2** were highly successful. With trumpeters Bill Coleman and Rex Stewart >**2**, the liaisons were not always as comfortable, but the pinnacle was reached with **Dicky Wells**. The brash worldliness of the trombonist on *Hangin' Round Boudon* >**3** and his no-nonsense assault on *Japanese Sandman* >**3** contrast wonderfully with Reinhardt's Romany whimsy. The Belgian's delicate line and lightly dancing step could not be further removed from the trombonist's approach, but together they are irresistible.

In 1947 Reinhardt took to the electric guitar and embraced bebop, the emerging jazz of the period. *Babik* >**4** and *Mobbin' The Bride* >**5** show that he adapted to the style well, but by his own standards it diminished his stature. For an eccentric original to become just another guitarist was sad and, despite a brief period when he joined the **Duke Ellington** Orchestra, this gifted monarch of the guitar will be remembered for his performances before the Second World War, not those after.

Lineage

Reinhardt first played violin but, after switching to guitar, rapidly established a jazz style at least tempered by his gypsy upbringing. Later his contact with American players led him to the music of **Louis Armstrong**, and in the forties his switch to the electric guitar was encouraged by his discovery of **Charlie Christian**.

A whole school of Reinhardt copyists has arisen – collectively in the persona of the group WASO, and very strongly in the playing of individuals such as British-born Martin Taylor and Frenchman Birelli Legrene.

Media

First-rate biography by Charles Delaunay, *Django Reinhardt*, published 1961. Reinhardt can be heard on the soundtracks of *Clair De Lune* (1932), *Eins* (1971), *Lacombe Lucien* (1974), *Alex And The Gypsy* (1976) and *L'Entourloupe* (1980). Wrote the score for *Le Village De La Colère* (1946).

Listening

1 50th Anniversary
  Quintet Of The Hot Club Of France/VJD 6950
2 Django Swing
  Django Reinhardt/Swaggie S 1252
3 Django Rhythms 1935-37
  Django Reinhardt/Swaggie S 1251
4 The Very Best Of Django Reinhardt
  Decca 6.28441 (2)
5 Django Reinhardt
  Xtra 1092

Jimmy Rushing

Born: 26th August 1902/Oklahoma City, Oklahoma, USA
Died: 8th June 1972/New York City, NY, USA
Instrument: Vocals, piano
Recording Career: 1929-1971
Nickname: Mister Five By Five

IN THE ART of blues shouting in front of a big band, James Andrew Rushing was the ultimate master. That gem of understatement reflects the genius of the man. The full truth was that putting the Oklahoman in a group of any size was enough to guarantee that it would swing remorselessly.

He had early swing experience on the West Coast, occasionally accompanied by **Jelly Roll Morton**, but returned home in 1925 to tour with the Billy King Revue, which included bassist Walter Page. In 1927 he joined Page's Blue Devils and made his recording debut with them in 1929, but it was his records with the **Bennie Moten** band from 1929 onwards that were significant.

As *New Orleans* >**1** showed, Rushing was the type of jazzman who, perhaps like **Louis Armstrong** and **Art Tatum**, had an irrepressible instinct for improvisation. His 1932 vocal was almost identical in phraseology and accenting to the version made in 1955 >**4**, and indicates that once he had satisfied himself with a conception he stayed with it.

After Moten's death, Rushing joined **Count Basie** and was a star attraction with the band until 1948. His performances with Basie were unsurpassed, a wholly ideal marriage of styles. There was the build-up of intensity at his vocal entrance to *Exactly Like You* >**2**; the transformation of trivia such as *London Bridge* and *Georgia* >**2**; the inspirational surge that Harry Edison sustained on the inane *You Be Good* >**2**; and the way in which Rushing's brief vocal on *Sent For You Yesterday* >**3** built up to the band's riff climax.

The list of such fine performances was almost endless, but after his break with Basie, Rushing never approached anything like that permanency of tenure again. He worked occasionally with Basie, toured with **Benny Goodman**, **Harry James** and **Eddie Condon**, but for the last fifteen years of his life was the constant companion of **Buck Clayton**. Trumpeter Clayton selected the appropriate musicians to represent each city in the 1955/6 *Odyssey Of James Rushing Esq* >**4** and wrote such exciting arrangements for *It's A Sin To Tell A Lie* and *Someday Sweetheart* >**5** from 1958.

The last chance to hear Rushing on record came in 1971 and, although there were frail moments, tracks like *Bei Mir Bist Du Schoen* >**6** recall him at his finest.

Lineage

Rushing began studying violin and piano but his singing was very much a product of the Middle West, even if he did concede the influence of **Bessie Smith** and Leroy Carr. The art of big band jazz singing more or less died with him, leaving only **Jimmy Witherspoon** to continue to carry the torch.

Media

Was in CBS film *The Sound Of Jazz* (1957) and in 1969 film *The Learning Tree*.

Listening

1 The Complete Bennie Moten Vols 5/6
Bennie Moten/RCA PM 45688
2 Good Mornin' Blues
Jimmy Rushing/Affinity AFS 1002
3 Swingin' The Blues
Count Basie/Affinity AFS 1010
4 The Jazz Odyssey Of James Rushing Esq
Philips BBC 7166
5 Rushing And The Big Brass
Jimmy Rushing/CBS 21132
6 The You And Me That Used To Be
Jimmy Rushing/RCA SF 5234

Artie Shaw

Born: 23rd May 1910/New York City, NY, USA
Instrument: Clarinet, saxophones, composer
Recording Career: 1928-

AFTER PLAYING in numerous big bands in the late twenties and early thirties, the erstwhile Arthur Jacob Arshawsky finally formed his own in 1936. Among the swing bands of the era it was something of an anomaly, in that it included a string section. Artistically, it was a worthwhile venture but, financially, it was less than viable and after only a year, Shaw returned to conventional swing band instrumentation.

In 1938, *Begin The Beguine* >**1** was an enormous hit: its success made him a rival to **Benny Goodman**. The two clarinet styles were very different, however, and each had its own following. Shaw's style was decorative rather than constructive; he had a pure singing tone and *Special Delivery Stomp* and *Summit Ridge Drive* >**2** (recorded with his Gramercy Five) show his flair for the well-sculptured solo.

This 'band-within-a-band' marked the high spot of Shaw's jazz career and was, in fact, reformed briefly after the Second World War. Shaw's interest in the band business wavered, however, and he went to live in Spain for some time. Then, astonishingly, after twenty years, he returned in 1983 to form a new

Artie Shaw

band, although only acting as a front man. It would seem the limpid sound of his clarinet has now been lost for ever.

Lineage
Shaw's early style suggests the playing of **Jimmie Noone**, but he had nowhere near as many disciples as **Benny Goodman**.

Media
Autobiography *The Trouble With Cinderella* appeared in 1952. Also wrote a book intriguingly called *I Love You, I Hate You, Drop Dead* (1965). Brigitte Berman produced a film about him entitled *Time Is All You Got* (1984). Role in film *Crash* (1978) and contributed to the soundtrack of *The Man Who Fell To Earth* (1976).

Listening
1 **Artie Shaw and His Orchestra 1938/39**
  RCA PM 43175
2 **The Indispensible Artie Shaw 1940/42**
  RCA NL 89774 (2)

Stuff Smith

Born: 14th August 1909/Portsmouth, Ohio, USA
Died: 25th September 1967/Munich, West Germany
Instrument: Violin, vocals
Recording Career: 1928-1967

JAZZ CRITIC Timme Rosenkrantz is reputed to have described Stuff Smith as the 'palpitating Paganini' and it seems to most observers that Smith devoted his entire life to proving this sobriquet appropriate.

Only seventeen when he joined Alphonso Trent's band, Hezekiah Leroy Gordon Smith remained with Trent (apart from a brief spell with **Jelly Roll Morton**) until the early thirties. After this, he formed his own band with Jonah Jones in the trumpet chair and in 1936 took them to New York. Quickly establishing himself at the Onyx Club, he began to use the amplified violin to burst through the ensemble of *Upstairs* >**1**, or dance alongside Buster Bailey's clarinet on *Onyx Club Spree* >**1**. Here was a violinist who could really swing, sawing his way to the hearts of the Onyx crowd until the middle forties when he went to Chicago.

In the fifties, Smith moved to the West Coast and was playing a Guarnerius, even then valued at $5,000. He came into contact with a new generation of players and while *Soft Winds* >**2** showed he could float over **Oscar Peterson**'s detailed bed of nails, *Paper Moon* >**3** took the listener into the gladiatorial arena for a head-to-head with **Dizzy Gillespie**. Smith came to Europe increasingly in the sixties where he took part in a 'violin summit' with **Stephane Grappelli**, **Jean-Luc Ponty** and Svend Asmussen >**4** in the last year of his life. He also made a stunning bop session with Kenny Drew and Neils-Henning Orsted Pedersen to show how completely modernised he had become. He once said 'I've always visualised myself playing trumpet, tenor or clarinet.' *Bugle Blues* >**5** from that session proved the point.

Lineage
His father, a multi-instrumentalist, made Smith his first violin at seven, and five years later welcomed him into his band. There are traces of his playing in most of the post-bop violinists, but **Billy Bang** tells not only of admiring his style, but of initially copying the way in which he held the instrument!

Media
Appeared in film *52nd Street* (1937).

Listening
1 **Golden Swing Years**
  (only four titles) Various/Brunswick (9) 87 525

Art Tatum

Born: 13th October 1910/Toledo, Ohio, USA
Died: 5th November 1956/Los Angeles, California, USA
Instrument: Piano
Recording Career: 1932-1956

THE INCREDIBLE Arthur Tatum was a child prodigy who formed his own small band at the age of sixteen. In 1932, he became accompanist to Adelaide Hall and made his recording debut with her in New York. While there, he caused quite a furore amongst local musicians who were amazed at his brilliant technique. Then came a two-year

residency at the Three Deuces in Chicago from 1935 to 1936, and a successful year in Hollywood. Tatum returned to New York just prior to a trip to England in 1938.

By the time that he first came to the studios in 1932, Tatum had already become the complete pianist. All that he did in the late thirties was to refine his remarkable craft. In so doing, he became the most wholly orchestral pianist in jazz history, his left hand an entire rhythm section, and the relationship between his two hands calling to mind the section interplay of a big band. Amazing though it was, *Elegie* >1, with its independent, two-handed counterpoint, was only a precursor for similarly ambidextrous performances that followed.

He played mainly as a soloist and, during the early years of the Second World War worked in California and New York. In 1943, he formed a trio with Tiny Grimes and Slam Stewart, although the constraints of a threesome did little to staunch his endless, melodic flow. If anything, the trio performances emphasised the very basis of Tatum's style. Bop may have been looming, but at no time did Tatum attempt to build new tunes on established chord sequences. The structure was always sacrosanct, surrounded by detailed counter-melodies; through them he proposed paraphrases of the time, without rewriting the original melody line. His roots in stride piano were never severed, and there were still times when he could swing out in a style that rivalled **Fats Waller**.

Tatum signed for Capitol in 1949, which led to four productive years. *Willow Weep For Me* >**2** showed that his structural awareness was as important as his flowing rhetoric, and *Someone To Watch Over Me* >**3** was a masterpiece of ballad care. A trio was again tried in 1952 but, in the following year, Tatum signed for Norman Granz and the Clef label.

An incredible 68 out of 100 musicians had voted him their number one in the *Encyclopedia Year Book Of Jazz* but he could have had no greater fan than Granz. The JATP man set about recording Tatum 'for posterity' and this meant, in real terms, giving the pianist freedom to record any tune he so desired. Tatum responded splendidly and a stream of masterful performances flowed from his fingers. The coquettish *Sittin' And A-Rocking* >**4**, the Waller-esque *You Took Advantage Of Me* >**4**, or the headlong *Tea For Two* >**5** are individual examples, but the consistency of inspiration was awesome.

In 1954, Granz hit upon the idea of recording Tatum with other major jazz figures. In the main they were horn men, but the establishment threw up its hands in horror. Surely this effusive egotist could not interrupt his flowing soliloquies to accommodate other stars? The answer was that he did not even try. It was left to the guests to make the adjustments: on *their* ability hung the success of the sessions. To take two extremes, there was little tangible difference between Tatum's playing with **Ben Webster** and with **Buddy de Franco** >**6**. Yet the former collaboration was highly successful and the latter was not. Webster worked with contrast, and made no attempt to compete on the pianist's own terms, while de Franco tried to play him at his own game. Unfortunately, a completely different case could be made by comparing the excellence of the titles recorded with the effusive **Lionel Hampton** >**6** with the slightly

uncomfortable air that prevailed on those with the gifted, but laconic **Benny Carter** >**6**.

Because of this series of recordings and the friendship of the two men, Granz set out to advance Tatum's career as much as possible. A Carnegie Hall concert was arranged (but did not take place) featuring the pianist with **Charlie Parker**. Granz then decided to arrange an impressive tour programme with the pianist billed simply as TATUM in the concert-hall tradition, and plans had progressed as far as the purchase of white tie and tails.

This was little more than a year before his death, however, and as his health began to fail, Tatum suggested that the plans be held in abeyance until he was stronger. But it was not to be, and Granz was finally forced to admit that the tour would never take place.

Considering the date of his first 'cut', Tatum made a comparatively small number of recordings. Had it not been for the foresight of Granz we would now have an inadequate testimonial to one of the music's finest pianists, a man that had brought to jazz a level of musicianship unrivalled on any other instrument.

Lineage

Tatum's original inspiration came from **Fats Waller** and **Earl Hines**, but he himself influenced only pianists who were capable of copying. That list hardly extends beyond Herman Chittison, Billy Taylor and **Oscar Peterson**.

Media

Tatum played a short but excellent piano part in the film *The Fabulous Dorseys* (1947) and also made a short for the *March Of Time* series.

Listening

1 Pure Genius
Art Tatum/Affinity AFFD 118
2 Art Tatum
Capitol LC 6524
3 Art Tatum
Capitol LC 6638
4 The Genius Of Art Tatum Vol 2
Clef MGC 615
5 The Genius Of Art Tatum Vol 8
Clef MGC 661
6 The Tatum Group Masterpieces
Pablo 2625-706

T-Bone Walker

**Born: 22nd May 1909/Linden, near
Texarkana, Texas, USA
Died: 17th March 1975/Los Angeles,
California, USA
Instruments: Guitar, piano, vocals
Recording Career: 1929-1973**

AARON THIBAUD Walker began as a
solo act and made his recording debut
with *Trinity River Blues* >**1** in 1929
under the colourful name of Oak Cliff
T-Bone. He spent time accompanying
Blind Lemon Jefferson, Ida Cox and
Ma Rainey before he met jazz guitarist
Charlie Christian in 1933. The two men
swopped ideas and T-Bone has
subsequently claimed to have been
using electric guitar as early as 1935.

In 1939 he joined the Les Hite band in
California and while with him recorded
his celebrated *T-Bone Blues* >**2**.
Throughout the forties he performed in
Los Angeles clubs, always playing
music that occupied that nebulous area
somewhere between jazz and pure
blues. His guitar style was unique, with
a biting attack full of jazz phraseology,
and the tone a gloriously metallic
tramcar jangle. In contrast, his voice
was a laid-back, blues-drenched
exercise in basic cynicism which found

its home in **Louis Jordan**-style jump
bands and is well heard in the
complaints of the *Hypin' Women
Blues* >**3** and *Midnight Blues* >**4** from
1947.

He continued to work solo and in
small blues bands in the fifties and
sixties, as well as touring Europe, as
often in fast jazz company as with blues
singers. Dramatic records continued to
appear, and Walker seemed
determined to update his presentation,
with titles like the 1967 *I'm Gonna Stop
This Nite Life* >**5**, showing his
awareness of current developments.

He was at home with jazz's finest
instrumentalists and appeared on stage
with the likes of **Dizzy Gillespie**, **Clark
Terry** and **Zoot Sims**. It was a salutary
experience to see all three of these
gentlemen return to the side of the
stage to observe this remarkable artist
during the course of a Norman Granz
concert in Britain in the late sixties.

Lineage

Walker learnt guitar within his family
circle, but was strongly influenced by
Blind Lemon Jefferson and Scrapper
Blackwell before later playing and
singing in a style reminiscent of Leroy
Carr. The influence of **Charlie
Christian** pushed him towards jazz and,
eventually, a wholly original style. His
influence on the whole of the blues and

gave the style a formal grammar, it was his protégé who turned it into poetry. He had a mighty stride left hand, but his treble explorations were delightfully unpredictable, and delivered with an irresistible delicacy.

Thomas Waller's career started in earnest when he won a talent contest playing Johnson's *Carolina Shout*. In the twenties, he played as house pianist in clubs, accompanied in silent movie houses, and later worked with Johnson in the *Keep Shufflin'* review. In the early thirties he recorded with **Fletcher Henderson**, **Jack Teagarden** and **McKinney's Cotton Pickers**, while 1934 saw the first of the Fats Waller And His Rhythm series of records. From that moment on, the man revered by his jazz peers became public property.

It was also a step that brought to everyone's notice the quality of his compositions, masterpieces such as *Honeysuckle Rose, Ain't Misbehavin', Black And Blue* and *Keeping Out Of Mischief Now* >**1**. In his case, however, the brilliant tunesmith was matched by dazzling improvising jazzmen and if, in the process, he made the world chuckle at his lyrics and his zany asides, everyone was delighted.

In 1938 he came to Europe, touring in 1941 with his own big band. Unfortunately Waller's health was not good and touring was imposing an extra strain. He had always enjoyed a drink, but the habit had reached prodigious proportions. In 1943 he was still far from well but, because of the war, embarked on a tour of military service camps. While travelling cross-country to one such job he died of pneumonia, on board the luxury train, the Santa Fe Chief.

Lineage

Waller was influenced by **James P. Johnson**, Luckey Roberts and Willie Gant, although it was almost a proxy arrangement that took him back to obscure New York pianists like Abba Labba, Jack The Bear, The Beetle and Jess Pickett. His own influence has spread into many fibres of jazz with his inimitable stride style appearing in the work of **Duke Ellington**, **Art Tatum**, Cliff Jackson and **Ralph Sutton**, his astoundingly detailed treble excursions in the playing of Hank Duncan and Johnny Guarnieri, and his compositional

---

rhythm and blues field has been enormous, from giants like **B. B. King**, Lowell Fulsom and Pee Wee Crayton through the entire fabric of contemporary blues.

Listening

1 Texas Country Music Vol 3
Various/Roots RL 327
2 T-Bone Blues
Les Hite Orchestra/T-Bone Walker/Varsity 8391 (78rpm)
3 T-Bone Jumps Again
T-Bone Walker/Charley CRB 1019
4 Plain Ole Blues
T-Bone Walker/Charley CRB 1037
5 Stormy Monday Blues
T-Bone Walker/Stateside SL 10223

Fats Waller

Born: 21st May 1904/New York City, NY, USA
Died: 15th December 1943/Kansas City, Missouri, USA
Instruments: Piano, organ, vocals, composer
Recording Career: 1922-1943

STRIDE PIANO was Fats Waller's modus operandi. If **James P. Johnson**

and melodic abilities frequently evident in the work, unlikely as it may seem, of **Thelonious Monk**.

Media

Waller made several short films and appeared in bigger productions such as *Hooray For Love!* (1935), *King of Burlesque* (1935) and *Stormy Weather* (1943). *Ain't Misbehavin'*, biography by Ed Kirkeby, published in 1966.

Listening

1 Ten Album Set
Fats Waller/RCA FATSCOF 1

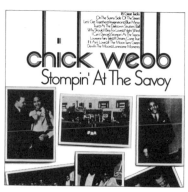

Chick Webb

Born: 10th February 1909/Baltimore, Maryland, USA
Died: 16th June 1939/Baltimore, Maryland, USA
Instrument: Drums
Recording Career: 1927-1939

THE LIFE of William Henry 'Chick' Webb was bound up with the 'Holy Land' – the Savoy Ballroom in Harlem. It was the scene of his greatest triumphs and his spiritual home. He was a diminutive and ailing man, a hunch-back as a result of tuberculosis of the spine, but he became the finest powerhouse big-band drummer of all time. Although only thirty when he died, he had breathed life into bands that would, without him, have been quite ordinary.

Something of a child prodigy, he was working on the Sheepshead Bay, Baltimore boats while still a teenager. In 1924, he went to New York and worked with the Edward Dowell Orchestra, but within two years was leading his own smaller units in clubs and dance halls of the city. His first spell as a leader at the Savoy came in 1927, and before the end of 1931, Webb had become something of a regular performer.

His fame as a drummer spread rapidly. The style was uncomplicated, but he possessed a tremendous drive, and was renowned for the resonance of his snare work; but, whether on snare or cymbals, he played with a light, staccato urgency. Breaks were played with all the alacrity of the New Orleans stylists, and the 'lift' that he gave to his band was phenomenal >**1**.

It was Chick Webb who, in 1934, discovered **Ella Fitzgerald** singing at an amateur talent contest; she became a member of the band, managing to increase its popularity even more >**2**. The band, however, remained an attraction in its own right, and it would be a brave leader who would take it on in the famed 'battles' that occurred at the Savoy.

The band was also becoming well known nationwide, and they broke attendance records at many venues. Unfortunately, Webb's health was suspect and, while touring Texas, he was taken ill with pleurisy. After hospitalisation, though, he continued to play and, appropriately, given his early exploits, the last date before his death was on a riverboat sailing from Washington.

Lineage

Webb was largely self-taught, but it might be easier to list drummers *not* affected by him. A direct and unmistakeable influence can be found in the work of Jo Jones, Sid Catett, Cozy Cole, James Crawford, Kenny Clarke, Gene Krupa, **Buddy Rich,** Alvin Burroughs, Louis Bellson and Dave Tough.

Listening

1 In The Groove
Chick Webb/Affinity AFS 1007
2 Forever Young Vol 1
Ella Fitzgerald/Swingtime ST 1006

Ben Webster

Born: 27th March 1909/Kansas City, Missouri, USA
Died: 20th September 1973/ Amsterdam, The Netherlands
Instruments: Tenor saxophone, piano, arranger
Recording Career: 1931-1973

IT IS ALMOST as if there were two Benjamin Francis Websters. One, the swaggering, aggressive soloist, capable of giving an up-tempo item a rough-tongued chastisement, the other a breathy balladeer who could move effortlessly into the field of pure romance.

His credentials were impeccable and **Bennie Moten**, Andy Kirk, **Fletcher Henderson** and **Benny Carter** were just four of the major leaders for whom Webster worked during the thirties. He also played briefly for **Duke Ellington** during this period, but reached the pinnacle of his career when he joined the Ellington band on a permanent basis in 1940. The new tenor man was featured prominently and he responded appropriately. For example, Webster caressed *Sittin' And A-Rockin'* >**1** with loving care and then treated *Cotton Tail* >**1** to a full frontal attack, and his distinctive tenor voice was heard on nearly every title in this productive period.

He left Ellington in 1943 and, from then on, was mainly occupied with small group work. He toured with Jazz At The Philharmonic and was involved in major recording dates. One, supervised by Norman Granz in 1956, with Webster partnered by pianist **Art Tatum**, displayed an amazing approach: he made no effort to match the pianist's extravagances, but merely placed his luxurious tenor lines above them. *My Ideal* and *My One And Only Love* >**2** are masterful performances and show just how well this contradiction of styles works. In a similar way he met the challenge of effusive **Oscar Peterson**, although on their 1959 date, *Touch Of Your Lips* >**3** for once demonstrated that Peterson was prepared to staunch his own outflow in order to support more consciously the tenor line.

The saxophonist had become hot property and his *Webster Meets* series of records sold well. Unfortunately, he became restricted by the formula and, after moving to Europe in 1964 began to put more emphasis on the heavy tone and breathy delivery than he did on any creative realisation. Yet, on up-tempo items, that original style that made him such an important player could still be frequently heard and appreciated.

Lineage
Webster graduated from the **Coleman Hawkins** school but was later influenced in his ballad playing by **Johnny Hodges**. His influence can be heard in tenor men like Paul Gonsalves and Flip Phillips.

Media
Webster appeared in several short films with Ellington, one with the Benny Carter Band, *Clash By Night* (1952), and in *Jazz On A Summer's Day* (1960) and *Quiet Days In Clichy* (1969).

Listening
1 The Indispensable Duke Ellington Vol 7/8
RCA NL 89274 (2)
2 Group Masterpieces
Art Tatum/Pablo 2310 737
3 Ben Webster Meets Oscar Peterson
Verve 2304 455

Dicky Wells

Born: 10th June 1909/Centerville, Tennessee, USA
Died: 12th November 1985/New York City, NY, USA
Instrument: Trombone, vocals, arranger, composer
Recording Career: 1927-1982

EVERY MUSICIAN should be judged at the height of his powers and for a timespan of almost ten years William 'Dicky' Wells deserved to be rated as one of the greatest of jazz trombonists. He made his professional debut while still a teenager and first recorded with Lloyd Scott in New York. He worked mainly with Lloyd's brother Cecil Scott until 1930, but his first really important move took him to **Benny Carter** in 1932 and coincidently into the Spike Hughes sessions of the following year. With the Englishman Hughes, his forthright, no-frills style was well in evidence on *Fanfare* >**1**, while his unforced blues melancholia put its stamp on *Sweet Sorrow Blues* >**1**. In all, this experimental band took part in three sessions, and on all Wells was a match for giants like Carter, **Coleman Hawkins** and **Henry Allen**.

Wells' next significant move was to Teddy Hill and he was in the band that came to Europe in 1937. While in France, he made a series of truly outstanding recordings: again his all-round ability showed through, and incomparably strong blues performances like *Dicky Wells Blues* and *Hangin' Around Boudon* >**2** come over as if slowly torn from the trombonist's body.

He was now indisputably in jazz's first division and in 1938 joined **Count Basie**. Playing alongside **Lester Young** and Harry Edison – modernists of the day – he examined with them the more linear aspects of the music. Straight items like *Taxi War Dance* >**3** showed Wells' excellent powers of construction, but his records with band-within-a-band Kansas City Sevens were even more impressive. He follows Young's offering on *Dicky's Dream* >**3** with a solo full of deliciously off-centre accents. The two *Complete Count Basie* sets of albums >**3, 4** with their alternative

takes, allow the listener the opportunity to examine the trombonist's inventive powers in detail.

After leaving Basie in 1945, Wells played alongside **Buck Clayton**, Sy Oliver, **Jimmy Rushing, Earl Hines** and – occasionally – back with Basie. However, his form was less than consistent and releases like *Bones For The King* >**5** showed that if his best moments were still outstanding, there were times when his playing became something of a caricature of itself.

Two trips to Europe with **Ray Charles** followed in the sixties, and despite being badly injured in a mugging attack in the seventies, he was still playing reasonably well and performing as a coherent soloist well into the eighties. Wells was often featured on the American festival circuit and as late as 1981 gave an exemplary performance at the New York Kool Festival.

Lineage

Wells studied music from the age of ten, flirted briefly with baritone horn, then took to the trombone at sixteen. His original influence was Jimmy Harrison, although he greatly admired the declamatory work of J. C. Higginbotham. His best known disciples were Vic Dickenson and George Matthews, but he influenced many swing-era style trombonists.

Media

Wells wrote a fine jazz book *The Night People* (1971). He worked with Elmer Snowden in the film *Smash Your Baggage* (1933), and played in *Hit Parade of 1943*. Wells was interviewed and played in John Jeremy's *Born To Swing* (1973), took part in the CBS *Sound Of Jazz* production (1957) and made several shorts with Count Basie.

Listening

1 Spike Hughes And His All-American Orchestra
Jasmine JSAM 2012
2 Dicky Wells In Paris 1937
Prestige 7593
3 The Complete Count Basie
CBS 88667/8
4 The Complete Count Basie
CBS 88672/3
5 Bones For The King
Dicky Wells/Felsted FAJ 7006

Mary Lou Williams

Born: 8th May 1910/Atlanta, Georgia, USA
Died: 28th May 1981/Durham, North Carolina, USA
Instrument: Piano, arranger, composer
Recording Career: 1927-1979

HERE was a lady that knew about hustling. Mary Lou Williams came of musical age on the demanding TOBA circuit, worked for various bands and, at one time drove a hearse for a living. She became best known for the association with Andy Kirk that began in 1929 when the erstwhile Mary Elfrieda Scruggs arranged *Messa Stomp* for his band >**1**. Her charts were imaginative, if not revolutionary, and suited the well-balanced section work of the Clouds of Joy. Marion Jackson was the regular (male) pianist in this band but, recognising her superior skills, Williams was used on almost all record dates: *Froggy Bottom* >**1** is an excellent example of her relaxed and bluesy style.

She remained with Kirk until 1941, maturing as an arranger, updating the Kirk image, but also freelancing for the likes of **Benny Goodman**, **Earl Hines** and **Tommy Dorsey**. Williams worked as a staff arranger with **Duke Ellington** in the fifties, becoming friendly with **Bud Powell** and **Thelonious Monk**. This greatly affected her musical

outlook and *Monk's Tune* >**2** shows just how she modified her style to accommodate the new musical language of bebop.

Critic Barry Ulanov considered that she 'had a great skill in all modern idioms'; she became a highly creative chameleon. She toured extensively in the sixties and seventies and, in the last decade of her life, taught at Duke University in North Carolina.

Lineage
Her early efforts were influenced by **Earl Hines** and **Fats Waller**, but later on it was mainly **Bud Powell** and **Thelonious Monk**, as well as altoist **Charlie Parker**. Her own influence as a pianist has been slight.

Media
Appeared in *Boy! What A Girl* (1947) and *The Benny Goodman Story* (1955).

Listening
1 Andy Kirk And His Clouds Of Joy
Andy Kirk/Hep 1002
2 I Have A Piano
Williams/Wilson/Powell/Esquire 304

Teddy Wilson

Born: 24th November 1912/Austin, Texas, USA
Died: 31st July 1986/New Britain, Connecticut, USA
Instrument: Piano, arranger
Recording Career: 1932-1985

THEODORE SHAW WILSON made his professional debut in 1929, and in the next seven years worked with leaders such as Speed Webb, Erskine Tate, **Louis Armstrong**, **Jimmie Noone**, **Benny Carter** and Willie Bryant. The different musical demands each made gave him a thorough musical grounding and by the time he joined **Benny Goodman** in 1936, he was a highly polished performer. His slick, busy lines sounded deceptively easy, while titles such as *China Boy* and *Nobody's Sweetheart* >**1** made clear just how well he fitted into Goodman's high speed chamber-like jazz trio.

Wilson's was a style that spoke little of emotional involvement. He was sometimes accused of being just a cocktail-bar pianist, and there were moments when his work did sound a trifle perfunctory. The highlight of his career came when – almost by accident – he became **Billie Holiday**'s musical director. Together they made a series of records that not only showcased Lady Day's tremendous talent but also showed what a sympathetic and involved pianist Wilson could be: listen to him tracking the singer on *Mean To Me* >**2**; sense them 'talking' to each other on *More Than You Know* >**2**; or hear just how much lift Wilson gives to the voice on *Sin To Tell A Lie* >**2**.

Wilson played a prominent part in the 1938 Carnegie Hall Concert and, after the Second World War, devoted a considerable amount of time to teaching and to studio work. Fine albums like *Prez And Teddy* >**3** from 1956 showed the way his playing was going, but he continued to tour and play club dates through the sixties and seventies. His tours were often with Goodman, including the well-publicised trip to Russia in 1962. Despite trouble with one hand, Wilson continued to play and in the eighties there were tours to Europe, South America, Japan and Australia.

Lineage

Wilson's style was an amalgam of **Earl Hines**, **Art Tatum** and **Fats Waller**. He in turn influenced pianists like Sonny White, Eddie Heywood, Billy Kyle and Clyde Hart.

Media

Wilson had a role in the film *The Benny Goodman Story* (1955). Also featured in *Hollywood Hotel* (1937) and *Something To Shout About* (1943).

Listening

1 The Complete Small Combinations
Benny Goodman/RCA PM 43176
2 The Golden Years
Billie Holiday/CBS 66301
3 Prez and Teddy
Lester Young/Teddy Wilson/Verve 2683 025

Right: Lester Young

Lester Young

Born: 27th August 1909/Woodville, Mississippi, USA
Died: 15th March 1959/New York City, NY, USA
Instruments: Tenor saxophone, clarinet
Recording Career: 1936-1959
Nickname: Pres, Prez (short for President), Red

LESTER YOUNG'S arrival on the jazz scene was a little traumatic: **Coleman Hawkins** had taught the world how to play jazz on a tenor saxophone and here was a newcomer questioning the rules. It was akin to changing the shape of a football. Young rejected the florid, multi-noted lines favoured by tenor men of the day; he played fewer notes, but delivered them with far less obvious definition.

On his first jobs, he played baritone and alto sax but, after switching to tenor, worked with eminent leaders such as **King Oliver** and Walter Page. In 1934, he had the misfortune to replace Hawkins in the **Fletcher Henderson** band and was greeted with some hostility – for *not* sounding like his predecessor. He worked briefly with Andy Kirk before joining the **Count Basie** Orchestra in 1936.

So began a series of records made with the band that stamped him not only as the band's finest soloist, but also as the man that gave its reed section a

totally distinctive sound. *Shoe Shine Boy* >**1** from the first session says it all: inherent sadness, the off-centre timing and the use of totally original phrase shapes. It was like telling stories by parable: the meaning came through clearly, but the delivery was one of innuendo and euphemism.

His tone, born of the C-melody sax, was unique. His vibrato was not pronounced and he made no attempt to be incisive within the ensemble. His solo entries were dramatic and tended to bask in the rhythmic shade provided by Basie's rhythm section rather than compete with them as his peers might have done. This was not to say that he could not be attacking: a title like *Honeysuckle Rose* >**2** shows how assertive he could be.

Young remained with Basie until the end of 1949, during which time he made a series of records with singer **Billie Holiday** that are the equal of the big band items. They were, however, very different – listening to titles such as *Without Your Love* >**3**, *Funny That Way* >**4** and *I'll Never Be The Same* >**5**, just three of a masterful series, it is impossible to say just who is the more dominant character. What is evident is that both artists had the same oblique way of phrasing. They also had the same relaxed, beat-dragging mastery, and the same inherent ability to organise their words or notes in such a way as to suggest that there could be no other way of doing so.

During the Second World War, Young worked with various leaders and in 1944 was conscripted into the US Army. This was an unhappy time for the Prez but, on release, he rapidly returned to playing. A West Coast session with **Nat King Cole** established that no musical damage had been done and, if anything, blues like *Back To The Land* >**6** showed an even more overtly emotional approach.

In 1946, Young joined Jazz At The Philharmonic and, for many years, was part of Norman Granz's travelling 'circus'. He led his own groups, however, and continued to record in other 'all star' sessions. For the first time, a few rather perfunctory performances began to creep in, usually when Young's musical compatriots were less inspiring.

An offering such as *Can't Get Started* >**7** from 1950 suggests for the first time that the great man could produce slight parodies of his own distinctive style.

Certain critics concluded such playing evidenced a total decline, but Young continued to confound them with performances like *Taking A Chance On Love* >**8** in the company of his old friend and pianist, **Teddy Wilson**. His health, however, began to suffer and, although still in his forties, he was hospitalised three times from 1955 to 1958.

During his last years, Young worked mainly as a soloist and, when the mood was right, could still be a considerable talent. It was by his best work that he will be judged, though, and Young must rate as one of the finest jazz musicians of all time.

Lineage

C-melody saxophonist Frankie Trumbauer was his first idol and Young strongly related to the sound of this instrument. From this, he devised a style totally at odds with the **Coleman Hawkins** tenor sound and became the most influential tenor up to the time of **John Coltrane**. His immediate disciples were **Wardell Gray**, Paul Quinichette, Gene Ammons and **Dexter Gordon**, but the cool school, led by **Stan Getz**, **Zoot Sims** and Al Cohn, took the message in a different direction.

Media

Young featured in the film, *Jammin' The Blues* (1944), the soundtrack issued on LP. He was in the CBS film *The Sound Of Jazz* (1957), as well as those with **Count Basie**.

Listening

1 Count And President
Count Basie/CBS 88667
2 Swingin' At The Daisy Chain
Count Basie/Affinity AFS 1019
3 Billie Holiday Story Vol 1
CBS 68228
4 Billie Holiday Story Vol 3
CBS 68230
5 Billie's Blues
Billie Holiday/CBS 72733
6 Genius Of Lester Young
Lester Young/Verve 2683 058
7 Pres Lives – Savoy Sessions
Lester Young/Savoy WL 70528
8 Prez & Teddy
Lester Young/Verve 2683 O25

The Second World War at first provided a stimulant to big band jazz. For troops travelling abroad it was a link with home and, although the emphasis may have been on the sentimentality of bands like those of Glenn Miller and Tommy Dorsey, there was no less interest in other big bands.

Unfortunately for jazz, the draft did not exclude musicians; gradually star performers were forced to leave bands and replacements were not always easy to find. A recording ban from 1943 to 1944 did not help, and jazz emerged from the war in something of a confused state.

However, an underground movement had existed among younger players, and New York became a hot house for burgeoning new talent. At clubs like Minton's and Monroe's Playhouse, jazz sessions were taking a new stance. Musical rules were being examined and, in many cases, replaced. Men like guitarist Charlie Christian, trumpeter Dizzy Gillespie and altoist Charlie Parker had experience with the big bands but now were looking for greater musical freedom.

The search led them to some very fundamental changes, away from the melodic mastery of the swing-era players and into an area that called for rebuilding rather than redesign. Most of these pioneers were versed in the art of melodic improvisation, the paraphrasing and the embellishing of a parent tune, but they were also aware that greater licence was available – and now they took it. Using the chordal structure of pieces as a base, they built entirely new musical edifices. *S'Wonderful* became *Stupendous* and the 'squares' did not know. Indeed, this exclusion of the unknowing became part of the musical 'game'. Breakneck tempos and difficult keys were chosen for no other reason than to deny access to the struggling outsider. Sartorial credibility was also required to gain admission, and some of the musicians and many of the followers adopted the uniform devised by Dizzy Gillespie: dark glasses, beret and goatee were *de rigueur* and it was Gillespie, the showman, who sold the music to a wider public.

It became known as bebop or re-bop, a title derived onomatapoeically from the bubbling quality of the phraseology, which was then simplified to bop. It received a very mixed reaction: establishment musicians saw it as a challenge to their livelihoods, while for much of the public it was too esoteric.

The strongest opposition, however, came from the New Orleans revivalists. A tentative return to the music of the twenties had begun in 1939 with trumpeter Muggsy Spanier, and gained impetus in the early forties with trumpeter Bunk Johnson and later trombonist Kid Ory. In the hands of such men, the music remained authentic, if not always as instrumentally proficient as one might desire. In contrast, the technical mastery of men like Louis Armstrong and Sidney Bechet meant that their brand of revivalism produced outstanding jazz, and it was not long before Europe, too, began to produce its own good quality Dixieland and New Orleans style music.

Good or bad, revivalism was inevitably a musical cul-de-sac, destined to go nowhere and, as men like Gillespie and Parker produced masterful recordings, it became obvious that, from being the creative avant-garde, bop had become jazz's true mainstream. It had even entered the fabric of dance music.

If anything, bop's strength as jazz's new musical direction was confirmed by its stylistic detours. Gillespie grafted on Cuban rhythms, Parker recorded with strings, but the main body of the music progressed through the discoveries at Minton's club in New York. At the end of the decade, any young musician of importance took his directions from the bebop signpost.

Left: Dizzy Gillespie poses at the junction of Sixth Avenue and the legendary 52nd Street

Louis Armstrong

ALTHOUGH THE motives behind Armstrong's change of musical direction in the forties could be questioned, there could be no doubting the quality of some of the jazz it produced. Interest in New Orleans jazz had begun to increase and, in 1940, Armstrong took part in a small group session with **Sidney Bechet**. The results were stupendous and *Down In Honky Tonk Town* and *Coal Cart Blues* >**1** can be compared with the masterly Blue Five dates. Rivalry between the main protagonists was not disguised and sparks flew as neither gave ground.

Armstrong continued to lead a big band too and a couple of delightful New Orleans-style sessions took place in 1946, associated with the making of the film *New Orleans*. Despite these, Armstrong (or his advisers) had become aware of the change in attitudes and, at New York's Town Hall in 1947, the Louis Armstrong All Stars made their debut.

In a strange way, this first date set a

seal on the band's style that was to remain throughout the All Stars' entire career. Little attempt was made to feature the collective New Orleans ensemble style: Armstrong had long since developed beyond that stage and it was a style that neither **Jack Teagarden** nor Peanuts Hucko had ever really mastered. All three were outstanding soloists, however, and it was this aspect of jazz, as well as Armstrong's singing, that *Ain't Misbehavin'* and *Save It Pretty Mama* >**2** showed off. This already fine unit was improved further in late 1947 when Barney Bigard took over the clarinet chair and further still when, in the following year, the mighty **Earl Hines** joined as pianist. 1951's *Indiana* and *That's A Plenty* >**3** tell of the band's verve, while still confirming the individuality of the soloists.

Unfortunately, Armstrong tended to feature the same melodies night after night and, on arduous one-night stands, this became wearing for his sidemen. Teagarden and Hines stood it until late in 1951, while Bigard, who left briefly in 1952, stayed on until 1955. These departures did not trouble Armstrong, though, who found excellent replacements: trombonist Trummy Young joined in 1952, pianist Billy Kyle

vocal on *Cotton Tail* >**7**; the moving counterpoint and Bigard's solo on *Mood Indigo* >**7**; and Armstrong's forthright version of **Bubber Miley**'s *Black And Tan Fantasy* >**7**.

Later in the sixties, frequent changes to his line-up, as well as the occasional health problem, meant that the Armstrong All Stars tended to coast. Ironically, vocal triumphs like *Hello Dolly* and *What A Wonderful World* introduced jazz's greatest figure to a whole new generation. Nobody ever thought Satchmo could die and he did perform to the last, still maintaining his dignity. But, on 6th July 1971 the impossible happened.

(For biographical information and lineage, see entry in The Twenties, page 21).

Media

Performances on film (post-1940): *Birth Of The Blues* (1941); *Cabin In The Sky* (1942); *Atlantic City, Jam Session* (both 1944); *The Glenn Miller Story* (1953); *The Beat Generation* (1954); *High Society* (1956); *Satchmo The Great* (1956); *Brother, Can You Spare A Dime?* (1975). Armstrong also appears in *New Orleans* (1947); *A Song Is Born* (1948); *The Five Pennies* (1959); *Paris Blues* (1961); *When The Boys Meet The Girls* (1965); *A Man Called Adam* (1966); *Jazz On A Summer's Day* (1960); *Hello Dolly!* (1969). Characterised in *Louis Armstrong – Chicago Style* (TV, 1975) and film *French Quarter* (1978), and his music can be heard in *On Her Majesty's Secret Service* (1969) and *The Man Who Fell To Earth* (1976); TV tribute *A Boy From New Orleans* (1971).

arrived in 1953 and both were present when the All Stars recorded their outstanding tribute to W. C. Handy >**4** in the following year. Armstrong, Young and Kyle played especially well, and were prompted to follow this with an equally outstanding salute to **Fats Waller** in 1955 >**5**. Both projects totally captured Armstrong's imagination and *St Louis Blues* >**4** and *Blue Turning Grey* >**5** are great performances by any standards.

During 1956 and 1957, Armstrong, now with Ed Hall on clarinet, made an outstanding four-album set – *Satchmo Musical Autobiography* – which featured newly-recorded versions of his past triumphs. Again, enthusiasm was the watchword and the trumpeter, freed from the tedium of his concert material, gave masterly readings of *Cornet Chop Suey, Hotter Than That* and *Gully Low Blues* >**6**.

The All Stars were still touring and, with a fairly stable personnel, continued to make good, if not inspired, records. Perhaps Armstrong's last real triumph came in 1961 when record producer Bob Thiele had the idea of teaming him with **Duke Ellington**. It was an unlikely partnership that nearly worked: the worst moments were chaotic, but jazz lovers will always treasure the scat

Listening

1 Struttin' With Some Barbecue
Louis Armstrong/Affinity AFS 1024
2 The Complete Town Hall Concert
Louis Armstrong/RCA NL 89746 (2)
3 Satchmo At Pasadena
Louis Armstrong/MCA (Japan) VIM 4621
4 St Louis Blues – Louis Armstrong Plays W. C. Handy
CBS 21128
5 Satch Plays Fats
Louis Armstrong/CBS 21103
6 Satchmo Musical Autobiography Vol 1
Louis Armstrong/RCA 2-4173
7 Louis Armstrong And Duke Ellington
Jazz Reactivation JR 133

immediate access to their music and he was given the early, if unofficial, accolade of being asked to join **Dizzy Gillespie**. In 1946, he came to Europe with Don Redman and, liking the slow pace of life, settled there until his death. He made odd trips to America but, in the main, did his recording in Holland. With age, Byas tended to simplify his solos, returning to the arabesques of the thirties, but he was always an inventive player. Outstanding albums like *Anthropology* >**3** document his progress and, despite a passing interest in the more modern outlooks of **John Coltrane**, he finished his career as he had begun: an effusive romantic.

Lineage
Byas was strongly influencd by **Coleman Hawkins** and for his part inspired players as diverse as **Roland Kirk** and Paul Gonsalves.

Media
Played in TV's *Just Jazz*, PBS 1971.

Listening
1 **Count Basie Vol 5 'Avenue C'**
   Count Basie/CBS 88674
2 **Charlie Christian Live 1939-41**
   Various/Festival ALB 377
3 **Anthropology**
   Don Byas/Black Lion BLP 30126

Don Byas

Born: 21st October 1912/Muskogee, Oklahoma, USA
Died: 24th August 1972/Amsterdam, The Netherlands
Instrument: Tenor saxophone
Recording Career: 1938-1972

LIKE MOST players of his generation, Carlos Wesley Byas had a grounding in basic skills with the big bands. In 1935 he joined the then little-known **Lionel Hampton** band and, as his reputation grew, had periods with Don Redman and Lucky Millinder. He was with Andy Kirk for more than a year, before tackling the unenviable task of replacing **Lester Young** in the **Count Basie** Orchestra in 1941.

Titles such as *Royal Garden Blues* and *Sugar Blues* >**1** show that he made no attempt to emulate his predecessor. Not for him the spare, drifting comment – here was an up-front tenor saxophonist. His full tone was ideal for his romantic approach to improvisation, although he did employ more oblique note placings than was normal in the **Coleman Hawkins** school.

This fact served him well when, in the forties, he became involved with Minton's and the bebop men >**2**. His instrumental facility allowed him

Wild Bill Davison

Born: 5th January 1906/Defiance, Ohio, USA
Instruments: Cornet, trumpet, vocals
Recording Career: 1924-
Nickname: Wild Bull, Defiant One (dubbed by Eddie Condon)

THE PROTOTYPE hot cornettist, William Edward Davison's tone is brassy, his stage manner aggressive and his timing on-beat and swinging. He was called the 'cockiest, sassiest, even blowsiest cornettist in jazz' by critic John S. Wilson, and has lived up to that reputation. There is, however, a Mild Bill trying to get out, and a title like the 1981 *Sweet And Lovely* >**1** shows a mellowed balladeer who can draw a tear with his melodic manoeuvrings.

Davison spent his early musical years in Cincinnati and Chicago but it was not until he moved to New York in 1941 that his career really blossomed. There, he led his own band at Nick's and became a regular with **Eddie Condon** at the latter's club in 1945. It was in 1945 that he made perhaps his finest recordings in Russian pianist Art Hodes' Hot Five. Matched against the power of soprano saxophonist **Sidney Bechet**, Davison responded magnificently, slugging it out toe-to-toe on minor masterpieces like *Save It Pretty Mama* and *Darktown Strutters Ball* >**2**.

His association with Condon was also productive on record, never better illustrated than by the Commodore 1946 version of *I'm Comin' Virginia* >**3**, or by titles like *Dippermouth Blues* and *Blues My Naughty Sweetie Gives to Me* >**4**, both recorded live at the Condon Club in 1951. Hearing these, it is most difficult to picture the man: his horn continually torn from his lips as he produced well-spaced phrases in the form of a controlled and drawn-out stutter. The style was simple in concept and spoke of a lifetime of experience.

Davison moved to California in 1960, but he missed the action of the Eastern seaboard. Since then, he has toured Europe regularly and the 1986 New York Festival had a tribute night in his honour in which he gave the lie to his eighty years, never coasting for a minute.

Lineage

Davison was inspired by **Bix Beiderbecke**, although his declamatory style was as far from Beiderbecke's lyricism as it is possible to imagine. In fact, there is more of **Freddie Keppard**'s frankness in Davison's own clearly spaced solos and he certainly would have heard Keppard in Chicago during his formative years. His own influence can be felt in most of the work of Johnny Windhurst but his growling tone and ferociously fragmented style found its staunchest devotees in the persons of Europeans such as Freddy Randall and Alex Welsh.

Media

Davison has appeared in short films with **Eddie Condon**, and in two *March Of Time* films (1946, 1950).

Listening

1 **All American Band**
   Wild Bill Davison/Sonet SNTF 880
2 **Sidney Bechet**
   Blue Note BLP 51203
3 **Tin Roof Blues**
   George Brunis/Commodore C 24294 AG
4 **The Individualism Of Wild Bill Davison**
   Savoy SJL 2229

Buddy De Franco

Born: 17th February 1923/Camden, New Jersey, USA
Instruments: Clarinet, bass clarinet, composer
Recording Career: 1943-

ALTHOUGH THERE were many contemporary clarinettists working in other established styles, only De Franco and Tony Scott remained loyal to the instrument in the modern jazz of the forties and fifties. Nevertheless, De Franco was often regarded with suspicion by European critics, for whom his impeccable technique was often a cudgel with which to beat him. Fortunately, this was not a view shared by the American writers and in one magazine he was voted top clarinettist on nineteen consecutive occasions from 1947.

Early training for Boniface Ferdinand Leonardo De Franco came in the big bands of Gene Krupa, Charlie Barnet, **Tommy Dorsey** and Boyd Raeburn, but it was in with the turmoil of the bebop revolution that De Franco threw his lot. Here he found the problems of adjusting his style to meet the requirements of the new music were greater than he had imagined. Translating **Charlie Parker** to the clarinet had functional snags: on the alto

the harder cutting edge gave an appealing sound, but the same process could make the clarinet sound empty and metallic. De Franco overcame the problem by the production of a quite beautiful tone, clear-cut articulation and a brilliant improvisational sense. His small groups in the early fifties were perfect examples, and with sidemen such as Kenny Drew on piano, and drummers like **Art Blakey** and Teddy Kotick, his quartet really took off. *Buddy's Blues* >**1** and *Carioca* >**2** are models of their kind and testify to a superb jazzman, showing how effectively he matched his inherent jazz ability with stunning technical accomplishments. De Franco's adaptibility was shown when he recorded with **Art Tatum** in 1956. Despite problems of compatability, the warmth of titles such as *Deep Night* >**3** confounds any suggestion of coldness. His 1964 session with the Jazz Messengers found him on bass clarinet and **Ornette Coleman**'s *Blues Connotation* >**4** proclaimed that De Franco was still very much a forward-looking player.

From 1960 to 1965 he was involved mainly in musical education, then from 1966 to 1974 fronted the Glenn Miller Orchestra. In more recent years he has toured as a single or with small combos, and has been a frequent visitor to Europe.

Lineage

Interested in his youth by **Artie Shaw**, De Franco's style has few copyists, with avant-garde clarinettists preferring more basic roots.

Media

Wrote *Buddy De Franco On Jazz Improvisation* and appeared in the film *The Wild Party* (1956). Also played on the soundtracks of *Ocean's 11* (1960) and TV's *Route 66* (1960-64).

Listening

1 Mr Clarinet
Buddy De Franco/Verve MV 2527
2 Buddy De Franco
MGM MM 2088
3 Art Tatum/Buddy De Franco
Pablo MTF 1064
4 Blues Bag
Art Blakey/Buddy De Franco/Affinity
AFF 55

Slim Gaillard

Born: 4th January 1916/Detroit, Michigan, USA
Instruments: Guitar, piano, organ, vibraphone, tenor saxophone, trumpet, vocals, composer
Recording Career: 1937-

THE CLOWN PRINCE of jazz, Bulee Gaillard is a one-off who has brought to the music considerable skill and a great deal of humour. In the early thirties he entered show business as a guitar and tap-dancing act. In 1937 he came to New York, formed the Slim and Slam act with Slam Stewart and came into contact with a jazz world that was hardly prepared for the shock. Gaillard was a jive-talker, even offering his alternative to Esperanto, a personal language called 'Vout' for which he actually produced a dictionary. It was a hipster's delight and could mean whatever was so desired.

In 1938 he enjoyed notable hits with *Flat Foot Floogie* and *Tutti Frutti*, was rewarded with a regular radio spot and gained nationwide notoriety. In performance, he was essentially a jazzman: on all of his instruments he swung remorselessly, and as a scat singer demonstrated a vocal dexterity that was later taken up by straight jazz singers. His humour was very much of

the forties, with the *Avocado Seed Soup Symphony* >**1** and *Opera In Vout* >**2** surrealistic dream sequences that ridiculed 'normal' behaviour.

Working the jazz clubs as well as the vaudeville circuit during the fifties and sixties, Gaillard found himself managing a hotel for a brief period. He appeared at the 1970 Monterey Jazz Festival with his one-time partner, Stewart, and continued to tour during the seventies. Visits to Europe became more frequent and currently he lives in London.

Lineage
Gaillard's was a vaudeville background but recording with **Charlie Parker** and **Dizzy Gillespie** brought him to bebop. He influenced similar humourists like Leo Watson and Harry 'The Hipster' Gibson.

Media
Appeared in *Hellzapoppin'* (1941), *Almost Married* (1942), *Star Spangled Rhythm* (1942), *Go, Man, Go* (1954), usually in zany situations. *Ovoutie O'Rooney* (1946) featured his trio and Gaillard played *Flat Foot Floogie* in *Malcolm X* (1972). Acting roles came in *Too Late Blues* (1961), *Roots* (1978) and *Absolute Beginners* (1986).

Listening
1 McVouty
  Slim Gaillard/Bam Brown/Hep 6
2 Opera In Vout
  Slim Gaillard/Verve 2304 554

Dizzy Gillespie

Born: 21st October 1917/Cheraw, South Carolina, USA
Instruments: Trumpet, piano, percussion, vocals, composer
Recording Career: 1937-

IT IS IMPORTANT to be aware that almost all of the finest bebop players had roots firmly planted in the swing era of the preceding decade, the thirties. This was especially true of John Birks Gillespie, a master who brought a new dimension to the art of virtuoso trumpet playing.

In his early days he had played in Philadelphia, but the big move came when he replaced his idol, **Roy Eldridge**, in the Teddy Hill Band and came to Europe as part of it. After the tour, Gillespie was unsettled for some time, before joining **Cab Calloway** in

1939. He was with the 'Hi Di Hi' man for two years and on titles like *Bye Bye Blues* >**1** added his own personality to the Eldridge tradition of jazz trumpet. Now blossoming as a soloist, he was in considerable demand among big-band leaders of the day, despite reports of a youthful but still excessively capricious personality.

He had already met, jammed with, and exchanged musical views with **Charlie Parker** but, in the more 'serious' pursuit of a career, Gillespie worked in the bands of Charlie Barnet, Lucky Millinder, **Earl Hines** and **John Kirby**. In 1944 he joined Billy Eckstine, a move that re-united him with Parker and introduced him to a musical organisation sympathetic to the new music, bebop. Later that year, he took what was reputed to be the first bop combo into New York's Onyx Club. For his part, Gillespie acknowledged the 'show biz' attitudes of former leaders like Calloway and had already adopted an eccentric form of dress. Beret, horn-rimmed glasses and goatee were *de rigueur* and, at the Onyx Club, his fans were similarly attired.

His critics latched onto this harmless distraction as proof of bop's musical poverty. Fortunately, they were confounded in the following year by records of the quality of *Dizzy Atmosphere* and *Shaw 'Nuff* >**2**, featuring both Gillespie and Parker. These laid the ground rules. The chord sequence had become the backbone of the style and both men built completely new tunes to fit the structure. No longer could the student of jazz speak of 'melodic improvisation'. In the new music a whole new musical edifice had to be constructed and a whole new vernacular forged to suit it.

In the 1944/5 period Gillespie began leading his own small groups on a permanent basis and made impressive recordings with saxophonists **Dexter Gordon** and Lucky Thompson, and vibraphonist Milt Jackson. More radically, he also formed his first big band in 1945, determined that it should propagate bop as serious music. The band's life was short, but in 1946 he reformed and with the new orchestra enjoyed both artistic and commercial success. This unit stayed together until 1950, while Gillespie became enamoured with a fusion of Cuban music and jazz that produced a musical alloy christened *cubop*. With the aid of conga master Chano Pozo, the band produced superb examples of the genre with *Manteca* and *Cubana Bop* >**3**.

In its more orthodox performances, the band combined many of the best features of earlier big-band traditions with the accents of bop. The attractive blues *Two Bass Hit* >**3** was especially traditional, yet it effortlessly accommodated Gillespie's uncompromising bop solo. The trumpeter was perhaps fortunate to enjoy the advantage of having arrangers of the quality of Gil Fuller, John Lewis, Tadd Dameron and the young **George Russell**.

After 1950, the trumpeter returned to combo leading, although he again assembled a big band during 1956 for tours of the Middle East and South America, sponsored by the US State Department. On his return Gillespie had to struggle to keep the band together finally forced to concentrate his talents on smaller units.

This led him back to JATP, with whom he had worked previously and through this into recording dates with **Roy Eldridge** and **Stan Getz**. With Eldridge, he produced an outstanding record in *Trumpet Blues* >**4**, a superb showcase for their joint talents, but the *Diz And Getz* >**5** date found the tenor wanting. Gillespie's touring group also brought out impressive records: *St Louis Blues* >**6**, with sparkling piano from Junior Mance, and *Moonglow* >**6** were typical.

In the sixties there were suggestions that Gillespie was coasting but, armed with a contract from Norman Granz's new Pablo label, the seventies saw a revitalised player. A brilliant duet album with Oscar Peterson >**7** and an excellent big band album with Machito >**8** showed that his light was undimmed. Throughout the eighties, he has toured constantly and, although more emphasis is placed on singing/resting, when his chops are up he is still a magnificent player.

Lineage

Gillespie had great admiration for both Charlie Shavers and **Roy Eldridge** and went on to influence two generations of horn men: **Fats Navarro**, **Howard McGhee**, **Miles Davis**, **Clifford Brown**, Donald Byrd and **Lee Morgan** are just a few and the list includes more recent players like Jon Faddis and **Wynton Marsalis**.

Media

Biography, co-written with Al Frazer, *To Be Or Not To Bop*, appeared in 1979.

Listening

1 Penguin Swing
  Cab Calloway/Jazz Archives JA 8
2 Dizzy Gillespie
  Phoenix LP 2
3 Dizzy Gillespie Vols 1/2
  RCA PM 42408
4 Trumpet Kings
  Dizzy Gillespie/Roy Eldridge/Verve 2683 022
5 Diz And Getz
  Dizzy Gillespie/Stan Getz/Verve 2610 045
6 Have Trumpet Will Excite
  Dizzy Gillespie/Verve MV 2696
7 Oscar Peterson And Dizzy Gillespie
  Pablo 2310 740
8 Afro-Cuban Jazz Moods
  Dizzy Gillespie/Pablo 2310 771

Dexter Gordon

**Born: 27th February 1923/Los
Angeles, California, USA
Instrument: Tenor saxophone
Recording Career: 1941-**

DESPITE BEING the first real bebop
tenor saxophonist, Dexter Gordon spent
the early forties working in the bands of
Lionel Hampton and **Louis
Armstrong**. His 'conversion' came in
1944 when, after leaving Armstrong, he
spent eight months in a Billy Eckstine
band full of bop luminaries. This led him
to the unofficial workshops of 52nd
Street in New York and to make
records like *Long Tall Dexter* and *Blow
Mr Dexter* >**1**, that demonstrated his
hard-edged tone and his ability to
swing powerfully. These cuts also
showed that he had fully grasped the
language of bop without surrendering
his laid-back approach to timing.

While with Eckstine, Gordon had
been involved in tenor battles with
colleague Gene Ammons and these had
evoked a favourable audience
response. This probably prompted his
next series of recordings, performances
that pitted his musical wits against
Wardell Gray and Teddy Edwards.

The Chase >**2** (with Gray) became
quite a hit but, in some ways, it
confirmed that he was prepared to be
typecast as a tenor gladiator.

Unfortunately, Gordon had far more
serious problems to contend with. His
involvement with narcotics had made
him somewhat of a furtive figure and, as
a smokescreen, he began to shuttle
between the East and West Coasts.
Records continued to appear but
consistency was lacking. 1955's *Daddy
Plays The Horn* >**3** confirmed that he
could still play with distinction, but it
was a series of records for the Blue
Note label that re-established him. As
always, his playing was littered with
quotes from other melodies.
Nevertheless, titles like *Cheese Cake*,
Love For Sale >**4** and *Shiny
Stockings* >**5** told of a return to grace.

He moved to Europe in 1962, later
taking up teaching posts in Scandinavia,
but this did not deter him from regular
trips to the United States for recording
dates, festivals and even club
appearances. He toured Japan in 1975
but, in the eighties, remained a major
asset to the European scene. He is still
regarded by his peers as the 'guvnor'
among tenor men.

Lineage

Gordon's original inspiration was **Lester
Young** but he was later deflected by
the playing of **Charlie Parker** and
Dizzy Gillespie. His own influence has
been widespread and is most evident in
the work of Allen Eager, Gene
Ammons, **Sonny Rollins** and **John
Coltrane**.

Media

Made TV film *Just Jazz* in 1971 and
appeared in *Atlantic City* (1944), *Pillow
To Post* (1945) and *Unchained* (1955).
Starred in 1986 Bertrand Tavernier film
Round Midnight.

Listening

1 Master Takes – The Savoy Sessions
  Dexter Gordon/Savoy WL 70814
2 The Chase And The Steeplechase
  Dexter Gordon/MCA 1336
3 Daddy Plays The Horn
  Dexter Gordon/Affinity AFF 103
4 Go
  Dexter Gordon/Blue Note BST 84112
5 Gettin' Around
  Dexter Gordon/Blue Note BST 84204

Wardell Gray

Born: 1921/Oklahoma City, Oklahoma, USA
Died: 25th May 1955/Las Vegas, Nevada, USA
Instrument: Tenor saxophone
Recording Career: 1945-

GRAY'S PLAYING represents a coming together of the progressive swing stylists and the boppers. Originally he had adopted the tonal sound of **Lester Young** and much of that laconical player's sense of note placement. After learning and working with **Charlie Parker**, he introduced aspects of the bebop vernacular into his basic language. The synthesis was wholly successful in avoiding the rather listless quality that afflicted certain young copyists. It also meant that there was no hint of the arid angularity found in players who misunderstood Parker's message.

Big band experience came with **Earl Hines**, **Benny Carter** and Billy Eckstine, but it is his small group recordings that mark Gray out as such an important player. Listening to him with Parker on the various takes of *Relaxin' At Camarillo* and *Cheers* >**1** provides the opportunity to assess his powers of improvisation, although it was significant that in the company of men from more orthodox backgrounds he tended to edge back towards the establishment. This was evident with J. C. Heard's 1948 septet which included Joe Newman and Benny Green.

Gray is perhaps most famous for his tenor duels with **Dexter Gordon**, of which *The Chase* >**2** is the best known; but, whatever the company, he was a saxophonist who always sounded relaxed. He overdosed at the age of thirty-four and the jazz world was a poorer place.

Lineage

Although the joint influences of **Lester Young** and **Charlie Parker** seem an unlikely combination, they produced a style that was instantly recognisable.

Listening

1 **Charlie Parker On Dial Vol 3**
   Spotlight 103
2 **The Chase And Steeplechase**
   Wardell Gray/MCA 1336

Woody Herman

Born: 16th May 1913/Milwaukee, Wisconsin, USA
Instruments: Clarinet, alto and soprano saxophones, vocals
Recording Career: 1932-

IT WAS at the age of eighteen that Woodrow Charles Herman first played for Isham Jones on record, and he was only twenty-one when he joined Jones' band on a permanent basis. Yet, when the leader quit two years later, it was Herman who was persuaded to take over the leadership of the band dubbed 'The Band That Plays The Blues' and, although Herman was not entirely happy with that billing, it was instrumental in bringing considerable commercial success. This was greatly enhanced when a storming version of *Woodchopper's Ball* >**1** became a smash hit and sold a million copies.

Right: Woody Herman

111

Nevertheless, Herman resented the band's old-time image and in the forties set about making it more modern. The arrival of Neal Hefti and Ralph Burns, with their arranging talents, produced a transformation and the First Herd came into being. Charts like *World On A String*, *The Good Earth*, and *Wild Root* >**2** made the band a hot property, and there was the bonus of outstanding soloists such as trombonist Bill Harris, tenor Flip Phillips and the leader himself. In all of his bands, Herman played somewhat strident but highly personal clarinet as well as **Johnny Hodges**-inspired alto. In theory, it was an anachronism, but for the Herds it worked.

The sound of the band was spectacular and the stinging brass brought many performances to wall-of-death climaxes. Surprisingly, the orchestra was disbanded in 1946 but, within a year, the Second Herd was in business. 1946 was also the year Herman first performed, at Carnegie Hall, the *Ebony Concerto* especially written for him by emigré Russian composer Igor Stravinsky. With saxophone stars **Stan Getz**, **Zoot Sims**, Herbie Steward and Serge Chaloff in the reed section it became known as the 'Four Brothers Band', a title taken from a tune of that name composed and arranged by Jimmy Giuffre and given a delightful performance by all concerned >**2**. The piece established a reed voicing for the band and completely changed its mood. Dramatic brass passages remained but there was a smoother, more legato air which was maintained, with different sidemen, in the Third Herd, of 1953.

Throughout much of the late fifties, Herman led smaller units, but in 1960 formed another big band. Jazz commentators had, by now, lost track of which Herd this particular one constituted, but by the late sixties he had soloists of the calibre of trumpeter Bill Chase and tenor sax player Sal Nistico >**3**. As the years progressed his bands seemed to get younger but their musical standards remained high. Herman survived a serious motor accident in 1977 and is still riding high with a shouting big band.

Lineage

Herman had listened to the New Orleans clarinettists but his alto sound was influenced by **Johnny Hodges**. His bands have become the models for many copyists throughout the world, among them the **Buddy Rich**, Thad Jones/Mel Lewis, Clarke Boland and Akiyoshi Tabackin Big Bands.

Listening

1 **The Band That Plays The Blues**
Woody Herman/Affinity AFS 1008
2 **The Thundering Herds**
Woody Herman/CBS 66378
3 **Woody's Winners**
Woody Herman/CBS 21110

Bunk Johnson

**Born: 27th December 1889/New Orleans, Louisiana, USA
Died: 7th July 1949/New Iberia, Louisiana, USA
Instrument: Trumpet
Recording Career: 1942-1947**

WHILE RESEARCHING their book *Jazzmen* in the late thirties, William Russell and Frank Ramsey came across the name Bunk Johnson. Although up to that time he had never been recorded, his name was linked with many of the great pioneers of pre-recording history and the two researchers sought him out. He claimed to have worked with the legendary Buddy Bolden, but this was later found to be untrue. Johnson had, however, played with many of the outstanding New Orleans musicians and remained musically active until the early thirties.

As the New Orleans revival took off in the early forties, Johnson assumed the mantle of guru and made a series of records for the American Music label >**1**,**2** which, perhaps erroneously, became yardsticks by which 'pure' New Orleans jazz was judged.

Johnson's playing was neither as good as this suggested, nor as bad as his detractors would have it. Obviously, the years of inactivity had taken their toll, but his somewhat sour tone had an appeal of its own and his note placements were far from being tediously metronomic. His approach to

improvisation was simple but effective, and he had genuine feeling for the blues. For his own part, he was unhappy with the choice of clarinettist **George Lewis** and trombonist Jim Robinson as sidemen. He played better in faster company and, despite the odd error, made superior records for Blue Note with **Sidney Bechet** and Sandy Williams, especially when involved with blues material like *Days Beyond Recall* >**3**. Significantly, when left to make decisions regarding his own band, he listened to trombonist Ed Cuffee, clarinettist Garvin Bushell, and bassist Wellman Braud, in preference to Lewis and Robinson.

Lineage

Johnson was influenced by the 'sweeter' side of Buddy Bolden's playing, and became father-figure to many of the European revivalists. His style certainly directs the work of men such as Ken Colyer, although his approach to solo improvisation differs greatly.

Listening

1 Bunk Johnson 1944 Vol 1
Dan (Japan) VC 4006
2 Bunk Johnson 1945
Dan (Japan) VC 4018
3 Jazz Classics Vol 1
Sidney Bechet/Blue Note BLP 1201

113

J.J. Johnson in duet with Richard Davis on bass

J. J. Johnson

**Born: 22nd January 1924/
Indianapolis, Indiana, USA
Instrument: Trombone, composer
Recording Career: 1945-**

AS THE JAZZ WORLD set about coping
with the discoveries of bebop, each
instrument was faced with different
problems and the trombone looked to
be the horn least equipped to cope with
rippling arpeggios and high-speed
delivery. Almost single-handed,
Johnson made a nonsense of any such
doubts.

He could be considered as the father
figure of post-bop trombone – in
adapting the saxophone language to the
needs of his seemingly ungainly
instrument, he produced a tone that
became a standard to which all
successors strived. Johnson ignored the
instrument's potential for slurred notes
and swooping glissandi and, as titles

like *Drifting On A Reed* and *Bongo
Beep* >**1** with **Charlie Parker** show,
perfected a style that drew attention to
his amazing articulation at fast tempos.

James Louis Johnson gained his early
training in the bands of Clarence Love
and **Benny Carter**, but his real tests
came as he joined the bop hurly-burly
of New York's 52nd Street in the late
forties. After a premature retirement
from music in the early fifties, he
returned in 1954 to team with Kai
Winding in the Jay and Kai Quintet. It
was a successful partnership and
Lullaby Of Birdland >**2** and *Hip
Bones* >**3** offer fine examples of their
delightful trombone 'arguments'.

After the group's break-up, Johnson
toured with his own bands and began
concentrating more on his writing. In
1970, he moved to California and wrote
numerous scores for TV and films. He
never lost his taste for playing,
however, and simply listening to his
trombone shouting behind **Big Joe
Turner** on the 1973 *Blues Around The
Clock* >**4** proves that he was still

2 **Live At Birdland**
  J. J. Johnson/Kai Winding/RCA PL 42069
3 **Early Bones**
  Various/Prestige P 24067
4 **The Bosses**
  Big Joe Turner/Count Basie/Pablo 2310 709

Stan Kenton

Born: 19th February 1912/Wichita, Kansas, USA
Died: 28th August 1979/New York City, NY, USA
Instrument: Piano, composer
Recording Career: 1937-1978
Nickname: Stan The Man

ASSESSMENTS OF Kenton's music are frequently jaundiced by generalisation. Critics who take ponderous, neo-classical works such as *City Of Glass* (1950, written by Bob Graettinger) as typical often ignore the fact that each of Kenton's bands had its own very separate, and by no means always similarly ponderous personality.

Stanley Newcomb Kenton gained early experience with Gus Arnheim and first led his own band in 1940. Though principally a dance band, it had genuine ambition and gained a degree of popularity at the Rendezvous Ballroom in Balboa. Singers like Anita O'Day and June Christy helped to popularise the outfit, but it was not until arranger Pete Rugolo joined in 1945 that the Kenton machine really began to move.

Kenton had first recorded *Artistry In Rhythm* >**1** in 1941 but this, together with *Unison Riff* >**2**, *Artistry in Bolero* >**3**, *Eager Beaver* >**4** and *Intermission Riff* >**4**, gave the band a new and exciting identity. The term 'progressive jazz' was coined and Kenton took this into his second important band in 1947. Ten brass players sat in the orchestra and the scores were devised to embrace dissonance. If nothing else, the band was noisy but it gained a following and had a massive hit with the unlikely *Peanut Vendor* >**4**. By this time, Kenton was using several arrangers ranging from the pretentious Bob Graettinger to

looming large. In the eighties he re-appeared on the festival circuit and, at the New York Festival of 1984, stole the show.

Lineage
Johnson was more influenced by altoist **Charlie Parker** and trumpeter **Dizzy Gillespie** than by any trombonist. His own influence was enormous, including not only established men like Benny Green and Bill Harris but also the whole generation that followed, including Kai Winding, Frank Rosolino, Milt Bernhart, Henry Coker, Benny Powell, Jimmy Knepper, Dave Baker and Curtis Fuller.

Media
Wrote film scores for *Man And Boy* (1971), *Top Of The Heap* (1972), *Across 110th Street* (1972), *Cleopatra Jones* (1973) and *Willie Dynamite* (1973); for TV, contributed to the series of *Barefoot In The Park* (1970), *Mod Squad* and *Harry O* (1974-6).

Listening
1 **Charlie Parker On Dial Vol 6**
  Spotlite 106

the unmannered Neal Hefti and Shorty Rogers. He had also ingratiated himself with the establishment and, as a result, had begun to enjoy the benefits of good reviews.

The 1947 band included the likes of trombonists Kai Winding and Milt Bernhart, and saxophonists Vido Musso, Bob Cooper and **Art Pepper**, but it still placed the main emphasis on collective playing. This displeased many jazz critics but proved to be a minor irritation in comparison with their reaction to his 1950 band, which was at times forty-three strong and gave concerts billed as 'Innovations In Modern Music'. Mercifully this horror was short-lived and, in complete contrast, Kenton followed it with a 1953 band that has been dubbed his most 'jazz-minded' unit. **Lee Konitz** and **Zoot Sims** were among its members and, for the best part of two years, the band put uncompromising jazz on record.

In 1961, Kenton and arranger Johnny Richards were looking for a new brass sound, and the mellophonium band was formed. Four of these unlikely instruments were used, and this bizarre line-up retained until 1965, the year that saw the birth of his Los Angeles Neophonic Orchestra. This, despite its name, took Kenton back into more orthodox climes.

The following year, Kenton began a series of campus clinics for university music students and teachers alike. In so doing, he was guaranteeing himself a supply of young sidemen, but was inevitably assisting his rivals as well in the nurturing of new, young talent.

Many Kenton-tutored youngsters turned up in the bands of **Woody Herman**, **Buddy Rich** and **George Russell**.

In the seventies Kenton's band continued to flourish, having rejected the more extreme elements. Up to the time of his death, he led a band that could still get on to its hind-hooves and whinny. No Kenton band had time for understatement, although one trumpet sideman tells of pretending to play all night without blowing a single note. Kenton is alleged to have been oblivious.

Lineage

Originally inspired by **Earl Hines**, Kenton featured on piano less and less. His band had several copyists, although many were ex-Kenton sidemen like Shorty Rogers and Maynard Ferguson. In Europe, his most devoted disciple was Vic Lewis.

Media

Played on the soundtrack of Road To Bali (1952). TV special The Crusade For Jazz made 1972. Biography Kenton Straight Ahead by Carol Easton published in 1973.

Listening

1 **The Kenton Era**
Stan Kenton/Creative World ST 1030
2 **By Request Vol 3**
Stan Kenton/Creative World ST 1062
3 **Artistry In Rhythm**
Stan Kenton/Creative World ST 1043
4 **Milestones**
Stan Kenton/Creative World ST 1047

George Lewis

**Born: 13th July 1900/New Orleans,
Louisiana, USA
Died: 31st December 1968/New
Orleans, Louisiana, USA
Instruments: Clarinet, alto saxophone
Recording Career: 1942-1966**

IT WOULD BE a mistake to judge
George Louis Francis Zeno by the same
standards as one might **Benny
Goodman**. Lewis was a genuine
primitive: his approach to melodic
improvisation was simple and his only
real asset was that he was a moving
blues player. He was perhaps fortunate
to be asked to record with **Bunk
Johnson** in 1942 because, despite
experience with Buddy Petit, **Henry
'Red' Allen** and Kid Rena when
younger, Lewis had never recorded
and was not highly regarded by his
peers.

The selection of Lewis for the session
by historian William Russell did not
please Johnson but the clarinettist
nevertheless flourished with his
reluctant leader. His technique became
more secure and, as early as 1944, there
were excellent trio performances like
Burgundy Street Blues >**1**. After
Johnson's death, Lewis took over the
band. Yet, despite being in a better
position to showcase his talents, he
never did so. He was a self-effacing
man whose bands always paid
considerable attention to ensemble
playing.

At his best in the fifties and sixties,
Lewis embarked on several world
tours. His trademarks were
unmistakable, his style heavy in clichés,
but 1954 titles such as *Panama* >**2**
showed his fluency in the chalumeau
register, while the likes of *Come Back
Sweet Papa* >**3** from the same period
show his skill at collective
improvisation. Kid Howard was perhaps
the most successful of the many
trumpeters Lewis employed although
one particular concert in Tokyo with
Punch Miller >**4** truly came to life.
Unfortunately, time was running out for
Lewis and he was often ill during his
latter years. It was perhaps appropriate
that he finished his playing days in the
Preservation Hall in New Orleans.

Lineage
A self-taught player, he did not follow
the playing tradition of that great
teacher Lorenzo Tio, a tradition which
prevailed in his hometown. He did,
however, become the model for a
legion of European revivalists intent on
looking at jazz from a static position.

Media
Biographies, *Call Him George* (1961) by
Jay Allison Stuart and *George Lewis* by
Tom Bethell (1977). Lewis took part in
the filming of *New Orleans* (1947) but
the sequence was cut from the final film.
He did, however, appear in *The
Cincinatti Kid* (1965).

Listening
1 George Lewis
  Storyville SLP 201
2 George Lewis And His Ragtime Band
  Storyville SLP 4022
3 George Lewis/Paul Barbarin
  Storyville SLP 4049
4 George Lewis In Tokyo
  King (Jap) KC 3009

Thelonious Monk

**Born: 10th October 1917/Rocky
Mount, North Carolina, USA
Died: 17th February 1982/New York
City, NY, USA
Instrument: Piano, composer
Recording Career: 1944-1975
Nickname: Melodious Thunk (as
dubbed by his wife)**

IN BROAD TERMS, the rapid
development of jazz can be traced to
the synthesis of personal inspiration and
group interaction. Inevitably, there
have been odd cliques that have
achieved high artistic levels without
greatly affecting the course of the
music's history. There have also been
individuals who, despite brilliantly
distinctive styles, have had few stylistic
disciples. One of the most outstanding
of these was the gifted pianist,
composer and band leader, Thelonious
Sphere Monk.

Unlike many of his contemporaries, Monk came from a comfortable home. He showed little interest in music as a youngster and it was not until he was almost twenty that he began to study the subject. Although a late starter, he became enraptured with jazz and it was not long before he was chancing his arm at New York's Minton's Play House and the Uptown House and anywhere else that encouraged the music he admired.

Through these clubs, Monk became part of the small musical conclave that gave birth to the, then unnamed, bebop. Togther with **Dizzy Gillespie**, **Charlie Parker**, **Bud Powell** and Kenny Clarke, he examined the harmonic and rhythmic ideas that each player pitched into the musical 'think tank'. Even at this early stage, however, Monk was something of a loner. He would come into the club before or after hours so that he could play alone.

Monk's method of playing defied comparison and was certainly that of an intuitive soloist. It was also a method that did not change and it would be safe to say that his solo style in the late forties remained with him throughout his chequered career. His brilliant 1952 trio dates could be taken as benchmarks for this style and they certainly raised questions from the fans. When hearing these performances for

the first time, it would be easy to believe the theory that the 'wrong' harmonies used were a result of musical error, rather than due to his highly individualistic 'ear'. What was important was that they were correct in the artistic sense and that Monk presented *Sweet And Lovely*, *These Foolish Things* and *Just A Gigolo* >**1** as he felt them.

In fact, it was this naive, yet paradoxically sophisticated feeling for harmony that fostered the string of magnificent compositions that flowed from his fingers. *Blue Monk*, *Rhythm-A-Ning* >**2**, *'Round Midnight*, and *Off Minor* >**3** were memorable by any standard but the list is much longer and very impressive. What was surprising was that, whereas his solo style had few devotees, his themes became the property of the entire jazz world.

In the early days, details of Monk's career were sketchy. He was with Dizzy Gillespie in Lucky Millinder's band in 1942 and he also played with **Coleman Hawkins** and Gillespie during that war period. In the main, he worked with a trio and was for many years a shadowy figure of jazz, known by musicians in New York but mainly overlooked by record companies. He led only nine record dates between 1945 and 1953 and that figure was only reached through the usual artistic perception of the Blue Note label.

Fortunately, things began to improve in the middle fifties. Monk was discovered by the media as well as by another generation of fans. He became a touring attraction and began to realise that the quartet was his best medium of expression. To this end, he employed several impressive tenor men in the late fifties: **Sonny Rollins** was the most relaxed and tended to simplify his solos to suit the surroundings. The influence on **John Coltrane** was more marked in that it drew his attention to space and to the fact that 'difficulty' is not an aesthetic criterion. **Johnny Griffin** was the least affected by the association, and tended to play in his normal, headlong fashion, often ignoring the subtle Monk nuance and riding roughshod over the most gentle tune.

In 1959, Monk was joined by Charlie Rouse and so began a long and fruitful association. The two men were together for almost eleven years and it was perhaps ironical, given their achievements as a quartet, that his first

Thelonious Monk – Live At The It Club

record date with Monk should be the famous Town Hall Concert as part of a ten-piece big band line-up. Hal Overton acted as musical director and tracks like *Monk's Mood* and *Off Minor* >**4** took on new and more profound meanings.

More usually, Rouse worked in the touring quartet and he virtually escorted Monk from his finest hour to the point at which he became a somewhat bored and cynical man. His outstanding grasp of Monk's music on titles such as *Well You Needn't* and *Bemsha Swing* >**5** from the live 1964 It Club recording mark the high point but the formula for performance became too stereotyped. Every number featured a lengthy solo from each player and Monk began to dry up as a composer. Finally, in 1970, Rouse left and Monk gave up his group.

In 1971 and 1972 Monk toured with Gillespie and **Sonny Stitt** in the Giants Of Jazz package and played quite superbly, and in 1974 he turned up at a New York concert devoted to his music and unexpectedly played all night. He reverted to the quartet format for a performance at the 1975 New York Festival, but at the same event the following year made his last public performance.

Lineage

Monk was a totally original player, whose playing was hardly touched by his bebop colleagues. His most obvious disciple is Britain's **Stan Tracey**, but something of his idiosyncratic chord work brushed off on **Duke Ellington** in the late part of that great man's career.

Media

Appeared in CBS *The Sound Of Jazz* (1957), was seen in *Jazz On A Summer's Day* (1960) and wrote music for *Les Liaisons Dangereuses* (1960).

Listening

1 Monk's Mood
  Thelonious Monk/Prestige OM 2018
2 Thelonious In Action
  Thelonious Monk/Milestone M 47043
3 Genius Of Modern Music Vol 1
  Thelonious Monk/Blue Note BST 81510
4 Thelonious Monk At Town Hall
  OJC 135
5 Live At The It Club
  Thelonious Monk/CBS 88584

Fats Navarro

Born: 24th September 1923/Key West, Florida, USA
Died: 7th July 1950/New York City, NY, USA
Instrument: Trumpet
Recording Career: 1943-1950
Nicknames: Fat Girl, Fat Boy

FOR MANY OBSERVERS, Theodore Navarro was the most complete of all bebop trumpeters: instrumentally more secure than **Miles Davis**, stylistically better organised than **Howard McGhee** and less eccentrically flamboyant than **Dizzy Gillespie**.

Starting out playing tenor in a Florida band, Navarro came to general notice when he joined Andy Kirk as a trumpeter in 1943. However he had to take second place to featured soloist McGhee and it was only on Gillespie's recommendation that he was considered eligible to join Billy Eckstine in 1945. He remained with Eckstine's band for nearly two years and made his most outstanding combo recordings.

Navarro's grasp of Gillespie's style had impressed Eckstine but, in the small groups, he blossomed as a major bebop soloist. He belonged to the school of players who remained loyal to their solos through several takes, but his splendidly brassy tone and faultless articulation made it all sound utterly spontaneous. *Our Delight* and *Dameronia* >**1** were outstanding examples of his ability to improvise a solo, while *Fat Girl* >**2** showed that, when it came to fiery delivery, bebop know-how and propulsive swinging, Navarro tipped his cap to no one.

Lineage

Originally inspired by **Dizzy Gillespie**, Navarro's influence has passed down to second-generation boppers like **Clifford Brown**, Donald Byrd, Kenny Dorham and **Lee Morgan**.

Listening

1 Fats Navarro With The Tadd Dameron Band
Milestone M 47041
2 Fat Girl – The Savoy Sessions
Fats Navarro/Savoy SJL 2216

Kid Ory

Born: 25th December 1886/La Place, Louisiana, USA
Died: 23rd January 1973/Hawaii
Instruments: Trombone, cornet, bass and alto saxophones, vocals
Recording Career: 1922-1971

CERTAIN INSTRUMENTAL styles in jazz do not make high technical demands on the player, calling for an economy of delivery rather than a facile show of skill. The obvious example is the tailgate trombone style with its wholly collective rôle and its position as the hub of the New Orleans ensemble. Rarely asked to carry a melody line, the tailgater is there to add colouration in the form of smears, glissandi and underlying bass harmonies.

One of its finest exponents was Edward 'Kid' Ory, a multi-instrumentalist whose speciality was trombone. He was also something of a natural leader and organised his first real band while still a child. After moving to New Orleans he employed, among others, **King Oliver**, **Louis Armstrong**, **Johnny Dodds**, **Sidney Bechet** and Mutt Carey. In 1919 he moved to the West Coast, continuing to lead his own units and recording under the improbable billing Spike's Seven Pods Of Pepper.

In 1924 Ory moved to Chicago and from then until 1929 played in the city's leading jazz and vaudeville bands. More importantly, he was one of the star musicians featured in Louis Armstrong's Hot Five, the Okeh recording group that made some of the greatest records in jazz history. Ory's punchy, if rustic, solos illuminated the likes of *Georgia Grind* and *Gut Bucket Blues* >**1** but it was *Your Next* >**1** that was the purest example of his tailgate playing. Much the same could be said of his masterful ensemble playing on *Gatemouth* >**2** with the New Orleans' Wanderers, or of the way he fitted effortlessly into **Jelly Roll Morton**'s marvellously organised *Black Bottom Stomp* and *Grandpa's Spells* >**3**. His former sideman, King Oliver, became his leader for a while and titles such as *Willie The Weeper* >**4** showed that the trombonist could up-date his style if needed.

In 1929, Ory returned to the West Coast and worked for three years before retiring from the music business.

It was a retirement that did not last, however, as he began taking odd jobs in 1940 and, two years later, joined Barney Bigard. Interest in New Orleans jazz was growing and, in 1944, Ory formed his own combo comprising, in the main, New Orleans veterans. His confidence returned rapidly and, with quality men like **Jimmie Noone**, Mutt Carey and Omer Simeon on hand, he made a completely successful comeback.

At first, his best solo outings were on slower items such as *Careless Love* >**5** and *Blues For Jimmie Noone* >**5** but as his 'chops' improved, he began to play solos that were even more assured than those of his heyday. His tailgate experience was a tremendous asset and he became a leader determined to have a good sound balance. Therefore, great attention was paid to dynamics and notorious flag-wavers such as *South Rampart Street Parade* and *Bill Bailey* >**6**, recorded in 1953, became models of well-modulated volumes and strategically-judged climaxes.

Ory brought to the revivalist movement of the forties and fifties a professionalism that was, in most cases, sadly missing.

Lineage
An early influence on Ory was Zue Robertson, while Ory himself left his mark on Honour Dutney, Roy Palmer, Geechy Fields, John Thomas, Charles Irvis and Wilbur de Paris.

Media
Ory appeared in films like *New Orleans* (1947), *The Benny Goodman Story* (1955), *Crossfire* (1947), *Mahogany Magic* (1950) and *Disneyland After Dark* (1962).

Listening
1 **VSOP Vols 1/2**
   Louis Armstrong/CBS (F) 88001
2 **The Immortal Johnny Dodds**
   VJM VLP 48
3 **The Complete Jelly Roll Morton Vols 1/2**
   RCA (F) PM 42405
4 **King Oliver and His Dixie Syncopators**
   Swaggie 822
5 **Kid Ory 1944**
   Joy 264
6 **This Kid's The Greatest**
   Kid Ory/Good Time Jazz M 12045

Charlie Parker

Born: 29th August 1920/Kansas City, Kansas, USA
Died: 12th March 1955/New York City, NY, USA
Instruments: Alto and tenor saxophones, composer
Recording Career: 1941-1954
Nicknames: Yardbird, Bird, Yard

IT WOULD obviously be wrong to attribute an entire musical revolution to the influence of one musician. When the face of jazz gradually changed in the middle forties, there were many outstanding players who played major roles. Established men like **Coleman Hawkins** and **Charlie Christian** shared the honours with newcomers like **Dizzy Gillespie**, **Thelonious Monk**, **Bud Powell** and Charlie Parker. Of these, Parker is sometimes singled out as the most important, and pianist Lennie Tristano is reputed to have said in 1960, 'If Parker had wanted to invoke plagiarism laws, he could have sued almost everybody who's made a record in the last ten years.' While it is perhaps true that Parker exerted the greatest influence, it would be a mistake to claim his pioneering work as exclusive.

Sadly, the pattern for the life of Charles Christopher Parker Jr was established at an early age: he encountered narcotics while still in his middle teens, having left school at fifteen to begin earning a living as a musician. Early reports were not encouraging, but his progress was rapid and, by the time he joined the **Jay McShann** band in 1937, he had become a proficient player.

Parker first went to New York in 1939 and worked at Monroe's Uptown House for a year. He rejoined McShann in Kansas during the following year before returning to New York on a more permanent basis in 1941. While there, he met Dizzy Gillespie and found in the trumpeter a kindred musical spirit. Both men had been experimenting independently to extend the harmonic range of jazz and they now began to combine their empirical findings.

After spells with Noble Sissle, **Earl Hines** and Andy Kirk in 1944, Parker joined Billy Eckstine and, for the first

Charlie Parker, with Miles Davis (right) and Tommy Potter on bass

time, found himself in a musical organisation that encouraged the new music. Gillespie was also in the band and both men had an influence on its policy. More significantly, the two began to work together in smaller groups and, despite the disadvantage of inappropriate drummers, produced outstanding records like *Groovin' High* and *Shaw 'Nuff* >**1**. This was bebop. The old chord sequences were retained but Parker's new, melodic lines transformed them into new tunes. His solos ploughed across bar lines with a rhythmic displacement that earned for his music the term 'ju-jitsu music'. This insult came, not only from establishment critics, but also from older musicians locked into inviolable traditions and frightened for their own futures.

Parker was hurt, and what followed was his unsatisfactory, but inevitable, reaction. He turned with greater intensity toward his habit and, in 1946, his drug-affected health collapsed completely. A lengthy spell in hospital was followed by some time with JATP. It was the small combo recordings that he made for Dial and Savoy, however, that were really more important. Even more than the early group with Gillespie, this series of records was the yardstick against which the style was judged. The

quintet had in **Miles Davis** a promising, but often diffident, young trumpeter, and though it was restricted by a predictable bassist in Tommy Potter, it became the model for all bebop quintets that followed. **Max Roach** was magnificent on drums, Duke Jordan had fully assimilated Bud Powell's piano interpretation of bebop and the leader was sublime.

It was Parker's magnificent attack, tremendous harmonic insight and brilliantly inventive flair that ensured that these recordings were not only the finest examples of the genre, but also great jazz records by any standards. *My Old Flame* >**2** was a beautifully laid-out ballad essay, *Dexterity* >**3** was self-descriptive, while *Bird Feathers* >**2** reminded us that there was still a trace of forties jump music in bebop. *Bird Of Paradise* >**3** even suggested that there was a little of the exotic in Parker's soul, but it really is invidious to select individual titles – whatever the line-up, the Parker combo records of the forties were uniformly excellent.

He visited France in 1949 and Scandinavia in 1950 but his health was now a major problem. Plagued by stomach ulcers and cirrhosis of the liver, he showed little inclination to fight back and was often incapacitated for

young Parker, although there were traces of the **Lester Young** style in his work with **Jay McShann**. Apart from obvious clones like **Sonny Stitt** and **Cannonball Adderley**, it is true to say that Parker influenced a whole generation of saxophone players, as well as muscians on other instruments. His influence even permeated all dance bands and pop groups of the day and elements of bebop survive in all departments of contemporary jazz.

Media

Parker's music has been used in the soundtracks of *The Connection* (1961), *Le Souffle Au Coeur* (1971), *Next Stop, Greenwich Village* (1975), *Passing Through* (1977), and *Sorcerer* (1977), while *Sweet Love, Bitter* (1966) is a film loosely based on Parker's life. Biographies: *Charlie Parker* by Max Harrison (1960), *Bird: The Legend Of Charlie Parker* by Robert Reisner (1962) and *Bird Lives!* by Ross Russell (1973).

Listening

1 Bird & Diz
Gillespie/Parker/Charlie Parker CP 512
2 Charlie Parker On Dial Vol 5
Spotlite 105
3 Charlie Parker On Dial Vol 4
Spotlite 104
4 Charlie Parker With Strings
Verve 817 442-1
5 The Greatest Concert Ever
Gillespie/Parker/Powell/Mingus/Roach/
Prestige 68319

months at a time. Only on projects that captured his imagination did he play enthusiastically, but he adapted well to the chance of being featured soloist in a big band when he recorded for Clef in 1952. This included work with strings, and on titles like *Just Friends* >**4** he pitched his inspired nervousness against the legato comfort of the conformist ensemble.

Parker broadcast with strings on several occasions, but his best work in the early fifties was still in his quartets or quintets, with musically sympathetic colleagues such as pianists Walter Bishop and Al Haig and drummers like Roy Haynes and Max Roach. In 1953, the amazing Quintet Of The Year with Gillespie, Powell, Roach and **Charles Mingus** gave him one last triumph >**5**. It was a timely reminder of Parker's immense contribution to bebop and to his mastery of the style. He had played a vital part in the development of all post-forties jazz and must be considered, together with **Louis Armstrong** and **Ornette Coleman**, as one of the greatest soloists in jazz history.

Lineage

By his own admission, it was altoist Buster Smith who most influenced the

Bud Powell

Born: 27th September 1924/New York City, NY, USA
Died: 31st July 1966/New York City, NY, USA
Instrument: Piano, composer
Recording Career: 1944-1965

THE POSITION of Earl 'Bud' Powell as the most outstanding of all bop pianists is not in doubt. 1944's *Floogie Boo* >**1** from his first recording date with Cootie Williams confirms his roots in the swing era, but even then there were eccentricities to suggest an empirical outlook. After leaving Williams, he secreted himself into the 52nd Street experimental scene and devoted himself to the new music. Almost single-handedly he gave the piano a bop language of its own, and captured for the keyboard the urgency of **Charlie Parker**'s alto and the fire of **Dizzy Gillespie**'s trumpet.

Powell did not operate with a low burn engine: he attacked with the urgency of a V-eight and coupled this with admirable creativity and a total emotional commitment. On his first trio album, the ferocious *Bud's Bubble* >**2** told of his technical supremacy while *I Should Care* >**2** was a model of ballad rebuilding. Whatever the tempo, Powell never coasted. He thought on his feet, took chances, and used errors as a stimulant to new directions. He had a nervous breakdown in 1945, but health problems rarely affected his playing before 1953. Indeed, his playing on the legendary Massey Hall Concert of that year was outstanding with his high-speed solo on *Wee* >**3** and the more leisurely *Hot House* >**3** both quite dazzling. Sadly, he had another breakdown in the following year and from then on there were problems in some of his performances. He settled in Paris in 1959, and albums with **Dexter Gordon** >**4** and **Coleman Hawkins** >**5** attest to his ability to play exceptionally well when the mood was right.

Unfortunately, other offerings were less spectacular and, although a 1964 trio release contained the moving *Blues For Bouffemont* >**6**, there were other, less secure items. In 1966, Powell returned to New York and died later that year.

Lineage
Powell's main inspiration came from **Earl Hines** and **Nat King Cole** but *My Old Flame* >**1** makes clear that he had listened constructively to **Art Tatum**. Apart from the **Thelonious Monk** school, he influenced just about all the bop and hard bop pianists.

Listening
1 Echoes Of Harlem
  Cootie Williams/Affinity AFS 1031
2 Bud Powell Trio
  Bud Powell/Columbia 33 SX 1575
3 The Greatest Concert Ever
  Charlie Parker/Dizzy Gillespie/Prestige 68319
4 Our Man In Paris
  Dexter Gordon/Blue Note BST 84146
5 Hawk In Germany
  Coleman Hawkins/Black Lion BLP 30125
6 The Invisible Cage
  Bud Powell/Black Lion BLP 30120

Buddy Rich

Born: 30th September 1917/New York City, NY, USA
Died: 2nd April 1987/Los Angeles, California, USA
Instrument: Drums, vocals
Recording Career: 1938-1986

A MASTER JAZZMAN, judged by his peers as technically the best-equipped of all drummers, Buddy Rich offered not only speed and accuracy, but an intuitive sense of swing. With this, he inspired bands of any size and had the ability to stir even the most ordinary musicians to play with real fire and passion.

Bernard Rich was a remarkable child prodigy, leading his own band at just eleven, but more serious training came in the bands of **Bunny Berigan**, **Artie Shaw** and, from 1939 to 1945, **Tommy Dorsey**. Rich formed his own big band in 1945, leading it intermittently during the remainder of the decade. He also toured with JATP, becoming famous for

Buddy Rich

the drum 'battles' much favoured by that organisation.

Although working on-and-off with **Harry James** through much of the fifties and sixties Rich still found time to lead bands of his own, albeit briefly. *Shorty George* >**1** and *Jumpin' At The Woodside* >**1** from his 1956 tribute to **Count Basie** give some idea of the quality of those outfits, while *Cherokee* >**2** from 1959 amply demonstrates the power of his ageless drumming.

In 1966, after reforming a big band on a more permanent basis, Rich rapidly achieved international success. Despite being briefly forced back to small group dimensions in 1974, he transformed a nucleus of one or two experienced 'hands' into a basically young band that enjoyed great success through the seventies and eighties. As late as the autumn of 1986, Rich was still touring, but his health failed rapidly at the start of the following year.

Lineage

The eighteen-month-old 'Baby Traps' learned his drum skills in vaudeville, growing up in the era of Sonny Greer and **Chick Webb**. His own influence can be felt in the work of Louis Bellson and Sonny Payne, but there are few dance band drummers who do not aspire to his flashy but undeniably phenomenal skills.

Media

Super Drummer: A Profile of Buddy Rich written by Whitney Balliett in 1968. Rich himself made a brief appearance in the film *Ship Ahoy!* (1942).

Listening

1 The Big Band Sound of Buddy Rich
Verve 2317 058
2 Richcraft
Buddy Rich/Mercury SMWL 21035

Max Roach

Born: 10th January 1925/Brooklyn, NY, USA
Instruments: Drums, vibraphone, composer
Recording Career: 1944-

ANY DISCUSSION of Maxwell Roach's drumming work must begin with Kenny Clarke, who was without doubt the man who established the drums' role in the pioneer days of bebop. In reducing the importance of the high-hat and switching attention to the top cymbal, Clarke provided a constant sound in which he could place accents. The beat was not defined, as it had been with the swing players; the high-hat was used sparingly and the bass drum employed only for 'bomb-dropping'.

Roy Haynes and Max Roach were the best of his followers, but it was the latter who was to surpass his mentor as he modified the style to suit his own requirements. Early records with **Charlie Parker** such as *Donna Lee* >**1** deviated very little from the Clarke model: the right hand on the top cymbal remained the vital element but his playing was to become more extravagant. The left hand began to gain in importance as he strove after an arid crispness with both brushes.

By the time he formed his brilliant quintet with **Clifford Brown** in 1954, he had forced his own personality into the general fabric of modern drumming. The top cymbal remained at the heart of the style, but the cross-rhythms of the left hand produced the headlong surge that was such a feature on titles like *The Scene Is Clean* >**2**. More significantly, this brilliant group with pianist Richie Powell and, first Harold Land and then **Sonny Rollins** on tenor, established Roach as a leader of stature.

Brown's death in 1956 came as a terrible shock to him, but he was now a committed leader and into his band of 1958 introduced another gifted trumpeter, Booker Little. Together with tenor George Coleman and tuba specialist Ray Draper, they made another series of fine records including an explosive three-tiered *You Stepped Out Of A Dream* >**3** and a masterful *Bemsha Swing* >**4**.

Max Roach

Roach's fearlessly outspoken political statement *We Insist, Freedom Now Suite* >**5** got him blacklisted from studio work in the sixties. Throughout the seventies and eighties, he led several valuable groups, which included men like trumpeter Cecil Bridgewater and tenor Odean Pope and a sample of their work can be found in 1982's stirring *Straight, No Chaser* >**6**, recorded in Italy. It offered both horn men ample solo space but did nothing to unseat Roach as master of his own groups. He is still rated as one of the finest of all jazz drummers.

Lineage

Roach was undoubtedly influenced by Kenny Clarke but he in turn inspired the entire generation of percussionists that followed including Elvin Jones, Billy Higgins, Ed Blackwell, Daniel Humair and, latterly Billy Hart, Jack DeJohnette, Sunny Murray and Milford Graves.

Media

Composed the musical *Another Valley.* The film *Freedom Now Suite* won first prize at the Locarno Film Festival.

Listening

1 The Complete Savoy Sessions Vol 3
Charlie Parker/Savoy WL 70548
2 Clifford Brown & Max Roach At Basin Street
EmArcy 6336707
3 Conversations
Max Roach/Milestone M 47061
4 Many Sides Of Max Roach
Mercury MCL 20029
5 We Insist, Freedom Now
Max Roach/Candid CM 8002
6 In The Light
Max Roach/Soul Note SN 1053

Pee Wee Russell

Born: 27th March 1906/Maple Wood, Missouri, USA
Died: 15th February 1969/Alexandria, Virginia, USA
Instruments: Clarinet, tenor saxophone
Recording Career: 1927-1968

IF THE WORK of Charles Ellsworth Russell prior to 1940 had been the yardstick, it is unlikely that his name would appear among the major figures in jazz. His wheezing tone and fragile technique make listening to his earliest recordings a painful experience. His timing was flat-footed and his eccentric note placements more a result of instrumental difficulties than jazz inspiration. Occasionally his playing was carried along by his colleagues even if his jinking run through *Hello Lola* >**1**, with the Mound City Blue Blowers, was a creditable exception. Similarly, his playing on the 1932 Rhythmakers dates achieved a useful standard and *Bugle Call Rag* and *Bald-headed Mama* >**2** have especially good clarinet moments.

Russell's tenor work was even less impressive but, after taking a residency at Nick's in New York during 1937, he became more consistent. Concentrating now on clarinet, his work with **Eddie Condon** in the forties could be classified as adequate, if not exactly earth-moving. He came into his own, however, on a series of mainstream sessions in the sixties with the likes of **Buck Clayton** >**3** and **Coleman Hawkins** >**4**.

Shortly after these recordings, claims were made that he was really a latent modernist, but his versions of **John Coltrane**'s *Red Planet* and **Thelonious Monk**'s *Round Midnight* >**5** display none of the qualities that would have supported such a contention.

Russell's idiosyncratic style had many fans and he has been dubbed the 'Poet Of The Clarinet', but in truth it is only his very finest work that can be rated that highly.

Lineage

Russell's original influences were

Johnny Dodds and Frank
Teschemacher but he did point the way
to certain European revivalists like
Archie Semple.

Media

Appeared in CBS film *The Sound Of
Jazz* (1957).

Listening

**1 The Indispensable Coleman Hawkins
(1927-56)**
RCA NL 89277 (2)

2 The Hottest Jazz Ever Recorded
The Rhythmakers/VJM VLP 53

3 The Memorial Album
Pee Wee Russell/Prestige HBS 6143

4 Jam Session At Swingsville
Pee Wee Russell/Coleman Hawkins/
Prestige 24051

5 New Groove
Pee Wee Russell/CBS BPG 62242

Sonny Stitt

**Born: 2nd February 1924/Boston,
Massachusetts, USA
Died: 23rd July 1982/New York City,
NY, USA
Instruments: Alto, baritone and tenor
saxophones
Recording Career: 1944-1981**

WITH AN ALTO STYLE near to that of
his idol, **Charlie Parker**, Edward
'Sonny' Stitt was an outstanding sax
player whose career was bedevilled by
criticism from certain quarters that he
was merely a Parker copyist. The
accusation was not without foundation:
his sound as well as his style was
undeniably very similar.

Stitt's first important professional job
was with bandleader Tiny Bradshaw
but, after discovering the scene on New
York's 52nd Street, he could not keep
away. He first heard Parker in 1943 and,
although he had been thinking along
similar lines, was forced to concede that
the Kansas man had developed them
further. New York was the testing
ground but titles like *Oop Bob
Sh'Bam* >**1** with **Dizzy Gillespie**,
showed that Stitt could make his own
important contribution to the new
music.

Personal problems took him away
from music in the late forties, but he
returned in 1949 in good health, and
ready to shake off the plagiarist tag. To
this end, he switched to tenor and
seemed to make a conscious effort to
get away from Parker's image. In the
early fifties, however, he resumed on
alto and in 1957 joined up for two years
with JATP.

The sixties found him with **Miles
Davis** for a spell, as part of an all-star
sextet which included **Clark Terry**. A
brief sojourn with **Zoot Sims** followed
and then it was back to the larger horn
for a two-tenor group with Gene
Ammons. The records made by this unit
are among the best in the saxophone
battle tradition and *Soul Summit* >**2** and
Together Again For The Last Time >**3**
demonstrate how well their styles
contrasted.

Teamed with Gillespie, **Thelonious
Monk** and **Art Blakey** in the Giants Of
Jazz during the early seventies, Stitt was
still playing extremely well. In his last
years he played alongside tenor
saxophonist Red Holloway and, on *Just
Friends* >**4**, they *were* just friends who
made some beautiful music.

Lineage

It is impossible to deny the tremendous
impact that **Charlie Parker** had on
Stitt's music but, in his tenor playing,
there were traces of **Lester Young**'s
phrasing. As a Parker disciple, he could
hardly be said to have had any
influence of his own.

Listening

1 In The Beginning
  Dizzy Gillespie/Prestige PR 24030
2 Soul Summit
  Gene Ammons/Sonny Stitt/Prestige PRLP 7234
3 Together Again For The Last Time
  Gene Ammons/Sonny Stitt/Prestige PR 10100
4 Just Friends
  Sonny Stitt/Red Holloway/Affinity AFF 51

Billy Strayhorn

Born: 29th November 1915/Dayton, Ohio, USA
Died: 31st May 1967/New York City, NY, USA
Instrument: Piano, composer, arranger
Recording Career: 1939-1963 (piano), 1967 (arranger)
Nickname: Swee' Pea

STRAYHORN FIRST offered compositions to **Duke Ellington** in 1938,

Above: Sarah Vaughan – The Divine Sarah

and after working briefly in the band of Ellington's son, Mercer, joined the Duke on a permanent basis a year later. As a pianist, however, he rarely appeared with the band and, despite some sessions with Ellingtonian sidemen, his principal contribution was in the field of writing and arranging.

Many observers were amazed that the autonomous Ellington should take on an arranging and composing 'assistant' but, such was the rapport which they rapidly achieved, it became difficult to distinguish one from the other. At first, Strayhorn introduced a romantic air to the band and *Chelsea Bridge* >**1**, *Day Dream* and *Passion Flower* >**2** had the luxurious Strayhorn hand on them. Nevertheless, *Take The A Train* >**1** and later *UMMG* >**3** gave notice that he was equally at home with medium tempo riff tunes.

After Ellington's return to grace in 1956, Strayhorn collaborated in many of Duke's finest extended works. The members of the band reacted to him much as they did to the leader, and it became a challenge for the listener to identify the individual writer. *Such*

Sweet Thunder >**4**, *A Drum Is A Woman* >**5**, *Nutcracker Suite* >**6** and *Far East Suite* >**7** were all superb examples, although it was perhaps Ellington's personal tribute *And His Mother Called Him Bill* >**8** that best illustrated jazz's immaculate trinity: Ellington, Strayhorn, and the orchestra.

Lineage
Strayhorn's lightly swinging piano style was very much 'of the era'. His composing and arranging, however, was originally inspired by **Duke Ellington** but, after joining the band, it could be said to have returned its own compliment to the leader.

Media
Strayhorn's skills were inextricably bound up with Ellington in films throughout his entire period with the band.

Listening
1 The Indispensable Duke Ellington Vols 7/8
RCA NL 89274
2 The Indispensable Duke Ellington Vols 9/10
RCA NL 89582
3 The Jeep Is Jumpin'
Duke Ellington/Affinity AFF 91
4 Such Sweet Thunder
Duke Ellington/CBS 84405
5 A Drum Is A Woman
Duke Ellington/CBS 84404
6 Nutcracker Suite
Duke Ellington/CBS 84413
7 Far East Suite
Duke Ellington/RCA PL 45699
8 And His Mother Called Him Bill
Duke Ellington/RCA NL 89166

Sarah Vaughan

Born: 27th March 1924/Newark, New Jersey, USA
Instruments: Vocals, piano
Recording Career: 1944-
Nicknames: Sassie, The Divine Sarah

THE MOST wholly beautiful voice in all jazz history belongs to Sarah Lois Vaughan. Her intonation is perfect, her control of vibrato and timbre unequalled, and she builds improvised solos with the logic of the most gifted instrumentalist.

As a child, she sang in her local Baptist Church, won an amateur singing contest at the Apollo Theatre in Harlem, New York, and shortly after her nineteenth birthday joined **Earl Hines**. In the following year she linked up with Billy Eckstine and came into contact with the bop pioneers, displaying an uncanny grasp of the 'new' music. 1945's *Lover Man* >**1**, recorded with **Charlie Parker** and **Dizzy Gillespie**, combined her feeling for the touching lyric with the equally finely-judged timing of her instrumental colleagues.

Sassie has known many triumphs since Columbia records launched her on the road to international stardom back in 1949. At times, her effortless mastery takes her to the brink of self-parody, and just occasionally she loses herself in her stagecraft. It hardly seems to matter. She is at her best with demanding material like the *Ellington Song Book* >**2** from 1979, or in stimulating company, as with the 'Basie-less' Basie Orchestra, on *No Count, Sarah* >**3**. Even with orchestral strings, she remains a jazz singer, providing her own power sources and commanding an unrivalled following of fans.

Lineage
She learnt the singing art from the horns of the bebop giants, but has developed a style so inimitable as to be virtually uncopied, and uncopiable. Plagiarists can only borrow what they can manage to use.

Media
Appeared in TV's *Wolftrap* (USA) and has made guest appearances on major TV interview programmes in three continents. Sang on the soundtrack of *Sharon* (1977).

Listening
1 In The Beginning
Dizzy Gillespie/Prestige PR 24030
2 Duke Ellington Song Book Vol 1
Sarah Vaughan/Pablo 2312 111
3 No Count, Sarah
Sarah Vaughan/Count Basie/Roulette 500012

The early fifties saw history repeating itself as a large number of white musicians, in the main concentrated on America's West Coast, took up the bebop cause and created their own somewhat parochial style. Most of the ingredients for their cool jazz were taken from the bop masters, although they had spiced it with flavouring derived from swing era musicians like Lester Young and Benny Carter.

The unquestionably cool image of their music incited the critical fraternity to use words like 'enervated', 'clinical' and 'emaciated'. The truth was very different. At their most detached, certain players worshipped improvisation at the expense of emotional projection. Weighed against this, saxophonists such as Stan Getz, Gerry Mulligan and Lee Konitz redirected their aims, ignoring the instrumental niceties and matching creative intent with warmth of delivery.

The East Coast reaction to cool jazz was at first slow. The West's Contemporary label had experienced tremendous success but, in the middle fifties, the Blue Note company began to put the earthier, more extrovert music of New York back on the map. Their music was a more direct descendant of bebop, but there was a shift in instrumental responsibilities and drummers found themselves nearer to the driver's seat. Art Blakey became a central figure in a movement that was

THE FIFTIES

Art Blakey

expression that maintained its own place in the mainstream of the music. Coltrane was a major figure: his playing was powerful and demanding, and he showed how brilliantly he could build solos from a permutation of minutely modified scales. The outcome was perhaps rightly described as *sheets of sound*.

Independently, however, there were other musical freedom-fighters. Almost as a reaction to the new formalism of the Coltrane method, a movement grew up in Forth Worth, Texas, and later in Los Angeles, around the talents of altoist Ornette Coleman. It ignored the tedium that could be a snare for those less gifted and less quick-thinking than a Coltrane. Coleman's clique returned jazz to the ideal of melodic improvisation – not to the essay-writing logic of the thirties but to a style that became known as free form.

This was, in fact, an aptly descriptive term which explained its exponents' aims in just two words. Melody was all important, but not as continuous melody. Starting with a basic and, in the old sense, tuneful theme statement, the soloists launched themselves on a course of melodic progression. Each motif stood on its own merits and, although successive phrases were related, each carried just the same autonomous responsibility. There was no chord structure as a harbour should navigation fail and, if a musical idea was crass or inappropriate, the soloist was lost.

The path taken by pianist Cecil Taylor was a degree more insular, but his particular brand of extravagant self-indulgence led jazz into equally creative fields. With Coleman, Taylor represented the way ahead and, as the fifties came to a close, it had to be acknowledged that, as a decade, it had only to touch its cap to the twenties as the most dramatic jazz era.

appropriately dubbed hard bop and a new generation of hard-hitting players like saxophonists Sonny Rollins, Jackie McLean and Johnny Griffin joined trumpeters Clifford Brown and Lee Morgan to give the music true direction. The mighty bass of Charles Mingus lay at the heart of an iconoclastic band which brought prayer-meeting intensity to a highly creative strain of music, and a mood of change was rife.

Bop pioneer Miles Davis emerged from the shadows to provide his own wing of the movement and, together with saxophonist John Coltrane, ushered jazz into the modal era. In so doing, he provided a useful tool for jazz musicians; the use of scales freed them from the straightjacket of chordal progressions and gave a lead in free

Cannonball Adderley

Born: 15th September 1928/Tampa, Florida, USA
Died: 8th August 1975/Gary, Indiana, USA
Instruments: Alto, soprano and tenor saxophones, trumpet, clarinet, flute, composer
Recording Career: 1955-1975

ONE OF that particular breed of American musician who arrived on the scene an already complete player, Julian Edwin Adderley came to New York as an unknown in 1955 and then packed more into the next four years than would have seemed possible. Within six months of joining bassist Oscar Pettiford, he had signed a record contract and formed a band with his cornet-playing brother Nat. He then spent eighteen months with **Miles Davis** in what proved to be the trumpeter's most creative period.

The modal *So What* >**1** and the bluesy *Freddie Freeloader* >**1** both demonstrate just how effectively Adderley's busy bop figures could be contrasted with Davis' spare and relaxed statements. The whole *Kind Of Blue* >**1** album became a landmark, yet within months Adderley left to join **George Shearing**. It was not long, however, before Cannonball Adderley (the nickname a corruption of 'cannibal' from his prodigious eating habits!) rejoined his brother. With the master of soul, Bobby Timmons on piano, their policy was not in doubt and the naming of material such as *Dat Dere* and *Work Song* >**2** was of significance. Joe Zawinul (later of **Weather Report**) replaced Timmons in the sixties, but a stable personnel was maintained and the group's *Mercy, Mercy, Mercy* >**3** became one of the best-selling jazz records of all time.

Adderley's own playing had changed while he was with Davis. It showed a greater awareness of space and assumed some of the trumpeter's relaxation. This was to prove an asset as he moved into the seventies with a wider knowledge of rock and its

electronic aids. His choice of keyboard players like **George Duke** and Hal Galper told its own story but, perhaps on the brink of another change of direction, Adderley had a fatal stroke while on tour.

Lineage
Adderley's first influences were **Benny Carter** and **Charlie Parker** but he was later greatly affected by the music of **Miles Davis** and **John Coltrane**.

Media
Appeared in films *Play Misty For Me* (1971), *Soul To Soul* (1971) and *Save The Children* (1973); played host on TV's *Go Minutes* and had an acting role in one episode of *Kung Fu*.

Listening
1 Kind Of Blue
Miles Davis/CBS 62066
2 Them Dirty Blues
Cannonball Adderley/Landmark LLP 1301
3 Mercy, Mercy, Mercy
Cannonball Adderley/Capitol T 2663

Count Basie

THE BASIE ORCHESTRA of the early fifties took time to settle but, by the time he had celebrated twenty years as leader in 1955, the personnel was new but stable. Thad Jones and Joe Newman were among the trumpets, Henry Coker and Benny Powell on trombones, and two impressive young tenor men in Frank Foster and Frank Wess continued the tradition of saxophone rivalry in the band. More significantly, the policy of the band had changed. There was a move away from the earlier loose-hipped gait, head arrangements were less favoured and a team of arrangers, headed by Ernie Wilkins, Neal Hefti and Johnny Mandel, were imported to tighten the loose musical screws.

Miraculously, it was achieved with no loss in swing power; if anything Basie's precision instrument of a band swung even more than the predecessors. Having retained the services of guitarist

Freddie Green, with bassist Eddie Jones and powerhouse drummer Sonny Payne making up the team, Basie had a genuinely propulsive unit. The icing on the cake was singer Joe Williams: no **Jimmy Rushing**, but hugely popular with the fans.

The so-called Dance Sessions demonstrated that the links with the old-style band had finally been severed. Moving over to the Verve label in 1956 and on to Roulette a year later, the new Basie band was launched. *Whirly-Bird* >**1** not only demonstrated the rifle-shot accuracy of the brass, but introduced another excellent tenor saxophonist – Eddie 'Lockjaw' Davis. *Splanky* >**1**, with its masterful brass slurs, reminded all that this was a blues band, while the leader's piano on *Lil' Darlin'* >**1** wrote its own legend. The reed section sang as one man on most selections, and Williams shouted *Alright, OK, Hallelujah, I Love Her So* and *Slap Dab In The Middle* night after night in concert.

This band simply could not lose. The sixties came and went with many superb live recordings, outstanding specials with guests like Frank Sinatra >**2** and **Ella Fitzgerald** >**3**, as well as the odd piece of trivia as the band went into a *Beatle Bag* >**4** with interpretations of Lennon and McCartney's hit songs. Bing Crosby >**5** was another notable guest in the early seventies but, by the end of the decade, although personnel changes had been kept to a minimum, few of the great Roulette team remained; Sonny Cohn was in the trumpet section, Al Grey had joined Hughes on trombone and Eric Dixon and Bobby Plater had come into the reeds.

The music had not really changed, however, and Basie and the faithful Freddie Green took the band into the eighties in style. Sadly, it was not long before the leader's health began to fail and, although he made wheelchair appearances to the end, William 'Count' Basie died in 1984.

(For biographical information and lineage, see The Thirties, page 56).

Listening

1 The Atomic Mr Basie
 Count Basie/PRT NFP 5503
2 Sinatra At The Sands
 Frank Sinatra/Count Basie/Reprise
 REP 64002
3 A Perfect Match
 Count Basie/Ella Fitzgerald/Pablo 2312 110
4 Basie's Beatle Bag
 Count Basie/Music For Pleasure MFP 1393
5 Bing And Basie
 Bing Crosby/Count Basie/Daybreak
 2932 007

133

Art Blakey

**Born: 11th October 1919/Pittsburgh,
Pennsylvania, USA
Instrument: Drums
Recording Career: 1944-**

THE TRANSITION from the bebop of
the forties to the hard bop of the fifties
was the result more of a change in
drumming attitudes than of a change in
the role of horn players. The drum kit
moved out alongside the frontline
instruments, the heart moved onto the
sleeve and the blood pressure was
increased. If one single man could be
said to be the personification of the
style, it is Art Blakey. His crash rolls
exploded only to recede like thunder,
his rim shots chattered noisily and his
ride-cymbal sound moved through a
range of tonal areas as his stick
explored almost every square inch of
metal.

To typecast him purely in this role,
however, would be a mistake. With
groups of all sizes, Blakey was capable
of producing work of great subtlety.
Almost all of his work with **Thelonious
Monk** was marked by its restraint and
hearing Blakey dragging at the pianist's
coat tails on the 1952 *Little Rootie
Tootie* >**1** is to appreciate why he has
been described as the most suitable
companion for this demanding pianist.

Solely as a drummer Blakey would
have been a major figure, but as the
leader of the Jazz Messengers he
became a giant. Playing with the big
bands of Billy Eckstine and Lucky
Millinder had given him the 'hard drive'
that never deserted him, but he
sharpened the quiet listening side of his
personality in clarinettist **Buddy De
Franco**'s Quartet and in the small
groups he led in New York in the early
fifties.

In 1954, Blakey formed a quintet with
pianist **Horace Silver**, which also
featured the mighty talent of the young
Clifford Brown on trumpet. The whole
venture was so successful that, in the
following year, Blakey and Silver
decided to make it a permanent
arrangement and they adopted the title
Jazz Messengers. Since that date, there
have been endless editions of the
group, each with its own charm and

with different approaches but all
dominated by the tremendous talent of
the drummer.

In the first real Messenger line-up,
the strangely watery-toned trumpet of
Kenny Dorham kept the poignancy of
the blues alive with the aid of Hank
Mobley's attractively warm but distant-
sounding tenor. The 1956-57 edition
introduced the puckishly busy lines of
Bill Hardman's trumpet and – on titles
like *Sam's Tune* >**2** – **Jackie McLean**'s
vinegary sharp alto improvisations. The
hurricane speed of tenor **Johnny
Griffin** arrived during 1957 and *Right
Down Front* >**3** gave first notice of
Blakey's interest in using the baptist
rock of his childhood. This aspect was
extended in 1958. The gifted twenty-
year-old **Lee Morgan** burst into the
band, together with tenor saxophonist
Benny Golson but, more significantly,
the piano chair became the property of
Bobby Timmons. Golson and Timmons
were both composers with strong
church links and Timmons' *Moanin'* and
Golson's *Blues March* >**4** ushered the
Messengers into the 'soul' movement
with a pianist in the band capable of
playing rolling 'downhome' gospel
piano.

Wayne Shorter brought his tenor
saxophone and his composing talents to
the band in 1959 and the personnel
remained stable from then until well
into 1961. Tours were undertaken and a
concert recorded in Tokyo's Sankei
Hall evidenced the extent of their
understanding. Later that year, **Freddie
Hubbard** replaced Morgan and for the
first time, Blakey used a trombonist in
Curtis Fuller. With Cedar Walton on
piano and Jymie Merrit on bass, this
was, for some, the best line-up since
1954. Certainly, the cleverly-arranged
Three Blind Mice and the driving
Plexus >**5** represented the Messengers
at their most powerful.

Morgan returned briefly in 1964 but,
in 1966, there was a clear-out of players.
Chuck Mangione came in to play better
than he has ever quite managed since
and, in 1968, Bill Hardman took over for
a stay that lasted on-and-off until 1976.
Another major shake-out took place in
1977. Russian trumpeter Valeri
Ponomarev's brassy tone announced
how well he had mastered an alien
idiom, tenor David Schmitter added his
John Coltrane-inspired cloud banks of
sound and the more rustic alto of Bobby

Watson danced on titles like *Jody* >**6** to a far more lighthearted tune. This particularly good edition of the Messengers lasted until 1980.

In that year, Blakey recruited the astounding trumpet prodigy **Wynton Marsalis**, followed within twelve months by brother Branford on tenor and alto. From a 1982 session at San Francisco's Keystone Corner *In Walked Bud* >**7** demonstrates what a gifted team Blakey had again assembled but, in this case, the Messengers acted as a restraint on a young trumpeter with aspirations beyond jazz and, in 1982, Marsalis left.

Word was soon about that the drum master had found another stunning young talent: Terence Blanchard appeared from New Orleans, already the finished article, and with Donald 'Duck' Harrison on alto and Bill Pierce on tenor, returned the Jazz Messengers to their rightful place at the top of the mid-eighties heap.

Good as all these players have been, the final accolade must be Blakey's. Nat Hentoff once commented that his 'backdrops resembled a brush fire' and nobody can complain about that. Although he may have been surpassed technically, Art Blakey (or Abdullah Ibn Buhaina, his adopted Muhammedan name) remains probably the most exciting drummer in jazz.

Lineage
Blakey was taught by thirties master **Chick Webb** and, in bringing the drums out in the open, made it possible for free drummers like Andrew Cyrille, Milford Graves and Sunny Murray to ply their trade without complaint.

Media
The Messengers recorded the soundtrack for the film *Des Femmes Disparaissent* (1959).

Listening
1 Thelonious Monk
  OJC 010
2 Ritual
  Jazz Messengers/Vogue LAE 12096
3 Buhaina – The Continuing Message
  Jazz Messengers/Affinity AFF 113
4 Moanin'
  Jazz Messengers/Blue Note BST 84003
5 Three Blind Mice
  Jazz Messengers/United Artists VAJ 14002
6 Gypsy Folk Tales
  Jazz Messengers/Roulette SR 5008
7 Keystone Three
  Jazz Messengers/Concord CJ 196

Ruby Braff

Born: 16th March 1927/Boston, Massachussetts, USA
Instruments: Cornet, trumpet
Recording Career: 1953-

UNFORTUNATELY for Reuben 'Ruby' Braff, being one of the most talented anachronisms in jazz has precluded him from working as regularly as his talent merits. It is not therefore surprising that, at times, he has become justifiably bitter about the jazz world. Originally, Braff built his reputation playing around Boston, before bursting on to the scene just as the 1953 Vic Dickenson sessions helped launch the mainstream jazz revival.

On these, Braff was outstanding: *Russian Lullaby* >**1** announced his warm, eloquent style; *Jeepers Creepers* >**1** was an object lesson in melodically flowing and creatively understated jazz; while *Keeping Out Of Mischief* >**1** best described his patchwork of styles, using the mingled yarn of **Louis Armstrong**, **Bix Beiderbecke** and Bobby Hackett. A brilliant trio date with Mel Powell followed in 1954 and offered in *You're My Thrill* >**2**, one of the most lyrical slow ballad performances of the decade.

It was undeniable that Braff, a young man of twenty-six, was playing in a style that was perhaps twenty years out of date, but he was doing it with such taste, such rhythmic subtlety and such inventiveness, that it hardly mattered. Regrettably, the public deemed otherwise and the late fifties saw him badly underemployed. There was an improvement in his fortunes during the succeeding decade, but with few recording opportunities, and it was not until a 1973-75 stint with guitarist

George Barnes that he began to enjoy the best of both worlds, the live performance and the recorded. Their excellent quartet produced its own kind of poetry on lovely ballads like *Old Folks* >**3**, and they stomped out together on jump tunes like *Liza* >**4**. Since then, Braff has worked New York clubs, toured extensively, and is playing as well as ever.

Lineage

Braff was influenced by **Louis Armstrong** and **Bunny Berigan** but there are times when his solo work has the ring of Jimmy McPartland or Bobby Hackett.

Listening

1 **Vic Dickenson Showcase**
Vanguard (JAP) K 18P 6186/7
2 **Mel Powell Trio**
Vanguard PPL 11000
3 **Plays Gershwin**
Braff/Barnes Quartet/Concord CJ 5
4 **The Best I've Heard**
Braff/Barnes Quartet/Vogue VJD 519

Clifford Brown

Born: 30th October 1930/Wilmington, Delaware, USA
Died: 26th June 1956/Bedford, Indiana, USA
Instruments: Trumpet, piano, composer
Recording Career: 1953-1956
Nickname: Brownie

HIS RECORDING CAREER may have lasted less than three years, but Clifford Brown nevertheless made a massive impact on jazz. He discovered bop as a teenager and, at the age of twenty, worked briefly with **Charlie Parker**. After a spell with Tadd Dameron's band, in 1953 he was part of **Lionel Hampton**'s touring band to Europe.

Brown had previously recorded with Dameron but, while in France, recorded with teammate Gigi Gryce without Hampton's knowledge or permission. His beautifully relaxed solo on *Strictly Romantic* >**1** was just one special performance from a session that announced yet another major jazz talent from the Manhattan hothouse.

After a short spell with **Art Blakey** in New York at the end of 1953, Brown was asked to join drummer **Max Roach** at the Lighthouse club in California. **Dizzy Gillespie** is reputed to have sung the praises of the brilliant youngster to Roach and encouraged the formation of the now legendary Roach/Brown Quintet. With first tenor saxophonist Harold Land and then **Sonny Rollins**, they made a stream of records that rate with any of that era. *Sandu* >**2** concentrated attention on Brown's control of vibrato at slow tempo, *Daahoud* >**3** showcased his sparkling articulation, while *Jordu* >**3** was an outstanding example of solo building through chance. His spirit of adventure produced daring phrases and seemed to permeate the entire ensemble. With Rollins, the group moved to an even higher plane and the masterful *What Is This Thing Called Love* >**4** introduced a sense of rivalry between Brown and the newcomer that added a further dimension.

Within months of this recording date, the trumpeter was killed in a motor accident. What his career still had to offer can only be a matter of conjecture.

Lineage

Brown was influenced by **Max Roach**

and **Fats Navarro**, the latter helping him tremendously – mostly in his means of attacking a phrase. To that he added his own unique lyricism, which can be traced in later hard bop players and most especially in the early work of men like Chuck Mangione, John Eckert, Herb Robertson and Tom Harrell.

Listening

1 Clifford Brown Vol 3
Jazz Reactivation JR 140
2 Study In Brown
Max Roach/Clifford Brown/EmArcy 6336 708
3 Clifford Brown/Max Roach Quintet
EmArcy 6336 322
4 Clifford Brown/Max Roach At Basin Street
EmArcy 6336 707

Dave Brubeck

Born: 6th December 1920/Concord, California, USA
Instrument: Piano, composer
Recording Career: 1948-

ALWAYS ONE of jazz's more controversial figures, Brubeck's piano

The Dave Brubeck Quartet, with its leader third from left

Right: Ray Charles

style, with its heavy chordal emphasis, made many enemies among the critical fraternity. Its harmonic complexity failed to convert them, and his great popularity with the general public (witness the pop chart success of *Take Five*) seemed to confirm their prejudices. And it has to be said the critics had it basically right: Brubeck's cocktail of Bach counterpoint, complex time signatures and straightforward jazz resulted in far too heady a brew.

In fairness, it must be acknowledged that the quartet that he led from 1951 to 1967 was not without its merits. Brubeck wrote good themes and in Paul Desmond he had an altoist whose smoothed-out **Lee Konitz** style was rich in melodic know-how. Titles like *Le Souk* and *Balcony Rock* >**1** show the band in its best light.

After the departure of Desmond, Brubeck worked for a while with **Gerry Mulligan** and *Blues Roots* >**2** and *Last Set At Newport* >**3** suggested a useful partnership. The new group's life was short, however, and from 1973 Brubeck began to tour with members of his family and to embrace the rock-fusion fashion of the day. *Blue Rondo A La Turk* >**4** wore the new uniform uneasily, and his loyalty to the style has continued to do little either for his group or for his still-excellent compositions. His 'popularity' with the critics remains constant.

Lineage
Brubeck studied for some time under French composer Darius Milhaud, but has had scant influence on jazz players.

Media
Film *Next Stop, Greenwich Village* (1975) used his early recordings as soundtrack.

Listening
1 Jazz Goes To College
Dave Brubeck/Phillips BBL 7447
2 Blues Roots
Dave Brubeck/CBS 63517
3 Last Set At Newport
Dave Brubeck/Atlantic SD 1607
4 Two Generations Of Brubeck
Dave Brubeck/Atlantic ATL 40 537 (SD1645)

Ray Charles

Born: 23rd September 1932/Albany, Georgia, USA
Instruments: Piano, organ, alto saxophone, vocals, composer
Recording Career: 1949-

BLIND FROM the age of six, Ray Charles Robinson emerged in the middle fifties to fill an important gap in the music world. Somehow he effected a synthesis of blues, gospel and bop-based jazz and created a personal style that was also a commercial commodity. Early records made while he was on the R & B circuit like 1953's *Mess Around* >**1** almost equalled the legendary boogie piano player Pine Top Smith in their in their naivety but, by 1954, Charles had his own band and was attracting a great deal of attention.

Initially, he featured himself extensively on piano and occasionally on alto but it was as a singer that he made his greatest impact. Soon Charles was touring as a self-contained show with his female vocal group, the Raelets. Charles struck up an immediate affinity with their leader, Margie Hendrix, and tracks such as *Lonely Avenue* and *What'd I Say* >**1, 2** became hit-parade material. The 1958 *Rockhouse* >**1** confirmed that Charles

appearance in *The Big TNT Show* (1966) and the title song for *In The Heat Of The Night* (1967). *Don't Tell Me Your Troubles* was used in *Who Is Harry Kellerman?* (1971).

Listening

1 His All Time Great Performances
  Ray Charles/Atlantic 2659 009
2 Early Ray Charles
  Charly R & B CRB 1071
3 Greatest Hits
  Ray Charles/Platinum LP 24002

Buck Clayton

Born: 12th November 1911/Parsons, Kansas, USA
Instrument: Trumpet, composer, arranger
Recording Career: 1937-

DURING THE middle fifties, there was a resurgence of interest in the swing-style music of two decades earlier. The 'mainstream' movement, as it was dubbed, helped re-establish many musicians who had become unwitting misfits in the pointless critical war that was raging between traditionalists and modernists. One of the most outstanding players to benefit from this healthy broadening of outlook was Wilbur 'Buck' Clayton.

To the fair-minded, Clayton had nothing to prove. He had already established a mighty reputation during a seven-year spell with **Count Basie**, a product of which was a particularly worthwhile musical relationship with singer **Jimmy Rushing**. After war service, Clayton played with JATP for a while but mainly freelanced around New York.

At first, suitable recording opportunities were few but in 1953 he recorded a jam session with the advantage of the then new long-playing record technology. *Hucklebuck* >**1** from that session became the anthem of the mainstream revival and showed that talented men like Clayton were better served by being able to stretch out in a way denied them on a three-minute single.

still had a taste for the jumping jazz group and his big band of the following year included players like Paul Gonsalves and **Zoot Sims**.

In 1960, he joined the ABC label and his move away from straight jazz began in earnest. String sections and 'heavenly' choirs formed the soft centre of *Georgia On My Mind* and *Ruby* >**1**, **3** but, as if to reassure the faithful, he recorded titles like *Hit The Road Jack, Busted* and *Let's Go Get Stoned* >**1**, **3**. The truth was that, like **Louis Armstrong**, all Charles' vocals became jazz, even if the material threatened to shackle him. Ray Charles' bands in the seventies and eighties varied a great deal but their featured vocalist remained the consummate artist.

Lineage

Instrumentally, Charles was strongly influenced by **Charlie Parker**, **Bud Powell** and **Thelonious Monk** but, as a singer, seemed affected in equal parts by blues singer Charles Brown and the velvet-toned **Nat King Cole**.

Media

Appeared in an acting role in the 1980 *Blues Brothers* film. Also featured in TV specials *Switched On Symphony* (1970), *NBC Follies* (1973) and *Cotton Club* (1974/5). Charles' other film contributions have been a leading role and songs for *Ballad In Blue* (1964), the title song of *The Cincinatti Kid* (1965), an

This change in musical climate suited the trumpeter; he re-established his contacts with Rushing and wrote arrangements for him. *Rosalie* and *Jimmy's Blues* >**2** attest to their quality, and there was always Clayton's own distinctive solo style to grace titles like *June Night* >**2**.

Clayton continued to make excellent records in this genre throughout the sixties and seventies. Players such as Emmett Berry, **Dicky Wells** and Buddy Tate were featured, and he was also captured to good effect in tandem with Britain's **Humphrey Lyttelton** on titles such as *Unbooted Character* >**3** and on a remake of *Hucklebuck* >**3**. In the eighties, bad health has restricted his playing but at the 1986 New York Festival he was at least prominent among the spectators.

Lineage

Clayton was influenced by **Louis Armstrong** and **Hot Lips Page**, and his own style is continued mainly through revivalists like Al Fairweather.

Media

Clayton featured in the film, *The Benny Goodman Story* (1955), and in *Jazz On A Summer's Day* (1960).

Listening

1 A Buck Clayton Jam Session Vol 1
CBS 21112
2 Little Jimmy Rushing And The Big Brass
CBS 21132
3 Buck Clayton With Humphrey Lyttelton 1964
Harlequin HQ 3005

Ornette Coleman

Born: 19th March 1930/Fort Worth, Texas, USA
Instruments: Alto and tenor saxophones, trumpet, violin, shenai
Recording Career: 1958-

ORNETTE COLEMAN was certainly not the first to attempt free form in jazz, but in providing the free language with a valid syntax, he became the personification of the music's finest ideals. He has been praised beyond words by devotees of his style – and dismissed as 'anti-music' by the sceptical. The parallel with **Charlie Parker** has been over-emphasised but, like the Bird, he began his main career to the accompaniment of much ill-considered abuse and had to wait several years to gain acceptance on a wide scale.

Coleman's early experience was obtained in the rhythm and blues field with leaders such as Clarence Samuels and Pee Wee Crayton. It was Crayton who, faced with his young sideman's musical 'experiments', actually paid him *not* to play! Undeterred, he made his first serious recordings in 1958 in the company of pocket trumpet specialist **Don Cherry**. It must be said that lack of consistent practice meant that his playing was not always technically secure but masterful performances like *Compassion* >**1** and the superb blues *Tears Inside* >**1** amazed the jazz world. The music was free, yet it had its own formal limits and its own logic. He wrote excellent themes, but used them merely as launching pads for his freely-developed blowing. The harmonics of the theme directed his solos without punctuating them. At times, he fashioned passages from scantily related, melodic statements, while on other occasions elaborated on each idea before passing to the next. There was no continuous 'storyline' and each adaptation resembled the original phrase only in its general design and interior balance.

In 1959, Coleman opened at New York's Five Spot Café to a storm of critical objection and slightly hysterical praise. Both he and Don Cherry were signed by Atlantic Records, who then sponsored their attendance at the School of Jazz at Lenox, Massachussetts. The irony of a situation in which the greatest contemporary jazz player took tuition needs no comment. What was important was that the quartet, with bassist **Charlie Haden** and drummers Billy Higgins or Ed Blackwell, made some of the finest records in jazz history. *Peace* >**2** was a model of the style, and has one of the leader's most brilliantly developed solos. *Ramblin'* >**3** is rhythmically vivacious, while *Embraceable You* >**4** shows how like **Thelonious Monk** Coleman could be when dismantling a popular standard. *Blues Connotation* >**4** was one of the most powerful performances, but the exquisite *Lonely Woman* >**2** remains the ultimate miniature masterpiece.

In 1960, he flirted briefly with Third Stream, the music alleged to bridge the gap between classical and jazz but, more significantly, he recorded *Free Jazz* >**5**. Using a double quartet, he made what was claimed, at the time, to be thirty-eight minutes of *ad lib* music. Later a 'blueprint' first take was found, but this did not detract from what was the first successful free form collective.

During 1963 and 1964, Coleman voluntarily withdrew from the scene to study trumpet and violin; when he re-emerged in 1965, playing both instruments, he was loyal to the trio of bassist David Izenzohn and drummer, Charlie Moffett, formed before his 'retirement'. This was the unit that made its memorable UK debut in 1965 at Croydon's Fairfield Hall. *Sadness* >**6** shows his alto power undiminished, while *Falling Stars* >**6** introduces his eccentric violin and trumpet skills. If anything, his playing on the two new instruments was yet more abstract, but it fitted his musical concept well and modified the pattern of his compositions.

In 1968, Coleman had a major personnel reshuffle: his young son, Denardo, became a permanent fixture on drums, and big-toned, tenor saxophonist Dewey Redman made it a two-reed front line. The considerable gulf between the two horn men's basic musical direction produced no stylistic antagonism and titles like *Rock The Clock* >**7** show that points of contact were easily achieved.

Even more drastic changes occurred in the seventies when a rock-influenced guitarist joined the group and Coleman coined the name 'Prime Time'. If anything, it concentrated the leader once more on his alto saxophone but as albums like the 1976 *Body Meta* >**8** and the 1979 *Of Human Feelings* >**9** show, he was occasionally lost in the clutter. The early eighties found Coleman an absentee from the recording studio, although Prime Time toured frequently. Nevertheless, his return to recording with *Song X* >**10** in 1985 was a triumph.

Ornette Coleman (second from left) fronts the New York Philharmonic

It was **Pat Metheny**'s date, and had Haden on bass and Jack DeJohnette and Denardo on drums, but the man who stole the show was Ornette Coleman.

Coleman has also been a major classical-style composer and performer and, although this side of his personality is outside the scope of this book, he excelled in the field. *Dedication To Poets And Writers* was a cleverly-wrought string quartet; *Forms And Sounds For Wind Quintet* showed a totally different side; while *Skies Of America* was performed by the London Symphony Orchestra.

Lineage

Coleman's early inspiration came from within his family, but the extent of his own influence has been comparable to that of **Charlie Parker** on bop. Almost all free-form players regard him with awe and the list of disciples is endless. More importantly, that list transcends the alto, tenor, trumpet and violin fields and embraces all instruments involved in free-form jazz.

Media

Film *Ornette – An American Experience* traced details of his life and he wrote a soundtrack for the film *Chappaqua* (1969), although it was replaced in the final editing. Coleman's music, however, does grace *Who's Crazy* (1965) and *Ornette – Made In America* (1981).

Listening

1 Tomorrow Is The Question
  Ornette Coleman/Contemporary S 7569
2 The Shape Of Jazz To Come
  Ornette Coleman/Atlantic LP 1317
3 Change Of The Century
  Ornette Coleman/Atlantic LP 1327
4 This Is Our Music
  Ornette Coleman/Atlantic SD 1353
5 Free Jazz
  Ornette Coleman/Atlantic SD 1364
6 Ornette Coleman In Europe
  Ornette Coleman/Freedom FLP 40103
7 Science Fiction
  Ornette Coleman/Columbia KC 31061
8 Body Meta
  Ornette Coleman/Artists House AH 1
9 Of Human Feelings
  Ornette Coleman/Antilles ANLP 2001
10 Song X
  Pat Metheny/Geffen 924 096-1

John Coltrane

Born: 23rd September 1926/Hamlet, North Carolina, USA
Died: 17th July 1967/New York City, NY, USA
Instruments: Tenor and soprano saxophones, bass clarinet, flute, composer
Recording Career: 1949-1967
Nickname: Trane

AS THE FACE of jazz changed in the fifties, certain players emerged as dominant voices: **Charles Mingus, Sonny Rollins, Miles Davis, Ornette Coleman** and John Coltrane became central figures in a jazz world that more than ever was fighting for its economic survival. John Coltrane was among the more fortunate, for his period under the aegis of Miles Davis gave him both the financial security and the fame to support his later ventures as a combo leader.

John William Coltrane made his musical debut in 1945, but spent much of his early career in the rhythm and blues bands of Eddie 'Mr Cleanhead' Vinson and Earl Bostic; periods with various **Dizzy Gillespie** and **Johnny Hodges** units were more rewarding. However, all of these challenges – great and small – helped to provide Coltrane with a grounding in both jazz and blues principles. In 1955, he joined Miles Davis and began a partnership that was to last, on and off, until 1960. In theory, they were imcompatible: Davis with his haunting tone and insinuating line and Coltrane steeped in ebullient overstatement. Indeed, there were problems which were not helped by Davis' refusal to discuss them. Early recordings such as *Just Squeeze Me* and *Stablemates* > **1** are not without tenor fumbles by Coltrane, but Davis pitched them around the middle register in which he felt comfortable, and this became a meeting-point for Coltrane's matt-toned tenor.

One of the factors that fostered a spirit of mutual co-operation was the way in which the bulk of the Davis quintet recordings were made. Most of the finest work was recorded in two sessions, in May and October 1956. It

improvisation. Kind Of Blue >**3** was as much a triumph for Coltrane as it was for his leader. He played movingly on the haunting *All Blues* >**3** and, on the modal *So What* >**3**, gave a clear indication that scales rather than chords would form the basis of his future musical experiments.

Concurrently, Coltrane had been leading his own groups; *Naima* and *Syeeda's Song Flute* >**4** showed that he had been working along similar lines away from Davis as well as with him. Once a leader in the full sense, however, he was free to direct his own destiny and, when the brilliant drummer Elvin Jones joined pianist McCoy Tyner and bassist Steve Davis, *the* quartet was complete. This group probably represented the high point in Coltrane's career. He was now released from the restrictions of normal extemporisational patterns even if, on the debit side, there were times when he was forced into a narrow channel of scale permutations. Whatever the theoretical restrictions, however, he would not be contained emotionally and 1960's *Village Blues* >**5** and *Blues To Elvin* >**6** have been judged among the most passionate performances in jazz history. Reed specialist **Eric Dolphy** spent most of 1961 in the band, although his very different outlook did not deflect it from its established musical policy.

After his departure, however, Coltrane made two recordings that were remarkably out of character, one with singer John Hartman, the other with **Duke Ellington**. His playing on both was conservative and presaged something of a change in attitude. *Wise One* and *Lonnie's Lament* >**7** were treated with similar circumspection, the tenor line staying close to Tyner's piano exactitudes, and scalar permutations avoided.

The powerful *A Love Supreme* >**8** came later that year and confirmed that changes were taking place, with Coltrane now writing down a great deal of his material. In 1965, he completely broke the mould with *Ascension* >**9**. Saxophonist Marion Brown told critic A. B. Spellman 'You could use this record to heat up the apartment on those cold winter days.' Certainly, much was made of the sustained high level of intensity but, too often, Coltrane's organisational know-how was ignored.

was as if the band reported to the studio and, on each occasion, placed a major part of its current repertoire on historical file. True, there were still times when Coltrane's elaborate lines sounded like three men playing in a telephone booth but titles like *Four* and *Trane's Blues* >**2** show greater maturity. A spell away from the band with **Thelonious Monk** furthered this process as Coltrane came to terms with that pianist's economy of movement.

Back with Miles, the two men found more and more common ground, as each expressed the desire to free jazz from normal, sequential, harmonic

Superficially, it seems a wild collective orgy of sound, but close examination reveals a clearly-defined formula for performance, one that could accommodate players like **Freddie Hubbard**, who were not normally associated with free music.

Ascension was the first record on which Coltrane employed tenor **Pharoah Sanders** and, after the session, Sanders became a permanent member of the band. Inviting this disciple and rival to join him was rather like throwing down the gauntlet but it proved to be a combination that worked. Coltrane certainly moved further toward free expression and a session like *Live In Seattle* >**10** gave irrefutable proof that the teacher had also been taught – at least in part.

Although the playing on such records evidences no frailty, Coltrane's health had begun to cause concern: in photographs taken on his 1967 Japanese tour he clutches his stomach in obvious discomfort. Diagnosed as a liver complaint, it forced him into hospital; sadly too late. Jazz was prematurely robbed of one of its great innovators, one whose influence continues to dominate all fields of music.

Lineage

Coltrane was largely influenced by **Dexter Gordon** and rated **Sonny Stitt**,

Sonny Rollins and **Stan Getz** as his favourite players.

His own influence was enormous, not only on major young players – **Pharoah Sanders**, Wayne Shorter, Billy Harper, Chico Freeman and Clifford Jordan amoung them, but, also on established players like **Don Byas** and **Dexter Gordon**.

Media

Coltrane, A Biography by C.O. Simpkins and *Chasin' The Trane* by J.C. Thomas both published 1975; *John Coltrane* by Bill Cole followed 1976.

Listening

1 **Green Haze**
   Miles Davis/Prestige 68-317
2 **Workin' And Steamin'**
   Miles Davis/Prestige PR 24034
3 **Kind Of Blue**
   Miles Davis/CBS 62066
4 **Giant Steps**
   John Coltrane/Atlantic 50239
5 **Coltrane Jazz**
   John Coltrane/Atlantic 1354
6 **Coltrane Plays The Blues**
   John Coltrane/Atlantic 1382
7 **Crescent**
   John Coltrane/Impulse A66
8 **A Love Supreme**
   John Coltrane/Impulse MCA MCL 1648
9 **Ascension**
   John Coltrane/Jasmine JAS 45
10 **Live In Seattle**
   John Coltrane/Impulse AS 9202-2

Kenny Davern

Kenny Davern

Born: 7th January 1935/Huntington, Long Island, NY, USA
Instruments: Clarinet, soprano saxophone
Recording Career: 1954-

LIKE TRUMPETER **Ruby Braff**, John Kenneth Davern is another gifted anachronism. He has usually been associated with Dixieland and its close relatives but, like Braff, he has an annoyingly consistent habit of being the best musician on stage in all sorts of company.

Miles Davis with Wayne Shorter (right)

Davern's credentials are unimpeachable: in the fifties he worked with **Jack Teagarden**, Pee Wee Irwin and Billy Butterfield, and in the sixties with **Eddie Condon**, **Wild Bill Davison** and Dick Wellstood. In 1973, he made a major contribution to Dick Hyman's brilliant tribute to **Jelly Roll Morton** >**1**, and two years later formed the excellent Soprano Summit with Bob Wilber. Tracks like *Lament* >**2** were outstanding, while perfect examples of the contrapuntal art (*Frog-I-More Rag* >**3** is typical) brought the Summit tremendous success over some five years.

In 1978, Davern made a free improvisation record with **Steve Lacy** which, against all the odds and despite poor recording quality, turned out to be remarkably successful: it was appropriately called *Unexpected* >**4**. Now with bassist Steve Swallow and drummer Paul Motian, Davern entered the free world and played without once resorting to a trite phrase. At 1986's 'Tribute To Wild Bill Davison' show at the New York Festival, Davern was the youngest man on stage – and shamelessly stole the show.

Lineage
Davern was influenced by **Louis Armstrong** and **Pee Wee Russell**.

Media
Appeared in the film *The Hustler* (1961).

Listening
1 Tribute To Jelly Roll Morton
   Dick Hyman/Columbia BL 32587
2 Soprano Summit
   Concord CJ 52
3 Soprano Summit
   World Jazz WJLP-S-13
4 Unexpected
   Kenny Davern/Kharma PK 7

Miles Davis

Born: 25th May 1926/Alton, Illinois, USA
Instruments: Trumpet, flugelhorn, composer
Recording Career: 1945-

IT SEEMS IMPOSSIBLE that a single musician could have *five* artistic peaks in one career, but this is just what has happened to trumpeter Miles Davis.

Davis came from an affluent family and was sent to study at New York's Juilliard School of Music. However, it was not long before he was working on 52nd Street and, in 1945, recording with **Charlie Parker** on the Dial and Savoy dates that are still placed by some among the finest jazz records made. In truth, the nineteen-year-old Miles Dewey Davis was hardly in the same class as Parker, and his playing on these sessions has always evoked mixed reactions. It cannot be denied that there was a degree of uncertainty in his work and Ross Russell, who organised the sessions, spoke of Davis as being slow to learn. There was, however, a distinct improvement between the November 1945 and March 1946 sessions, and a still greater one by the end of 1947, when titles like *Embraceable You* >**1**, *Out Of Nowhere* and *My Old Flame* >**2** show Davis in excellent form introducing gentle, almost reflective moods into the turmoil of bop.

During 1947, Davis met arranger **Gil Evans** and, in the following year, joined the coterie of musicians who talked jazz at Evans' apartment. Davis had just left Parker and had made a base at New York's Royal Roost. Somehow he persuaded the management to take on the band that had been the talking point at Evans' place. In simple terms, it was a pared-down version of the Claude Thornhill band with the advantage of stronger jazz soloists. Capitol Records were convinced that they should record them, and three sessions under Davis' name took place in 1949 and 1950.

The line-up of four brass and two reeds included tuba and french horn, the available range was three and a half octaves and there could easily have been a sameness about the outcome. In fact, the various arrangers found no difficulty in giving each selection a personality of its own. All took advantage of the tonal depth available, but whereas *Godchild* >**3** used the scope of the sound to draw Davis from the inner reaches of the ensemble, *Move* >**3** was something of a jam session. *Venus De Milo* >**3** moved imperceptibly from chart to solo, while *Israel* >**3** could almost be classed as an orthodox arrangement.

However, the essence of the band was that it deliberately set out to achieve a refined and calm mood of delivery through the beautiful way in which the horns were collectively voiced. In some circles, the result was

seen as the torchbearer for the emerging cool school. It may have been an artistic success, but the exercise was a total financial failure and the early fifties were something of a disaster for Davis. His health had not been good, and there had been other personal problems, but his success at the 1955 Newport Jazz Festival marked something of a turning point. He began to get together another band and the *new* Davis Quintet featured **John Coltrane**, Red Garland, Paul Chambers and Philly Joe Jones. This line-up was not without its collective problems but, very soon, ballad adaptations of *There Is No Greater Love* >**4** and *Surrey With The Fringe On Top* >**5** evidenced great progress. Davis, who had taken to the 'harmon mute', was playing superbly – his tone had a mysterious, 'smoked glass' quality and the rhythm section had overcome its early difficulties to emerge as a major strength.

In 1959, with altoist **Cannonball Adderley** added to the line-up, the band enjoyed its finest hour. Davis and Coltrane had been working towards modal ideals, freeing jazz from its chordal base and using scales to form the basis of their solos. The album, *Kind Of Blue*, was the culmination of their experiments, and nowhere better heard than on tracks such as *So What* and *All Blues* >**6**.

At the same time, Davis had been collaborating with Gil Evans and setting similar ideas in a big-band context. *Milestones* >**7** with a nineteen-piece orchestra had been a brilliant first try, but a later re-working of Gershwin's *Porgy And Bess* >**8** showed that there were still discoveries to be made. The pinnacle came with 1960's *Sketches Of Spain* >**9**, when all the elements fused together to give not only a jazz performance of indisputable stature, but a genuine work of art, too. Notable on this recording is the now-famous arrangement of the slow movement from Spanish composer Joaquin Rodrigo's *Concierto de Aranjuez*, originally scored for guitar and orchestra.

Davis' fifth and final peak seemed to sneak up on him. After the excitement of the Coltrane band and the Gil Evans triumphs, Davis used a number of different saxophone players, tending to play old material, and in the early sixties had undoubtedly got into a rut. Then, in 1964 Wayne Shorter joined him from **Art Blakey**'s Jazz Messengers and with recent newcomers Tony Williams, **Herbie Hancock** and Ron Carter in the band, Gil Evans was tempted to call them 'the best new group in the world'. *ESP* >**10** and *Nefertiti* >**11** gave clear evidence of the quality, and such was the leader's confidence in his men that some performances did not feature a Davis solo.

When Coltrane died in 1967, Davis was re-instated as the unofficial leader of the avant-garde's 'right-wing'. He reacted to this by winning greater acceptance with his own people. He became friendly with rock star Jimi Hendrix, and moved his music toward the rock field. Early in 1969, *In A Silent Way* >**12** suggested this might be a valuable musical seam to mine. Then, a dismal 1971 concert in London rather demonstrated that Davis had settled for compromise. The very poor *On The Corner* >**13** album confirmed this and there was talk of Davis being finished as a musical power. In fact, his health was not good and he retired for some time in the seventies but, just as the faithful were about to give up, Davis re-emerged. In the eighties, his music-making has failed to reach previous heights, but he presents an excellent rock-oriented package and still plays well.

Lineage
Davis was originally inspired by **Clark Terry**, but was greatly affected by his meetings with **Dizzy Gillespie** and **Charlie Parker**. His own influence is most discernible in hard-bop players such as **Art Farmer**, **Clifford Brown**, Blue Mitchell and Woody Shaw.

Media
Books, *Miles Davis – A Musical Biography* (1974) by Bill Cole, and *Miles Davis* (1982) by Ian Carr. Took a part in one episode of the TV series *Miami Vice* and performed the soundtrack of *Lift To The Scaffold* (1957).

Listening
1 **Charlie Parker On Dial Vol 4**
   Spotlite 104
2 **Charlie Parker On Dial Vol 5**
   Spotlite 105
3 **Birth Of The Cool**
   Miles Davis/Capitol CAPS 1024

4 **Green Haze**
   Miles Davis/Prestige 68317
5 **Workin' And Steamin'**
   Miles Davis/Prestige PR 24034
6 **Kind Of Blue**
   Miles Davis/CBS 62066
7 **Milestones**
   Miles Davis/CBS 85553
8 **Porgy And Bess**
   Miles Davis/CBS 32188
9 **Sketches Of Spain**
   Miles Davis/CBS 32023
10 **ESP**
   Miles Davis/CBS 85559
11 **Nefertiti**
   Miles Davis/CBS 85551
12 **In A Silent Way**
   Miles Davis/CBS 63630
13 **On The Corner**
   Miles Davis/CBS 85549

Eric Dolphy

Born: 20th June 1928/Los Angeles, California, USA
Died: 29th June 1964/Berlin, West Germany
Instruments: Alto saxophone, bass clarinet, clarinet, flute
Recording Career: 1958-1964

BY TAKING PART in the contentious *Free Jazz* >**1** experiment in 1960, Eric Allan Dolphy became linked with the music of **Ornette Coleman**, but, in reality, he had very little in common with the Texan master of free form. Dolphy was far more orthodox, his approach to tonality more legitimate and his solos possessed a more narrative logic. His early experience came in the bands of George Brown, Gerald Wilson and Buddy Collette but, in 1958, he joined Chico Hamilton's forward-looking quintet. When he departed less than two years later, by now a more radical player, he began a musical association with **Charles Mingus** that was to last on and off until the time of Dolphy's death.

During 1961, he briefly led a band with fiery trumpeter Booker Little and showed his alto teeth on an aptly titled *Aggression* >**2**. There was also an exquisite 1961 *Stolen Moments* >**3** with Oliver Nelson that challenged the jazz

world to name a more creative or more animated flautist. Almost all of the 1964 Blue Note album *Out To Lunch* >**4** was excellent, but it was still with Mingus that Dolphy's genius truly flourished. His bass clarinet was every bit as outstanding as his other horn playing and the solo with Mingus on *What Love* >**5** assumed the conversational cadence of a street-corner orator. Only months before he died came the recording of the sadly prophetic *So Long Eric* >**6**, again with Mingus, and as we now listen to his alto shimmying and feinting around the rhythmic centre it seems impossible to believe that Dolphy was making his last record at the age of thirty-six.

Lineage
Dolphy's favourite players were Buddy Collette and **Charlie Parker**, but there is little evidence of his own influence on the next generation of saxophonists.

Media
Appeared in the film *Jazz On A Summer's Day* (1960).

Listening
1 **Free Jazz**
  Ornette Coleman/Atlantic SD 1364
2 **Eric Dolphy At The Five Spot**
  Prestige PR 7294
3 **Blues And The Abstract Truth**
  Oliver Nelson/Jasmine JAS 20
4 **Out To Lunch**
  Eric Dolphy/Blue Note BST 84163
5 **Mingus At Antibes**
  Charles Mingus/Atlantic 60146
6 **Charles Mingus Sextet – Concertgebouw Amsterdam**
  Ulysses AROC 50506/7

Duke Ellington

WITH THE return of **Johnny Hodges** to the band in 1955, the old sound was revived. It was tenor saxophonist, Paul Gonsalves, however, whose performances changed the band's fortunes. His twenty-seven electrifying choruses on *Diminuendo and Crescendo in Blue* >**1** at the 1956 Newport Jazz Festival re-established the Ellington Orchestra in the eyes of the jazz world.

Popularity gave Ellington renewed confidence and fired a spate of composing that continued until his death in 1974. In 1957, he first performed *Such Sweet Thunder* >**2**, a suite devoted to Shakespearian characters: it seemed *Lady Mac*(beth) had 'a little ragtime in her soul'; Gonsalves and Hodges became 'The Star-Crossed Lovers'; while trumpeter Cat Anderson showed where Hamlet's mental breakdown led him in *Madness In Great Ones*.

In 1960 Duke flirted with the 'Ellingtonisation' of the classics, arranging Tchaikovsky's *Nutcracker Suite* >**3** and the suite from Grieg's *Peer Gynt*. The former was most successful, and titles like *Dance Of The Floreadores* show how intuitively Ellington could balance his own impeccable taste with an element of satire.

The band had now begun worldwide tours on a grand scale and the leader was greatly affected by the music he heard on his travels. In his 1966 *Far East Suite* >**4**, baritone saxophonist Harry Carney offered *Agra*, his musical portrait of the Taj Mahal, and Hodges took *Isfahan* into the realms of poetry. Back home, the brilliant *New Orleans Suite* >**5** allowed trumpeter Cootie Williams, bassist Joe Benjamin and Paul Gonsalves to pay their homage to **Louis Armstrong**, Wellman Braud and **Sidney Bechet** respectively.

In his last years, the great man gave several religious performances, of which his Third Sacred Concert, *The Majesty of God* >**6** at London's Westminster Abbey, was perhaps the most widely publicised. It was also his own fitting epitaph. (For biographical information and lineage, see entry in The Twenties, page 28).

Media

Ellington wrote film scores for or contributed to the soundtracks of *Anatomy Of A Murder* (1959), *Paris Blues* (1961), *Assault On A Queen* (1966), *Change Of Mind* (1969), and *England Made Me* (1972). His music was also used on the soundtrack of *Zoot Suit* (1981) and he wrote the theme for the 1960-61 TV series *The Asphalt Jungle*. Outstanding books include *The World Of Duke Ellington* by Stanley Dance (1973) and *Duke Ellington* by Peter Gammond (1986) as well as the autobiographical *Music Is My Mistress* (1973).

Listening

1 At Newport
  Duke Ellington/CBS 84403
2 Such Sweet Thunder
  Duke Ellington/CBS 84405
3 Nutcracker Suite
  Duke Ellington/CBS 84413
4 Far East Suite
  Duke Ellington/RCA PL 45699
5 New Orleans Suite
  Duke Ellington/Atlantic 2400 135
6 The Majesty Of God
  Duke Ellington/RCA A PL 1-0785

Ella Fitzgerald

Born: 25th April 1918/Newport News, Virginia, USA
Instrument: Vocals
Recording Career: 1935-

WHEN DISCOVERED in an amateur show in New York, Ella Fitzgerald was just sixteen. She joined **Chick Webb**'s band, becoming the idol of Harlem's Savoy Ballroom and, on his death, took over the band. However, the difficulties of this forced her in 1940 to give it up and become instead a solo act in vaudeville.

In 1946, she began to work for JATP and to tour worldwide. If anything, her voice had improved, and she began to set standards that were beyond all but the likes of **Sarah Vaughan**. Her intonation was precise, her articulation like a perfect line of type and her ability to swing equal to that of most top horn players. She used scat in her more jazz-filled moments, and brought to many trite, popular songs a dignity that they did not deserve.

In 1955, Ella first recorded for Norman Granz who led her to embark on a series of 'Song Books' that set

Duke Ellington and, opposite page, Eric Dolphy

Erroll Garner

Born: 15th June 1923/Pittsburgh, Pennsylvania, USA
Died: 2nd January 1977/Los Angeles, California, USA
Instrument: Piano, composer
Recording Career: 1945-1976

IN COMMON WITH **Fats Waller**, Garner was a pianist whose style proved acceptable to the general public. His secret lay probably in a choice of material encompassing popular songs and the odd, highly-melodic original, while his delivery was also particularly effective. The dragged, single notes of the right hand were supported by a guitar-like effect with the left, and the whole was dressed up with an abstract opening cadenza. This complex blend is heard at its most persuasive and lucid in titles like *I'll Remember April* and *Autumn Leaves* >1 from his famous *Concert By The Sea* recording.

Erroll Louis Garner first recorded with Slam Stewart's Trio and made a considerable number of records in the late forties. His dates with **Charlie Parker** presented an uneasy compromise; the otherwise rewarding *Birds Nest* and *Cool Blues* >2 were disrupted by the clash of Garner's gently contoured lines with Parker's natural angularity.

During the fifties, Garner changed record companies several times but albums, including *Concert By The Sea*, continued to appear. He took part in a *Piano Parade* with **Art Tatum**, **Meade Lux Lewis** and Pete Johnson and continued to tour with his own trio. In the sixties he frequently came to Europe and continued to appear with major symphony orchestras as a star soloist. *Misty* >3 from 1959 proved to be a popular hit and became an evergreen, but the peak for Garner in the seventies was a 1974-75 season that teamed him with the National Symphony in Washington. Sadly, health problems also began in 1975 and he spent much of the following year convalescing in California. This remarkable little man left many friends. He had been a total musician, combining head and heart in equal

standards that were hard to match. The albums of **Duke Ellington** >1, George Gershwin >2, and Cole Porter >3 were perhaps the best, but all had many moments of the highest quality.

After a bout of eye trouble in the seventies, she has moved into the eighties still happy to perform at concerts and jazz festivals, although illness again troubled her in 1986.

Lineage
Fitzgerald is largely self-taught and, because of her daunting musical standards, has had few disciples.

Media
Featured in the film *Pete Kelly's Blues* (1955) and has made TV appearances with Frank Sinatra. Sang the title track of *But Not For Me* (1959) and featured in *Let No Man Write My Epitaph* (1960).

Listening
1 **The Duke Ellington Song Book Vol 1**
Ella Fitzgerald/Verve 2683 059
2 **The George Gershwin Song Book Vol 1**
Ella Fitzgerald/Metro 2682 044
3 **Ella Sings The Cole Porter Song Book**
Ella Fitzgerald/Verve 2683 004

proportions and it was no coincidence that one of his best albums was called *Play It Again, Erroll* >**4**.

Lineage

There is much of **Art Tatum**'s romanticism in his playing, but his influence was mainly on cocktail pianists who prostituted the style outrageously.

Media

Garner composed for and performed on the soundtracks of *A New King Of Love* (1963), *Play Misty For Me* (1971), *Drive-in* and *Poto And Cabengo* (both 1979). Biography *The Most Happy Piano* (1985) written by James N. Doran.

Listening

1 Misty/Concert By The Sea
Erroll Garner/CBS 22185
2 Charlie Parker On Dial Vol 1
Spotlite 102
3 Erroll Garner
Phillips 6338978
4 Erroll Garner
CBS 88129

Stan Getz

**Born: 2nd February 1927/
Philadelphia, Pennsylvania, USA
Instrument: Tenor saxophone
Recording Career: 1944-**

ONE OF JAZZ's truly great improvisers, Stanley Getz mastered the art of rebuilding a standard tune in the days of the three-minute single. Perhaps, as a result, he resented anything that wasted time and space and, when LPs gave him more of both in with which to work, he did not squander the opportunity.

Getz's musical grounding came in big bands and included over a year with **Stan Kenton**. In 1947, however, he joined **Woody Herman** and, with **Zoot Sims**, Herbie Steward and Serge Chaloff, became part of the *Four Brothers* >**1** sax section. Jimmy Giuffre's tune, and the Herman band's interpretation of it, certainly helped his career and in the early fifties he was a much sought-after combo leader.

Although conceding that items like *There's A Small Hotel* or *My Old Flame* >**2** emphasised the cool, slightly unemotional side of his jazz, they nevertheless remained models of inventive, new-tune realisation. Touring with JATP in 1957 and 1958 seemed to bring this fact home to Getz and, from that date onward, there was an increased emphasis on emotional projection and less inclination to stick to the safe phrase.

Some of the most successful 'horn plus strings' recordings were made in 1961, with quite brilliant arrangements by Eddie Sauter >**3**. In the following year, Getz recorded *Desafinado* >**4** and began concentrating on the music of the bossa nova dance. This was never a totally happy marriage of styles and the jazz world was delighted when he returned to a more straight-ahead musical policy in the late sixties.

Despite the inclusion of men with rock-fusion reputations, Getz's seventies groups made few concessions. Though he performed in rock clubs, his own personal manner of playing remained constant and, at the 1986 New York Festival, he led an orthodox quartet with all his old dash; the tone was heavier, but still beautiful, and his flair for melodic development flowed out of every chorus.

Lineage

Getz is unquestionably of the **Lester Young** school although he, in the main, influenced men from the cool school like Richie Kamuca, Bill Perkins, Bob Cooper, Dick Hafer, Jerry Coker and Don Lanphere.

Media

Featured in the films *The Benny Goodman Story* (1955), *The Hanged Man* (1964), *The Exterminator* (1980). Wrote soundtrack for *Mickey One* (1965).

Listening

1 The Thundering Herds
Woody Herman/CBS 66378
2 Stan Getz Quintets
OJC 121
3 Focus On Stan Getz
Verve SVSP 29/30
4 Getz/Gilberto
Verve 2304 071

Johnny Griffin

Born: 24th April 1928/Chicago, Illinois, USA
Instruments: Tenor saxophone, composer
Recording Career: 1946-

NOT WITHOUT REASON has Griffin been dubbed the fastest tenor in the (mid)West. Almost from the moment he emerged on record he has shown himself to be a brilliant technician, an improviser who can think clearly at speed and a swinger who almost took hard bop back to the rhythmic climate of two decades earlier.

He came from the unsung (they had few recording opportunities) Chicago bebop school, had experience with the big band of **Lionel Hampton**, then worked with Joe Morris, Jo Jones and Arnett Cobb. In 1957, he joined **Art Blakey**'s Jazz Messengers and thereby began his true education. The drummer introduced him to the baptist rock of *Right Down Front* >**1** and encouraged Griffin to go holy rolling in a more simplified tenor style. The message certainly seemed to have got across and Griffin's own *Purple Shades* >**2** gets a similar treatment.

Thelonious Monk was guest on that session and, in the following year, Griffin spent almost a year in the pianist's band. Unfortunately, the baptist rock had a hold and it led rather too comfortably into the soul movement in the late fifties. The sixties proved more positive, however, and Griffin joined forces with fellow tenor Lockjaw Davis, made a series of records that contained a substantial proportion of Monk material and returned to more 'straight ahead' virtues.

In 1962, Griffin took up residency in Europe, living first in Paris but then buying a farm in Holland. Records like *Leave Me Alone Blues* >**3** with fellow expatriates continued to appear and he was always prominent at European jazz festivals. *At The Montreux Festival, 1975* >**4** was one such example and there were still albums with Europeans to show his superiority to the locals. In the early eighties he began working with the Paris Reunion Band, with whom

he appeared at the 1985 Pendley Jazz Festival in England.

Lineage
Charlie Parker was his favourite tenor but Griffin also exchanged ideas with fellow Chicagoans like the late Nicky Hill.

Media
Played on the soundtrack of *Des Enfants Gâtés* (1977).

Listening
1 Buhaina – The Continuing Message
   Art Blakey/Affinity AFF 113
2 Jazz Connection
   Art Blakey/Atlantic K 50248
3 You Leave Me Breathless
   Johnny Griffin/Black Lion BLP 30134
4 At The Montreux Festival
   Dizzy Gillespie/Pablo 2310 749

Lee Konitz

Born: 13th October 1927/Chicago, Illinois, USA
Instruments: Alto, soprano and tenor saxophones
Recording Career: 1947-

ONE OF JAZZ's true mavericks, Lee Konitz emerged from the clinical atmosphere of the Claude Thornhill band, and was almost unique in ignoring the all-pervading influence of **Charlie Parker** in the process of becoming a highly distinctive altoist. He had a minor role in the **Miles Davis** Capitol recordings, but made a massive contribution to the music of Lennie Tristano.

Konitz first recorded with Tristano in 1949 and was immediately sympathetic with the pianist's unique style. Neither was about to burst open the gates of delirium, but Konitz's seductively allusive style, with its naturally thin tone and occasionally imperceptible tensions, was an ideal match for the leader's piano. Relaxation seemed to be an unacceptable commodity and improvisation was all-important. The

Lee Konitz

Tristano school was a thing apart from the mainstream but its insistence on inventiveness did lead to daring experimentation. The appropriately named *Intuition* >**1** was an exercise in unshackled expression, devoid of any harmonic base and literally an abstract exercise that came nearly nine years before **Ornette Coleman**'s free-form revolution.

Although he never became an effusive romantic, Konitz did begin to warm up the tonal aspect of his music. His skill as an improviser remained unimpaired, while his slightly 'beefed-up' style was able to accommodate the demands of the 1952 **Stan Kenton** Orchestra where he was featured as a soloist. He made a guest appearance with the **Gerry Mulligan** Quartet in 1953, enjoying richly inventive outings on *Can't Believe That You're In Love With Me* and *Lover Man* >**2**.

For the remainder of the fifties and most of the sixties, Konitz was either a combo leader in New York or on tour in Europe. He was always delighted to work with Tristano and, even with his former mentor, he displayed more warmth on the 1955 *You Go To My Head* >**3** than would have previously seemed possible. The musical partnership between the two men had

always threatened to become permanent and in 1954 they had a well-publicised reunion for concert and club dates.

The change in the emotional climate of Konitz's playing had made him a distinctly more animated player, and this was a condition that he carried into the seventies with some particularly impressive nonet recordings. In this bigger unit, he had the chance to shout a little: the band boasted four brass and although Konitz the leader was still conscious of sound blends, he could turn up the volume tastefully when required to achieve the desired effect. *Moon Dreams* >**4**, arranged by **Gil Evans**, is hardly raucous but his own *April* >**4** jumped with heavier shoes, while *Primrose Path* >**5** almost took an excitingly dissonant **Charles Mingus**-like route.

The Konitz of the eighties is back with smaller units as well as touring as a solo but, whatever the environment, the altoist seems able to transmute even the most ordinary musical copper into the cool beauty of improvised gold.

Lineage

Konitz was more influenced by the Claude Thornhill band and by pianist Lennie Tristano than by any saxophonist. His own influence was most felt in the middle fifties and can be traced in the gentle side of altoists **Art Pepper**, Lennie Niehaus, Bud Shank and Johnny Dankworth, as well as tenor saxophonist Hans Koller and baritone specialist Lars Gullin.

Media

Wrote film soundtracks for *A Place For Lovers* (1968), *Desperate Characters* (1971) and *Cops And Robbers* (1973).

Listening

1 Crosscurrents
Lennis Tristano/Tadd Dameron/Affinity
AFF 149

2 The Complete Pacific Jazz & Capitol Records of The Original Gerry Mulligan Quartet And Tentette With Chet Baker
Mosaic MR 5-102

3 That's Jazz Vol 15
Lennie Tristano/Atlantic ATL 50245

4 Live At Laren
Lee Konitz/Soul Note SN 1069

5 Yes Yes Nonette
Lee Konitz/Steeple Chase SCS 1119

153

Humphrey Lyttelton

Born: 23rd May 1921/Windsor, Berkshire, England
Instruments: Trumpet, clarinet, piano
Recording Career: 1948-
Nickname: Humph

BEGINNING his playing career with George Webb's Dixielanders, Lyttelton formed his own band in 1948 and went on to become one of the world's outstanding New Orleans revivalist leaders. By 1949, his band included trombonist Keith Christie and clarinettist Wally Fawkes, and his repertoire mixed jazz standards with excellent original material. Fine renditions of *Irish Black Bottom*, *Snake Rag* >**1** and *Tom Cat Blues* >**3** rubbed shoulders with *Trog's Blues* >**2** and *Suffolk Air* >**3** and all showed how well-integrated the band had become.

In 1951, Lyttelton joined forces with members of the Graham Bell band from Australia and the following year produced novel fusion music in the Grant–Lyttelton Paseo Jazz Band. At the heart of all of these bands was the leader's excellent **Louis Armstrong**-inspired trumpet and Fawkes' warm-toned clarinet; this was further strengthened in the mid-fifties by the introduction of altoist Bruce Turner, a quirky soloist who at the time occupied the stylistic hinterland between **Johnny Hodges** and **Lee Konitz**.

Unfortunately, this presaged the band's move toward mainstream jazz, an area where Lyttelton was less comfortable. His first band in the style, with Joe Temperley, Jimmy Skidmore and Tony Coe, came over well on *Triple Exposure* >**4** but personnel changes, rather than bringing fresh ideas, instead led to a somewhat repetitive pattern. The inspiration of tourists such as **Jimmy Rushing** and **Buck Clayton** did help, but this was not the leader's most successful style. Even today, his band sounds happiest when it slips back to more traditional material.

Lineage
Lyttelton followed the **Louis Armstrong** style with great success but the later influence of **Buck Clayton** was assimilated less easily.

Media
Lyttelton has own BBC radio programme *Best Of Jazz On Record*. He is an excellent raconteur and has appeared on various TV panel shows. He played on the soundtrack of *It's Great To Be Young* (1956) and featured in *The Tommy Steele Story* (1957).

Listening
1 A Tribute To Humph Vol 1
   Humphrey Lyttelton/Dormouse DM 1
2 A Tribute To Humph Vol 2
   Humphrey Lyttelton/Dormouse DM 2
3 A Tribute To Humph Vol 3
   Humphrey Lyttelton/Dormouse DM 3
4 Triple Exposure
   Humphrey Lyttelton/Parlophone PMC 1110

Howard McGhee

**Born: 16th March 1918/Tulsa,
Oklahoma, USA
Instruments: Trumpet, clarinet,
piano, tenor and alto saxophones,
composer
Recording Career: 1942-
Nicknames: Maggie, McGoo**

BEFORE THE ADVENT of 'modern'
jazz, Howard McGhee learned his trade
in the bands of **Lionel Hampton**, Andy
Kirk, Charlie Barnet and **Count Basie**,
prior to the important move that took
him into the **Coleman Hawkins** Band of
1944. Hawkins had become involved in
bop and, if anything, 1945 titles like
Rifftide and *Disorder At The Border* >**1**
show McGhee as the man most
prepared to throw himself whole-
heartedly into the new music.

    Charlie Parker certainly thought so
and poached him in 1947 for excellent
performances like the aptly titled
Relaxin' At Camarillo >**2** and *Carvin'
The Bird* >**2**. McGhee seemed to be
everyone's choice at the time and he
even drew blades with the daunting
Fats Navarro to produce sparkling
duels on *Double Talk* and *The
Skunk* >**3**. There was power to
McGhee's playing, too, acquired in the
big bands, which proved useful when
he played with JATP in 1947 and 1948.

    In the fifties, drug addiction forced
him off the scene for some time but, on
his return in 1961, the excellent
Maggie's Back In Town >**4** with pianist
Phineas Newborn Jr presented a wiser
man, and a more restrained but no less
inventive trumpeter. *Willow Weep For
Me* >**4** was an especially moving ballad
performance and typical of his small
group work in the sixties. He fronted a
big band briefly in 1966, but continued
to lead his own group in clubs in and
around New York through the
seventies. Despite major surgery in
1982 his resilience and personal
courage enabled him to undertake a
European trip later that year. At
London's Canteen in June 1982 he was
careful rather than inspired but, for a
man of sixty-eight, played impressively.

Lineage
McGhee's initial inspiration came from
Louis Armstrong and **Roy Eldridge**,
but he later turned toward bop and
Dizzy Gillespie.

Listening
1 **Disorder At The Border**
   Coleman Hawkins/Spotlite 121
2 **Charlie Parker On Dial Vol 3**
   Spotlite 103
3 **The Fabulous Fats Navarro**
   Blue Note BLP 1532
4 **Maggie's Back In Town**
   Howard McGhee/Contemporary SCA 5030

Jackie McLean

**Born: 17th May 1932/New York City,
NY, USA
Instruments: Alto saxophone, flute,
composer
Recording Career: 1955-**

ONE OF THE outstanding hard bop
musicians, John Lenwood McLean
studied with pianist **Bud Powell** and
came to prominence with Paul Bley and
Charles Mingus; but it was as one of
Art Blakey's Jazz Messengers, and
later as a small combo leader, that he
made his indelible mark on jazz.

    McLean joined Blakey in 1956 and
made an immediate impression with
nimble improvisations, a light
distinctive tone and, on titles like *Scotch
Blues* >**1**, a ready sense of fun. He also

Jackie
McLean
ACTION
ACTION
ACTION

made records under his own name while part of the Messengers and tracks like *McLean's Scene* >**2** confirm his abilities as a master of the blues. This aspect of his style became yet more evident when he left the group in 1958 and began a programme of records with Blue Note that continued until 1967.

These records might not have appealed to the general public, but *Jackie's Bag* >**3**, *Bluesnick* >**4** and *Vertigo* >**5** became highly popular with the jazz *cognoscenti*. They demonstrated how hard bop should be played, with plenty of attack, the alto riding strongly on the crest of the beat, and solos that built to a climatic finish. The results were exciting, but never contrived, and it came as something of a shock when 1963's *One Step Beyond* >**6** announced that McLean had adjusted his sights. In attempting to assimilate the message of **Ornette Coleman**, something of McLean's lightly bouncing authority was lost. In 1967, he actually used Coleman as his trumpeter on a record date, but most observers were relieved when he returned to the formula he had mastered.

During 1972 he taught full time at Hartt College of Hartford University, building up their Afro-American Music Dept, then helped form The Artist Collective to teach inner-city children music, dance and the visual arts.

McLean spent some time in Europe and, after 1975, often worked with his son Rene on tenor sax. No record has appeared under his name since 1979 but live performances have shown he is still playing with the same effortless fluency and contagious enthusiasm.

Lineage

McLean's favourite players are **Charlie Parker** and **Sonny Rollins**; although undoubtedly influenced by the former, he has never been a slavish copier.

Media

Acted and performed in play *The Connection* 1959-60 and in its later film version (1961).

Listening

1 Ritual
Jazz Messengers/Vogue LAE 12096
2 McLean's Scene
McLean/Original Jazz Classics OJC 098

3 Jackie's Bag
Jackie McLean/Blue Note BLP 4051
4 Bluesnick
Jackie McLean/Blue Note BST 84067
5 Vertigo
Jackie McLean/Blue Note LT 1085
6 One Step Beyond
Jackie McLean/Blue Note BST 84137

Charles Mingus

Born: 22nd April 1922/Nogales, Arizona, USA
Died: 5th January 1979/Cuernavaca, Mexico
Instruments: Bass, piano, cello, composer
Recording Career: 1943-1978
Nickname: Chazz

AN INNOVATORY bass player and influential composer, arranger and band leader, Charles Mingus was an important figure in jazz history. Moreover, he was also an inspiration to young musicians whom he coached to maturity.

As a young man himself Mingus worked with **Louis Armstrong**'s big band and with New Orleans trombonist **Kid Ory**. More important was his grounding with **Lionel Hampton** and **Red Norvo** but it did not deter his more modern-minded personal friends from kidding him about his taste for 'old tyme' music. In fact, he had an interest in more modern forms from the middle forties and had a complete grasp of the harmonic principles of bop long before he began recording with its leading exponents. One has only to listen to him behind **Dizzy Gillespie** or during his own solo on *Hot House* >**1** to be reassured, and newcomers might appreciate the extent of his mastery by humming *What Is This Thing Called Love* above his bass line.

His style exhibited different priorities from those of early bop men Tommy Potter, Curley Russell or Al McKibbon. Mingus sought to lose the feeling of the metronome and said: 'Imagine a circle surrounding each beat – each guy can play his notes anywhere in that circle and it gives him a feeling he has more space.' This theory was certainly borne

out by his playing, providing not only greater flexibility but also the driving intensity that became his trademark.

The ability to analyse his own music was obviously an advantage as a band-leader and, when he formed his first 'Jazz Workshop' in 1953, he exploited it. However, his first recording date under the Workshop banner offered nothing really experimental other than a front line made up of four trombones.

The 1954 unit was very different and was particularly significant in representing a complete change in musical emphasis. The arrangements were prepared down to the last detail and members of the band came to regard any inclusion of unwritten solos as laziness. Cool jazz was still in vogue and in selecting ethereal reed players like John La Porta and Teo Macero, Mingus was keeping face with fashion. The arrival of the more volatile Thad Jones meant the addition of a trumpet, and a loosening up in the group's policy; titles like *Minor Intrusion* >**2** gave a first glimpse of Mingus the stylistic iconoclast.

In the following year, 1956, the full impact was felt when Mingus recorded *Pithecanthropus Erectus* >**3**, a stormy musical description of the first man to stand upright. For the bassist, it meant almost a complete about-face. In **Jackie McLean** and J. R. Monterose, he chose saxophonists with far more fiery styles,

abandoned written parts and encouraged his sidemen to regard their solos not as personal moments of expression but as intrinsic parts of a volatile whole.

The jazz world was left in shock, but Mingus showed no sympathy and this was to be the pattern of performance right to the time of his death. For Mingus it was like an act of exorcism: the door had been slammed on the cold, clinically analytical approach and his music became as flamboyant as the man himself. His band of 1957, with trumpeter Clarence Shaw and trombonist Jimmy Knepper, showed how much he enjoyed making music. *Tijuana Gift Shop* >**4** was full of musical bric-a-brac and argumentative traders, *Ysabel's Table Dance* >**4** flashed its rhythmic underskirt for the lady who was half-stripper and half-whore, while *West Coast Ghost* >**5** finally rejected the spectre of cool jazz in his make-up.

If anything, his 1959 output was even more dynamic. When Shaw left, Mingus did not replace him, which put considerable pressure on trombonist Knepper. He met the challenge triumphantly, leading the congregation into a frenetic *Wednesday Night Prayer Meeting* >**6** and playing a quite brilliant part in Mingus' tribute to **Jelly Roll Morton**, *My Jelly Roll Soul* >**6**. Other musical portraits, including *Goodbye Pork Pie Hat* >**7** for **Lester Young**, *Open Letter To Duke* >**7** for

Duke Ellington and *Eat that Chicken* >**8** for **Fats Waller**, showed just how well Mingus understood his dedicatees. In 1960, saxophonist **Eric Dolphy** joined the band and began an exciting on-off partnership that was terminated only by Dolphy's death. One of its highlights was the 1960 *What Love* >**9** but almost every recording they made together was a success. Mingus, for his part, was becoming increasingly interested in bigger line-ups. He felt that they would be able to transform his ideas from pastel shades to garish hues with more drama; and so it proved.

The remarkable *Black Saint And The Sinner Lady* >**10** was recorded with an eleven-piece and can now be seen as a prototype for other cosmopolitan works like **Charlie Haden**'s *Liberation Orchestra*, Clifford Thornton's *Gardens Of Harlem* and **Carla Bley**'s *Escalator Over The Hill*. In a way, *Black Saint* synthesised the early formal experiments and the hedonistic abandon of the *Prayer Meeting* >**6** period. Jaunty and simplistic ideas were built into complex collectives, his well-loved 'accelerating locomotive' effect was conjured up on *Hearts Beat* >**10**, and Jay Berliner even offered dazzling flamenco guitar.

Such was the impact of Mingus' music in the years from 1956 to 1963 that it has been described as a purple patch. Certainly he was inactive for almost four years in the late sixties but during the seventies toured extensively, often in Europe, and had sidemen as eminent as saxophonists Charlie McPherson and Bobby Jones and trumpeters Jon Faddis and Eddie Preston.

Despite occasional accusations that he was merely repeating old material and wallowing in the comfort of his established formula, new material did emerge. A 1977 concert, sadly destined to appear as the *Charlie Mingus Memorial Album* >**11**, gave a clear indication of his direction. Old and new jostled for the audience's approval, the result a draw. By then, however, multiple sclerosis had exerted its grip on one of jazz's greatest figures. A poignant moment occurred when Mingus visited the White House, President Carter putting his arm affectionately around the ailing bassist. Within the year Mingus was dead.

Lineage

Mingus learned bass with Red Callander and greatly admired **Jimmy Blanton**, Milt Hinton and Oscar Pettiford. For his part, he claimed that his music came from **Duke Ellington**, **Art Tatum**, **Charlie Parker** – and the church. His influence on bass players was tremendous, but the true spirit of his style can best be appreciated in the work of free players like Henry Grimes and Malachi Favors. As a leader he influenced the conservative wing of the sixties' new-wave musicians, but had no influence on the abstract expressionists.

Media

Appeared briefly in the film *Higher And Higher* (1943). Wrote the soundtrack for *Shadows* (1958/9) and his autobiography *Beneath The Underdog* in 1971. Book, *Mingus-A Critical Discography* by Brian Priestley (1982).

Listening

1 The Greatest Jazz Concert Ever
Gillespie/Parker/Powell/Mingus/Roach/Prestige 68319
2 Abstractions
Charles Mingus/Atlantic AFF 135
3 Pithecanthropus Erectus
Charles Mingus/Atlantic SD 8809
4 Tijuana Moods
Charles Mingus/RCA NL 89593
5 East Coasting
Charles Mingus/Affinity AFF 86

Modern Jazz Quartet

Original Line-up:
**Milt Jackson (vibes)/John Lewis
(piano)/Percy Heath (bass)/Kenny
Clarke (drums)**
Career: 1952-1974*
Nickname: MJQ
*(*Reunion concerts have been held
after this date.)*

IT WAS IN 1952 that vibraphonist Milt
Jackson had a record date on which he
used pianist John Lewis, bassist Percy
Heath and drummer Kenny Clarke. All
four relished the outcome and, as a
result, decided to stay together as a
group. Organised as a co-operative,
they chose the anonymity of the name
Modern Jazz Quartet.

The initial impact of the group was
tremendous: here was a group with a
latent inner fire, but one that gave the
superficial impression that every
phrase had been weighed, measured,
and prepared for immaculate
presentation. The dancing *All The
Things You Are*, the moving *Django*,
and beautifully paced *Delauney's
Dilemma* >**1** showed the extent of their
versatility and left no one in doubt about
their commitment.

In 1955, Clarke was replaced by
Connie Kay, and as long as items like
the evocative *Concorde* >**2** and
Bluesology >**3** remained in the
programme, all was well. There was,
however, a refinement of outlook that at
times threatened to reduce their music
to the level of a formula, albeit a
creative one. Their appeal to those on
the fringe of jazz prompted some rather
gimmicky efforts: their version of *God
Rest You Merry Gentlemen* >**4** is one
example.

Their best records tended to be
those that involved guests, but a session
with **Sonny Rollins** only drew attention
to his easy genius and to MJQ's rather
contrived pomposity. By the time they
disbanded in 1974, most jazz followers
were of the opinion that the group had
run its full course. Revival concerts in
the eighties have confirmed that
opinion.

Media
Lewis wrote, and the MJQ performed
the score for the Venice-based film
Sait-on Jamais? (1957). MJQ played on
the soundtracks of *Maidstone* (1970),
Little Murders (1971), *The Age Of
Peace* (1974).

Listening

Modern Jazz Quartet

Lee Morgan

**Born: 10th July 1938/Philadelphia,
Pennsylvania, USA
Died: 19th February 1972/New York
City, NY, USA
Instrument: Trumpet, composer
Recording Career: 1956-1971**

A TRUMPETER cast in the classic
hard-bop mould, Morgan possessed an
excellent technique, an embouchure
that never tired and the confidence to
attack his improvisations without
excessive preparation. He had his own
record date for Blue Note at just
eighteen, was allowed solo space on a
Dizzy Gillespie record session one
year later and, at the age of twenty,
joined **Art Blakey**'s Jazz Messengers.
   This was the ideal place for the young
lion, who now had the freedom to fulfil
his own record obligations and continue
to learn his trade under the master,
Blakey. On only his second recording
date, a muted, **Miles Davis**-like
Whisper Not and a slurringly moody
Moanin' >**1** showed that Blakey himself
was not short-changed. Under Morgan's
own name, contrasting albums like the
straight-ahead *City Lights* >**2**, and the
more soul-influenced *The Cooker* >**3**
defined the course of his career, while a
single title like *Easy Living* >**4** showed
the extent of his personal adaptability,
as he moved from the gently
conversational to the effectively
outspoken in one single trumpet
showcase.
   Morgan left the Messengers in 1961,
only to return in 1964 for another two
years' stay. This came abruptly to an
end when Morgan had a massive hit
record with *Sidewinder* >**5**. Originally
recorded in 1963, it made Morgan a
very exploitable property, and sadly
severed his connections with the
Messengers for good. It also set a
pattern for later performances: the likes
of *Soulita* and *Caramba* >**6** perhaps
showed more consciousness of the hit
parade. However, Morgan, always
keen to spread the message of his
music to as wide an audience as
possible, became an activist within the
'Jazz And Peoples' movement of 1970-
71.
   In 1972, Morgan was shot and killed

on stage at 'Slugs' in New York by a
former woman friend. He was still only
thirty-three and jazz had lost a major
talent.

Lineage
Morgan took inspiration from **Dizzy
Gillespie**, **Miles Davis**, **Fats Navarro**
and **Clifford Brown**. In turn, he
influenced second generation hard-
boppers like Randy Brecker.

Listening
1 The Olympia Concert
  Art Blakey/Epic LN 16009
2 City Lights
  Lee Morgan/Blue Note BST 84071
3 The Cooker
  Lee Morgan/Blue Note BST 81578
4 Expoobident
  Lee Morgan/Affinity AFF 134
5 The Sidewinder
  Lee Morgan/Blue Note BST 84157
6 Caramba
  Lee Morgan/Blue Note BST 84289

Gerry Mulligan

**Born: 6th April 1927/New York City,
NY, USA
Instruments: Baritone and soprano
saxophones, clarinet, piano,
composer
Recording Career: 1948- (1947 as
arranger)**

AS COMPOSER, arranger, player, or
latterly as leader, Gerald Joseph
Mulligan has excelled in all
departments of his craft. He has always
delivered a sense of quality. His first
playing experience really came with
Gene Krupa but, in 1948, he played with
the **Miles Davis** Capitol Band. In this
experimental unit, Mulligan played
baritone sax but, more significantly,
wrote arrangements for superb
performances such as *Jeru*, *Boplicity*
and *Godchild* >**1**.
   In the early fifties, he wrote for and
played with Elliott Lawrence and
Claude Thornhill but it was in 1953 that
he introduced his lightly swinging,
pianoless quartet with trumpeter Chet
Baker. The trumpeter played quite

beautifully on *Funny Valentine* >**2**, and on titles like *Nights At The Turntable* and *Bernie's Tune* >**2** the mood was of diluted bebop with a rhythmic relaxation akin to quality Dixieland. The group was a considerable success and throughout the sixties Mulligan led combos of varying sizes that took it as their inspiration. His gruff-toned but melodically uncomplicated baritone was well featured in all of them and it remained a style that was ageless.

In 1960 he formed a thirteen-piece band, for which he wrote superbly evocative scores. The instrumentation was imaginative and Mulligan used every tonal colour at his disposal. He returned to small groups in 1966, working with **Dave Brubeck** for a spell, but always seemed to return to the 'small big band' during the seventies.

Throughout his career, Mulligan made a series of recordings in tandem with other star performers. It is not surprising that those that brought the silky skills of Paul Desmond (1957) >**3** and **Johnny Hodges** (1960) >**4** scored over the untidy item with **Thelonious Monk** >**5**. Mulligan the soloist was always affected by those around him but he remains one of the best baritone saxophonists in jazz.

Lineage

Mulligan was perhaps as much affected by Claude Thornhill's band as he was by baritone Harry Carney. He himself influenced Pepper Adams, Lars Gullin and Ronnie Ross as well as many lesser-known West Coast players.

Media

Appeared in CBS film *Sound Of Jazz* (1957), and was also in *Jazz On A Summer's Day* (1960). He was seen and heard in the films *I Want To Live* (1958), *The Subterraneans* (1960) and *The Rat Race* (1960) and made early films as a member of the Gene Krupa Orchestra. Mulligan has also been responsible for the title song of *A Thousand Clowns* (1965), and the soundtracks of *Luv* (1967), *The Final Programme* (1973) and *La Menace* (1977). He plays on the soundtrack of *Pele* (1977).

Listening

1 **The Birth Of The Cool**
Miles Davis/Capitol CAPS 1024
2 **The Complete Pacific Jazz And Capitol Records Of The Original Gerry Mulligan Quartet And Tentette With Chet Baker**
Mosaic MR 5-102
3 **Gerry Mulligan Meets Paul Desmond**
Verve 2304 329
4 **Gerry Mulligan Meets Johnny Hodges**
Verve 2304 476
5 **Round Midnight**
Thelonious Monk/Gerry Mulligan/Milestone 68 136

for spells in the fifties.

On his return in 1957, Pepper recorded in Los Angeles with the current **Miles Davis** rhythm team and *Pepper Meets The Rhythm Section >2* proved to be a revelation. It introduced a far more emotional player to the jazz world. The Hollywood High School undershirt and its associated image was discarded and an altogether more mature player had emerged. One brilliant date, arranged by Marty Paich for a twelve-piece, showed how potent the 'new' Pepper could be in bigger band context. His great depth of expression made *Round Midnight >3* an exceptionally moving experience and, as a bonus, there was a sample of his idiosyncratic clarinet on *Anthropology >3*.

This set the pattern for the sixties. He used **Ornette Coleman**'s *Tears Inside >4* on one excellent session and, as the seventies rolled on, made records that were increasingly unromantic. A taste had developed, too, for powerful rhythm sections and Pepper used men like **Charlie Haden**, Shelly Manne and Elvin Jones. A 1977 version of *Cherokee >5* with Jones recorded live at the Village Vanguard showed just how far Pepper had come since his 'surf jazz' of the early fifties.

Art Pepper

Born: 1st September 1925/Gardena, California, USA
Died: 15th June 1982/Los Angeles, California, USA
Instruments: Alto, tenor and soprano saxophones, clarinet, flute
Recording Career: 1943-1982

THE FIRST recording by Arthur Edward Pepper was made in 1943, with **Stan Kenton**. After a four-year break he became a feature of Kenton's orchestra, on and off, in the period 1947-52, finally departing to concentrate on leading somewhat smaller combos. Records from this latter period show him to be a light-toned, highly melodic altoist, and an extremely inventive improviser: *These Foolish Things* and *Chili Pepper >1* from 1952 are typical. In fact, he could almost have been considered a prototype cool jazz player with a clean-cut 'Beach Boys' image! Unfortunately, his personal life was not so wholesome: he had a narcotics problem which forced him off the scene

Lineage

Throughout his career, Pepper's influences were **Lester Young**, **Zoot Sims** and **John Coltrane**.

Media

Powerful autobiography *Straight Life* (1979) told much about his personal life and Don McGlynn's excellent film *Notes From A Jazz Survivor* (1981) helped complete the story. Pepper played on the soundtracks of *Bells Are Ringing* (1960), *The Enforcer* (1976) and *Heart Beat* (1979).

Listening

1 Discoveries
Art Pepper/Savoy WL 70507 (2)
2 Pepper Meets The Rhythm Section
Art Pepper/Boplicity COP 004
3 Pepper Plus Eleven
Art Pepper/Boplicity COP 007
4 Smack Up
Art Pepper/Contemporary 68.613
5 Saturday Night At The Vanguard
Art Pepper/Contemporary 68.608

Oscar Peterson

**Born: 15th August 1925/Montreal,
Quebec, Canada
Instruments: Piano, organ
Recording Career: 1945-**

BEFORE JOINING JATP in 1949, Oscar
Emmanuel Peterson had already
acquired a hefty reputation in his native
Canada. As part of Norman Granz's
touring party, however, he was able to
reach a world market, giving him the
opportunity to record as he wished.
Despite his brilliant pianistic skills, his
early records were disappointing –
they were often live with JATP, which
discouraged careful preparation.

During the fifties, Peterson mainly led
trios in the company of guitarists such as
Barney Kessel, Irving Ashby and Herb
Ellis, but it was the excellent 1954
session with **Lionel Hampton** that
showed him in the best light. Early
recordings had made technique the
all-important thing but *Love For Sale*
and *Midnight Sun* >**1** were typical
examples of the way Peterson used his
tremendous talent for accompanying
other soloists.

In 1959, Peterson replaced his
guitarist with a drummer, Ed Thigpen,
and in so doing changed the outlook of

the trio. He now approached his solos
more directly, and with Thigpen a
permanent member for five years
seemed freer to examine the attacking
side of his playing. This was reflected in
a series of records originally made
privately for Hans Georg Brunner-
Schwer in Germany but which,
fortunately, were later issued publicly.
His first wholly solo album *My Favourite
Instrument* >**2** was one of them and,
like the remainder, presented Peterson
at his brilliant best.

Subsequently he moved back to
Granz's new label Pablo and, in 1974,
recaptured the spirit of the old JATP
with excellent albums featuring **Dizzy
Gillespie** >**3** and **Roy Eldridge** >**4**.
Latterly, he has tended to appear in
concerts more often as a solo pianist,
but such is his virtuosity and sense of
swing that a rhythm section is never
missed.

Lineage
Peterson is one of the very few pianists
with enough technique to be influenced
by **Art Tatum**, but he also listened
constructively to **Nat King Cole**.

Media
TV chat show *Oscar Peterson Presents*,
introduced other leading jazzmen.
Biography *Oscar Peterson* (1984)
written by Richard Palmer and

Peterson. Compiled and published *Jazz Exercises And Pieces* and *Peterson's New Piano Solos*. Played on the soundtrack of *Play It Again, Sam* (1972).

Listening

1 The Jazz Ambassadors
Hampton/Peterson/Rich/Brown/Verve 2683 050
2 My Favourite Instrument
Oscar Peterson/MPS BMP 20671-8
3 Oscar Peterson And Dizzy Gillespie
Pablo 2310 740
4 Oscar Peterson And Roy Eldridge
Pablo 2310 739

Sonny Rollins

Born: 7th September 1929/New York City, NY, USA
Instruments: Tenor and soprano saxophones, composer
Recording Career: 1948-
Nickname: Newk

THE DEVELOPMENT of jazz seems to occur in sporadic bursts: the years of fiercest creative rebellion inevitably followed by periods of consolidation. The early fifties must qualify as one of the arid periods, with the concentration of recording outlets on the West Coast giving an unbalanced view. One name which became synonymous with the return to greater musical imagination and integrity in the mid-fifties was Theodore Walter Rollins.

Early efforts with **Art Blakey**, **Bud Powell** and **Miles Davis** had not been overly impressive. The young saxophonist had mastered neither his instrument, nor the language of **Charlie Parker**. As a result, he spent most of 1955 'woodshedding', and working only occasionally in Chicago away from the centre-stage glare. The move proved beneficial and he emerged in the **Clifford Brown**-**Max Roach** quintet of 1956 as a far more complete jazzman. Moreover, Roach was present on Rollins' own *Saxophone Colossus* >**1** album from that year and the drummer gave steadfast aid to the player who had become, in little more than a year, a

virtuoso. Many observers consider it an album that typifies the jazz of the period: an irresistible swing was generated on *St Thomas*, and the rolling *Blue Seven* represented blues playing of the highest order.

Rollins had grown immeasurably in confidence and, in the following year, his sardonic wit was shown on parodies of tunes such as *I'm An Old Cow Hand* >**2** and *Toot Toot Tootsie* >**3**. Now he had become a pacesetter whose humour in no way disguised his massive talent as an improviser. In fact, the mastery of his material was daunting – he placed his notes with uncanny insight and used his muscular tone to lend credibility to every phrase.

Notably, years later **Miles Davis** voted him as the greatest tenor of all time yet, incredibly, Rollins was plagued with self-doubts. He embarked on a second sabbatical to ponder **John Coltrane**'s challenge to his 'supremacy' and to consider the musical direction taken by his friend, **Ornette Coleman**. The effect of this re-think was not immediate but 1962's *Oleo* >**4** illustrates how well Rollins was able to compromise between thematic loyalty and free form. The development evidenced by this album continued to mature over the next few years; titles like the 1965 *Three Little Words* >**5** show that he could think along freer lines even at a very fast tempo. However, Rollins made sure there were no self-imposed limitations, and on *East Broadway Run Down* >**6** from 1966, he abandoned the inherent blues structure and instead took it along modal lines.

A five-year retirement now followed but on his return Rollins continued where he had left off. *Playing In The Yard* >**7** took him into the funk field and *The Way I Feel* >**8** showed that he was capable of adding real artistry to fusion. Certainly Miles Davis is not alone in rating him so highly.

Lineage

Coleman Hawkins was Rollins' first and major influence, but **Charlie Parker** and, later, **Ornette Coleman** made a considerable impact. His own influence has spread to the likes of **Archie Shepp**, David S. Ware, Joe McPhee, **David Murray** and, together with that of **John Coltrane**, through to the whole field of sixties and seventies saxophonists.

Media

Made an hour long BBC TV special in 1974, mainly in Ronnie Scott's club. Wrote the soundtrack for the film *Alfie* (1966).

Listening

1 Saxophone Colossus
Sonny Rollins/Prestige 7326
2 Way Out West
Sonny Rollins/Boplicity COP 006
3 The Sound Of Sonny
Sonny Rollins/Riverside 68938
4 Our Man In Jazz/What's New
Sonny Rollins/RCA 741091/2
5 Sonny Rollins On Impulse
Sonny Rollins/Jasmine JAS 2
6 East Broadway Run Down
Sonny Rollins/Jasmine Jas 69
7 Next Album
Sonny Rollins/Milestones MSP 0042
8 The Way I Feel
Sonny Rollins/Milestones M 9074

George Russell

Born: 23rd June 1923/Cincinnati, Ohio, USA
Instruments: Drums, piano, composer
Recording Career: 1947-

DESPITE AN early life plagued by tuberculosis, George Allan Russell joined the **Benny Carter** Orchestra as a drummer at the age of twenty. Lengthy spells in hospital, however, diverted him toward the theoretical side of music. He studied composing and arranging and it was in this guise that he returned to the jazz arena. **Dizzy Gillespie** used his *Cubana-Be* and *Cubana Bop* >**1** on a big band session in 1947.

Flushed by their success, Russell began turning out more work and had arrangements accepted by Charlie Ventura, **Artie Shaw** and Claude Thornhill. Somehow, this was not enough, and in the early fifties he left the music scene to complete his *Lydian Concept Of Tonal Organisation*. In this esoteric theory, based on the ancient Lydian mode, Russell transformed chords into scales and took his music into the field of pan-tonality.

In practice, the music was still accessible to the layman and *The Lydiot* >**2** from Russell's own big band in 1960 and *Ezz-Thetics* >**3** from his sextet in 1961 could be taken as typical examples. In fact, the early sixties was a productive period for him; he was leading his own band and, as *Kige's Tune* >**4** proves, playing fine piano in it. He took the sextet to Europe in 1964 and later settled in Scandinavia. He remained there until the early seventies, playing, writing and teaching his LCTO to local musicians.

Russell's musical thinking during the late sixties became evident when his *Electronic Sonata For Souls Loved By Nature* >**5**, recorded in 1966 and 1967, was remastered with the aid of the modern mixing studio and issued in 1982. Back in America from the mid-seventies, Russell continued to play out his theories and rework old favourites: *Living Tune* >**6** was given a 1978 face-lift and *Ezz-Thetics* >**7** was reassessed in 1982 as the Lydian man continued to look forward. Both now used big bands in more detailed arrangements.

Lineage

Originally taught arranging by a fellow patient in hospital, Russell was later inspired by the compositions of **Thelonious Monk**. His Lydian theories have been used by many serious music composers and, within the jazz world, by educators like Dave Baker.

Media

The Lydian Chromatic Concept is the official text of the University of Indiana Music School and Russell has produced both LP and book *Listen To The Silence*

Listening

1 Dizzy Gillespie Vols 1/2 (1946-1948)
RCA PM 42408
2 Jazz In The Space Age
George Russell/Affinity AFF 152
3 Ezz-Thetics
George Russell/OJC 70
4 The Stratus Seekers
George Russell/Riverside RLP 412
5 The Essence
George Russell/Soul Note SN 1044/5
6 New York Big Band
George Russell/Soul Note SN 1039
7 Live In An American Time Spiral
George Russell/Soul Note SN 1049

Ronnie Scott

Born: 28th January 1927/London, UK
Instruments: Tenor and soprano
saxophones
Recording Career: 1946-

PROBABLY MOST FAMOUS as the owner of one of the world's finest jazz clubs, a London venue which has played host to a virtual 'Who's Who' of jazz dignitaries over its twenty-odd years' existence, Ronnie Scott has been as willing to feature the avant-garde of **Ornette Coleman**, **Cecil Taylor** and **Archie Shepp** as he has, say, **Sarah Vaughan**, **Ruby Braff** and George Melly.

Ronnie Scott on saxophone, leading his
orchestra

As a player, Scott is no less admirable. He worked with Ted Heath and Jack Parnell in the early fifties, forming his own band in 1953. The highlight of his playing career came in the years 1957 to 1959 when, with Tubby Hayes, he worked as co-leader of the Jazz Couriers **>1**, but he also enjoyed a spell as featured soloist with the Kenny Clarke–Francy Boland Big Band.

Currently he leads a quintet featuring trumpeter Dick Pearce and pianist John Critchenson, and continues to make his club the best musical oasis in London.

Lineage
Scott was originally impressed by the bop pioneers but it was Hank Mobley and **Sonny Rollins** who had the more lasting effect on his style.

Media
A regular broadcaster on British radio, Scott also appeared in the TV short *Archer Street* (1985). The story of his jazz club is told in John Fordham's *Let's All Join Hands And Contact the Living* (1986).

Listening
1 The Jazz Couriers
  Ronnie Scott/Tubby Hayes/Jasmine JASM 2004

George Shearing

Born: 13th August 1919/London, UK
Instrument: Piano, composer
Recording Career: 1937-

BLIND FROM BIRTH, George Albert Shearing was a highly successful player in Britain before permanently moving to America in 1947. At first, he worked as a single but, in 1949, the normally empirical process of organising a new group led him into a formula that was to change his career. Using a locked-hand chordal style as the best way of interlacing his piano lines with those of vibist Margie Huyams, and guitarist Chuck Wayne, he achieved a sound that captured the imagination of fans worldwide and the quintet became extremely popular >**1**.

Shearing remained loyal to small groups through most of his career although he did update his sound. He made guest appearances with many symphony orchestras and, in the early eighties, often stood in for the ailing **Count Basie** in his big band.

Lineage

Originally inspired by hearing **Fats** **Waller** and **Teddy Wilson**, Shearing later turned his attention towards bebop men like **Bud Powell**.

Media

Appeared in *Jazz On A Summer's Day* (1960) and made educational TV series with Father O'Connor in 1957. Wrote the score for the film *80 Steps To Jonah* (1969). Wrote own book, *Shades Of Shearing*.

Listening

1 Lullaby Of Birdland
George Shearing/Verve 2683 029

Horace Silver

Born: 2nd September 1928/Norwalk, Connecticut, USA
Instrument: Piano, composer
Recording Career: 1950-

THE EVOLUTION of jazz in the fifties owed much to the vital contribution of Horace Ward Martin Tavares Silver. With **Art Blakey** he was co-leader of the Jazz Messengers and together they redirected jazz from the millpond niceties of cool jazz into the turbulent waters of hard bop. Indeed, there was something drum-like in Silver's own percussive piano style and, when he formed his own quintet in 1956, he became the power source for that group.

An early line-up with Donald Byrd on trumpet and Hank Mobley on tenor provided a blueprint: the moody *Senor Blues* >**1** gave notice of things to come. In 1958, Junior Cook took over on tenor while Blue Mitchell replaced Byrd on trumpet. This group remained intact well into the sixties and produced what is now regarded as the classic Silver sound. Vital to the group were the brilliant compositions by its leader. *The Preacher* >**2** had featured in a 1955 Messengers' date, and its soul-searching stance still proved highly popular ten years on. *Sister Sadie* >**3**, *Let's Get To The Nitty Gritty* >**4** and even *Tokyo Blues* >**5** followed the same emotional path as *The Preacher*

and the adjectives 'funky' and 'soulful' became inseparable from Silver's name.

When they left in 1964, Cook and Mitchell continued to play in the Silver mode, while the pianist himself became more interested in lyric writing. However, the quintet he led remained a highly potent outfit. Exhaustive tours occupied much of the seventies, although Silver did 'retire' briefly in 1974. The eighties show his powers undiminished: a group with saxophonist Ron Bridgewater enjoyed a 1980 season at London's Ronnie Scott's Club and another with Ralph Moore (tenor) and Brian Lynch (trumpet) proved that Silver had lost none of his selective know-how when it stopped the show at the 1984 New York Festival.

Silver remains the archetypal, hard bop pianist: even a flowing melody like *The Dragon Lady* >**4** is attacked, and this aggression has permeated every group he has led. His great quality is to trade in excitement without surrendering his gifts as a tunesmith.

Lineage
Silver was strongly influenced by **Bud**

Powell and has himself been the model for younger pianists like Mulgrew Miller, James Williams, Billy Gault and George Cables, the favourite sideman of **Art Pepper**.

Listening
1 Sterling Silver
   Horace Silver/Blue Note BN-LA 945 H
2 The Jazz Messengers
   Horace Silver/Blue Note BST 81518
3 Blowing The Blues Away
   Horace Silver/Blue Note BST 84017
4 Silver's Serenade
   Horace Silver/Blue Note BST 84131
5 Tokyo Blues
   Horace Silver/Blue Note BST 84110

Zoot Sims

Born: 29th August 1925/Inglewood, California, USA
Died: 23rd March 1985/New York City, NY, USA
Instruments: Tenor, alto and soprano saxophones, clarinet
Recording Career: 1944-1984

ALTHOUGH A West Coast musician by birth, John Haley 'Zoot' Sims never

Below: Horace Silver
Opposite: Zoot Sims

completely fitted the cool West Coast mould. As a member of **Woody Herman**'s famous 1947 'Four Brothers' saxophone team, he gained early fame and his contribution to **Stan Kenton**'s 1953 'swinging' band was more significant than any other single player. Sims played well in big bands, but his real home was in small, blowing jazz combos. In the fifties he worked with **Benny Goodman**, **Gerry Mulligan**, Bob Brookmeyer and Al Cohn and the story was always the same: Sims was the player who always had time to get his ideas across; the delivery sounded almost accidental, and the solos were a very personal combination of melodic redesign, whispered asides, slurred blue notes and the merest of breath passing through the horn. Listening to him play a ballad like *Ghost Of A Chance* >**1** is like hearing it as a new tune.

A partnership with fellow saxophonist Al Cohn was particularly productive and 1960's *You 'n' Me* >**2** was typical of the recordings that they made together. Nevertheless, Sims began to change in the sixties, using a bigger tone and playing with greater economy. He played with JATP and as he moved into the seventies, began recording for Pablo. The outcome was highly successful: his sound became almost deliberately luxurious and he mixed small group sessions with work in larger units. *Basie And Zoot* >**3** and *Hawthorne Nights* >**4** are particularly

fine, although his delightful soprano playing on *Soprano Sax* >**5** is proof of his wide range of expression.

Lineage

Like many West Coast tenors, Sims was influenced by **Lester Young** and came nearer the spirit of Prez than any other player.

Media

Appeared in TV special with **Benny Goodman**, and as guest in one of **Oscar Peterson**'s jazz shows for TV.

Listening

1 One To Blow On
Zoot Sims/Biograph BLP 12062
2 You 'n' Me
Zoot Sims/Al Cohn/Mercury 6336 525
3 Basie And Zoot
Zoot Sims/Count Basie/Pablo 2310 745
4 Hawthorne Nights
Zoot Sims/Bill Holman/Pablo 2310 783
5 Soprano Sax
Zoot Sims/Pablo 2310 770

Jimmy Smith

Born: 8th December 1925/Norristown, Pennsylvania, USA
Instrument: Organ
Recording Career: 1956-

JAZZ MUSICIANS are usually products of their era, and this is certainly true of James Oscar Smith. By the middle fifties, an adverse reaction to the cool school was developing and a return to the roots of jazz became an exaggerated, but satisfactory, alternative. From this background, Smith emerged to put his chosen instrument, the organ, firmly on the jazz map.

Despite the claims made on behalf of **Fats Waller** and **Count Basie** in earlier times, the organ had had no jazz language of its own and, generally, was without a traceable tradition. Not until Smith exploded on to the record lists of the Blue Note label was a real identity established.

His earliest studies had been on

Above: Jimmy Smith

piano and bass, and in 1952 he joined Don Gardner And His Sonotones primarily as a pianist, before later switching to organ. In the three years to 1955, when he formed his own group, he formulated a style that was to revolutionise the organ's role in jazz. Fortunately, for both Smith and Blue Note, he began recording in the following year and produced a stream of albums that shored up the slightly ailing record label and made Smith a household name in black America.

Distinguished by the use of a far greater variety of stops than normal, Smith's style showed him to be inventive at all tempos and able to make telling use of instrumental devices unique to the organ. Trio items such as *The Preacher* >**1** and *The Champ* >**2** established his reputation,

but the introduction of horns set the pattern for the organ-based groups which swamped small American clubs in the sixties. Listening to Smith, however, never became a boring experience and titles like *Summertime* >**3** with Lou Donaldson, *Big Fat Mamma* >**4** with Ike Quebec, and *Back At The Chicken Shack* >**5** with **Stanley Turrentine** became big successes.

Inevitably, Smith sought to extend his musical spectrum and in 1962 switched to the Verve label. They set him into big band contexts but with mixed results. At his best on items like *Walk On The Wild Side* >**6** he used the shouting qualities of the organ to good effect but, on other occasions, listeners became conscious of a musician seeking refuge in the comfort of his own well-known formula.

By the seventies, Smith was in semi-retirement but has recently made a comeback. The methods remain the same, but nothing can detract from his pre-eminent position in the evolution of jazz organ.

Lineage

Smith's earliest influences were pianists **Bud Powell** and **Horace Silver** but, after switching to organ, he left his mark on players such as Shirlie Scott, Jackie Davis, Groove Holmes, Eddy Louiss and Lonnie Smith, not to mention a whole generation of amateur club players.

Media

Played in the films *Get Yourself A College Girl* (1964), *Where The Spies Are* (1966) and on TV in *Black Omnibus, The Mike Douglas Show* and *Dating Game*.

Listening

1 The Incredible Jimmy Smith At Club Baby Grand
Blue Note BST 81528

2 The Champ – Jimmy Smith At The Organ Vol 2
Blue Note BST 81514

3 All Day Long – Jimmy Smith At The Organ Vol 1
Blue Note BST 81551

4 Jimmy Smith's Greatest Hits
Blue Note BST 83367/8 X

5 Bashin' The Unpredictable Jimmy Smith
Verve 823 308-1

6 Walk On The Wild Side
Jimmy Smith/Metro 2682 025

Ralph Sutton

Born: 4th November 1922/Hamburg, Missouri, USA
Instrument: Piano
Recording Career: 1947-

FOR MOST of his life Ralph Sutton has looked like a bank president and played piano like a whorehouse wastrel. He began playing in public in St Louis at the age of fourteen and had worked with **Jack Teagarden** for three years before he joined the US Army. After demob, he returned to playing in St Louis, rejoining Teagarden briefly before talking over as intermission

pianist at **Eddie Condon**'s club in New York in 1948. This gained him popularity and a recording date, although his first titles did give a misleading impression: he was persuaded to record a series of ragtime tunes and for some time after was considered a specialist in this field.

In reality, what Sutton did best was to play stride piano, keeping alive the memory of **Fats Waller** and showing that a 'dated' style could still be an effective mode of expression. *Snowy Morning Blues* and *Fussin'* >**1** illustrate how well Sutton played the style: left hand pumping out a rhythmic base, the right balancing it with beautifully articulated arpeggios.

He made a little bit of history by being one of the first two American musicians to play legally in Britain after the Second World War.

In the sixties, he moved first to Monterey and then to Aspen, Colorado but continued to tour and record. In 1965, he became associated with the Ten Greats Of Jazz and remained with the ensemble for nine years after they became the World's Greatest Jazz Band – so called.

Sutton has since returned to working as a single, sometimes with a rhythm section but, as titles like the 1975 *T'ain't So Honey, T'ain't So* and *Changes* >**2** evidence, he is equally efficient without. Over the years he has also built up a considerable rapport with **Ruby Braff**, with titles such as 1968's *Someday Sweetheart* >**3** or 1980's *Keeping Out Of Mischief* >**4** rivalling the outstanding duet performances of the past.

Lineage

Sutton's influences were **Fats Waller** and **James P. Johnson**.

Media

Piano Man, The Story Of Ralph Sutton (1975) written by James D. Shacter.

Listening

1 Stacy 'N' Sutton
Ralph Sutton/Jess Stacy/Affinity AFS 1020

2 Changes
Ralph Sutton/77 S 57

3 On The Sunny Side Of The Street
Ralph Sutton/Hermosa BJAC 501

4 R & R
Ralph Sutton/Ruby Braff/Chaz Jazz CJ 101

Clark Terry

Born: 14th December 1920/St Louis, Missouri, USA
Instruments: Trumpet, flugelhorn, vocals
Recording Career: 1947-

ALTHOUGH ESSENTIALLY a musician's musician, Clark Terry plays with an easy lyricism that appeals to even the most superficial listener. In his early years he worked with **Lionel Hampton**, Charlie Barnet and Charlie Ventura, before joining **Count Basie** in 1948. He remained with Basie until 1950, even when the leader had reduced the band to septet proportions.

In the following year, Terry joined **Duke Ellington** and began a musical association that benefited both. The Duke wrote brilliantly for the newcomer: the 1955 remake of *Harlem Airshaft* >**1** and 1957's *Lady Mac* >**2** were tailor-made for Terry's particular gifts, as well as being typical of a long line of arrangements in the fifties. For his part, Terry produced a smoothness of line more in keeping with a reed instrument, but the bopper in him was never to be wholly denied and long legato phrases were usually punctuated by fiercely rippling arpeggios.

After leaving Ellington, Terry enjoyed a brief spell with Quincy Jones before becoming a staff musician for NBC in 1960. This meant a residency in New York and led to him forming a group with trombonist Bob Brookmeyer. Their partnership produced some impressive records, of which the *Power Of Positive Swinging* >**3** was typical. The situation also left Terry free for other recording projects and noteworthy albums were made with **Thelonious Monk**, **Ben Webster** and, most especially, **Oscar Peterson**. With the latter, the trumpeter introduced his own unique form of scat >**4**, although he preferred to call it 'mumbling', for reasons soon obvious to those who heard it. 'Mumbling' became a feature of his concert appearances through the sixties and seventies. For promoters George Wein and Norman Granz, many of these were perfect examples of what was liable to occur at a Clark Terry concert. Terry continues to play well in the eighties, but tends to work mainly as a single.

Lineage
Terry was initially inspired by Shorty Baker and **Dizzy Gillespie** but he has the distinction of being an acknowledged influence on **Miles Davis**.

Media
Active for years in US TV's *Johnny Carson Show*.

Listening

1 Ellington Showcase
Duke Ellington/Capitol T679 (ECR-(JAP)-88063

2 Such Sweet Thunder
Duke Ellington/CBS 84405

3 Power Of Positive Swinging
Clark Terry/Bob Brookmeyer/Fontana TL 5290

4 Oscar Peterson Plus One
Mercury 20030 MCL

172

Joe Turner

Born: 18th May 1911/Kansas City, Missouri, USA
Died: 24th November 1985/ Inglewood, California, USA
Instrument: Vocals, composer
Recording Career: 1938-1985
Nickname: Big Joe

ONE OF THE great blues shouters, Joseph Vernon Turner did not flourish (unlike **Jimmy Rushing**) in the world of big bands, and perhaps his finest work was to the accompaniment of outstanding pianists. His career was more or less launched by his early association with Pete Johnson in Kansas City and 1941's *Wee Wee Baby* and *Rock Me Mama* >**1** with **Art Tatum**, still rate among his best records.

Turner had little more than a four-note range, but he had a big voice and a vibrant sense of swing. He addressed audiences powerfully, cutting through the racket of Kansas City's hard drinking crowds with uncanny ease. For some observers, he typified this pure Kansas feeling, never better displayed than on the late forties *Old Piney Brown's Gone* and *Trouble Blues* >**2**.

In the fifties, Turner moved over to rhythm and blues and had a big hit with *Chains Of Love*. By now a very influential figure in the field, he never totally deserted the earthier end of the blues spectrum. He was part of the brilliant Johnny Otis show that rocked the legendary 1970 Monterey Festival >**3**, but it was the pure jazz dates that provide his most lasting obituary. The presence of Pete Johnson, Lawrence Brown and Joe Newman make *Low Down Dog* and *Morning Glories* >**4** on the 1956 *Boss Of The Blues* triumphs of the blues shouting art. In 1973, Turner made a sadly underpraised session with **Count Basie**, **J.J. Johnson** and Harry Edison that produced an irresistible *Flip Flop And Fly* and *Blue Around The Clock* >**5**. Turner spent his last years on crutches but featured at the New York Festival right until the last. He seemed as happy singing for blues buffs at clubs like the Ginger Man as he did standing on stage at Carnegie Hall.

Lineage
Turner was influenced by the records of **Bessie Smith** and Leroy Carr, and provided inspiration for jazz singers like Walter Brown, Cleanhead Vinson and **Jimmy Witherspoon**, as well as countless rock singers, including Elvis Presley, Mick Jagger and Shakin' Stevens.

Media
Appeared in brilliant *Last Of The Blue Devils*, a retrospective film about Kansas City jazz made between 1974 and 1979. Turner also featured in film *Boulevard Du Rhum* (1971).

Listening
1 Pure Genius
  Art Tatum/Affinity AFFD 118
2 Jumpin' The Blues
  Joe Turner/Arhoolie R 2004
3 Live At Monterey
  Johnny Otis/Epic 66295
4 Boss Of The Blues
  Joe Turner/Atlantic K 50244
5 The Bosses
  Joe Turner/Count Basie/Pablo 2310 709

Dinah Washington

**Born: 29th August 1924/Tuscaloosa,
Alabama, USA
Died: 14th December 1963/Detroit,
Michigan, USA
Instrument: Vocals, piano
Recording Career: 1943-1963
Nickname: The Queen**

EVEN THOUGH over-studious critics
found her success in the pop field and
popularity with the general public
something of an embarrassment, there
was no denying that Dinah Washington
– or Ruth Jones to give her real name –
was one of the really outstanding jazz
singers. Her only problem was that she
was good at everything she did,
whether it was rhythm and blues,
gospel, jazz, or just plain ballad-singing.
Fortunately, she always seemed able to
concentrate on whatever style was
required at any given time.

Her early vocal training came
through the church, but the idea of
becoming a singer was planted when
she won an amateur singing contest at
the age of fifteen. In 1943, she joined
Lionel Hampton and her career was
launched. At first the emphasis was on
the blues, and some impressive titles
were recorded both with the full band

fifties, enjoyed working with big bands and with arrangers as eminent as Quincy Jones and Ernie Wilkins.

Her 1957 salutes to **Fats Waller** >2 and **Bessie Smith** >3 are high watermarks of her recording career, and she was still in magnificent voice when a tragic medication mix-up resulted in her premature death.

Lineage

Washington always acknowledged her debt to **Bessie Smith** and **Billie Holiday**, but her own influence was felt more strongly in the rhythm and blues and soul music worlds, particularly in the music of Aretha Franklin.

Media

Appeared in the film *Jazz On A Summer's Day* (1960) and can be heard on the soundtracks of *Slumber Party* (1976) and *The Line* (1980).

Listening

1 Test Pilot
Lucky Thompson/Swingtime ST 1005
2 The Fats Waller Song Book
Dinah Washington/EmArcy 818 930-1
3 Dinah Washington Sings Bessie Smith
EmArcy 6336328

Muddy Waters

Born: 4th April 1915/Rolling Fork, Mississippi, USA
Instrument: Guitar
Recording Career: 1941 (Library of Congress), 1943-
Nickname: Sweet Lucy Carter

and on small sessions away from it. *Rich Man Blues* and *Pacific Coast Blues* >1 showcase her bluesy voice, her relaxed delivery and her well-controlled but wide vibrato.

In 1946, Dinah Washington went solo and developed into a more extrovert singer. Her gospel background became more evident and, for a while, she concentrated on her forthright rhythm and blues style. Even when occupied in this field, her interest in jazz remained and well-loved tenors like **Wardell Gray**, Paul Quinichette and Paul Gonsalves appeared on sessions at regular intervals. In 1958 she stole a large portion of the show at the *Jazz On A Summer's Day* edition of the Newport Jazz Festival and, throughout the late

IT WAS A TUNE by Muddy Waters, *Rollin' Stone,* that gave its name both to the British rock group and the American magazine, but Waters' own musical importance is far greater than either. From the time he was discovered by folklorist, Alan Lomax, McKinley Morgan Field (his real name) became one of the most famous of all blues singers. He was the genuine article, having *really* worked and sung on cotton fields and, after moving to Chicago in 1943, sweated it out in the teeming juke joints and clubs on the South Side.

It was there that he built up his singing power in a style full of unashamed drama. In 1951 he teamed up with harmonica (harp)-playing, Little Walter Jacobs, and formed a band that included Otis Spann on piano and Freddy Bellow on drums. A residency was obtained at Smitty's Corner, a large club in Chicago, and records made. *Hoochie Coochie Man, Manish Boy* >**1** and *Young Fashioned Ways* >**2** were typically big hits in the rhythm and blues charts. There were tours, including Britain in 1958, but for most of the fifties, Waters remained in Chicago. Then, as the blues revival of the sixties took off, he assumed his rightful position in the vanguard. His fame was now so widespread that he played and was

recorded at jazz as well as blues and rock festivals. His *Got My Mojo Working* >**3** made a tremendous impact at the 1960 Newport Jazz Festival, and became an essential encore for the rest of his career.

Waters was nearly killed in a road accident in 1969, but recovered completely and in the seventies continued to top the bill at blues events all over the world. A flirtation with electronic funk, *Electric Mud* >**4** was unsuccessful, but did at least introduce his talents to a whole new generation of fans.

Lineage
Waters always named pianist and half-brother Otis Spann as his greatest influence, while his own music inspired nearly all subsequent blues singers, not to mention a legion of soul and rock performers.

Media
Appeared on the soundtracks of *Mandingo* (1975) and *The Last Waltz* (1978).

Listening
1 Chess Masters
  Muddy Waters/Chess CXMD 4000
2 Chess Masters
  Muddy Waters/Chess CXMD 4015
3 Muddy Waters Live At Newport
  Vogue 515039
4 Electric Mud
  Muddy Waters/Cadet LP 314

Above: Muddy Waters

Jimmy Witherspoon

Born: 8th August 1923/Gurdon, Arkansas, USA
Instrument: Vocals
Recording Career: 1945-
Nickname: Spoon

NO ONE WAS more surprised than James Witherspoon when, as a serving conscript, he sang at the Grand Hotel Winter Garden in Calcutta, India, in the band of Teddy Weatherford. It was with

far greater confidence that he replaced Walter Brown as the singer with the **Jay McShann** Orchestra in 1944. With that band he made his mark, recording contemplative, older blues like *How Long* >**1** and social complaint belters such as *Money's Getting Cheaper* >**1**.

Concentrating on the rhythm and blues market in the early fifties, he enjoyed big hits with *Big Fine Girl* and *No Rollin' Blues*. In fact, it was not until he sparked the Monterey Festival in 1959, that he really began to attract the attention of jazz followers. Exciting remakes of *No Rollin'* and *Big Fine Girl* >**2** had him in good voice and he was supported by the likes of **Earl Hines**, **Roy Eldridge**, **Coleman Hawkins** and **Ben Webster**. The partnership with Webster was particularly productive and in 1962 they recorded *Outskirts Of Town* >**3**, an object lesson in voice and horn rapport.

Although Reprise Records teamed him with a big band in the early sixties, he was happy to return to small backing groups. He toured Japan in 1973, Britain the following year and, in 1980, recorded in Australia >**4**. In 1981, a London recording >**5** introduced the crooning Spoon but, although his singing lacked its normal whisky-

soaked realism, his rapport with saxophonists Peter King and Hal Singer made it an ideal musical exercise.

He underwent throat surgery in the early eighties but, happily, is now singing again, his voice deeper than before but still full of superb blues feeling.

Lineage
Witherspoon was influenced by **Joe Turner** and aspects of his style have always stayed in Spoon's music.

Media
Played the title role in *Black Godfather* (1974) and has made TV features *Midnight Special* and *An Evening With Spoon*.

Listening
1 Ain't Nobody's Business!
Jimmy Witherspoon/Black Lion BLP 3014
2 The 'Spoon Concerts
Jimmy Witherspoon/Fantasy F 24701
3 Jimmy Witherspoon/Ben Webster
Warner WB 56 295
4 Spoon In Australia
Jimmy Witherspoon/Jazzis R0100
5 Big Blue
Jimmy Witherspoon/JSP 1032

THE SIXTIES

Hard bop had continued to flourish alongside the free experiments and had, quite wrongly, been seen by the conservatives as the continuing mainstream. Its importance was never in doubt but, in retrospect, the more significant music of the early sixties was the expanding free form movement. Rejection, even more intense than that endured by the boppers, had to be faced by the free axis, which responded by being even wilder, and even less impressed by the old consonance.

Black pride became an important factor in the earlier stages, and performers like Archie Shepp were associated with the growing 'black power' movement. The frenetic 'all-in', with upwards of three horns playing contrapuntally, became more than a mere weapon, and whole concerts were given over to this challenge to orthodoxy.

In stark relief to this attitude, the mid-sixties saw the flourishing of the Chicago school. Here the emphasis was more on abstract musical expression than on racial passion, and Sun Ra and Muhal Richard Abrams were recognised father-figures. Acceptance was still a problem, however, and a large number of free-form players moved to Europe to seek recognition. In

truth, this was rather less forthcoming than they had expected, but it did mean that free pioneers like Shepp, Don Cherry, and the Art Ensemble Of Chicago were on hand to inspire local musicians involved in similar experiments.

At first, the European Free Improvisation School borrowed the vernacular of their American brothers, but it was not long before they devised a language of their own. The Globe Unity Orchestra and the Spontaneous Music Ensemble became important voices in the newer music, and gifted individuals like guitarist Derek Bailey and trombonist Paul Rutherford took free expression to the limits of abstract performance. In America the 'flower-power' rebellion, so influential in pop music, barely touched jazz. There was the lightweight artistry of vibist Gary Burton's Quintet, the flower-in-the-hair good humour of altoist John Handy and the 'love-in' intensity of tenor Charles Lloyd. All used the musical utensils available, but none made progress in the mainstream of the music.

Almost oblivious to these developments, the hard-bop players were not about to surrender centre-stage easily. Though the free movement had gained in power, the two musics walked hand in hand, often exchanging players on a temporary basis. The big band scene was dead in the real sense, but the Duke Ellington and Count Basie revival of the late fifties continued unabated and, in the case of the former, produced a stream of quite outstanding compositions. Most of the other big bands coasted along in the traditions of the past and had little to contribute to the evolving mainstream of the music.

Miles Davis, always a barometer of the climate of jazz, led a superb quintet through the middle sixties but, as the decade came to a close, set about re-evaluating his position. Sensing that jazz was losing contact with its own people, he began making his music more accessible. Davis embraced the electronic world of rock, and turned the jazz world on its head, literally with just one record: *In A Silent Way*.

The initial breakthrough in free form had been by horn players, but the sixties had seen the role of the rhythm section strengthened. In many cases, the responsibility for hearing the pulse had been transferred to the audience, with the listener asked to be his own metronome. Inevitably, the move to rock reversed this procedure and the insistent beat returned, through both bassist and drummer.

The Art Ensemble Of Chicago: left to right, Lester Bowie, Famoudou Don Moye, Malachi Favors, Roscoe Mitchell and Joseph Jarman

Muhal Richard Abrams

Born: 19th September 1930/Chicago, Illinois, USA
Instruments: Piano, clarinet, cello, composer
Recording Career: 1955-

SAXOPHONIST Joseph Jarman described himself, *before* meeting Muhal Richard Abrams, as a 'hip ghetto nigger who took dope'. Jarman's rehabilitation came about as a result of that encounter and was typical of many that occurred in Chicago's jazz scene in the sixties. Abrams emerged as a father figure and was regarded as something of a guru by the black artistic community.

Musically, he was very much a product of his background in a city that, during the fifties, could almost be said to have had its own individual piano style. That style had bebop at its heart, was strongly influenced by contact with the blues, and was typified by players like Abrams, and pianists Jodie Christian and Junior Mance. Abrams moved out from the pack when he formed Modern Jazz Two + 3 with tenor sax man Eddie Harris in 1955. The group played uncompromising hard bop with the inevitable strong blues overtones and when the gifted young Nicky Hill took over the tenor chair, the band's fame spread well beyond Chicago.

When it folded, Abrams did a considerable amount of woodshedding before re-emerging in 1961 to form the Experimental Band: a large line-up, it undertook the difficult task of playing free jazz with an indeterminate number of musicians. In addition to its musical aspirations, however, the band was committed to the social, financial and artistic welfare of its players. This altruistic body then graduated into a permanent organisation, the Association for the Advancement of Creative Musicians being formed in 1965 with Abrams as its first president.

An excellent opportunity to assess Abrams' own playing at the time was provided by *Young At Heart* >**1**, a solo

piano exercise in which the pianist provided a thinly disguised potted history of piano styles from **James P. Johnson** to the brink of **Cecil Taylor**. His bands were no less striking, although *Levels And Degrees Of Light* >**2** was disrupted by an inappropriate 'straight' singer, and by too much space on the powerful *Bird Song* >**2** given over to sounds of birds themselves. Such art music elements did creep into the early Chicago free records but by the late seventies Abrams was making each record date count. 1977's *1−OQA+19* >**3** brought together saxophonists **Anthony Braxton** and **Henry Threadgill** in a contest that took them through deft arhythmic space walks as well as straight-ahead swing. Another important change came about in Abrams' music in the eighties. A great deal of preparation went into the 1980 *Mama And Daddy* >**4** date; as a result, its unisons were texturally rich and even the contrapuntal passages sounded well-prepared. It was clear that more attention had been paid to the written note, and the even more beautifully balanced *Blues Forever* >**5** seemed to sum up fully this new musical direction.

Lineage

Abrams' early piano inspiration came from **Nat King Cole**, **Art Tatum** and **James P. Johnson**, but his own influence is of a spiritual as well as musical nature. Groups like the **Art Ensemble Of Chicago** and individuals including **Leroy Jenkins**, **Anthony Braxton** and **Henry Threadgill** owe much to the climate of musical free expression that he engendered in Chicago.

Listening

1 Young At Heart
Muhal Richard Abrams/Delmark DS 423
2 Levels and Degrees Of Light
Muhal Richard Abrams/Delmark DS 413
3 1−OQA+19
Muhal Richard Abrams/Black Saint BSR 0017
4 Mama And Daddy
Muhal Richard Abrams/Black Saint BSR 0041
5 Blues Forever
Muhal Richard Abrams/Black Saint BSR 0061

A E of C's Lester Bowie

Art Ensemble of Chicago

Original Line-up: Lester Bowie (trumpet)/Joseph Jarman (saxophones)/Roscoe Mitchell (saxophones)/Malachi Favors (bass) Recording Career: 1968-

ALMOST AS much a travelling theatre as a jazz group, the face make-up used by the Art Ensemble of Chicago is a permanent feature of the band's presentation and has a purpose. Joseph Jarman believes that it frees the player from human considerations and allows his spirituality greater freedom. The notion may verge on the pretentious, but the AE of C are a type of black Dada movement in their own right and the ghost of painter Marcel Duchamp stalks their blatant challenges to the establishment. Their only formula for performance is that there is none. Just as audiences feel they know what to expect, they are confounded with something entirely different.

Musically, the Art Ensemble can be as melodic as **Duke Ellington**, as tragic as **Bessie Smith** or as irreverent as **Eric Dolphy**. The noise of a pinball machine walks arm-in-arm with a jazz tradition as old as **Louis Armstrong**'s Hot Five and their collective playing can be as intricate or as simplistic as seems appropriate to them at the time. Despite Jarman's philosophy they do not take themselves too seriously.

The group, formed in 1968, grew out of the Association For The Advancement Of Creative Musicians: Bowie (born 1941) came from Frederick, Maryland via St Louis; Jarman (born 1937) was from Pine Bluff, Arkansas; Mitchell (born 1940) was a Chicago native and Favors (born 1937) hailed from Lexington, Mississippi. Acceptance was slow at first and, in an effort to reach an appreciative audience, the group moved to France in 1969. Ironically, Europe's most jazz-minded country was among the last to react favourably to free jazz, and support for the group was restricted to a coterie of devoted specialists.

It did at least offer an opportunity to record, giving people outside France a chance to appreciate the amazing scope of their music. The richly soulful opening to part two of *People In Sorrow* >**1** confirmed their bluesy roots; they took a serious look at bebop on *Dexterity* >**2** and Mitchell's beautiful *Horn Web* >**3** was used to show how their collective playing could be at once exciting and uncluttered.

Drummer William Howell was added in 1970 for a Paris recording session which also featured harmonica player Julio Finn and tenor Chicago Beau. In the event, it was not a successful experiment. Howell accented in too obvious a manner and, with the extra bodies, the Ensemble's clean-lined counterpoint became jumbled. More successful was the introduction of another drummer, Famoudou Don Moye (born 1946) from Rochester, New York. He became a member of the group in 1970 and when AE of C returned to the United States a year later, made the Ensemble a permanent quintet. All of the original four had accepted percussion duties in the past, but the presence of a specialist drummer who grasped their music was of immeasurable help, and never more so than in the frenetic, contrapuntal atmosphere of *Dautalty* >**4** where the criss-crossing melody lines of the horns were anchored by his ferocious, but controlled, drumbeat.

On their return, the Ensemble were at last taken seriously by American audiences and an approach free of stylistic constraints added to their credibility. They had placed themselves in a musical time warp that allowed them to move in any direction: 1973's tone-poem *Tnoona* >**5** reflected their admiration for Ellington and showed a capability to produce their own avant-garde 'jungle style'.

In the middle seventies, the Ensemble's touring became ever more demanding and wide-ranging. On *Cyp* >**6** they created a European free music atmosphere as horn lines meandered through a spatial void, giving space itself definition. Even more unlikely was *JA* >**6** with its injection of West Indian calypso jive.

No subject proved sacred and all subjects were worthy of the Ensemble's attention. A studio recording date in 1980 must rate as one of their finest. It offered the thrilling *Charlie M* >**7** to show off the group's collective talents but, most especially, to underline the importance of Favors' power behind the horns. Jarman exploited the full range of his skills, from the melancholy of his bassoon on *Magg Zelma* >**7** to the quicksilver of his soprano on *Old Time South Side Dance* >**7**, while Mitchell (usually heard from the right channel) also paraded his full talents on *Magg Zelma*, his tenor a mixture of bebop insight and downhome blues.

Bowie (pronounced Boo-y), always attired in a white doctor's coat, remained the most dominant voice. Of them all, he was the most ruthless master of parody and many new listeners have questioned why an outstanding trumpeter should deliberately convey the impression of being an inspired amateur. It is necessary to look beneath that doctor's coat to find the musician who is no stranger to the world of burlesque. Is the real Bowie the trumpeter who plays the brilliantly articulated solo on *Urban Magic* >**8**, or the one that jumbles through corny pop songs?

Each player adds his own personality to the group while accepting the restrictions that it can impose. The Art Ensemble remains one of the most potent forces in jazz and its claim to produce 'Beautiful Black Music' is not an empty one.

Lineage

There were no musical precedents for The Art Ensemble Of Chicago. If

art ensemble
of chicago
a.a.c.m. great black music
message to our folks

actuel
28

Above: Albert Ayler

anything, their roots can be traced to the world of French satirical theatre and art.

Media

Wrote music for and appeared in French/Canadian film *Les Stances À Sophie* (1970) and performed in the soundtrack for *Passing Through* (1977).

Listening

1 People In Sorrow
Art Ensemble of Chicago/Nessa 3
2 Message To Our Folks
Art Ensemble of Chicago/Affinity AFF 77
3 With Fontella Bass
Art Ensemble of Chicago/America 30 AM 6117
4 Live At Mandel Hall
Art Ensemble of Chicago/Delmark DS 432/433
5 Fanfare For The Warriors
Art Ensemble of Chicago/Atlantic ATL 50 304
6 Nice Guys
Art Ensemble of Chicago/ECM 1126

7 Full Force
Art Ensemble of Chicago/ECM 1167
8 Urban Bushmen
Art Ensemble of Chicago/ECM 1211/2

Albert Ayler

Born: 13th July 1936/Cleveland, Ohio, USA
Died: 25th November 1970/New York City, NY, USA
Instruments: Tenor, alto, and soprano saxophones, bagpipes
Recording Career: 1962-1970

PULLED FROM New York's East River, dead at the age of thirty-four, the facts regarding the death of Albert Ayler

183

have remained a mystery but, even before this tragedy, he had become one of the most controversial figures in jazz. A Swedish promoter had actually pulled him off the stage early in his career, and his sternest critics likened his tone to a foghorn!

Ayler's first experience came in the rhythm and blues field and throughout his career he seemed intent on reproducing on saxophone the sounds he encountered there. At times he whined like a Texas blues guitarist, shouted like **Joe Turner** or honked like an exaggerated **Lester Young**. His compositions were distinctive, titles like *Holy Holy* and *Spirits* >**1** being aptly described by critic, LeRoi Jones, as 'churchified chuckle tunes'.

He was greatly affected by the men with whom he played and had a particular affinity with drummer Sonny Murray. *Spiritual Unity* >**2**, with Murray and bassist Gary Peacock, was perhaps his finest recording. It took him as far from the European musical 'ideal' as was possible, and screamed unequivocally that 'black was beautiful', but did so within an emotional range stretching from tenderness to brutality. Nevertheless, his reception in America was mixed and it seemed that the wide vibrato and excessive romanticism of, say, 1964's *Mothers* >**3** was too bathetic for certain ears.

Although continuing to tour successfully in Europe, Ayler spent more time in America after joining the Impulse record stable in 1966. He had built up something of a cult following, and his first three albums for the new label were exceptional. *Change Has Come* and *Truth Is Marching In* >**4** find him at his most inventive but all were never less than involving and, as always, his themes and his solos were an incongruous mixture of naivety and magniloquence. However the Impulse records of 1968 and 1969 were disappointing. They took him into the funk field and found him dressing his signature tune, *Ghost* >**5**, in a new and somewhat inappropriate musical shroud. A French tour in 1970 confirmed his return to more creative climes but, within months of his return to America, he was dead.

Lineage

Ayler listed **Lester Young** and **Sidney**

Bechet as his main infuences and, although he often used a wide, Bechet-like vibrato, titles like *I'll Remember April* >**6** suggest a more than passing knowledge of the phrase shapes and tonal emphasis of **Sonny Rollins.** His own influence has been strongest on altoists like Charles Tyler and Trevor Watts, but his expansive attitudes have affected many departments of free jazz.

Media

Ayler made a film for the BBC that was considered 'inappropriate for use'.

Listening

1 Spirits
Albert Ayler/Debut DEB 146
2 Spiritual Unity
Albert Ayler/ESP-Disk 1002
3 Vibrations
Albert Ayler/Debut DEB 144
4 In Greenwich Village
Albert Ayler/MCA Impulse AS 9155
5 New Grass
Albert Ayler/Impulse AS 9175
6 The First Recordings
Albert Ayler/Sonet SNTF 604

Derek Bailey

Born: 29th January 1932/Sheffield, Yorkshire, UK
Instruments: Guitar, electric guitar
Recording Career: 1961-

THERE IS something strangely Gauginesque about a guitarist who gives up a stable, if not altogether lucrative, career as a dance-band, nightclub and theatre musician, to enter the precarious world of free music. Yet, after fifteen years of such security, this is what Derek Bailey did.

He was thirty-one when he met drummer Tony Oxley and bassist Gavin Bryars and consequently began to re-examine the musical rules that he had previously accepted without thought. He started to question his adherence to orthodox techniques and to look for a new avenue of expression, choosing free music as the best vehicle for his experiments; although it was

Right: Derek Bailey

significant that he remained loyal to the traditional instrument rather than follow, say, Jimi Hendrix into the world of electronic manipulation with guitars especially constructed for the purpose.

Bailey's records can prove a culture shock for newcomers, but albums like *Lot 74* >**1** and *Drops* >**2** outline the nature of his style. They exhibit no episodic continuity but instead represent chromatic music played with scrupulous accuracy. Bailey is concerned with the beauty of sound and the space around it and his splintered-glass angularity has caused him to be described as an 'avant-garde bottleneck' guitarist. Despite the highly personal nature of his solo work, he has proved himself to be a good player in the company of others. Playing on and off for ten years with the **Spontaneous Music Ensemble**, Bailey showed on works like *Karyobin* >**3** that the formula worked. From 1968 to 1971 he pitted his musical wits against Hugh Davies' electronics in the Music Improvisation Company >**4** and scaled remarkably creative heights with trombonist **Paul Rutherford** on *Iskra 1903* >**5**.

He continues to present his esoteric solo skills in club and concert alike but his best work is perhaps found with Company. This group of some twelve or more musicians agreed, in 1976, to present concerts permutating the available personnel in JATP style, but playing only uncompromisingly free music. A series of records document the project and the work of **Anthony Braxton**, Leo Smith, **Evan Parker** and the leader himself make *Company 5* >**6** and *Company 7* >**7** outstanding among them.

Lineage

Bailey's playing was without precedent but he has influenced a whole troup of free-form guitarists including Eugene Chadbourne, Fred Frith, John Russell and Richard Coldman, as well as blues-based players like **Sonny Sharrock**.

Media

Bailey has written a lucid and informative book *Improvisation* (1980) which outlines his ideals.

Listening

1 Lot 74 – Solo Improvisations
Derek Bailey/Incus 12
2 Drops
Derek Bailey/Andrea Centazzo/Ictus 003
3 Karyobin
Spontaneous Music Ensemble/Island IPLS 9079
4 Music Improvisation Company 1968-1971
Incus 17
5 Iskra 1903
Incus 314
6 Company 5
Incus 28
7 Company 7
Incus 30

185

considerable, displaying astonishing control of false high-note production. His solos were full of elbow-nudging rhetoric, and he wielded excitement like a branding iron. At times he was repetitious and occasionally ignored the thematic and rhythmic latitude that the style offered, but there was an acute awareness of timbre, and his variations in tone colour went a long way towards explaining his preoccupation with repeated figures.

In 1967, his first album as a leader provided a chance to examine his improvisational powers closely. As the sole horn in a quartet, he had to sustain a performance single-handed but, as *In Search Of Mystery* >**3** demonstrates, his soapbox authority did not justify slightly hysterical pronouncements and failed to disguise the paucity of ideas.

In 1970 he returned to Argentina and his music began to adopt a more Latin-based stance. It was not without rock overtones either, but a collaboration with Chico O'Farrill in 1974 showed that Barbieri was not averse to playing the role of the tenor paramour. On *Milonga Triste* >**4** the luxurious side of his tone is exploited in a busy Latin maze from which he makes little attempt to escape.

This has remained the pattern into the eighties and the conclusion must be that, although he never quite mastered the challenge of free jazz, his best work was done in making the attempt.

Gato Barbieri

Born: 28th November 1934/Rosario, Argentina
Instrument: Tenor saxophone, composer
Recording Career: (1955) 1965-

AS A YOUTH, Leandro J. Barbieri was a fanatic record collector and jazz was the common link in everything he bought. Inevitably, he channelled his musical skill in the same direction but when, as a teenager, he set about making it his career, he immediately came up against the establishment: the Argentinian government had decreed that the repertoire of all home-bred groups should consist of fifty per cent native music.

For a committed jazzman, the problems this posed were obvious but a reasonable compromise was reached when Barbieri was able to play in the dynamic Perez Prado Orchestra and work with smaller groups in Brazil. In 1962, he came to Europe, met the touring **Don Cherry** and **Sonny Rollins** and joined them for the rest of their tour. Stimulated by free music, he joined Cherry on a permanent basis, in 1965 playing on the *Complete Communion* >**1** suite and in the following year on the *Symphony For Improvisers* >**2**.

Barbieri's contribution was

Lineage
Barbieri listened a great deal to **John Coltrane** and **Pharoah Sanders**, but it was his studies under **Don Cherry** that added the finishing touches to his style.

Media
He would have gained fame if he had done nothing else but compose the music for the film *Last Tango In Paris* (1972) in which he also appeared. The soundtrack won him a Grammy award.

Listening
1 Complete Communion
   Don Cherry/Blue Note BST 84226
2 Symphony For Improvisers
   Don Cherry/Blue Note BST 84247
3 In Search Of Mystery
   Gato Barbieri/ESP-Disk 1049
4 Chapter Three – Viva Emiliano Zapata
   Gato Barbieri/Impulse AS 9279.

Carla Bley

**Born: 11th May 1938/Oakland,
California, USA
Instrument: Piano, composer
Recording Career: 1964-**

EARLY PIANO STUDIES had equipped
Carla Borg for something better than
the job of cigarette girl in a New York
jazz club. Yet this was the menial job
that supported the freelance writer and
arranger while she became more
involved in creative composition. It was
the supreme instance of the jazz fan
becoming a performer in her own right.
In 1959, she married pioneer free-form
pianist Paul Bley and with him became
involved in the Jazz Composers Guild, a
'musicians' protective' that grew out of
jazz's own 'October Revolution' which
erupted in the Autumn of 1964. Like its
Russian predecessor, it was the
proletariat's (in this case, jazz
musicians) stand against the
establishment. Although she divorced
Bley, she kept faith with the Guild's
principles and, with new husband,
trumpeter Mike Mantler, became a
founder member of the Jazz Composer's
Orchestra Association (JCOA). After
presenting the orchestra at the 1965
Newport Jazz Festival, Carla Bley
toured Europe with saxophonist **Steve
Lacy** in the Jazz Realities Quintet.
On piano she was something of an
avant-garde Hoagy Carmichael: quirky
lines delivered with an infectious lilt but
the direction often disguised in an
imaginative jumble of space, naive runs
and grace notes. *Gospel Ballade* >**1**
remains a fine example of the way in
which she promised a continuously
flowing line only to disrupt it with
deliberate dissonance and conscious
metronomical denials.
It was as a writer, however, that she
excelled. The monumental *Escalator
Over The Hill* >**2** was begun in 1968
and took three years to complete.
Lyrics were provided by Paul Haines
and the work, described as a
'chronotransduction', presented a Bley
score full of atmospheric defiance,
jingle-time flippancy and a touch of
traditional rock-and-roll extravagance.
It set the pattern for other works like
Tropic Appetites >**3** and established

Bley as a jazz leader who could move to
the fringe of the idiom with effortless
ease. *Enormous Tots* and *Funnybird* >**3**
established an element of humour and
this became an important ingredient in
the music of her touring bands. The
increasingly important international
spirit of the music was emphasised by
the multi-national line-up on the 1977
Europe Tour Band >**4**.
In the eighties, she has continued to
tour extensively, including
performances with **Charlie Haden**'s
Liberation Music Orchestra, and her
tongue-in-cheek versions of items like
The Pink Panther theme rub shoulders
with jazz pieces of more serious intent.

Lineage
As an arranger, Bley was very aware of
Gil Evans, but as a writer drew
inspiration from outside the field of jazz.

Media
With Mike Mantler, formed her own
record company, WATT, and produced
a newsletter for the New Music
Distribution Service of JCOA.
Participated in the film score for
Jodorowsky's *The Holy Mountain* (1973)
along with other members of the JCOA.

Listening

1 **The Gardens Of Harlem**
Clifford Thornton/JCOA J 2004
2 **Escalator Over The Hill**
Carla Bley/ECM 2641802
3 **Tropic Appetites**
Carla Bley/Watt 1
4 **Europe Tour Band 1977**
Carla Bley/Watt 8

Anthony Braxton

**Born: 4th June 1945/Chicago,
Illinois, USA
Instruments: Alto, soprano,
contrabass and c-melody
saxophones, clarinet, bass and
contrabass clarinets, sopranino flute,
musette, composer
Recording Career: 1967-**

DESPITE THE enormous contrast in
their personalities, Braxton is the
modern counterpart of **Jelly Roll
Morton**. The similarity arises from the
fact that, just as the volatile Creole took
to the pool table to augment his musical
earnings, Braxton hustled chess! There
were other common factors, though,
because at some time both men were
disillusioned with jazz and both moved
home as a means of solving the
problem.

While at college, Braxton met young
saxophonist Roscoe Mitchell and,
although previously interested only in
classical music, was greatly impressed
by this persuasive jazz fanatic.
Nevertheless, his newly-found passion
for jazz did not extend to the free-form
field and it was not until the AACM
came into being that Mitchell brought
Braxton into the fold. Mitchell
commenced a course of re-
indoctrination and soon had his protégé
prepared to 'lose Coltrane'. Braxton's
earliest attempts were slightly tentative,
although 1968's *Three Compositions Of
New Jazz* >**1** showed that his lighter,
Paul Desmond-like sound, with its **Dave
Brubeck** Quartet overtones, was no
barrier to the delivery of the free
message.

Braxton was certainly pleased with

the outcome but, although he was now
fully involved with AACM at their
Chicago home in Lincoln Center, he
had to earn a living. Chess hustling
gave him breathing space but he was
becoming increasingly disillusioned
and, when the **Art Ensemble Of
Chicago** came to Europe in 1969,
Braxton was not far behind.

This move to the old world was to
prove of immeasurable significance to
the young saxophonist. He had left
Chicago, with its pressure-cooker
induction into black 'free' music, to join
a European scene, itself unsure of its
routes to freedom. Braxton's reaction to
the problem was to ignore it. In 1970, he
formed Circle, a quartet with pianist
Chick Corea, bassist Dave Holland and
drummer Barry Altschul. Their musical
policy was divided between orthodox
and free music and the group finally
broke up because of arguments about
style. Ironically, it is the rumbustious
Duet >**2**, featuring antagonists Corea
and Braxton, that remains one of the
group's most exciting performances.

Braxton certainly had no objections to
playing tunes as well as open-ended,
free solos and the 1974 performances
on *Just Friends* and *Lush Life* >**3** were
taken straight. What he wanted was to
be free to choose, which led him
toward compatible European players.
His partnership with guitarist **Derek
Bailey** was particularly productive and
a 1974 Wigmore Hall Concert >**4**
demonstrated just how their differences
brought them together. There were no
melodies for the audience to follow, but
Braxton's stream of disconnected
phrases flowed effortlessly over Bailey's
harmonic bed of nails.

Duos proved to be a good means of
expression for Braxton. On the 1976
H(07−G√NB) >**5** George Lewis's
robustly bucolic trombone churned up
the gentle contours of Braxton's
chamberish theme. The 1977 Canadian
recording with Roscoe Mitchell
exhibited the intimacy to be expected
from such old friends and a title such as
Five Twenty One Equals Eight >**6**
delights with its perfectly interwoven
counterpoint. *Birth* >**7** with **Max Roach**
(1978) brought together two masters of
timing and it would be difficult to
imagine any other drummer of Roach's
generation so able to adapt to the
requirements of Braxton's music. In fact,

the Braxton/Roach collaboration was so successful they became a regular festival, teaming in Europe for a brief time.

Braxton himself continued to tour extensively, always making himself available for his commitment to Company, an avant-garde version of JATP, formed by **Derek Bailey** in 1976. These have been well-documented and Braxton's self-effacing mastery has never been better revealed than on *Akhrajat* >**8**.

Back in the States, Braxton became aware that a new generation of players had emerged. Typically, he welcomed the chance to help as well as to record with them, and 1981's *40B* and *52* >**9** found Braxton in stunningly creative form in the company of pianist Anthony Davis, bassist Mark Helias and veteran drummer Ed Blackwell. In particular, young rhythm-section players seemed to welcome the challenge of Braxton's timeless music. The 1983 *105A* >**10** presented not only trombonist George Lewis playing with almost **Roswell Rudd**-like flamboyance but also the young team of bassist John Lindberg and drummer Gerry Hemingway, playing the music with genuine understanding.

Braxton continues to be one of the major jazz voices. His music can be difficult for anyone new to free jazz, but he remains the champion of the unexpected. However, whether playing a standard or challenging himself with a free improvisation, Braxton always knows where he is – and where he is going.

Lineage

Braxton's early influences were Paul Desmond, Warne Marsh, **Eric Dolphy** and **John Coltrane**, but the impact of **Ornette Coleman** (via Roscoe Mitchell) changed his musical direction.

Media

He improvised the film scores for the French films *Paris Streets*, *La Coupe À Dix Francs* (1975) and *Vues D'Ici* (1978).

Listening

1 **Three Compositions Of New Jazz**
  Anthony Braxton/Delmark DS 415
2 **Paris Concert**
  Circle/ECM 1018/9
3 **In The Tradition**
  Anthony Braxton/Steeplechase SCS 1015
4 **Duo**
  Anthony Braxton/Derek Bailey/Emanem 601
5 **Elements Of Surprise**
  Anthony Braxton/George Lewis/Moers Music 01036
6 **Duets With Anthony Braxton**
  Roscoe Mitchell/Sackville ST 3016
7 **Birth And Rebirth**
  Max Roach/Anthony Braxton/Black Saint BSR 0024
8 **Company 2**
  Incus 23
9 **Six Compositions (Quartet)**
  Anthony Braxton/Antilles AN 1005
10 **Four Compositions (Quartet)**
  Anthony Braxton/Black Saint BSR 0066

Don Cherry

Born: 18th November 1936/Oklahoma City, Oklahoma, USA
Instruments: Pocket trumpet, cornet, flute, percussion, composer
Recording Career: 1958-

THE DELIGHTFUL, QUIXOTIC Cherry ranks as one of the most important trumpeters in jazz history. After his immense contribution to the **Ornette**

Coleman Atlantic recordings, Cherry continued to spread the free gospel as player and proselytiser. He worked briefly with **Steve Lacy** and took **Sonny Rollins** on his first excursion into the style, a partnership documented by *Our Man In Jazz* >**1** from their 1962 live session at New York's Village Gate.

With **Archie Shepp** and John Tchicai he was, in 1963, a founder member of the New York Contemporary Five. He brought to it Coleman material and, as befits a master of free improvisation, was the dominant figure. On either pocket trumpet or cornet, he produced a small, though infectious tone, but his agitated attack lent excitement to his delivery and his ability to extend a simple idea through several choruses was best illustrated on *Cisum* >**2**.

After the premature demise of the NYCF in 1964, Cherry formed a group with Argentinian tenor **Gato Barbieri** and used him in what probably amounts to the high spot of his career, certainly in terms of his writing and his organisational ability: *Complete Communion* and *Elephantasy* >**3** were both four-part suites and, although the interaction between individual movements did not always flow, they were outstanding pieces of melodic composition for quartet. *Symphony For Improvisers* >**4**, from the following year, went further; the line-up was increased to septet proportions and the sense of total unity achieved.

In the late sixties, Cherry was a frequent visitor to Europe – a brilliant 1969 session with Ed Blackwell produced *Mu* >**5**, a trumpet and drum conversation to rival any of the great duo performances of the past.

In 1971, settling in Sweden with artist wife Moki, Cherry became involved in mixed media events. Musically it was not a satisfying time for him but, in 1976, together with Coleman alumni Dewey Redman (tenor), Charlie Haden (bass) and Ed Blackwell (drums), he formed Old And New Dreams. Musically the style was based on *the* Ornette Coleman Quartet and, although a superb Coleman title like *Lovely Woman* >**6** brought out the best in them, so did excellent originals like Haden's *Chairman Mao* >**7**. The group stayed together into the eighties but, in 1985, Cherry formed a group called Nu with Blackwell, altoist Carlos Ward and

percussionist Nana Vasconcelos which appeared at the 1986 Bracknell Festival.

Lineage

Originally influenced by the bebop trumpet majors, Cherry met altoist **Ornette Coleman** and fell completely under his spell. His adaptation of the style to the trumpet has been passed down to all free-form players, but is most evident in Olu Dara's phrase organisation, Baikida Carroll's rhythmic lay-out and the late Mongezi Feza's attack. **Jan Garbarek**'s quartet paid their tribute to Cherry with a recording of his *Desireless* for the ECM label.

Media

Played in the film soundtrack of Michael Snow's *New York Eye And Ear Control* (1964) >**8** and wrote music for *Zero In The Universe* (1965) and for Alexander Jodorowsky's film, *Holy Mountain* (1973).

Listening

1 Our Man In Jazz/What's New
Sonny Rollins/RCA 741091/2
2 Cisum
Archie Shepp/Storyville SLP 1010
3 Complete Communion
Don Cherry/Blue Note BST 84226
4 Symphony For Improvisers
Don Cherry/Blue Note BST 84247
5 Mu – Part 1
Don Cherry/Ed Blackwell/BYG 529 301
6 Old And New Dreams
ECM 1154
7 Old And New Dreams
Black Saint BSR 0013
8 New York Eye And Ear Control
Albert Ayler/ESP-Disk 1016

Chick Corea

Born: 12th June 1941/Chelsea, Massachusetts, USA
Instruments: Piano, organ, synthesizer, composer
Recording Career: 1962-

AS A COMMITTED Scientologist, Armando Anthony Corea believes his

music has a mission. What would seem to be unsure is the route that he needs to take to fulfil it. He has been a straight, hard-bop leader; has worked in the exotic company of Latin specialist Mongo Santamaria; has played high quality jazz-rock and has flirted with the uncompromising avant-garde. Surprisingly, he has performed well in all of these guises, and followers hooked at one stage of his development seem ever-willing to accept the others.

In the quintet, used for his first session as a leader, Corea chose the darting, **Freddie Hubbard**-like trumpet of Woody Shaw and the fast-flowing tenor of Joe Farrell. His own playing on items such as *Straight Up And Down* >**1** was full of assertive, chordal strength: the melody line was never disguised and his fleet, right hand did a fine job of re-landscaping as his improvisations took him away from the harmonic landmarks. Less concern for extemporisation was apparent on the more formal *Trio For Flute, Bassoon And Piano* >**1**, but he made a major contribution to **Stan Getz**'s brilliant 1967 *Sweet Rain* >**2**. In 1968, Corea joined **Miles Davis** at yet another important transitional stage in his career. The trumpeter had introduced a rock-influenced guitarist, **John McLaughlin**, into the band and he seemed to answer the uncertainty he felt about his line-up by using more than one pianist. Corea became part of the resulting 'keyboard choir' and was associated with *In A Silent Way*, *Bitches Brew* and *Live At Fillmore East*. From Corea's point of view, the skitteringly inventive *Toy Room* >**3** trio performance (1970), or the 1971 solo *Departure From Planet Earth* >**4** give a better indication of his talents.

In 1970, the group Circle was formed with altoist **Anthony Braxton**, bassist Dave Holland and drummer Barry Altschul and brilliant performances like *Nefertiti* and *No Great Love* >**5** only served to make the group's eventual break-up the greater musical tragedy. Circle was one of the best creative units of the early seventies and Corea's own contribution was both percussively rhythmic and creatively consistent. He renewed his associations with Joe Farrell in 1972 when, with **Stanley Clarke**, Airto Moreira and Flora Purim, they formed Return To Forever. Corea

was now playing electric piano, and graceful performances like *Crystal Silence* >**6** advised of an important new group. Regrettably, the middle seventies saw a change in policy. The group pushed up its sound level, became completely electrified and consciously moved over to a rock world that granted it 'supergroup' status.

As compensation for his jazz following, Corea made a series of solo and duo albums in the late seventies and eighties. These presented him with pianist **Herbie Hancock** >**7** and vibist **Gary Burton** >**8** (a frequent touring partner at the time) and contain some quite outstanding jazz piano.

Lineage

His early interest in Bach, Beethoven and Chopin grew while studying with classical pianist Salvatore Sullo, but Corea's main jazz influences were **Bud Powell**, **Horace Silver** and, latterly, **McCoy Tyner**. The impact of working with **Miles Davis** was also important, especially in terms of band-leading.

Media

Appeared briefly in *Sweet Love, Bitter* (1966).

Listening

1 Inner Space
  Chick Corea/Atlantic K 60081
2 Sweet Rain
  Stan Getz/Polydor 2317115
3 The Song Of Singing
  Chick Corea/Blue Note BST 84353
4 Piano Improvisations Vol 2
  Chick Corea/ECM 1020 ST
5 Paris Concert
  Circle/ECM 1018/9 ST
6 Return To Forever
  ECM 1022 ST
7 C And H Homecoming
  Chick Corea and Herbie Hancock/Polydor 2672049
8 In Concert, Zurich October 28 1979
  Chick Corea/Gary Burton/ECM 1182/3 ST

191

Bill Evans

Born: 16th August 1929/Plainfield, New Jersey, USA
Died: 15th September 1980/New York City, NY, USA
Instrument: Piano, composer
Recording Career: 1956-1979

A BRILLIANT PIANIST who somehow managed to disguise the fact, Bill Evans never paraded his technique but, like all true virtuosi, he made no mistakes. His home was the piano trio and he brought to piano, bass and drums an orchestral awareness and an expansiveness that belied the size of the group.

Despite this, he first came to international attention through his role in three important recordings with other leaders. Evans' contribution to **Charles Mingus**' *East Coasting* >**1** and *Tijuana Moods* >**2** was slight, his playing sounding almost too studied for the turmoil of the bassist's evocative musical portraits. With **Miles Davis**, his involvement was more substantial. He actually finalised all of the arrangements for the *Kind Of Blue* >**3** session (and claimed to have originally written *Blue In Green* and *Flamenco Sketches* >**3**). Nevertheless, his playing on the date sounds a trifle passionless against the slow burn of Davis and **John Coltrane**.

Evans' finest hour came in the 1959-1961 trio with fleet-fingered bassist Scott LaFaro and the ever adaptable drummer Paul Motian. *Gloria's Step* and *Waltz For Debbie* >**4** were perfect examples of the piano trio art. His distinctive touch marked out both, a combination of imaginative vision and inexorable logic. The freedom given to his colleagues was finely judged: each was allowed his solo and collective say, yet there was no lapsing into incontinent jangling. No other line-up ever quite equalled the 1959 group, although in fairness, the 1963 >**5** and 1965 >**6** trio with Chuck Israels and Larry Bunker on bass and drums came close.

During the seventies, a gifted newcomer, Eddie Gomez, took over the bass chair and sometimes Evans and he worked as a duo. Evans also made records with saxophonists like Harold Land, **Lee Konitz** and Warne Marsh, but concerts from Paris in 1979 confirmed that his heart still belonged with the trio format. The November concert of the series >**7** also showed that Evans' brilliance as a trio pianist had not diminished, something borne out by his season at London's **Ronnie Scott** Club only months before his death.

Lineage

Evans always quoted **George Shearing** as his inspiration, but there seems little doubt that his basic style was more influenced by **Bud Powell**. In his legacy to the trade, he passed on his lyricism to **Herbie Hancock** and **Keith Jarrett**, his harmonic insight to Paul Bley, and his latent power to **Chick Corea**.

Media

Three books of solo piano transcriptions published. Performed in the 1959 film *Odds Against Tomorrow*.

Listening

1 East Coasting
    Charles Mingus/Affinity AFF 86
2 Tijuana Moods
    Charles Mingus/RCA NL 89593
3 Kind Of Blue
    Miles Davis/CBS 62066
4 Sunday At The Vanguard/Waltz For Debbie
    Bill Evans/Milestone 68101
5 1963 Club Performances
    Bill Evans/Milestone M 47068
6 Trio '65
    Bill Evans/Verve 2304 517
7 The Paris Concert
    Bill Evans/Elektra Musician 60164

Gil Evans

Born: 13th May 1912/Toronto, Canada
Instrument: Piano, arranger,
composer
Recording Career: 1941-

AS AN ARRANGER, the career of Ian Ernest Gilmore Green has been a series of triumphs. Using other people's compositions, he has managed to create a style that is uniquely his own; yet he has never overpowered the work of the individual he has chosen to showcase, nor caused his various bands to lose their identity.

He led his first band in Stockton, California for more than five years and literally learned the arranger's art by trial and error. In fact, when Skinnay Ennis assumed leadership of the band in 1938, he retained Evans as his arranger. A spell of military service interrupted his progress, then from 1941 until 1948 he was with Claude Thornhill.

This was a band that occupied a strange position in the musical world. More of a show band than a jazz unit, it numbered among its personnel at various times such committed jazzmen as trumpeter Red Rodney and reed specialists Danny Polo and **Lee Konitz**. More significantly, beautiful charts like *Robin's Nest* and *Polka Dots And Moonbeams* >**1** pointed to the route that future Evans projects would take. With overtly jazz-slanted items like *Donna Lee* and *Anthropology* >**1** the direction was obvious but, oddly, it was the slightly detached air of the standards that highlighted the variety of tonal textures used.

This was the basis for what was known later as the **Miles Davis** Capitol sound. In the late forties, Evans' apartment had become a meeting place for forward-looking musicians including Davis, pianist John Lewis and saxophonist **Gerry Mulligan**. Their discussions ranged over all aspects of music but focused on achieving the Thornhill sound with the minimum number of players. In the event a band was formed and, with Davis fronting, they appeared briefly at New York's Royal Roost. Capitol were persuaded to record them, and some of the most

talked-about recordings of the era were made. Artistically it was a triumph: Thornhill's misty, edge-of-the-forest mood was achieved on many but never more so than on Evans' *Moon Dreams* >**2**, and critic Andre Hodier rated *Boplicity* >**2** as one of the masterpieces of arranged jazz.

Miles Davis' understated mode of delivery made him an ideal trumpeter to feature in this type of group and, in 1957, Evans had an important reunion with him. It led to *Miles Ahead* >**3**, a nineteen-piece band venture that placed the trumpeter in a totally new context. The Capitol issues had always been a group project but this was a musical exercise solely devoted to Davis' flugelhorn. The title track, in particular, was a superb blues arrangement in which Davis' solo could hardly fail. Evans' attention to detail during the recording was phenomenal, with members of the band seated to ensure that the ensemble texture was just as he 'heard' it in his head.

This was an achievement of some magnitude yet, in 1958, the two principals introduced an additional challenge. They repeated the operation but, this time, restricted themselves entirely to George Gershwin's opera *Porgy And Bess* >**4**. It represented a logical advance on the ideas expounded in *Miles Ahead*, although it must be said that, had Davis not been able to interpret the various singing roles in such a varied manner, the whole performance could have foundered.

In his reviews, the perceptive writer and critic Stanley Dance did raise the question of the jazzmen's 'old inferiority complex', the need to compete with classical music and to gain conservatoire approval. Their next assignment confronted this question. *Sketches Of Spain* >**5** was to be built around the *Concierto De Aranjuez* of contemporary Spanish composer Joaquin Rodrigo which Davis had fallen in love with. Evans answered the challenge completely: all the elements came together and, with Davis at his best, the result was a genuine work of art as well as an impressive jazz performance.

Almost as effective have been the projects under Evans' own name. The 1958 *New Bottle, Old Wine* >**6** presented trumpeter Johnny Cole and altoist **Cannonball Adderley** on jazz standards like *St Louis Blues* and *King Porter Stomp*, while Cole was featured to even better effect on *Out Of The Cool* >**7** from 1960. In the early sixties, Evans continued to appear in concert but, as the decade progressed, concentrated on writing. In 1969 he formed a group for recording and in the following year performed once a week at New York's Village Vanguard.

In the seventies, this master of musical innuendo and veiled strength demonstrated how effectively he could use new electronics. A powerful 1978 touring band added Evans' magic to Jimi Hendrix's *Up From The Skies* >**8** and later that year a smaller, but even better, line-up, with saxophonists **Steve Lacy**, **Arthur Blythe** and trumpeter Lew Soloff, brought a new dimension to the rock guitarist's *Stone Free* >**9**.

Evans continued to tour into the eighties as well as travelling alone. He has never been averse to organising bands on site and since 1984 has repeated history with a weekly date at the Sweet Basil club in New York. Regular visitors there can vouch that the music produced at this 'public workshop' offers quality consistent with earlier triumphs. Establishment recognition has come with the award of a Guggenheim Fellowship in composition in 1968 and a Composer Commission by the N.Y. State Council On The Arts in 1974, as well as election as a founding artist at the J.F. Kennedy Center For The Performing Arts.

Lineage

Although self-taught, Evans has a great admiration for **Duke Ellington**.

Media

Evans wrote film scores for Nogata's *Fragments* (1967). Gittler's *Parachute to Paradise* (1969) and Lee's *The Sea In Your Future* (1970).

Listening

1 Claude Thornhill And His Orchestra 1947
London HMP 5040
2 The Birth Of The Cool
Miles Davis/Capitol CAPS 1024
3 Miles Ahead
Miles Davis/CBS 62496
4 Porgy And Bess
Miles Davis/Gil Evans/CBS 32188

5 Sketches Of Spain
Miles Davis/Gil Evans/CBS 32023
6 New Bottle, Old Wine
Gil Evans/Blue Note LA 461 H2
7 Out Of The Cool
Gil Evans/Impulse As 4
8 The Rest Of Gil Evans – London 1978
Mole Jazz MOLE 3
9 Parabola
Gil Evans/Horo HDP 31-32

Art Farmer

Born: 21st August 1928/Council Bluffs, Iowa, USA
Instruments: Trumpet, flugelhorn
Recording Career: 1949-

A MUSICIAN whose assets do not always endear him to the jazz fraternity, Arthur Stewart Farmer is no revolutionary; neither does he possess a highly personal style. However, he is at home in most musical company, and his impeccable taste never countenances the spectacular. He must wince every time he hears himself described with the old cliché 'a musician's musician' but that is exactly what Farmer is.

His early experience could not have been more diverse: it embraced the big band of Horace Henderson, the rhythm and blues hurly-burly of Johnny Otis, the smooth swing of **Benny Carter** and the bebop of **Wardell Gray**. He was with hard boppers Gigi Gryce and **Horace Silver** in the fifties and, in 1959, formed the Jazztet with Benny Golson. Although the group folded in 1962, the sixties saw Farmer emerge as a successful record maker.

The immaculate playing on the 1965 album, *Sing Me Softly Of The Blues* >**1**, the surprisingly successful 1966 *Baroque Sketches* >**2** and the unlikely 1967 *The Great Jazz Hits* >**3**, all have much to recommend them. In 1968, he moved to Vienna and, although he often returned to the United States for festivals, remained in Europe until 1975. Since then, there has been a welcome spate of recordings, mostly of American origin but including beautifully produced albums like *Manhattan* >**4**

Art Farmer

and *Mirage* >**5**, recorded in Italy for Soul Note.

A reunion of the Jazztet came about in 1982, an event documented by *Moment To Moment* >**6** in the following year, and the group remains in wide demand for clubs and festivals.

Lineage

Despite the evidence of his own style, Farmer was influenced by trumpeters **Louis Armstrong**, Ray Nance and Rex Stewart, tenor saxophonist **Lester Young**, and pianist **Duke Ellington**. However, only grudgingly does he acknowledge boppers **Dizzy Gillespie** and **Charlie Parker**.

Media

Appeared with **Gerry Mulligan** in the films *I Want To Live!* (1958) and *The Subterraneans* (1960). Also played in *Jazz On A Summer's Day* (1960).

Listening

1 Sing Me Softly Of The Blues
  Art Farmer/Atlantic SD 1442
2 Baroque Sketches
  Art Farmer/Columbia CL 2588
3 The Great Jazz Hits
  Art Farmer/CBS 63113
4 Manhattan
  Art Farmer/Soul Note SN 1026
5 Mirage
  Art Farmer/Soul Note SN 1046
6 Moment To Moment
  Art Farmer/The Jazztet/Soul Note SN 1066

Charlie Haden

Born: 6th August 1937/Shenandoah, Iowa, USA
Instrument: Bass, composer
Recording Career: 1958-

OVER A PERIOD of almost thirty years, Charles Haden has proved to be the ideal bassist for **Ornette Coleman** and his music. He 'grew up' musically with the original quartet in the period 1958 to 1960, as he abandoned conventional bass positions and reacted to the free flow of the horn lines. He was never 'melodically independent and non-chordal' as Coleman suggested, but a title like *Lonely Woman* >**1** shows how he remained a harmonic cornerstone while still providing the beat and offering solos that were on an equal melodic footing with the horns.

In the early sixties, Haden played in the conventional combo of **Red Norvo**, losing a brief battle of the decibels with **Archie Shepp**. When he rejoined Coleman in 1966, however, he had the additional responsibility of compensating for the wayward time-keeping of child drummer Denardo Coleman. Though not immediately successful, he had certainly mastered the problem by the time a New York University Concert was recorded live in 1969 >**2**. In the same year, Haden made his debut as a leader: the Liberation Music Orchestra recording >**3** was a personal triumph, exploiting the cosmopolitan aspects of his music and linking the battle cries of the Spanish Civil War with the anguish of the American avant-garde. His glorious composition *Song For Che* >**3** was the crowning moment and perhaps explains why he was such an obvious choice to assist in **Carla Bley**'s similarly ambitious project *Escalator Over The Hill* >**4**.

Never a mere rhythm bass player, Haden re-surfaced in **Keith Jarrett**'s trio in 1971. The association flourished and, when horns were added for later performances like *Back Hand* >**5** or *Rotation* >**6**, it was Haden and drummer Paul Motian who dominated the proceedings. During 1976, the bassist embarked on a series of duets

195

Charlie Haden

which mark the high point of his career. All were outstanding but the session with Ornette Coleman in *O.C.* >**7** was perhaps the very best. A fine balance was achieved with Jarrett >**7**, and Alice Coltrane (widow of **John Coltrane**) was also allowed room for her rococo embellishments >**7**. However, it was Archie Shepp who inspired the best bass solo >**8**.

Haden was nothing if not versatile and, on a 1978 session with trumpeter Leo Smith, he showed himself master of the European free school's 'conversations in space' concept by 'waiting and listening' as he played. Since 1976, Haden has been involved with Old And New Dreams, the group devoted to Ornette Coleman's Atlantic (fifties) style which has proved to be an ideal musical environment for him. He has also worked successfully in a pastorally lyrical trio partnered by Norwegian saxophonist **Jan Garbarek** and Brazilian guitarist and pianist Egberto Gismonti >**9**.

Ornette Coleman himself once said 'Charlie's music brings one stranger to another and they laugh, cry and help each other to stay happy'. The altoist was as good as his word and Haden was the bassist he recruited upon his return to the recording studios in 1985 >**10**.

Lineage

Haden was an orthodox bassist before coming under the spell of **Ornette**

Coleman**'s music. He has himself influenced the next generation of outstanding free bassists such as Fred Hopkins, William Parker and Ed Schuller.

Media

Haden performed on the soundtracks of *Last Tango In Paris* (1972) and *The Holy Mountain* (1973).

Listening

1 **The Shape Of Jazz To Come**
   Ornette Coleman/Atlantic 1317
2 **Crisis**
   Ornette Coleman/Impulse AS 9187
3 **Liberation Music Orchestra**
   Charlie Haden/Jasmine JAS 55
4 **Escalator Over The Hill**
   Carla Bley/ECM 2641802
5 **Back Hand**
   Keith Jarrett/Jasmine JAS 67
6 **Mysteries**
   Keith Jarrett/Impulse IMPL 8026
7 **Closeness**
   Charlie Haden/Horizon SP 710
8 **The Golden Number**
   Charlie Haden/Horizon SP 727
9 **Magico**
   Charlie Haden/Jan Garbarek/Egberto Gismonti/ECM 1151
10 **Song X**
   Pat Metheny/Ornette Coleman/Geffen 924 096-1

Andrew Hill

Born: 30th June 1937/Port Au Prince, Haiti
Instruments: Piano, baritone saxophone, composer
Recording Career: 1955-

WHEN HE BEGAN recording for Blue Note in 1963, Andrew Hille (the original spelling) represented an organising talent in an avant-garde jazz world that was slanted strongly toward free-form. He wrote powerful themes like the seven/eight-time *Siete Ocho* >**1**, the mambo-based *Catta* >**2** and the soul march, *Les Noirs Marchent* >**2**, taking his musicians through the harmonic minefield of free expression to the haven of near-mainstream.

Hill's early training was in Chicago where he first recorded. The piano style was relentlessly percussive, as befitted a man with rhythm and blues experience, and he utilised that aspect of his playing in his composing. Directing his groups in an authoritative manner, he formed a particularly rewarding partnership with vibist **Bobby Hutcherson**. In addition to the titles cited above, *The Groits* >**3** illustrates how the two men drew upon each other's rhythmic strength and were mutually inspiring in the art of tune re-building.

Although Hill's music was highly original, 1968's *Grass Roots* >**4** – withou totally jettisoning his composing trademarks – did incline its head toward hard bop. This became something of a pattern in the late sixties but, following his last Blue Note session in 1970, he did not record for more than four years. On his return, and with his instrumental glitter as bright as ever, he made his first trio album, from which *Catfish* and *Invitation* >**5** evidence that he was still the master of the fiercely-stabbed, chorded blocks.

His loyalties remained to the smaller group after that date and, although the solo *Reverent DuBop* >**6** distilled his expression to an even more concentrated level, the eighties have seen Hill return to the potential of the trio once again.

Lineage

His first teacher was saxophonist Pat Patrick but, although he claims as influences Barry Harris, **Bud Powell**

and **Thelonious Monk**, it is only the latter's heavily chordal style that is reflected in Hill's playing.

Media

Composed an opera *Golden Spook*, wrote the TV score for *Lenox Avenue Sunday* and was a member of the CBS Repertory Theatre.

Listening

1 Judgment
Andrew Hill/Blue Note BST 84159
2 Dialogue
Bobby Hutcherson/Blue Note BST 84198
3 Andrew
Andrew Hill/Blue Note BST 84203
4 Grass Roots
Andrew Hill/Blue Note BST 84303
5 Invitation
Andrew Hill/Steeple Chase SCS 1026
6 From California With Love
Andrew Hill/Artists House AH 9

Freddie Hubbard

Born: 7th April 1938/Indianapolis, Indiana, USA
Instruments: Trumpet, flugelhorn, piano, composer
Recording Career: 1959-

WHEN HIS musical family brought him to New York in 1958, Frederick Dewayne Hubbard was already a useful trumpeter but stints with **J. J. Johnson**, **Max Roach** and **Sonny Rollins** sharpened his city teeth. In 1961, he joined the Jazz Messengers and, with tenor Wayne Shorter and trombonist Curtis Fuller alongside, it was rated as highly as any other **Art Blakey** line-up. Hubbard was fresh from taking part in **Ornette Coleman**'s *Free Jazz* >**1** experiment where his carefully laid out solos and clean articulation had been a rather superfluous commodity. With the Messengers it was different: his confident legato lines caressed the waltz-time *Up Jumped Spring* >**2**, drove *Plexus* >**2** remorselessly over his leader's drum barrage and, on his own *Kyoto* >**3**, showed his easy lyricism.

While with Blakey, Hubbard made a

STEREO
BST 84 203
THE MUSIC OF ANDREW HILL
BST 4203
BLUE NOTE
ANDREW!!!

Freddie Hubbard

number of good records for Blue Note but, in 1966, he joined an Atlantic label in its transitional stage. A more bluesy approach was needed and, although *Lonely Soul* >**4** was a reasonably successful track, too many commercial offerings such as *Midnight Soul* >**4**, with its **B. B. King**-like guitar, were demanded. In 1972, Hubbard moved to California, but had already said that 'it was difficult to stay out of rock and make a living' and the policy on the West Coast proved no different. For this reason, much of the seventies was an artistic desert for him but, as the decade came to a close, he was able to make more orthodox jazz recordings. 1978's *Super Blue* >**5** pointed the way, and a 1983 move back to an Atlantic label which had returned to the old values helped further. There were also regular concert appearances with VSOP, a group including **Herbie Hancock** and Ron Carter, devoted to uncompromising, hard-bop principles. Freddie Hubbard had returned home.

Lineage

Hubbard's main influence has been **Clifford Brown**, but most of his own disciples have been more interested in Hubbard the seventies rock player rather than the jazz musician.

Media

Featured in **Herbie Hancock**'s soundtrack for the film *Blow Up* (1966), and on the soundtrack of *The Pawnbroker* (1964), *The Bus Is Coming*

(1971), *Shaft's Big Score* (1972), and *The Anderson Tapes* (1971).

Listening

1 Free Jazz
Ornette Coleman/Atlantic 1364
2 Three Blind Mice
Art Blakey/United Artists UAJ 14002
3 Thermo
Art Blakey/Milestone 47008
4 The Atlantic Years
Freddie Hubbard/Atlantic ATL 60 053(2)
5 Super Blue
Freddie Hubbard/CBS 82866

Bobby Hutcherson

Born: 27th January 1941/Los Angeles, California, USA
Instruments: Vibraphone, marimba
Recording Career: 1961-

THE PRESENCE OF Earl Griffith on a 1958 **Cecil Taylor** record date meant that the vibraphone had at least a foot in the free-form door. In fact, it did not kick that door open until the early sixties and by then the boot doing the kicking was worn by Bobby Hutcherson. Even more than Griffith, he sensed how easily the instrument's percussive qualities could be used. Only rarely did he fully cross the threshold into free-form, but he was never afraid to embrace dissonance nor to embark on rhythmically free voyages.

Hutcherson had moved to New York in the mid-fifties, and it was his musical open-mindedness that accounted for his inclusion on experimental sessions like **Andrew Hill**'s *Judgment* >**1**, **Eric Dolphy**'s *Out To Lunch* >**2**, **Jackie McLean**'s *One Step Beyond* >**3** and Grachan Moncur's *Evolution* >**4**. Certainly, the middle-sixties found Hutcherson in great demand and capable of responding to most jazz situations. In 1969, he returned to the West Coast and for two years played in a straight-ahead style as co-leader of a group with Harold Land.

He continued to be an avid experimenter but, during the seventies, he became involved in the Blue Note label's commercially-slanted programme. *Linger Lane* >**5**, with its theme from MASH as well as pop vocals was perhaps the nadir, but the 1982 *Solo/Quartet* >**6** album returned Hutcherson to his rightful, forward-looking position. Certainly he has always been an innovator, and it could be argued that his chiming vamp on **Archie Shepp**'s 1965 *Scag* >**7** was something of an inspiration for similar devices used prolifically in the later work of **Weather Report**.

Lineage
Influenced by Milt Jackson, Hutcherson broadened the scope of his instrument and later inspired free players like Khan Jamal and Paris Smith.

Listening
1 Judgment
Andrew Hill/Blue Note BST 84159
2 Out To Lunch
Eric Dolphy/Blue Note BST 84163
3 One Step Beyond
Jackie McLean/Blue Note BST 84137
4 Evolution
Grachan Moncur III/Blue Note BST 84153
5 Linger Lane
Bobby Hutcherson/Blue Note LA 369-G
6 Solo/Quartet
Bobby Hutcherson/Contemporary 14009
7 New Thing At Newport
Archie Shepp/Jasmine JAS 22

Leroy Jenkins

Born: 11th March 1932/Chicago, Illinois, USA
Instruments: Violin, viola, xylophone, recorder, composer
Recording Career: 1968-

JENKINS' early instruction was in both the academic and the practising blues field. He himself taught string instruments in colleges, but it was with Chicago's AACM – Association for the Advancement of Creative Music – that he came to the notice of a wider audience. In the late sixties, his Creative Construction Company included **Anthony Braxton** and **Muhal Richard Abrams** and its music >**1**, built on the principle of collective improvisation, graphically captured the mood of the seventies avant-garde.

Critic Nat Hentoff wrote that 'Jenkins had so expanded the conceptual dimensions of improvisatory violin as to be beyond category'. Jenkins certainly had become the ultimate spokesman for the instrument in the era and the formation of the Revolutionary Ensemble in 1971 presented his creative talents in the ideal trio format. His violin sound remained unadulterated, but the stark reality of his music on a title such as *Chicago* >**2** demonstrates just how the musical laboratory of his home town had burnished it with black ghetto realism.

In 1974 he won the Down Beat critics' poll for the first time and on *For Players Only* >**3** showed how well he was equipped to be featured star in the big band of the Jazz Composers' Orchestra. He also played remarkable solo concerts and at one in New York made a stunning recording of **Billy Strayhorn**'s *Lush Life* >**4**.

Sting, his strongly jazz-based fusion group, was formed in 1981, played the 1983 New York Jazz Festival and has enjoyed considerable popularity in the more general musical field.

Lineage
Jenkins took his ultimate inspiration from **Charlie Parker**, but it was classicist Jascha Heifetz who fired his ambition to master his instrument, and **Ornette Coleman** who provided him

with the musical syntax. Most modern jazz violinists reflect something of his irresistible passion but his influence is used most productively in the playing of **Billy Bang**.

Media

Appeared briefly in *Borsalino* (1970).

Listening

1 **CCC**
   Creative Construction Company/Muse MR 5071
2 **164 11 tc**
   Revolutionary Ensemble/Enja 3003
3 **For Players Only**
   Leroy Jenkins/JCCA Record J 2006
4 **Solo Concert**
   Leroy Jenkins/India Navigation IN 1028

B. B. King

Born: 16th September 1925/Itta Bena, Mississippi, USA
Instrument: Guitar, vocals
Recording Career: 1949-
Nickname: Blues Boy (B.B.)

THE MOST SUCCESSFUL of living blues singers, in concert Riley B. King resembles a preacher with his flock and controls his congregation at a music festival as though in his baptist church at home. The vocal style is simple, but it is powerful and moving, and he is not ashamed to trade in drama.

He would be an important figure in the blues world if all he did was sing, but his real strength is as a guitarist. He speaks himself of bending notes like **Lester Young** and that is exactly how his solos appear. Often set in uninspired backgrounds, King's dramatic solos swoop and delay like Prez and, on titles like *Sweet Sixteen* or *Going Down Slow* >**1**, it is his guitar with its judicious note-placing that is more riveting than his singing.

King's early records were made in Memphis and Houston >**2** but, in 1956, he switched to Los Angeles, still with Modern's RPM label. At that time, some of his material was slanted toward the rock and roll market but, after 1961, when he moved to ABC Paramount, he became more aware of his parallel jazz following. ABC recorded him in concert and this proved a successful formula, with the 1964 *Live At The Regal* >**3** one of the really outstanding live blues albums. In contrast, albums like *Indianola Mississippi Seeds* >**4** teamed him with non-blues artists such as Carole King and Leon Russell and, although they have novelty appeal, do not do full justice to the man. He did, however, perform at pop as well as blues festivals in the seventies, a practice which he discontinued as he took his place in the jazz events of the eighties.

Lineage

King's first vocal influences were his cousin Bukka White and, on record, **Blind Lemon Jefferson**. Instrumentally, it was the work of **T-Bone Walker**, Lowell Fulsom and Elmore James that initially inspired him but he always had a great admiration for **Charlie Christian** and **Django Reinhardt**. His own influence on modern blues guitar is enormous and has spilled into the world of 'blue-eyed blues' with disciples like Eric Clapton and Mike Bloomfield.

Media

Authorised biography *The Arrival of B.B. King* (1980) by Charles Sawyer is both thorough and entertaining. Played on the soundtrack of *The Seven Minutes* (1971) and *FM* (1978) and appeared in *When You Comin' Back, Red Ryder?* (1979).

Listening

1 B. B. King's Greatest Hits
America 30 AM 6079
2 B. B. King – The Memphis Master
Ace CH 50
3 Live At The Regal
B. B. King/Ace CH 86
4 Indianola Mississippi Seeds
B. B. King/Probe SPBA 6255

once, claimed to breathe through his ears and then asserted that he was out to 'catch the sound of the sun'. Yet Roland Kirk was a brilliant musician; he *did* play tenor, manzello and stritch simultaneously, and did so with genuine skill and much good taste. His circular breathing was more advanced than any other player, allowing him to blow constantly throughout a whole number – without giving trouble to his ears. The inescapable feeling was that, given time, he would have heard the sun.

Kirk led a rhythm–and–blues band at the age of fourteen, gradually building up his armoury of musical tricks, starting with two horns, and ending up wearing a contraption around his neck to carry all of his instruments and tools. On his first date as a leader, there remains some suspicion that overdubbing was used (the overlaying of separately-recorded tracks onto a single tape): but at least on the up-tempo blues *Roland's Theme* >**1** there seems to be genuine unison playing. However, from that date onwards, Kirk unquestionably eschewed all studio trickery. Most of his records categorically state that no multi-tracking took place and one has only to listen to the spontaneity of *Kirk's Work* >**2** or *We Free Kings* >**3** to know that here was the genuine article. Almost as fascinating as the horn 'unisons' was his amazingly achieved 'voice-over' flute. *Three For The Festival* >**3** was a perfect example, as Kirk brought the instrument to life by

Rahsaan Roland Kirk

Born: 7th August 1936/Columbus, Ohio, USA
Died: 5th December 1977/ Bloomington, Indiana, USA
Instruments: Tenor saxophone, manzello, stritch, flute, nose flute, clarinet, trumpet, composer
Recording Career: 1956-1977

IT HAS TO BE difficult to take seriously a blind man who played three horns at

singing across the mouthpiece.

Briefly in 1961, he worked with **Charles Mingus** and on *Hog Callin' Blues* >**4** gave an exhibition of straight-ahead blues playing to silence all who questioned his ability to play in more orthodox circumstances. His first trip to Britain came in 1963 with a residency at **Ronnie Scott**'s, and Kirk spent much of the sixties either shuffling between New York and the West Coast or touring abroad. He formed his Vibration Society which he led through most of the seventies but, in 1975, had a stroke and was paralysed down one side. Astonishingly, he continued to play with one hand, while exercising to regain the strength in the other but, just as signs of improvement began to appear, he was cut down by a second stroke.

Lineage

Kirk always had a great admiration for **Don Byas** but, although Dick Heckstall Smith, Barbara Thompson and Vladimir Checksin are among those who play more than one horn simultaneously, there cannot be said to be a true disciple of this remarkable man.

Media

Appeared in US TV's *Soul* programme 1972 and in BBC TV's *Tempo* show 1967.

Listening

1 Early Roots
Roland Kirk/Affinity AFF 121
2 Pre-Rahsaan
Roland Kirk/Prestige P24080 (2)
3 You Did It, You Did It
Roland Kirk/Mercury 6336384
4 Oh Yeah
Charles Mingus/Atlantic 40387

Steve Lacy

Born: 23rd July 1934/New York City, NY, USA
Instrument: Soprano saxophone, composer
Recording Career: 1956-

THE SOPRANO SAXOPHONE occupies a strange position in the firmament of jazz's star instruments. Men like **Johnny Hodges**, **John Coltrane** and Wayne Shorter made major statements on it, but all three remained specialist saxophonists *who also played soprano*. **Sidney Bechet** and Steve Lacy have been the only two major jazzmen prepared to channel the whole of their musical ethos through this one instrument.

Steve Lacritz (Lacy's real name) began as a Dixielander and made a good living working with Max Kaminsky, Jimmy McPartland and Rex Stewart. Despite this success, he abandoned the style in 1955 and joined avant-garde giant **Cecil Taylor**. *Song* >**1**, from a Boston session shortly after his arrival, suggested that he was uncomfortable with the harmonic freedom on offer and barely more at ease with the pianist's unremitting rhythmic attitudes. In contrast, *Change 'Em Blues* >**1**, from the same date, gave encouraging evidence that he could match Taylor's melodic explosions, darting runs and harmonic paradoxes with similar contortions on the saxophone.

The more prosaic side of his personality was given rein in his two-year spell with **Gil Evans**, but work was irregular and, in 1959, the two men parted company. Lacy's interest in the music of **Thelonious Monk** was made tangible in 1960 when he actually joined his idol. Learning was done 'on site', and the rhythmic side of Lacy's personality developed rapidly; so much so that, when he formed his own group with **Roswell Rudd** in 1961, he was able to do full justice to his mentor's compositions. *Bye-Ya* >**2** suggested that he was mining the same creative seam as saxophonist **Eric Dolphy**, although on *Monk's Dream* >**2** he displayed a more naive, folkish quality.

Both approaches were eschewed in the middle sixties when Lacy fully committed himself to free improvisation. He was in Europe in 1965 with **Carla Bley** in Jazz Realities, although a 1966 recording from South America showed that he was still inclined to cover his naivety in the new style behind a ferocious, multi-noted smokescreen. From 1967 he spent three years in Rome before moving to Paris in 1970 where he remained for the next five years. The result was a protracted exposure to the European free music scene.

It is worth noting that by the early seventies, the European school had moved some distance from the American model. It had also turned from the blues and adopted a more upright and rigid approach to timing. This more static approach was not at first to Lacy's liking but *The Breath* and *Josephine* >**3** from 1972 reveal that he had a mature grasp of the principles involved.

Lacy's technical control was daunting and, in the seventies, he formed a group with saxophonist Steve Potts devoted to abstract jazz improvisation. 1977's *Stamps* >**4**, with its surrealistic unisons, floating counterpoint and high, creative standards, showed just how inventive the group could be but, inevitably, a free music group could not, by definition, exist on a permanent basis.

Time was still given to solo, duo and trio jobs and, as the isolated horn, Lacy's tremendous talent was given excellent exposure. New listeners to free music might well be bewildered by hearing Lacy's disjointed and, at times, anguished solos: they might also miss that storytelling continuity possessed by the swing-era masters. Lacy, the saxophonist, knows no compromise: each idea must stand on its own merits and his infallible sense of timing makes his music impervious to unsympathic support musicians. Fortunately, he has rarely had to work with any and, as on the 1979 *Quirks* >**5** has usually enjoyed the help of men like the late Ronnie Boykins (bass) and Dennis Charles (drums) who know the rules.

Lineage

Lacy learnt much from reed man Cecil Scott but, perhaps, his real training came from the fingers of pianists **Thelonious Monk** and **Cecil Taylor**. His own favourites include **Miles Davis**, **Sonny Rollins** and **Pee Wee Russell** and it would be fair to say that he cross-pollinated musical ideas with saxophonists like **Evan Parker** and Trevor Watts. His influence on Steve Potts was considerable.

Media

Was in the Italian short film *Free Fall*

(1972) and composed the soundtrack of the Swiss film *Alfred R* (1972).

Listening

1 In Transition
Cecil Taylor/Blue Note LA 458-H2
2 School Days
Steve Lacy/Emanem 3316
3 Solo
Steve Lacy/Emanem 301
4 Raps
Steve Lacy/Adelphi Jazz Line AD 5004
5 Capers
Steve Lacy/Hat Hut FOURTEEN (2 R 14)

Cleo Laine

Born: 27th October 1927/Southall, Middlesex, UK
Instrument: Vocals
Recording Career: 1951-

AFTER MAKING her professional debut with Johnny Dankworth, Clementina Dinah Campbell then went on to marry him. Shortly after that event in 1958, she left Dankworth's band to concentrate on a solo acting and singing career. It was, in fact, a highly

successful step to take and, although she continued to win jazz polls and to appear occasionally with her husband, Cleo Laine was lost to jazz for some time.

In the face of her considerable talent as a jazz singer, this was unfortunate and, had she not had such success during a 1972 tour of America, she might well have abandoned her singing career. The tour, with Dankworth, brought her greater fame on both sides of the Atlantic, however, and in the following year she justified a Carnegie Hall booking. This was brilliantly documented on *Live At Carnegie Hall* >**1** and here was the chance to hear the fully mature artist; her range was exceptional, the tonal quality of her voice a delight, and the musical gymnastics of her style had the grace of an Olympic floor exercise specialist.

Laine was the mistress of musical agility and this new success turned her life around. She involved herself with her husband's work in musical education, but it was the fleet duets with Dankworth's alto that were making her increasingly popular. Albums such as *Themes* >**2** began to reach listeners outside the world of jazz, while the musical dexterity of the principals remained the main attraction for the committed jazz listener.

Lineage

Laine was mainly influenced by the musicians heard during her early days in London, like husband John Dankworth, Peter King and Tubby Hayes, although there is something of **Sarah Vaughan**'s audacious note placement in her style.

Media

Her first stage role was in *Flesh To A Tiger* (1958); she took the title role in Ibsen's *Hedda Gabler* (1970) and played in several London Shakespeare productions. She acted in the film *The Roman Spring Of Mrs Stone* (1961) and sang on the soundtracks of *The Criminal* (1960), *The Third Alibi* (1961) and *The Servant* (1963).

Listening

1 Live At Carnegie Hall
Cleo Laine/Sierra FEDD 1006
2 Themes
Cleo Laine/Sierra FEDC 2000

Chris McGregor

Born: 24th December 1936/Somerset West, South Africa
Instrument: Piano, composer
Recording Career: 1963-

SON OF A British missionary, McGregor's musical training came at the Capetown College of Music as well as at the feet of Xhosan musicians. He gained an international reputation in the sixties by bringing his Blue Notes to play at the Antibes Festival and then by taking a residency in Switzerland. The pianist's sidemen were the explosive Mongezi Feza on trumpet, the effusive altoist Dudu Pukwana and the propulsive rhythm duo of Johnny Dyani (bass) and Louis Moholo (drums). Their brand of hard bop was tinged by the South African veldt but, after moving to London in 1965, they began to update their act.

Feza, in particular, donned the mantle of free-form trumpeter **Don Cherry**, but the whole quintet introduced a looser approach to improvisation, well illustrated on the 1967 *Don't Stir The Beehive* >**1**. This title, with its pleasing synthesis of styles, was typical and went some way towards explaining just why the band exerted such influence on Britain's own emerging free movement. *Beehive* showed that, while themes were rarely wholly eradicated, they were often quickly jettisoned, freeing the group to move out into territory rich in its own special brand of musical anarchy.

In 1970, McGregor expanded to big-band proportions and, in the wake of **Mike Westbrook**'s big band experiments, formed The Brotherhood Of Breath. His band was the wilder of the two and brought together elements of free-form, bebop tune transformation and the Kansas City riffs of the thirties. Performing with one long line of musicians across the stage, they were visually dramatic but the musical mixture was equally extraordinary. *Mra* >**2** had insistent simplicity; *Sunrise On The Sun* >**3** offered a solo sequence and frenetic all-in build-ups; while *Tungis Song* >**4** confirmed the band's ability to play tunes.

The economic problems of leading a

Wes Montgomery

big band finally proved too great in the mid-seventies but, despite the tragic deaths of Feza in 1975 and Dyani in 1986, sidemen like Pukwana have continued to keep the spirit of the Blue Notes alive into the eighties.

McGregor, the pianist, was no less arresting than the bands he led. Equally at home in small groups, his jabbing, harmonic instructions and his flowing clusters made him ideal for the compact unit and his almost telepathic understanding with Moholo is nowhere better appreciated than on the second movement of 1975's *Blue Notes For Mongezi* >**5**. A move to Paris came in the eighties, but regular visits to Britain have included the 1986 Bracknell Festival.

Lineage

Initially inspired by second Viennese School classicists such as Schoenberg and Webern, McGregor's style was almost in direct contrast to fellow South African Abdullah Ibrahim (a.k.a. Dollar Brand). Ignoring the folk element that informed Ibrahim's essentially melodic style, McGregor was influenced by **Bud Powell** and **Horace Silver** and later came under the spell of **Cecil Taylor** and **Don Cherry** as a result of following them into Copenhagen's Montmartre Club.

Listening

1 Very Urgent
  Chris McGregor/Polydor 184 137

2 Chris McGregor's Brotherhood Of Breath
  RCA Neon NE 2
3 Procession
  Brotherhood Of Breath/Ogun OG 524
4 Live At Willisau
  Brotherhood Of Breath/Ogun OG 100
5 Blue Notes For Mongezi
  Chris McGregor/Ogun OGD 001/2

Wes Montgomery

Born: 6th March 1925/Indianapolis, Indiana, USA
Died: 15th June 1968/Indianapolis, Indiana, USA
Instrument: Guitar, composer
Recording Career: 1948-1968

JOHN LESLIE MONTGOMERY was a thumb, rather than a plectrum guitarist, and his parallel octaves style of playing was exactly what that technique suggests. His solos, however, were never exercises in the easy lyricism which characterised the post-**Charlie Christian** school.

He spat out rapid single note phrases in a way that was compatible with the hard bop jazz of the early sixties. It was as if he wanted to rival horn men such as **John Coltrane** and in doing so he gave to jazz guitar a degree of tension that was immediately exciting.

Montgomery played with **Lionel Hampton** from 1948 to 1950, but was thirty-four before he came to the notice of the jazz world as a result of his work for the Pacific Jazz label. In the following year, he moved to New York and rapidly integrated with local musicians. He also moved over to the Riverside label and made quite beautiful recordings like *Movin' Along* and *Ghost Of A Chance* >**1** with the kicking rhythm team of bassist Sam Jones and drummer Louis Hayes.

In the early sixties Montgomery led his own trios and quartets and on record used men like pianist Tommy Flanagan, bassist Percy Heath and drummer Albert Heath. This particular unit was on hand to confirm his natural skills with the twelve-bar on the 1960 *D. Natural Blues* >**2**, which achieved with ease the synthesis of relaxation and latent tension – a hallmark of the blues.

A change of record label in the late sixties proved significant: he moved to Verve who seemed intent on submerging his brilliant talent in a welter of strings and romanticism. The 1965 *Smokin' At The Half Note* >**3** showed that they were still, on occasions, prepared to issue him a combo setting but, in 1967, he moved on to A & M and was offered no such artistic clemency. From that date until his death in 1968, he recorded with cumbersome orchestras that gave him little room to parade his true improvisational skill.

Lineage

Montgomery's jazz style borrowed most from horn men like **John Coltrane** and **Sonny Rollins**. He has himself been described as the most copied guitarist since **Charlie Christian** but he certainly influenced men like Grant Green and **George Benson**.

Media

Wrote and performed the soundtrack for *Maidstone* (1970).

Listening

1 Movin' Along
   Wes Montgomery/Riverside 68951
2 The Incredible Jazz Guitar of Wes Montgomery
   Riverside VDJ 1538(CD)
3 The Smallest Group Records
   Wes Montgomery/Verve VE2-2513

Joe Pass

Born: 13th January 1929/New Brunswick, New Jersey, USA
Instrument: Guitar
Recording Career: 1962-

THERE ARE TIMES when being a talented musician is not enough. The line between fame and obscurity is finely drawn and often all that is missing is luck. Joseph Anthony Passalaqua, a gifted guitarist, played with **George Shearing**, Earl Bostic, Gerald Wilson and Bud Shank in the sixties, as well as working for some time in the West Coast studios. Through this he could point to recordings with Frank Sinatra, Billy Eckstine and **Sarah Vaughan**. Yet despite this track record, his name was barely known outside the studios and then only to a small circle of musicians and record collectors.

Pass recorded for Blue Note in 1963, with the memorable *For Django* >**1** (a tribute to **Django Reinhardt**) appearing in the following year, but it was not until a trip to Germany in 1970 that his career turned the corner. He recorded *Intercontinental* >**2** for MPS and began to reach a wider audience. A guitar duo with Herb Ellis occupied the period from 1972 to 1974 and Pass then had the good fortune to join Norman Granz's Pablo label.

Granz was greatly taken by this virtuoso performer and, in fact, called his first release simply *Virtuoso* >**3**. This solo album paraded all of Pass' talents: his rhythmic strength up-tempo, imaginative chordal work with ballads, and a natural aptitude for improvisation. Later came *Virtuoso 2* and *Virtuoso 3*, but Granz also teamed him with individual giants like **Oscar Peterson** and Milt Jackson.

Good as these associations were, it remained the solo albums (*I Remember Charlie Parker* >**4** was one of the most notable) that showed Pass at his best. He looks and sounds right when he is in a club, sitting almost unobtrusively centre stage, simply playing solo. Enjoying his effortless artistry in such surroundings, it is often necessary to be reminded just how famous a performer Joe Pass has now become.

Lineage

Pass has a rather personal style, although an early inspiration was **Charlie Christian**.

Media

He has published several guitar tutors of which *Joe Pass Guitar Style, Chord Book, Jazz Guitar Solos* and *Jazz Duets* are the best known. Pass played on the soundtrack of *Shaft's Big Score* (1972).

Listening

1 For Django
 Joe Pass/Pacific Jazz LN 10132
2 Intercontinental
 Joe Pass/Memoir MOIR 105
3 Virtuoso
 Joe Pass/Pablo 2310 708
3 I Remember Charlie Parker
· Joe Pass/Pablo 2312 109

Jean-Luc Ponty

**Born: 29th September 1942/ Avranches, France
Instruments: Violin, electric violin, violectra, piano, composer
Recording Career: 1964-**

THIS FRENCH VIOLINIST'S contribution to jazz lasted for only a limited period. Ponty began as a classical musician, and burst onto the jazz scene at the 1964 Antibes Festival but, by the late seventies, had deserted the medium for popular music. He told

Down Beat that it had taken him more than three years to adjust to jazz; but, after his initial breakthrough, he freelanced in Europe with great success.

During 1969, Ponty visited America and worked with **George Duke**, a pianist who, at the time, was making his own progress with the scalar discoveries of **Miles Davis**. It was the ideal environment for a musician translating the modal message of saxophonists to the violin and *Cantaloupe Island* >**1** preserves Ponty's success for posterity. It was a move that applied the finishing touches to his style. He came into direct contact with the players who, like himself, were working in the post-Miles Davis rock idiom and flirted briefly with the rock groups of Frank Zappa and the Mothers Of Invention. In 1974, Ponty joined **John McLaughlin** in the Mahavishnu Orchestra. It was the second edition of the group but *Visions Of An Emerald Beyond* >**2** showed how well the now fully-amplified violinist helped shape its policy.

Since that time, Ponty has moved away from jazz entirely, although his standing in the rock world remains high. His remarkable contribution to the 1966 *Violin Summit* >**3** with Svend Asmussen, **Stuff Smith** and **Stephane Grappelli** gives a frustrating taste of his jazz potential and his musical inventiveness can be seen in the violectra, an instrument he created. Its sound is pitched between a viola and a cello and comes from tuning a baritone violin one octave lower than a normal fiddle.

Lineage

Ponty was influenced more by tenor saxophonist **John Coltrane** than by violinists. His own disciples are in the field of rock.

Media

Played on the soundtrack of *Take It To The Limit* (1980).

Listening

1 Cantaloupe Island
George Duke/Jean-Luc Ponty/Blue Note BNLA 632
2 Visions Of An Emerald Beyond
Mahavishnu Orchestra/CBS 69108
3 Violin Summit
Ponty/Smith/Asmussen/Grappelli/MPS 821 303-1

Don Pullen

Born: 25th December 1944/Roanoke, Virginia, USA
Instruments: Piano, organ, composer
Recording Career: 1964-

THE GENUINE all-rounder, Donald Gabriel Pullen can develop a theme in the accepted bebop manner or play a solo in a way that rapidly denies its links with the starting theme and takes him into the field of free expression. Due solely to a quirk of circumstance, his earliest records led the jazz world to believe that his commitment was exclusively to free music: he overshadowed his teacher Giuseppi Logan on his first studio session and on *Dialogue* >**1** produced an extremely mature free solo.

More dynamic still was his duo with the brilliant drummer on that date, Milford Graves. It took place at Yale University and, as *Nommo* >**2** shows, was a genuine duet. Graves was never shackled to the timekeeper's role and Pullen flooded the music with **Cecil Taylor**-like tone clusters. Between them, they ignored legitimate punctuation and, with Graves' ringing cymbal patterns, as abstract in their way as the pianist's melodic flurries, they produced a major performance.

To the amazement of an expectant jazz world, there was no true follow-up, and for the next ten years Pullen worked as accompanist to singers Arthur Prysock and Nina Simone. However, a spell with **Art Blakey**'s Jazz Messengers in 1974 rekindled his jazz fire and in 1973 he had begun two years with **Charles Mingus**. The hypercritical Chazz was not about to encourage 'free jive' in his band and Pullen played in the legitimate hard bop manner. In this role, he surprised many with his clever, melodic variations and fine chordal work supporting the horns.

After leaving Mingus, he toured extensively and while in Canada recorded a personal progress report: *Big Alice* >**3** was orthodox solo piano while *Song Played Backwards* >**3** took him out into free country. A tour of Europe followed and found him in the company of saxophonist George Adams and drummer Danny Richmond, a team that has stayed together on and off until the present.

Pullen has never quite got the piano-and-drums duo idea out of his head, however, and in a 1978 session with Famoudou Don Moye from the **Art Ensemble of Chicago**, he recaptured the magic of that earlier Yale date with *Conversation* >**4**. On the same session, *Milano Strut* >**4** was a simple dialogue for his post-**Jimmy Smith** organ and *Curve Eleven* >**4** an arhythmic piece of free piano, with Pullen occasionally strumming the strings beneath the lid of the piano.

His eighties touring band is co-led with George Adams and teams bassist Cameron Brown with Danny Richmond in the rhythm section. The whole of *City Gates* >**5** would serve as an introduction to the band, and shows exactly how this excellent quartet presents a concert or club performance.

Lineage

Pullen's influences are hard to understand. Firstly, he claims Clyde 'Fats' Wright, his pianist cousin; he then lists the vastly different **Ornette Coleman** and **Eric Dolphy**, but ignores **Cecil Taylor**. Certainly, there are strong elements of Taylor in all of *Nommo* >**2** and on titles like *Conversation* >**4**.

Listening

1 The Giuseppi Logan Quartet
ESP-Disk 1007

2 Nommo
Milford Graves/Don Pullen/SRP LP 290

3 Solo Piano Album
Don Pullen/Sackville 3008

4 Milano Strut
Don Pullen/Famoudon Don Moye/Black
Saint BSR 0028

5 City Gates
George Adams/Don Pullen/Timeless
SJP 181

Roswell Rudd

**Born: 17th November 1935/Sharon,
Connecticut, USA
Instruments: Trombone, french horn,
piano, bass, drums, congas, composer
Recording Career: 1955-**

ROSWELL HOPKINS RUDD JR is the
man who makes a nonsense of stylistic
barriers. He began as a Dixieland
trombonist, then discovered free-form
jazz and, while making some of the most
important avant-garde records of the
sixties, nevertheless continued to play
his adapted brand of tailgate in
traditional jazz clubs.

Rudd bypassed the swing era
completely although, for a brief period,
he played in a 1963 **Steve Lacy** group
devoted to the music of **Thelonious
Monk**. It was a chance meeting with
trumpeter Bill Dixon, however, that took
him into the world of free expression.
Through him he met Danish altoist John
Tchicai and in 1964 the two men formed
the New York Art Quartet (NYAQ) with
drummer Milford Graves and bassist
Lewis Worrell. The title implies a
gentle chamber unit, but works like
Mohawk >**1** leave no doubt about the
group's collective passion. More
importantly, the ensemble allowed
room for solo expression and Rudd was
able to use his newly acquired skill as a
free, melodic improviser. *Rosmosis* >**2**
(actually track two on side one, but
wrongly labelled on all issues!) showed
just that, but it also made use of Rudd's
tremendous facility in the upper
register and his ability in delicate

obbligato passages.

The lifespan of NYAQ was little more
than a year and, in 1965, Rudd joined
the group of tenor saxophonist **Archie
Shepp**. It was an ideal environment for
the trombonist, encouraging him to use
his rustic tone and contrasted his
'gutbucket' vulgarity with Shepp's fleet
saxophone musings. *Where-ever June
Bugs Go* >**3** showed just how well he
succeeded, and how completely he had
countered the smooth precision of the
J.J. Johnson school. His solos were pure
atavism and made copious use of
smoothly-oiled glissandi and pulse-
defying slurs. His ensemble
contribution was even more important.
Shepp was heavily involved in
collective playing, and featured this
style at the British Jazz Expo of 1967.
The quintet finished to a barrage of
boos, but received a comparable
number of ecstatic cheers.

In 1968, Rudd formed the Primordial
Quintet with **Lee Konitz** on electric
tenor. The group grew to nonet
proportions, and worked regularly in
New York for almost a year. Rudd
teamed briefly with **Gato Barbieri** but
they had parted company by the time
the Jazz Composers' Orchestra
commissioned the Numatik Swing Band
project in 1973. This took the form of the
normal JCO session with Rudd featured
prominently on *Circulation* >**4**, but the
whole work was designed to feature
other soloists, working with material
written by Rudd.

He toured continously in the late
seventies and eighties and was
recorded by leading European labels
like ECM, Horo and Soul Note. The 1979
Horo album was in one sense a novelty
record. With the aid of over-dubbing,
Rudd played the part of the one-man-
band producing dazzling counterpoint
in *Up Front* >**5**, relishing the tasteful
ballad on *Laughing On The Outside* >**5**
and capping it all with explosive blues
playing on *Zeibekiko* >**5**. All were the
work of a master trombonist, but Rudd
still seems more at home in an orthodox
group. His 1982 *Monk's Mood* >**6** was
one such case and, with the aid of Steve
Lacy and Misha Mengelberg, he shows
how he can get under the skin of a real
jazz classic.

Lineage

Rudd was influenced by Dixieland

trombonists like Cutty Cutshall, **Jack Teagarden** and Brad Gowans, but his whole musical outlook was turned around by Bill Dixon, **Steve Lacy** and John Tchicai.

Media

Appeared as a musician in the film *The Hustler* (1961).

Listening

1 Mohawk
NYAQ/Fontana 681 0092 L

2 New York Art Quartet
NYAQ/ESP-Disk 1004

3 Live At San Francisco
Archie Shepp/Jasmine JAS 75

4 Numatik Swing Band
Roswell Rudd/JCOA J 2002

5 The Definitive Roswell Rudd
Horo HZ 12

6 Regeneration
Roswell Rudd/Soul Note SN 1054

Paul Rutherford

Born: 29th February 1940/London, UK
Instruments: Trombone, euphonium,
piano, composer
Recording Career: 1964-

INVOLVED IN the British free music scene since its inception, Paul Rutherford's contribution to the overall European free improvisation world has been almost as important.

His earliest experience in the New Jazz Orchestra was discouraging; torn between admiration for **J.J. Johnson** and the need to say something on his own behalf, he foundered. Fortunately, drummer John Stevens and altoist Trevor Watts, both of whom he had met earlier during his military service, were facing similar problems. They formed the **Spontaneous Music Ensemble**, Rutherford joined them, and they made their home in London's Little Theatre Club. Their aim was to play free music and, although the trombonist's solo on *After Listening* >**1**, from their first recording session, could have been more ambitious, it did show that he had completely broken his ties with Dixieland and bop.

An involvement with **Mike Westbrook**'s Concert Band followed and it can now be seen as more crucial than it appeared at the time. It allowed him the breathing space to formulate a coherent style and to gain confidence in his own ability. In a perverse way, it also offered him a discipline against which to react, especially on titles such as the 1968 *Folk Song* >**2** where he had complete freedom to express himself. Good as this was, it was his brilliant work in drummer Tony Oxley's sextet that evidenced the first flowerings of his mature, free style. The 1970 *Amass* >**3** found him totally free, using his voice as well as his lips, and presenting a unique sound.

In 1970, Rutherford formed Iskra 1903 >**4** with guitarist **Derek Bailey** and bassist Barry Guy, and within the group he also played piano. During the two-year life of this challenging group, its involvement in free improvisation was total and shamelessly chromatic. Rutherford was in his element and, for the first time, emerged as an influential figure inspiring fellow Europeans with the possibilities of his voice-and-horn style. Unfortunately, playing music that was unacceptable to the cosy conservatives was not a lucrative pastime and a great deal of travelling had to be undertaken to remain in employment. He worked in Europe with Alex von Schlippenbach's Globe Unity in the middle seventies and – as if to convince the doubters – even recorded a straight *Creole Love Call* >**5** with a re-formed Westbrook band in 1976.

It was as solo trombonist on the European circuit that he began to make his mark in the seventies, however, and the 1974 *Gentle Harm Of The Bourgeoisie* >**6** confirmed that his solos could only have been conceived on the trombone. Even better was *Old Moers Almanac* >**7**, recorded live at Moers Festival. His vocabulary of voice and trombone accents remained the same but the scope of his bucolically relaxed improvisation was somehow broader. To prove his links with the distant past, he played his breaks with the alacrity of a Dixielander and delivered his glissandi with the near alcoholic slur of the tailgate primitives.

He formed an excellent trio in the eighties, with bassist Paul Rogers and drummer Nigel Morris, but could not get regular employment. Once again, one of jazz's most daringly inventive players was struggling for work because his method of self-expression was not 'nice'.

Lineage

His early inspiration was trombonist, **J.J. Johnson**, but there are traces of **Roswell Rudd**'s explosive delivery in his style. He has strongly influenced men like Albert Mangelsdorff and Gunter Christian as well as the second-generation of free players in Britain such as Nick Evans.

Media

Played on the soundtrack of *Steppenwolf* (1974).

Listening

1 The Spontaneous Music Ensemble
   Eyemark EMPL 1002
2 Release
   Mike Westbrook/Deram SML 1031
3 Four Compositions For Sextet
   Tony Oxley/CBS 64071
4 Iskra 1903
   Incus 3/4
5 Love/Dream And Variations
   Mike Westbrook/Transatlantic TRA 323
6 The Gentle Harm Of The Bourgeoisie
   Paul Rutherford/Emanem 3305
7 Old Moers Almanac
   Paul Rutherford/Ring 01 014

Pharoah Sanders

Born: 13th October 1940/Little Rock, Arkansas, USA
Instruments: Alto, soprano and tenor saxophones, contrabass, clarinet, flute, piccolo, percussion, vocals
Recording Career: 1964-

BURSTING onto the jazz scene in the middle sixties, Farrell 'Pharoah' Sanders was hailed as the new jazz messiah and invited into the bosom of the **John Coltrane** musical family, but he never quite fulfilled his initial promise. He joined Coltrane in 1965, playing a prominent part in the legendary *Ascension* >**1** recording. In some ways, it was a case of the teacher taught: Sanders encouraged Coltrane

along the transcendental path and it was no coincidence that *Kulu Se Mama* >**2** and *OM* >**3** were devised while he was in the band. Coltrane's style changed, the emotional outpouring seemed less controlled and, rhythmically, neither player seemed to place their notes with due care.

Their best work together was on location and 1965's *Live In Seattle* >**4** album recorded at the Penthouse, Seattle, was not surpassed. After Coltrane's death, Sanders worked with his widow Alice, but mysticism still clouded musical issues. He had recorded *Tauhid* >**5** under his own name while with Coltrane, but titles like *Upper Egypt And Lower Egypt* >**5** were spuriously exotic. The pattern continued when he became a leader in his own right and *Karma* >**6** and *Jewels Of Thought* >**7** still failed to showcase the virile tenor he had once been.

This sadly remained the pattern through the seventies, although occasional club and festival performances were couched in more straight-ahead jazz language.

Lineage

Sanders was first inspired by **John Coltrane** and **Sonny Rollins**, yet he could be said to have influenced Coltrane in his last years.

Listening

1 Ascension
John Coltrane/Jasmine JAS 45
2 Kulu Se Mama
John Coltrane/Jasmine JAS 51
3 OM
John Coltrane/Impulse AS 9140
4 Live In Seattle
John Coltrane/Impulse AS 9202-2
5 Tauhid
Pharoah Sanders/Impulse AS 9138
6 Karma
Pharoah Sanders/Impulse AS 9181
7 Jewels Of Thought
Pharoah Sanders/Impulse AS 9190

Archie Shepp

Born: 27th May 1937/Fort Lauderdale, Florida, USA
Instruments: Tenor and soprano saxophones, composer
Recording Career: 1960-

AN ARTICULATE speaker, author, poet and playwright as well as musician, there have been times when Archie Shepp has wished that the list of his talents had not included the last category. Rejection by critics unaware of his aims, audience response based on similar prejudice and irregular employment, have often made him sorry to be a musician. However, this is the thing he does best, and there is no doubting that he was one of the most important players to emerge in the sixties.

There is no denying either that he was thrown into the deep end when asked to make his first recording with **Cecil Taylor**. Shepp was utterly confused on titles like *Air* or *Lazy Afternoon* >**1**, but he was already a musical street-fighter and not liable to go down under pressure. He hid his comparative harmonic naivety behind an air of detachment, a policy that also

disguised his rather ponderous, rhythmic manner.

In 1962, Shepp co-led a quartet with trumpeter Bill Dixon and displayed a marked improvement. **Ornette Coleman**'s free message had been fully grasped when they recorded *Peace* >**2** in 1962, and in 1963 Shepp became a founder member of the New York Contemporary Five. Its trumpeter, **Don Cherry**, had come from Coleman, bringing with him some of the great altoist's book and this was the basic, musical stance that the NYCF adopted. Shepp was perhaps the man apart. He was developing a highly personal style, one that allowed him to be a verbose romantic while still delivering his message with almost savage violence. This was not inappropriate to his role on the **John Coltrane** *Ascension* experiment but, in his own bands during the mid-sixties, things were to become more restrained and organised. Certain pieces such as *Call Me By My Rightful Name* and *Sentimental Mood* >**3** received gentle treatment and Shepp even used phrase patterns that owed much to swingsters like **Johnny Hodges** and **Ben Webster**.

However, it was only the lull before the storm and Shepp's 1967 quintet caused havoc at London's Jazz Expo. They played a ferocious, collective set with only the brief *Shadow Of Your Smile* for solo relief and the pattern was repeated on *One For Trane* >**4**. About a quarter of the audience walked out, leaving the remainder to cheer wildly at the end. At the time, Shepp's name was linked with the Black Power movement, and his poems did speak of racial resentments. In 1967, during the height of the Vietnam war, he described his own playing as 'a burst of Vietcong machine-gun fire' but, in the main, his music remained nearer to the jazz mainstream than he cared to admit.

During most of 1969 and 1970, Shepp was in Europe and, while there, came into close contact with the **Art Ensemble of Chicago**. There was an exchange of ideas, and performances together, but when he returned to the States, he turned away from playing to become a college professor at the University of Buffalo and later at the University of Massachusetts in Amhurst. He was more-or-less off the music scene until 1975, when the 'new' Archie Shepp appeared. In fact, it was the old version with the avant-garde cloak thrown off. The romantic that had always threatened to burst out now appeared and, while performances like *Steam* >**5** were anything but soft-centred, they had returned to certain pre-free standards.

This became the pattern through the seventies and into the eighties as performances like 1977's *Green Dolphin Street* >**6** and 1979's *Loverman* >**7** supported his self-held theory that he was the last astylistic tenor whose mission in life was to let the world hear the evolution of the tenor through the bell of his horn. Challenging projects like the duo with **Max Roach**, *The Long March* >**8**, and his quasi-fusion duo with Jasper Van't Hof, *Mama Rose* >**9** from 1982, confirmed his continuing forward outlook, but concerts were given over to Shepp the history book.

Lineage

Shepp was influenced by **Sonny Rollins** and **John Coltrane**, but was trained to some extent by pianist **Cecil Taylor**. He has never lost sight of the men from earlier eras, however, and traces of **Ben Webster** and **Coleman Hawkins** continue to appear.

Media

Has written several off-Broadway plays and musicals and collaborated with Cal Massey on *Lady Day – a Musical Tragedy*. Also frequently played the part of jazz critic himself.

Listening

1 The World of Cecil Taylor
Candid 9006
2 Archie Shepp/Bill Dixon Quartet
Savoy MG 12178
3 Live In San Francisco
Archie Shepp/Jasmine JAS 75
4 One For Trane
Archie Shepp/Polydor 583 732
5 Steam
Archie Shepp/Enja 2076
6 On Green Dolphin Street
Archie Shepp/Denon XY 7524 ND
7 Bird Fire
Archie Shepp/Sun SR 22-119
8 The Long March
Max Roach/Archie Shepp/Hat Hut
THIRTEEN (2R 13)
9 Mama Rose
Archie Shepp/Jasper Van't Hof/
Steeple Chase SCS 1169

Spontaneous Music Ensemble

Original Line-up:
Kenny Wheeler (trumpet)/Paul Rutherford (trombone)/Trevor Watts (alto saxophone)/Bruce Cale (bass) Jeff Clyne (bass)/John Stevens (drums)
Recording Career: 1966-

THE SME WAS a tremendous training ground for British modernists. In addition to those players listed above, guitarist **Derek Bailey**, saxophonist **Evan Parker**, bassist Dave Holland and trumpeter Ian Carr also passed through its ranks.

Formed in 1965, the SME was fortunate to acquire a regular home in London's Little Theatre Club. This was a loft venue before the New York loft scene; there were often more musicians than spectators present but it provided a rallying point and a sense of unity. The flourishing New York avant-garde had made a powerful impact and, initially, the group's approach was along eclectic lines. Watts had done his **Eric Dolphy** homework for *ED's Message* >**1** and the inspiration for *2B Ornette* >**1** needed little investigation.

Yet, almost at once, the group set out to achieve its own identity, at first through total group music. The 1968 *Karyobin* >**2** was a brilliant success: Parker, Bailey and Holland joined Wheeler and Stevens in an intriguing five-way conversation, with no argument to settle and no decision to be reached. It could well have offered a basis for further development but Stevens, the eternal empiricist, was already looking elsewhere. Disappointingly as it turned out, it led to his use of the human voice as an expressive medium in his music. The development was compatible with his desire to transcend the concept of musical notes, but *Oliv 1* >**3** failed because of the creative limitations of the voices used. No such criticism could be levelled at the non-vocal music which continued to flourish alongside these attempts. Watts formed his own group, Amalgam, at first without a drummer – but when Stevens and the saxophonist got together again, the banners of Amalgam and SME were virtually interchangeable. Amalgam's first recording maintained a very high creative level and *Prayer For Peace* >**4**, in particular, must rate as one of their most inspired collective performances.

Self-discovery still remained of paramount importance and in 1973 a daring experiment was recorded at the Little Theatre Club. Only Stevens and Watts were involved: they sat opposite one another and set about reacting to each other musically. The performance extended the concept of playing without ego: Stevens' cleverly fragmented drum style was totally exposed and Watts showed on *Face To Face* >**5** that he could match it for emotional involvement. By its very nature, such jazz earned the sceptics' jibe of being 'grunts and clicks' music, but its absolute lack of continuous melody was as the players intended.

In 1975, a London concert introduced an enlarged SME with, at one time, twenty musicians on stage. In the true tradition of SME, the Spontaneous Music Orchestra covered new ground and, despite the inclusion of inexperienced free-formers, the outcome was chaotically exciting >**6**.

In the late seventies, the SME ceased to appear under that banner but, as 1979's *Endgame* >**7** proves, the presence of free improvisation giants such as Stevens and Watts was enough to guarantee a return to the old values.

Lineage

There were no true precedents for the Spontaneous Music Ensemble. Its musical policy came from every branch of jazz; from the tailgate of New Orleans, the rhetoric of **Eric Dolphy** and the freedom of **Ornette Coleman**.

Listening

1 Challenge
Spontaneous Music Ensemble/Eyemark EMPL 1002
2 Karyobin
Spontaneous Music Ensemble/Island IPLS 9079
3 Oliv
Spontaneous Music Ensemble/Marmalade 608 008
4 Prayer For Peace
Amalgam/Transatlantic TRA 196
5 Face To Face
Trevor Watts/John Stevens/Emanem 303
6 SME+
Spontaneous Music Orchestra/A Records A 003
7 Endgame
Trevor Watts/John Stevens/JAPO 60028

Sun Ra

Born: c1910/Birmingham, Alabama, USA
Instruments: Piano, organ, synthesiser, space harp, composer
Recording Career: 1948-

HERMAN SONNY BLOUNT (Le Sony'r Ra) of the huge cloak, the forehead brooch and the large sun on his chest, is a genuine original. His musical career has gone almost full circle, from arranger with **Fletcher Henderson** and **Stuff Smith** in the forties, to band leader whose concerts in the eighties combine mixed media events, free improvisation and the playing of Henderson classics like *Christopher Columbus* and *Yeah Man*.

Sun Ra, deriving his new name from ancient Egyptian mythology, moved to Chicago in the late thirties and wrote music for speciality acts at the Club DeLisa. He played with **Coleman Hawkins** and also led his own trio but his real claim to fame dates from the early fifties. As early as 1953, he maintains he was using the electric piano and, in that year, led his own combo at Shepp's Playhouse in Chicago.

In the following year, he augmented the group to big-band proportions and took a residency at the famous Grand Terrace in the city. His sidemen, including saxophonists John Gilmore, Marshall Allen and Pat Patrick, trombonist Julian Priester and trumpeter Art Hoyle, were to play an important part in the next stage of his development. On the band's first recording date in 1956 >**1**, his arrangements were somewhat exotic – but hardly revolutionary in the real sense. Gilmore insists, however, that **John Coltrane** sought the pianist's help in formulating his own style and as Sun Ra moved into the late fifties, he began to introduce freer elements into his band's collective playing. This became more evident in the early sixties and he formed his own record label, Saturn, to document progress. The results were rather parochial; they suggested that his experiments were just as valid as were those of **Ornette Coleman** and **Cecil Taylor**, and titles like *Solar Differentials* >**2** confirmed that this was music of a high creative standing.

His obsession with intergalactic matters deterred the sceptics. He made pronouncements about space travel, wrote rather naive poetry about the universe and billed his band as the Astro Infinity Arkestra and Solar Arkestra. The band dressed in 'school play' space uniforms and titles were adapted from science fiction language like *Space Aura, The Cosmos* and *Nebulae*.

The music was better than the image, however, and Sun Ra's own playing had become powerfully authoritative. His fiery organ solo on the 1960 *Atlantic* >**3**, in particular, was full of innovative, electronic effects that would later be taken for granted in all branches of jazz. Sidemen Gilmore and Allen were also charting new territory: Allen by the kind of diverse route he takes on *Love In Outer Space* >**2** and Gilmore in a more all-embracing style.

Gilmore, in fact, became the band's major soloist and his contribution to Sun Ra's most successful works was inestimable. On the outstanding 1966 *Heliocentric Worlds Of Sun Ra* >**4** he captured the essence of the parent style completely yet his own playing was full of individual personality and free expression. His command of scalar development was daunting and the Arkestra gave him the licence he needed.

In concerts, Sun Ra's approach became more diversified. He began to combine orthodox big band arrangements with freer items and the 1968 *Pictures Of Infinity* >**5**, recorded live, took the listener through free form, ordinary big band charts and busy **Charles Mingus**-like 'all-ins'.

It was as if Sun Ra was renewing his cabaret card and looking back to the tent shows of early Negro vaudeville.

The danceable quality of *Friendly Galaxy* >**6** from his 1970 tour suggested further entrenchment and concerts began to assume the character of 'happenings': dancers and fire eaters were introduced and more swing-era arrangements appeared. The 1977 *Unity* >**7** featured, in addition to a strangely folky *Favourite Things*, Sun Ra's astylistic versions of *King Porter Stomp* and *Lightnin'*. It had become obvious that he was looking to attract a wider audience and his work during the eighties followed this path with intensity.

Recordings from the period did not always show the band in the best light. The Arkestra concert of the eighties was very much a visual performance and the odd moments of sloppy execution, hidden by the 'occasion', were put into sharp relief on record. The suspect vocal intonation of the Ra choir became all too apparent and releases like the 1983 *Dreams Come True* >**8** and *Live At Praxis* >**9** evidence a distinct decline from his highest standards.

Nevertheless, Sun Ra has been a major influence in the development both of free-form jazz generally and in the build up of the Chicago scene in particular. His experience in all walks of jazz life has proved invaluable, with playing guru to musicians in trouble a vital aspect of his popularity.

Lineage

As an arranger Sun Ra was influenced by **Fletcher Henderson**, **Duke Ellington** and **Gerry Mulligan** but his

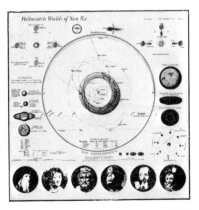

insular style had few imitators. As a keyboard player his influence was tremendous and later players of the electronic piano, such as **Herbie Hancock** and **Chick Corea**, owe him a tremendous debt.

Media

Documentary film about Sun Ra *A Joyful Noise* (1980).

Listening

1 Jazz By Sun Ra
Sonet SLP 23
2 Secrets Of The Sun
Sun Ra/Saturn 9954
3 Atlantis
Sun Ra/Impulse AS 9239
4 Heliocentric Worlds Of Sun Ra Vol 2
ESP 1017
5 Pictures Of Infinity
Sun Ra/Black Lion BLP 30103
6 Nuits De La Fondation Maeght Vol 2
Sun Ra/Shandar SR 10 003
7 Unity
Sun Ra/Horo HDP 19-20
8 Dreams Come True
Sun Ra/Saturn 11
9 Live At Praxis '84 Vol 1
Sun Ra/Praxis CM 108

John Surman

Born: 30th August 1944/Tavistock, Devon, UK
Instruments: Baritone and soprano saxophones, bass clarinet, piano synthesizer
Recording Career: 1967-

A VIRTUOSO saxophonist, John Surman has done a great deal to establish the baritone as an instrument capable of playing free form. He shed the 'bags-of-sand-on-the-back' image associated with the big horn and took it into the rarified atmosphere of high harmonics with consummate skill.

He was also at home in more orthodox surroundings, coming to prominence with the **Mike Westbrook** Concert Band. Titles like *Portrait* >**1** and *Tension* >**2** have typical Surman contributions, the tone heavy, the ideas delivered with stunning dexterity and the improvisations tinged with just a taste of malice. There was, however, a gentle side to his personality and his soprano on the 1975 *Tender Love* >**3** shows him as an altogether different player.

Although he took part in that session, Surman had left Westbrook in 1968 and had worked impressively with the bands of Graham Collier, David Holland, **Ronnie Scott** and **Chris McGregor**. The 1968 *Incantation* >**4** introduced his skill in a smaller unit and in the following year he formed The Trio with bassist Barre Phillips and drummer Stu Martin. This was a magnificent group where Surman's playing was outstanding. His bass clarinet weaved chamber-like counterpoint with string bass on *In Between* >**5** and on the big horn in *Green Walnut* >**5** he used his incredible range – not to dull the senses, but to add just about every tonal colour to his musical palette.

The trio's break up in 1972 was greeted with general regret but, in the following year, it was replaced by SOS, another challenging group. Consisting of Alan Skidmore, Mike Osborne and Surman, it was an all-saxophone trio, but one with a difference. Surman programmed synthesizer parts in advance and the saxophones were added in performance. The process worked well and a 1975 recording like *Goliath* >**6** proved how valid the electronic contribution could be. *Country Dance* >**6** was made by a straight saxophone choir before such a style became fashionable.

Later in the seventies, Surman became disappointingly over-involved with the synthesizer. *Cloud Line Blue* >**7**, with singer Karin Krog, did little justice to either performer, although the five-octave range of Aina Kemanis helped the re-united Surman and Phillips to make *Music By* >**8** a more successful exercise. In the eighties, Surman has also worked in the quartet of bassist Miroslav Vitous and in recent years seems to have succeeded in balancing his massive talent as a saxophone improviser with his proficiency as a synthesizer operator: 1982's *Such Winters Of Memory* >**9** confirms this creative synthesis.

Lineage
Surman lists as his influences clarinettist **Johnny Dodds** and saxophonists Harry Carney, **Charlie Parker**, **John Coltrane** and **Sonny Rollins**.

Media
Wrote the ballet music for *Sablier Prison* for the Paris Opera and played on the soundtracks of *Mado* (1976), *Spoiled Children* (1977) and *Merry-Go-Round* (1977/8).

Listening
1 Celebration
Mike Westbrook/Derum SML 1013
2 Marching Song Vol 2
Mike Westbrook/Derum SML 1048
3 Citadel/Room 315
Mike Westbrook/RCA SF8433
4 John Surman
Derum SML 1030
5 The Trio
Dawn DNLS 3006
6 SOS
Skidmore/Osborne/Surman/Ogun OG 400
7 Cloud Line Blue
Karin Krog/Surman/Polydor 2382 093
8 Music By
Barre Phillips/Surman/ECM 1178
9 Such Winters Of Memory
John Surman/ECM 1254

Cecil Taylor

Born: 15th March 1933/New York City, NY, USA
Instrument: Piano, composer
Recording Career: 1956-

THE ESOTERIC nature of free-form jazz has resulted in even its most outstanding exponents finding it difficult to maintain regular employment. None has suffered quite as badly as Cecil Percival Taylor, yet here was the first man genuinely to challenge **Art Tatum**'s mastery of the piano. In terms of the normal 'paying of dues' demanded by his peers, Taylor made a bad start. He first studied piano, composition and harmony at the New York College Of Music and then, for a further four years, continued his academic career at the New England Conservatory in Boston. He had no interest in jazz, to the extent of regarding the process of jazz improvisation with real suspicion.

It was not until saxophonist Andrew

McGhee convinced Taylor that improvisation was also for him that he showed any inclination to become a jazz musician. Nevertheless, when the decision was made, it was for keeps and, when he returned to New York from college, he played on sessions with men like **Johnny Hodges** and **Hot Lips Page**. Though Taylor derived satisfaction from such work, he was more interested in establishing his own style. This was not as straightforward as he had hoped, although as early as 1956, a Boston recording pointed the direction he was taking. Significantly, this first session included *Bemsha Swing*, a **Thelonious Monk** composition and *Sweet And Lovely* >**1**, a tune that Monk loved to decimate. Taylor extended the dismantling process and the basis of his style had been established.

Times proved hard for Taylor, but he was not without friends and in 1956 enjoyed a six weeks' residency at New York's Five Spot. The following year, he was invited to appear at the Newport Festival and soon after he revamped his quartet, bringing in vibist Earl Griffith. It was a line-up that made a considerable impact on record. The 1958 *Wallering* >**2** and *Excursion On A Wobbly Rail* >**2** confirmed his interest in modernising stride piano and in retaining the rhythmic thrust of the style. Between 1959 and 1960 less than satisfactory record dates followed with trumpeter Kenny Dorham and saxophonists **John Coltrane** and **Archie Shepp**, but in the main, this must be put down to musical incompatibility. However, they perhaps prepared the ground for his final flowering.

On tour in Denmark in 1962, Taylor was recorded in a bass-less trio including altoist Jimmy Lyons and drummer Sunny Murray. The outcome was sensational and *D. Trad That's What* >**3** could be cited as among the finest performances in piano jazz history. It was apparent that, in Taylor's hands, free jazz was not a haphazard collection of disconnected ideas, but rather a build-up in which statements progress from one to another even if not developing in the thematic sense. On this track it is only necessary to listen to his insistent left hand to realise that, while there are harmonic signposts, the story-telling aspect of solo building has been systematically rejected. To overcome the fixed pitch of the piano, he used his own chromatic devices, swamping the stabbing left-hand guide lines with a swirling mass of right-hand 'clusters'.

Lyons became a permanent musical companion and, as if to confirm the structural validity of his music, Taylor experimented with a more formalised group approach in the sixties. There was certainly no diminution of piano power in *Unit Structures* >**4** and *Conquistador* >**5** but Taylor had set about examining the relationships between the tonal values of various instruments. Both players used structure of a very loose kind but abandoned the idea of playing by chance.

This concept was extended in 1968 when Taylor was featured on record with the Jazz Composers' Orchestra >**6** but, as he moved into the seventies, he began to appear increasingly as a solo pianist. The strongly orchestral aspect of his style made this a logical step although, in earlier times, he had used drummers like Murray and Andrew Cyrille as a re-directional buffer when his more angular exercises threatened to become becalmed. The 1974 *Silent Tongues* >**7** was like *Unit Structures*, another of the Taylor suites; one of the most fluent he had put together, it made full use of his long and elaborate lines. The 1976 *Air Above Mountains* >**8** was similar, its ferocious flight of fancy taking on an apparently abstract route but the fact of being unaccompanied seeming to concentrate his mind on the work's architectural needs.

Despite these solo ventures, Taylor continued to work with Lyons and to form groups for specific jobs. They were together at New York's Fat Tuesday's Club in 1980 to record an impressively integrated *It Is In The Brewing Luminous* >**9** with a sextet that included violinist Ramsey Ameen, as well as two drummers – Jerome Cooper and Sunny Murray. Perhaps because of the line-up, the performance called to mind the small group works of the sixties, although it was to be something of a one-off.

In other ventures Taylor was widening his horizons, occasionally indulging in mixed-media events and writing for contemporary dance groups. With this in mind, the solo *Garden* >**10** was significant. His right hand still inflicted its daring chromatic plunder but there was a greater awareness of composition shapes – perhaps with a view to eventually accommodating a dance team.

Taylor is still a phenomenal power in jazz piano. His opponents refuse to concede that his jazz even qualifies as *music* but, among his peers, he is regarded with awe. It would be difficult to imagine any young modernist playing today without some reference to his style.

Lineage

Taylor's earliest inspiration came from **Bud Powell**, **Thelonious Monk** and **Duke Ellington**. He has strongly influenced players like **Don Pullen**, **Chris McGregor**, Alex von Schlippenbach and Marilyn Crispell, but aspects of his playing are to be found in almost all post-free form pianists.

Listening

1 In Transition
Cecil Taylor/Blue Note BN-LA 458-H2
2 Looking Ahead
Cecil Taylor/Boplicity COP 030
3 Innovations
Cecil Taylor/Polydor 2383 094
4 Unit Structures
Cecil Taylor/Blue Note BST 84237
5 Conquistador
Cecil Taylor/Blue Note BST 84260
6 The Jazz Composers' Orchestra
JCQA LP 1001/2
7 Silent Tongues
Cecil Taylor/Arista 1005

8 Air Above Mountains
Cecil Taylor/Enja 3005
9 It Is In The Brewing Luminous
Cecil Taylor/Hat Hut SIXTEEN (2R16)
10 Garden
Cecil Taylor/Hat Hut 1993/94

Stan Tracey

Born: 30th December 1926/London, UK
Instruments: Piano, vibes, accordion, composer
Recording Career: 1952-

EXPERIENCE WITH the finest of Britain's big bands made Stan Tracey a good choice as resident house pianist when **Ronnie Scott** opened his London jazz club in 1960. It was a job that he held down for eight years, accompanying all American visitors, be they friendly, irascible, quiet, loud, gifted musically, incompetent or just plain impossible.

During this time, he wrote his own inspirational version of the Welsh poet Dylan Thomas' *Under Milk Wood* >**1**. From this, the haunting *Starless And Bible Black*, the quizzical *Nantucket* and the rocking *AM Mayhem* showed his wide range of expression but, if anything, his piano solos said even more about him as a jazzman. Tracey was heavily into the harmonic side of bebop and his strongly chordal playing took each solo into his own uncharted area.

For some time, Tracey was involved in touring with his combo and a big band; then, in 1971, he formed Tandem with the late Mike Osborne. The young altoist had long since emerged from the shadow of **Ornette Coleman** and, with Tracey stepping into the chromatic shallows, performances like *Ballad Forms* >**2** were essentially dynamic. Tracey had always been a superbly rhythmic player, but his move to freer climes put even greater emphasis on that aspect of his style. His mid-seventies quartet, with saxophonist Art Themen, bassist Dave Green and drummer Brian Spring, was just the place to parade it and *Captain Adventure* >**3** could not have been more appropriately named.

Tracey continued to compose with style and his commission for the 1976 Bracknell Festival was later recorded at London's 100 Club. For this performance the quartet became an octet, but *Fraggie Bar Waltz* >**4** captured all the immediacy of the open-air event.

In the eighties, his son Clark took over the drum stool and was on hand to record *The Crompton Suite* >**5**, commissioned for the Bolton Festival of 1979 but not recorded until two years later.

Interestingly, Tracey is the only British jazzman to have been elected an honorary member of the Royal Academy of Music.

Lineage

Tracey drew much inspiration from **Thelonious Monk** but his adaptation to the needs of more modern styles was very much by instinct.

Media

Performed on the soundtrack of the film *Alfie* (1966).

Listening

1 Under Milk Wood
Stan Tracey/Steam SJ 101
2 Live At Bracknell Festival
Stan Tracey/Mike Osborne/Ogun OG 210
3 Captain Adventure
Stan Tracey/Steam SJ 102
4 The Bracknell Connection
Stan Tracey/Steam SJ 103
5 The Crompton Suite
Stan Tracey/Steam SJ 109

Stanley Turrentine

Born: 5th April 1934/Pittsburgh, Pennsylvania, USA
Instrument: Tenor saxophone
Recording Career: 1950-

A PLAYER who has courted fashion for most of his playing career, in pure jazz

sourroundings Stanley William Turrentine produces uncompromising jazz solos. While he can be a very impressive player, he has also accommodated compromise rather too consistently.

Turrentine began his career in the commercially-slanted bands of **Ray Charles** and Earl Bostic but a period from 1959 to 1960 with drummer **Max Roach** was extremely productive in terms of his ultimate style. The 1960 *Drum Conversation* >**1**, recorded in Germany, introduced his essentially masculine style; the harmonic source was hard bop, the rhythmic source somewhat earlier and the improvisational aspirations simple but extremely effective.

Fortunately, in his forays away from the jazz path, he never deserted these jazz principles completely and, sometimes almost by accident, he made records that could be rated highly as jazz performances. His work with organist **Jimmy Smith** had much to recommend it and titles like the 1960 *Back At The Chicken Shack* >**2** were well-suited to his full-throated sound and to his forthright, rhythmic style.

In fact, Turrentine rarely traded in the language of the cocktail lounge: his brusque tone was distinctive and certainly contributed to his overall popularity. It especially suited the blues, and items like *Z T's Blues* >**3**, from his 1961 band, showed how he could communicate without extravagant gesture. This was a particularly good band for him, featuring young guitarist Grant Green, but it did not survive Turrentine's commercial preoccupations. During most of the sixties, he followed the 'organ and tenor' path to popularity with his wife Shirley Scott >**4**. Although achieving higher standards than were normally associated with the style, it was a restrictive environment and they were often glad to introduce light relief in the form of trumpeters like Blue Mitchell and brother Tommy Turrentine.

In the seventies, husband and wife split up and Turrentine again followed the popular route, this time into the funk world. His records for the Fantasy and Elektra labels sold well but rarely showed the tenor man at his best. 'Crossover' was the term used to describe them but the music fell

Stanley Turrentine

between two stools, satisfying neither rock nor jazz followers.

Although the eighties saw no end to this policy, on solo appearances he continued to play straight jazz in clubs on both sides of the Atlantic.

Lineage
Turrentine lists as his favourite tenors **Don Byas, Coleman Hawkins** and **Sonny Rollins**.

Media
Played on the soundtrack of *One Flew Over The Cuckoo's Nest* (1975)

Listening
1 Drum Conversation
  Max Roach/Enja 4074
2 Back At The Chicken Shack
  Jimmy Smith/Blue Note BST 84117
3 Z T's Blues
  Stanley Turrentine/Blue Note BST 84424
4 Blue Flames
  Shirley Scott/Prestige PRLP 7338

Grover Washington

Born: 12th December 1943/Buffalo, NY, USA
Instruments: Alto, baritone, soprano and tenor saxophones, clarinet, electric bass, piano, flute
Recording Career: 1971-

THE MIDDLE BROW listener's idea of a jazz musician, Grover Washington Jr's improvisations are melodically simple, his mode of delivery rhythmically strong and his soul-based tone acceptably 'heated'. At his worst he typifies all that is bad in rock-jazz fusion and titles like *I Loves You Porgy* **>1** are lugubriously sentimental. At his best, however, whole albums such as *Winelight* **>2** take the jazz element more seriously and offer crossover

Grover Washington Jr

music worthy of consideration: never complicated, but with lift from the rhythm team and solos that develop well.

Washington left his home town at sixteen and played out of Columbus, Ohio with the Four Clefs. The group folded in 1963 and, during his national service, Washington was able to freelance with rock groups in Philadelphia. He was with organist Charles Earland in 1971 and, as a result of a recording date with another organist, Johnny Hammond, landed his own recording contract.

His work throughout the seventies enjoyed considerable popularity but, disappointingly, his debut for the re-activated Blue Note label was something of a flop. In the company of Kenny Burrell, Ron Carter and Jack DeJohnette, 1984's *Togethering* >**3** offered little more than a rehash of sixties soul and perhaps confirmed what the jazz world had always known: that Grover Washington is an accomplished follower of fashion.

Lineage

His influences were **John Coltrane** and Joe Henderson, but any second-generation Washingtons belong to the crossover field.

Listening

1 Inner City Blues
  Grover Washington/Motown STMS 5055
2 Winelight
  Grover Washington/Elektra 256262
3 Togethering
  Grover Washington/Blue Note BT 85106

Mike Westbrook

**Born: 21st March 1936/High Wycombe, Buckinghamshire, UK
Instruments: Piano, baritone horn, tuba, composer
Recording Career: 1967-
Nickname: Westy**

WHEN HE CAME to London in 1962, Michael John David Westbrook brought with him baritone saxophonist **John Surman** who was destined to be his star soloist in the ensuing years. His first five years gained him a large and vociferous local following, but his real breakthrough came in 1967 when he recorded *Celebration* >**1** and, in the

Rutherford and Malcolm Griffiths remained and the excellent trumpet of Henry Lowther had been drafted in, but Surman had moved on and his authoritative voice was missed.

Sadly, the economics of running the Concert Band had become an even greater problem and Westbrook offered an alternative with the smaller Brass Band. As a group, it transcended jazz, drawing its material from folk music, poetry, art music as well as from almost any national style to create concerts that resembled a variety show. Phil Minton's strange vocalese was a special attraction and *The Paris Album* >**6** from 1981 gives a good illustration of the style.

Westbrook's heart remained with the more ambitious eleven-piece, however, and, although opportunities were rare, a work commissioned in France was performed in 1984. *On Duke's Birthday* >**7** was a triumph: Westbrook made no attempt to write like **Duke Ellington** but captured the mood of the dedicatee and did so with a band that was no mere up-date of Westbrook's old sound.

Lineage
Westbrook drew something from the great swing bands but most especially from **Duke Ellington**.

Media
Wrote *Tyger*, a stage musical for Britain's National Theatre, *Citadel/Room 315* >**5** for Swedish radio and *On Duke's Birthday* >**7** for Le Temps Du Jazz, Amiens and Jazz En France, Angoulême. A documentary on Westbrook was made by the Arts Council of Great Britain (1978).

Listening
1 Celebrations
Mike Westbrook/Derum SML 1013
2 Release
Mike Westbrook/Derum SML 1031
3 Marching Song
Mike Westbrook/Derum SML 1047/8
4 Love/Dream And Variations
Mike Westbrook/Transatlantic TRA 323
5 Citadel/Room 315
Mike Westbrook/RCA SF 8433
6 The Paris Album
Mike Westbrook/Polydor 2655 008
7 On Duke's Birthday
Mike Westbrook/Hat ART 2012

following year, *Release* >**2**. The pattern of these performances was continuous, with themes loosely linked and solos deftly cushioned. In this department, Westbrook was fortunate and in Surman, altoist Mike Osborne and trombonist **Paul Rutherford** his band had genuinely creative voices.

His arrangements were geared to such men and, although ensemble parts were occasionally a trifle pedestrian, the excitement generated in concert transferred well to records. The 1969 *Marching Song* >**3** was a total celebration of the style; swaggering ensembles brought together circus ring drama, military pomp and jazz's own ageless marching band tradition. Quality soloing emerged from the turmoil and there were even gentle interludes to showcase the reflective piano skills of the leader.

In the seventies, a rhythm team of pianist Dave McRae, bassist Chris Lawrence and guitarist Brian Godding was introduced and its arrival hinted on *Love/Dream And Variations* >**4** that Westbrook was thinking of a change in musical direction. This was confirmed when *Citadel/Room 315* >**5** ushered the band into the fusion age, at least to the extent of using rock-based rhythms. The impressive trombone team of

THE SEVENTIES & EIGHTIES

The fusion of rock and jazz was a feature of the early seventies. Miles Davis moved further from jazz and played less himself, while his sidemen sensed the commercial potential of the style and broke away to form groups of their own. Chick Corea's Return To Forever, John McLaughlin's Mahavishnu Orchestra, and Larry Coryell's Eleventh House showed the scope available within the style, and Wayne Shorter made a major contribution to Weather Report, the most satisfying ensemble of them all. Unfortunately, a whole legion of second-division fusion groups emerged, and the fashion for heavy, leather-tongued saxophone players and four-square rhythms gained ground.

Jazz, the injured animal, slunk away to lick its wounds, and its response came from New York. A new generation of creatively-minded young musicians was arriving who needed somewhere to play. The establishment clubs, happy with well-known artists and a guaranteed following, were not about to risk their trade by employing unknowns.

With the aid of stalwarts like Sam Rivers, however, the problem was overcome. A large number of disused warehouse lofts were available, too small for major industrial use, but ideal for conversion into recital rooms. These surroundings were less than ideal, but little expense was involved in setting them up for jazz performances. The loft movement had been born and although it did smack of artists starving in garrets, it gave a jazz world, in danger of suffocation by rock rhythms, genuine breathing space.

The new wave of young players included saxophonists such as Oliver Lake, David Murray, Hamiet Bluiett and Henry Threadgill; trumpeters like Olu Dara and Baikida Carroll; and string players, among them Billy Bang and Abdul Wadud. These musicians were to guide the jazz mainstream through the troubled waters of the late seventies, using the language of the free pioneers but increasingly organising their music and moving away from the mayhem of open-ended, or themeless, free playing.

European jazz, though, was not free from rock influence, represented at its best by the Miles Davis-inspired Nucleus but, in the main, bogged down by uncreative hornmen and cluttered rhythm sections. Its most creative strain came from the unlikely area of Scandinavia. The German ECM label captured players like guitarist Terje Rypdal, bassist Arild Andersen and saxophonist Jan Garbarek in performances of at times quite cold and clinical beauty. This was music without the passion of black jazz: its structure was more formal but it spoke of high creative standards.

The ECM recording engineers aspired to a clean, well-defined, but rather sterile sound which, to some extent, accounted for the 'cold-blooded' critical jibe that it suffered. In reality,

V.S.O.P. II, left to right: Herbie Hancock, Wynton Marsalis, Ron Carter and Tony Williams

the sound suited the music: the players involved were highly inventive and, since ECM also embraced the work of other outstanding internationalists like Eberhard Weber, Egberto Gismonti, Kenny Wheeler and Enrico Rava, there could be no real support for the theory that it was a one-style label. ECM's later involvement with groups like the Art Ensemble Of Chicago finally confounded its critics and it moved into the eighties equipped to represent various jazz factions.

In America, the young lions of the lofts had themselves become establishment. It was not that their music had become bland but – as always happens – their audiences had come to know them more intimately. In one sense, however, their music returned to certain older values. The path of organisation had been followed with more vigour and a crop of saxophone groups, without rhythm sections, appeared. They were all capped by the World Saxophone Quartet, but most of the emerging groups of the eighties used their own compositions and arranged their jazz with care.

To show the range of expression available, Arthur Blythe introduced an element of old-time swing; Billy Bang advanced the case for street-wise musical cunning, while Carla Bley favoured satirical comedy. David Murray led both a brilliant octet and a colourful big band and, although all put the emphasis on solos and soloists, it was their arrangements which gave depth to the performances.

The early eighties were a period of consolidation. A vernacular established in musical rebellion had been put to more conservative use and, in the process, jazz had become truly international. Inevitably, America remained the all-important source of inspiration, but a genuine cross pollination of ideas now existed. Trombonist George Lewis, trumpeter Leo Smith and guitarist Fred Frith were just three influenced by the European free improvisation axis.

Ray Anderson

Born: 16th October 1952/Chicago, Illinois, USA
Instruments: Trombone, tuba, percussion, vocals, composer
Recording Career: 1977-

LIKE MANY young musicians in the eighties, Ray Anderson is a man of many parts: a serious jazzman who is also well-equipped to play music outside the jazz field. His jazz style lives somewhere in the creative avenue between the architect-designed precision of master trombonist Britt Woodman and the more rustic **Roswell Rudd**. His outlook is modern but there is more than a trace of 'gutbucket' in his soul.

Early musical studies at high school alongside fellow trombonist George Lewis led to a mutual interest in the music of Chicago's South Side and that city's laissez-faire attitudes encouraged Anderson's own cosmopolitan attitudes. After college he quit music for a year but, in the early seventies, played in a funk band. He then spent time in California, working with Stanley Crouch and **David Murray**, before moving to New York in 1973.

This brought him into the lively 'loft scene' where he played with men like **Sam Rivers** and Bennie Wallace. From 1977 to 1979 he toured, on and off, with **Anthony Braxton** and the quality of their partnership was well captured at the 1979 Willisau Festival in Switzerland >**1**. Braxton's detailed compositions tested the trombonist's technique but it was the dense textures of the group's collective passages that challenged his improvisational skills and his ability to listen to a contrapuntal rival. He passed the test with ease but one could not help but feel that his barnstorming talents were better displayed in Barry Altschul's looser combos. *Irina* >**2**, in particular, offered the soulful side of Anderson's personality, while *Orange Was The Colour* >**3** showed that he was no stranger to the bluesy 'plunger mute' world of **Tricky Sam Nanton**.

In the eighties, he began leading his own units and his records proclaimed his versatility. *Portrait Of Mark Dresser* >**4** was a satirical funeral march, *Paucartambo* >**4** took him into steel band territory, while the well-spaced *Boxcar* >**5** showed his grasp of the more static elements of the European school.

His funk/dance band the Slickaphonics (formed in 1984) offers the complete contrast. With bassist Mark Helias in a rock role, the group sings and jives like so many sidewalk buskers. They produce a music that completes the picture of a man who can be profound or flippant without embarrassing the listener.

Lineage
Anderson was originally inspired by his father's Dixieland collection and lists Vic Dickenson and Trummy Young as his main influences. The later influence of saxophonist **Anthony Braxton** turned him into more formal areas.

Listening
1 Jazz Festival At Willisau
Anthony Braxton/Hat Hut NINETEEN (2R19)
2 Brahma
Barry Altschul/Sackville 3023
3 For Stu
Barry Altschul/Soul Note SN 1015
4 Right Down Your Alley
Ray Anderson/Soul Note SN 1087
5 You Be
Ray Anderson/Minor Music 007

Billy Bang

Born: 20th September 1947/Mobile, Alabama, USA
Instruments: Violin, drums, flute, composer
Recording Career: 1977-

AT BOARDING SCHOOL, the young Billy Walker hated the violin: he felt that its image was unhip and he told critic Lee Jeske that he had only been given it 'because he was small of stature'. He also felt his name to be anonymous and he changed to Billy Bang on the strength of the theory that it would never be forgotten. This apart, he had become quite proficient on the violin and it was only out of petulance that he turned his attention to drums and flute. This was not a wholly successful move, however, and as he became more serious about his music in the late sixties, he was forced to concede that he could express his musical ideas more easily on the violin than on flute.

The result was a return to the bow and, when he became a professional in 1972, the violin was his chosen axe. By then, living in New York, he took some ego-denting knocks from establishment musicians, although he had begun to make his mark. He maintains that he did not find his real direction until 1977, the year in which he formed the String Trio Of New York (STONY) with guitarist James Emery and bassist John Lindberg. This group was a delicious mixture of gypsy whimsy, recital-hall formalism and speakeasy jazz. Emery likened the music to that of the New Orleans spasm bands but the technical expertise shown on titles like the 1980 *Strawberries* >**1** and Bang's own superb solos on the 1983 *Open Up* and *Penguins* >**2**, make nonsense of such a comparison.

This was only one aspect of Bang's talent, however, and he used his versatility to look at jazz from other standpoints. His improvisational awareness was always acute and his fertile mind flourished in an area best described as post-**Ornette Coleman** orthodoxy. His was a tune-playing version of free form: the tonality was modern, but the storytelling element was traditional, and the whole was coloured with a realism that was bred in the ghetto but comfortable in the concert hall.

In fact, he gave concerts as a solo recitalist and *Loweski* >**3** illustrated what a versatile performer he could be. He also led uncompromising jazz quintets and sextets and, on material like *Rainbow Gladiator* >**4** and *Loverman* >**5**, his powerful and inventive violin style dominates even a hard-hitting, modern group. In 1984, his working combo adopted the name Jazz Doctors. They donned white coats but made no attempt to make their music correspondingly clinical. Ornette Coleman's *Lonely Woman* >**6** retained its strength and urgency and demonstrated perhaps that Bang had found his most satisfying musical environment.

Working with other leaders was a different matter: with Ronald Shannon Jackson's Decoding Society, Bang fitted uneasily into the crossover atmosphere but as part of Material, **Sonny Sharrock**'s more earthy band, he entered fully into the free funk spirit, using his dashing, rhythmic powers to the utmost. In 1986, Bang left the STONY but continues to be active in his other musical areas; he nurtures the desire to work with a larger string ensemble and is convinced that this will be possible in the near future.

Lineage

Bang greatly admired violinist **Stuff Smith** and from photographs of his idol acquired the bad habit of bowing his instrument straight down his chest. Lessons with **Leroy Jenkins** cured this, while also allowing him access to the music of the Chicago free form school.

Listening

1 Area Code 212
String Trio Of New York/Black Saint BSR 0048

2 Rebirth Of A Feeling
String Trio Of New York/Black Saint BSR 0068

3 Distinction Without A Difference
Billy Bang/Hat Hut FOUR (1R04)

4 Rainbow Gladiator
Billy Bang/Soul Note SN 1016

5 Invitation
Billy Bang/Soul Note SN 1036

6 Intensive Care
Jazz Doctors/Cadillac SGC 1011

George Benson

Born: 22nd March 1943/Pittsburgh, Pennsylvania, USA
Instrument: Guitar, vocals
Recording Career: 1963-

BENSON'S CAREER finds an unlikely parallel in the work of the late **Nat King Cole**. Like the pianist, he built up a considerable reputation as a jazz instrumentalist only to find that a new generation had become enamoured of his vocal skills.

He first emerged as a guitarist in the

sixties when organ-based combos were popular. After three years with organist Jack McDuff, he went on to record with **Miles Davis** on 1968's *Miles In The Sky* >**1**, with Jaki Byard on *Byard With Strings* >**2** from the same year, and with **Freddie Hubbard** in the 1971 *Straight Life* >**3**. His playing followed the Barney Kessel and **Wes Montgomery** lineage and had its heart in the hard bop style of the day. He was not unaware of other developments, however, and in 1970 he began a musical association with record producer Creed Taylor, at first with A & M, and then with the CTI label.

Taylor set about commercialising Benson, surrounding him with large orchestras and, as on *White Rabbit* >**4**, turning him into a formula product. At first his inherent skill as a jazz player

won the day, but he showed himself willing to simplify his improvisational process for mass consumption and a move to Warner Brothers in 1978 only intensifed the process. *Breezin'* >**5**, his first album for the label was a tremendous hit and he has seen no reason to re-adjust his artistic sights since.

Benson still wears his jazz hat at festivals and for the odd concert date and even jammed in a London wine bar for one night in the eighties. Despite these occasional forays, he is lost to jazz and continues to play in a simplified way that complements a pleasing, if unspectacular, vocal style.

Lineage

Benson was inspired by **Charlie Christian** but has exerted little influence in the jazz world.

Media

Took part in a TV tribute to producer John Hammond and has also appeared with the **Count Basie** Orchestra on TV. Two of his songs were used in the film of boxer Muhammed Ali's life *The Greatest* (1977), and Benson appeared in the film of The Beatles' *Sgt Pepper's Lonely Hearts Club Band* (1978). He featured in *All That Jazz* (1979).

Listening

1 Miles In The Sky
Miles Davis/CBS 85548
2 Jaki Byard With Strings
Jaki Byard/Prestige PR 7573
3 Straight Life
Freddie Hubbard/CTI 6007
4 White Rabbit
George Benson/CTI 6015
5 Breezin'
George Benson/Warner Bros. K 56199

Ran Blake

Born: 20th April 1935/Springfield, Massachusetts, USA
Instruments: Piano, keyboards, composer
Recording Career: 1961-

BLAKE'S MOST EXCITING discovery was the singing of the Pentecostal Church. There they 'sang the music of God with the most beautiful blues scales', and Blake became an instant convert. His further education occurred when he heard **Thelonious Monk** while waiting table in New York's Greenwich Village during school vacation. In the fifties his interests fell between the rolling accompaniments of gospel queen Mahalia Jackson's pianist Mildred Falls and the work of classical composers Béla Bartók, Charles Ives and Anton Webern. This strange dichotomy certainly affected his musical life, yet his ability to play storefront piano was well illustrated by *Church On Russell Street* >**1** from his first record with singer Jeanne Lee. Between this 1961 date and 1975 he

recorded only twice, but it was his work in the late seventies that established him as a gifted if eccentric maverick of the piano.

Fortunately, his devotion to Monk sired a highly original approach. He never played more than the bare bones of a tune and *You Stepped Out Of A Dream*, *Sophisticated Lady* >**2** and *Lush Life* >**3** confirmed his refusal to flesh out a ballad with empty rhetoric. His command of keyboard techniques was free from false aspirations, always employed to further the musical content of his work. He has since worked in duets with **Anthony Braxton** and the superb hard bop trumpeter Ted Curson and, as the 1980 *Film Noir* >**4** proved, he is no stranger to lighter, more modern, forms with even a hint of rock.

Lineage

Blake's Mother Earth is **Billie Holiday** and his three favourite pianists **Thelonious Monk**, Thelonious Monk and Monk! He listened to **James P. Johnson** for stride and to **Mary Lou Williams** for her blues, but has influenced few players himself.

Listening

1 The Newest Sound Around
Jeanne Lee/Ran Blake/RCA PL 42863
2 Breakthru
Ran Blake/Improving Artists Inc. 37 38 42
3 Third Stream Re-composition
Ran Blake/Owl 017
4 Film Noir
Ran Blake/Arista AN 3019

Hamiet Bluiett

Born: 16th September 1940/Lovejoy, Illinois, USA
Instruments: Baritone saxophone, clarinet, flute
Recording Career: 1972-

SOME HAVE SEEN in Hamiet Bluiett the new Messiah of the baritone saxophone, the man who extended the chain that began with Harry Carney and carried through with **Gerry Mulligan**, Serge Chaloff and Pepper Adams.

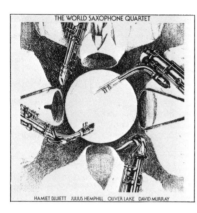

THE WORLD SAXOPHONE QUARTET

HAMIET BLUIETT   JULIUS HEMPHILL   OLIVER LAKE   DAVID MURRAY

These men adapted the language of bop to the needs of their own instrument, but Bluiett's requirements were somewhat different. He was neither innovator nor consolidator, his inspirational sources were disparate, his links with tradition very strong and his musical associations with avid experimentalists misleading. Bluiett's success in the jazz vanguard of the late seventies was based more on adaptability and instrumental facility than on his own barrier-breaking impetus.

Early experience with St Louis' Black Artists Group brought him into the company of men like Julius Hemphill and records like *Hard Blues* >**1** show him more as a steadfast bandsman than as a soloist. At the age of twenty-nine he went to New York and played a prominent part in the loft movement at clubs such as Studio Rivbea. Stimulated by the musical infighting of these sessions, he began to play with an all-embracing expressiveness. *Sobra Una Nube* >**2** from his 1976 debut as a leader introduced him as a marauding samurai of his instrument, vocalising his protest on the baritone sax, dredging honks from his very soul and using overtones with superb control.

These rallying cries did not disguise his planned musical strategy, however, and such solo performances as *My Father's House* >**3** were models of formal design while *Between The Raindrops* >**4** confirmed his commitment to melody.

In 1977, Bluiett became a founder member of the World Saxophone

Quartet in which, if only because he played the lower pitched horn, he provided the bass continuity. Despite imaginative solos like *Scared Sheetless* >**5** which paraded his individual skills, he underpinned his colleagues in the way that tuba specialist Cyrus St Clair had dominated **Clarence Williams**' rhythm sections in the early thirties. Although Maurice McIntyre (a.k.a. Kalaparush) probably did more to tailor the needs of the baritone to free-form jazz, Bluiett was the complete bandsman, the cornerstone of the WSQ and a soloist with a foot in the door of every decade's mainstream style.

Lineage
Eric Dolphy's bass clarinet not only inspired Bluiett, but also deterred him from playing the instrument; it was while working with men such as Lester Bowie, Julius Hemphill and **Oliver Lake** that he came to create his own musical language.

Listening
1 Coon Bid'ness
  Julius Hemphill/Freedom FLP 41012
2 Endangered Species
  Hamiet Bluiett/India Navigation IN 1026
3 Birthright
  Hamlet Bluiett/India Navigation IN 1030
4 Dangerously Suite
  Hamiet Bluiett/Soul Note SN 1018
5 Point Of No Return
  World Saxophone Quartet/Moer's Music 01034

Arthur Blythe

Born: 5th July 1940/Los Angeles, California, USA
Instruments: Alto and soprano saxophones, composer
Recording Career: 1971-
Nickname: Black Arthur

BLYTHE emerged from the obscurity of the West Coast in the middle seventies to make a very special mark on jazz. His dues had been paid with the bands of Horace Tapscott and **Ray Charles** as well as in the experimental environment of the Owen Marshall musical workshop. It was his move to New York in 1974, however, that brought him to prominence. His advantage was that he was already the finished article and it was not long before he was working with Chico Hamilton, as well as freelancing with **Gil Evans**.

As an improviser he set no hard and fast rules. He shunned open-ended or abstract playing completely and, as a title such as *Lower Nile* >**1** shows, had the ability to build a solo with the structural consistency of a **Coleman Hawkins**. He was equally at home moving away from the parent theme, implying a new direction yet retaining the melody in his head, merely as an umbilical option and a contact with source.

He had a natural affinity with players of an organised disposition and his group formed in 1979 with tuba specialist Bob Stewart and brilliant cellist Abdul Wadud had a personality of its own. It stayed together well into the eighties and *Metamorphosis* >**2** illustrates its genuine collective awareness. Blythe's powerful oratory makes strong points but they are set in a musical debating club where everyone has a say. Arrangements were a loose but vital part of the altoist's musical policy and in 1983 he recorded a superb tribute to **Thelonious Monk** >**3**. Before hearing Monk, Blythe claims to have directed his musical identity to being a 'blues' saxophonist but a title such as *Epistrophy* shows just how totally immersed in the jazz mainstream he had become.

Recordings with **Gil Evans** >**4** and Lester Bowie >**5** describe how selflessly he could work with other leaders and, even on more commercially-slanted recording projects >**6**, Blythe's solos exhibit shape, creativity and, perhaps above all else, an ineluctable sense of swing.

Lineage
Blythe lists his main influences as **John Coltrane**, **Thelonious Monk** and **Eric Dolphy** but has, himself, played an important part in the career of **David Murray**.

Listening
1 The Grip
Arthur Blythe/India Navigation IN 1029

2 Metamorphosis
Arthur Blythe/India Navigation IN 1038
3 Light Blue
Arthur Blythe/CBS 25397
4 Parabola
Gil Evans/Horo HDP 31–32
5 The 5th Power
Lester Bowie/Black Saint BSR 0020
6 Elaborations
Arthur Blythe CBS 85980

Gary Burton

Born: 23rd January 1943/Anderson, Indiana, USA
Instruments: Vibes, piano, organ, composer
Recording Career: 1961-

ALTHOUGH Gary Burton is an outstanding jazz musician, the music he makes and the groups in which he works are not always so easy to classify. His jazz grounding was thorough, having worked with **George Shearing** and **Stan Getz**, but when he formed his own quartet in 1967, his motives were less clear.

He played superbly on titles like *The*

Beach and *June The 15, 1967* >**1**, his solos jinking and side-stepping their way through the material and his four-mallet technique adding harmonic richness to the overall group sound. In contrast, guitarist partner Larry Coryell's rock background denied him Burton's improvisational fluency, yet the music they made together was a melodic delight.

Burton's brilliant solo work in the early seventies underlined his jazz qualities and the 1973 quartet, with Michael Goodrick on guitar, proved that Burton could produce a uniquely personal group sound with any sidemen.

It was this unit which recorded with the NDR Symphony Orchestra in Hamburg, but the outcome lacked the flexibility and sustained creativity of the straight quartet's *Open Your Eyes* or *Mallet Man* >**2**. These were strong performances, although there always lurked the danger of Burton's playing tipping into romanticism. He loved elaborate embellishment and his *Children's Songs* >**3**, in duet with **Chick Corea**, indulged this side of his personality.

The Corea-Burton duo was otherwise a productive team and they toured together successfully. This became a pattern of Burton's musical life in the eighties and 1981's *One* and *Autumn Leaves* >**4** presented another potent partnership, on this occasion with Ahmad Jamal. He brought to all of these associations a natural gift as a composer but also that of a canny improviser, one who could make all his 'new' tunes sound more valid than the original from which they were taken.

Lineage

Burton successfully translated **Bill Evans**' piano style to the vibes and has since seen his four-mallet skills borrowed by many contemporary vibraphonists. He no doubt left his mark, too, on the students of Berkeley College of Music in California, where, for some time, he was on the permanent staff.

Media

Appeared in *Get Yourself A College Girl* (1964) and *The Hanged Man* (1964), both with **Stan Getz**.

Listening

1 Lofty Fake Anagram
   Gary Burton/RCA SF 7923
2 The New Quartet
   Gary Burton/ECM 1030 ST
3 Duet
   Gary Burton/Chick Corea/ECM 1140
4 Live At Midem
   Ahmad Jamal/Gary Burton/Kingdom GATE 7006

Stanley Clarke

Born: 30th June 1951/Philadelphia, Pennsylvania, USA
Instruments: Bass, electric bass, cello, keyboards, sitar, percussion, vocals, composer
Recording Career: 1971-

MUCH PRAISE has been heaped on the head of this child prodigy since he played for **Horace Silver** at the age of eighteen. Inevitably this has been welcomed by his sycophantic followers but has also been regarded with unreasonable suspicion by the critical fraternity. The truth is that Clarke is a very good musician, and one who has successfully bridged the gulf between jazz and rock.

As a star member of Return To Forever >**1** he could show his jazz 'chops', build solos with sure-footed logic and use his easy, rhythmic manner to infect the whole group. In contrast, his own albums like *School Days* >**2** acknowledged equal enthusiasm for the electric bass and for its more rudimentary application. Such records replaced the supple flow of his pure jazz voice with a heavily propulsive, 'beat-making' line, simplifying his music for more general consumption.

Clarke has worked with the likes of **Art Blakey**, **Stan Getz**, **Dexter Gordon** and Joe Henderson, recorded with **Gato Barbieri**, Joe Farrell, Aretha Franklin and **Pharoah Sanders** and, in 1984, was often on the festival touring circuit in a bass duo with ex-**Weather Report** bassist Miroslav Vitous. Clarke tends to be a man for all seasons but, when the company is right, is a very impressive bassist.

Stanley Clarke

Lineage

Clarke lists his influences as **Jimmy Blanton**, Oscar Pettiford and Scott LaFaro, but also concedes that their message has been filtered through **Miles Davis**, one-time Jimi Hendrix bassist Billy Cox, and by the whole Motown sound. If one single album can be said to show just where these diverse routes have led, it is *Journey To Love* >**3**.

Listening

1 Return To Forever
  ECM 1022 ST
2 School Days
  Stanley Clarke/Epic 32094
3 Journey To Love
  Stanley Clarke/Epic 32093

Billy Cobham

**Born: 16th May 1944/Panama
Instruments: Drums, percussion, composer
Recording Career: 1967-**

IN MOVING FROM hard bop drumming powerhouse to rock drum superstar, William C. Cobham has left very few casualties on the way. He had early experience with **Grover Washington** in 1967, chased Billy Taylor's fleet Tatum-isms around the Hickory House in New York and, in 1968, after his military release, joined the **Horace Silver** Quintet. Here he played exceptionally well on the album *Serenade To A Soul Sister* >**1** and later took part in important **Miles Davis** record dates like *Bitches Brew* >**2** and *Live-Evil* >**3**.

In 1971, Cobham joined **John McLaughlin**'s Mahavishnu Orchestra and played a major part in *Inner Mounting Flame* >**4**. What was surprising was that he had completely changed his style. Gone was the ringing cymbal of the hard bop drummer, and, in its place, the heavy afterbeat of the rock percussionist. Although on such records, his attention to time keeping was thorough, in some live performances, showmanship led to erratic tempos.

The original edition of the Mahavishnu folded in 1973 but, armed with an Atlantic recording contract, Cobham began to work under his own name. Eminent sidemen like trumpeters Randy Brecker and Marvin Stamm, pianist **George Duke** and guitarists John Abercombie and Jon Scofield were used but, as commercial success came, this band distanced itself from jazz. The depths of gimmickry were reached with *A Funky Thide Of Signes* >**5**, although Cobham's Glass Menagerie band did redress the balance somewhat with *Smokin'* >**6**, recorded live at the 1982 Montreux Festival.

233

Cobham's speed of execution and his naturally rhythmic style are not put to their best use in the funk-crossover style but he remains a very exciting performer, and a drummer with the ability to completely control the line-ups in which he works.

Lineage

Cobham cites drummers Jo Jones, Gus Johnson and Sonny Payne as inspirations but his own influence has been mainly on rock and show players.

Media

Played on the soundtracks of *Jack Johnson* (1970), *Shaft* (1971) and *Flic Ou Voyou?* (1978). Can also be heard in some episodes of TV series *Mission Impossible* (1966-73).

Listening

1 Serenade To A Soul Sister
Horace Silver/Blue Note BST 84277
2 Bitches Brew/Sanctuary
Miles Davis/CBS 66236
3 Live-Evil
Miles Davis/CBS 67219
4 Inner Mounting Flame
Mahavishnu Orchestra/CBS 64717
5 A Funky Thide Of Signes
Billy Cobham/Atlantic 50189
6 Smokin'
Billy Cobham's Glass Menagerie/Electra 960 233.1

Steve Coleman

Born: 20th September 1956/Chicago, Illinois, USA
Instruments: Alto and soprano saxophones, clarinet, flute, vocals, percussion, composer
Recording Career: 1980-

ALTHOUGH HE GAINED a local reputation in Chicago when he began appearing with the Thad Jones-Mel Lewis Orchestra in 1978, Steve Coleman has had to wait until the eighties to reach a more international audience. He is, however, a remarkable young saxophonist, well-versed in musical styles that transcend jazz, but nevertheless a jazzman of considerable potential.

In 1979, he moved to New York and, for a time, settled for busking on the city's streets. In the early eighties, he worked with drummer Doug Hammond and further developed his composing talents. In 1984, he joined bassist Dave Holland and made a tremendous impact on European audiences during a tour that year.

With his own group, the 1985 *Cud Ba-Rith* and *On This* >**1** show Coleman's Chicago bop roots but it is his playing on items such as *Another Level* >**1** that mark him out as a creative improviser. More importantly, this title identifies him as an eighties player, a user of mainstream continuity but a musical painter who shades his finished canvas with the colourful vernacular of the freer players. Like many of his performances, it is a piece of pulpit-preaching alto that never allows its passion to override its powers of oratory. As an accompanist to singer Cassandra Wilson, he had exhibited similar understanding and the manner in which he crests the jagged, rhythmic background of *Desperate Move* >**2** is particularly impressive. The fusion atmosphere of *On The Edge Of Tomorrow* >**3** is a less challenging environment for him and, as a response, he resorts to a simplistic disco language. It is a dissipation of talent rather than a bad performance but it suggests that he is content to produce the empty wail of formula rock saxophonists when the occasion demands. He remains, nevertheless, a very promising musician and one who, in the right company, can produce jazz solos of genuine maturity.

Lineage

Coleman names saxophonists Von Freeman and Bunky Green as his instrumental influences, but **Henry Threadgill** and **Sam Rivers** as his writing models.

Listening

1 Motherland Pulse
Steve Coleman/JMT 850001
2 Point Of View
Cassandra Wilson/JMT 850004
3 On The Edge Of Tomorrow
Steve Coleman/JMT 860005

George Duke

Born: 12th January 1946/San Rafael, California, USA
Instruments: Piano, clarinet, organ synthesizer, composer
Recording Career: 1966-

TO CLASSIFY George Duke is almost impossible. He has played jazz extremely well in fast company and taken part in experimental, avant-garde music, yet he must now be considered a pop/rock superstar.

Duke's early experience in San Francisco was gained backing famous visiting musicians like **Dizzy Gillespie** and **Bobby Hutcherson**. He played with **Jean-Luc Ponty** in 1969 and, after eight months with the Don Ellis Band, joined Frank Zappa. From 1971 to 1972, he toured with **Cannonball Adderley** and showed on *Pretty Paul* and *Walk Tall* >**1** just how well he could perform within a hard/soul quintet. His playing was relaxed, yet the latent urgency of the baptist rock flowed through his well-lubricated improvisations. It was his mastery of this conflicting aspect of the music that marked him out as a man who could have personally progressed the soul movement.

It was not to be, however, and Duke was back with Zappa from 1973 to 1975 and soon leading his own groups. His 1975 recording for Eddie Henderson, *Sunburst* >**2**, gave warning of what was to come and, when he signed for the Epic label in 1976, almost all jazz ties were severed. The 1978 *Don't Let Go* >**3** and 1980's *From Me To You* >**4** told the story. Both were confused by busy, Latin/rock beats and swamped by vocal extravagances. Jazz had lost itself a highly talented son and George Duke had become a rich man.

Lineage
Duke names **Miles Davis**, Les McCann, Ahmad Jamal and Frank Zappa among his influences.

Media
Played on Zappa's soundtrack for the film *2000 Motels* (1971) and appeared with the vocal group Third Wave in *Hollywood Palace*.

Listening

1 At Congresshall
Cannonball Adderley/PST Z-SXL 0546
2 Sunburst
Eddie Henderson/Blue Note BN-LA 464-G
3 Don't Let Go
George Duke/Epic 82821
4 From Me To You
George Duke/Epic EPC 81850

Vyacheslav Ganelin

Born: 1944/Vilnius, USSR
Instruments: Piano, bass, guitar, organ, trumpet, percussion, composer
Recording Career: 1976-

GANELIN'S SERVICE to Russian jazz has been inestimable. He persuaded the state-controlled Melodiya label to issue records by his free jazz trio, has toured successfully throughout Europe with the group and even appeared in the 1986 New York Festival. In so doing, he did much to correct the impression that jazz beyond the iron curtain was merely a matter of derivative revivalism. In fact, the Ganelin Trio's music, a mixture of American avant-garde, Willem Breuker laugh-in and European free improvisation, has charted much new territory. It is often extremely formal and although compositions are structured to allow free solo expression, they are structured nonetheless.

In the trio, saxophonist Vladimir Chekasin doubled on trombone and violin, played two saxophones simultaneously, and introduced elements of dance in the form of self-parody. He is at best when roaring full-throatedly on tenor, as on *Live In East Germany* >**1**, but proves a consistently inventive player in the free manner on all the group's recordings. Vladimir Tarasov is a tight and muscular drummer who can play a whisper or, as he showed on *De* >**2**, introduce a feeling of whirlwind power. Ganelin himself is the conservative, seeming

Vyacheslav Ganelin

happier when the theme remains in sight and describing his own playing as 'lyrical avant-garde'. *New Wine* >**3** demonstrated what he meant by this, with its mood of general understatement.

Ganelin did not become fully committed to free improvisation until the middle seventies but has, since then, established his trio as the most significant in a promising Russian jazz scene. At times, the group overplay the comic element in their music, with on-stage postures that transcend parody, become banal and lead the players to the brink of university rag-week pranks. Weighed against this, there are suites, like the imaginative *Ancora Da Capo* >**4**, to confirm that here are three alert and highly sophisticated minds. The Ganelin Trio, as a whole, has received a great deal of western media attention, although one suspects this is more because of their Russian background than for their undoubted musical quality.

Lineage

Despite claims to the contrary, Ganelin and his men were inspired both by American avant-garde figures like **Ornette Coleman** and **Archie Shepp** and by European bands such as the Globe Unity Orchestra and the Willem Breuker Kollektief.

Listening

1 Live In East Germany
Ganelin Trio/Leo LR 102
2 Vide
Ganelin Trio/Leo LR 117
3 New Wine
Ganelin Trio/Leo LR 112
4 Ancora Da Capo
Ganelin Trio/Leo LR 108/9 (2)

Jan Garbarek

Born: 4th March 1947/Mysen, near Oslo, Norway
Instruments: Bass, soprano and tenor saxophones, clarinet, flute, composer
Recording Career: 1966-

JAN GARBAREK is very sceptical of the 'Nordic ice-horn' image with which he is sometimes branded. Atmospheric performances like *Vandrere* >**1**, where he reacted to an unmanned wind harp and to the wind coming in from the North Sea, were wrongly taken as typical, ignoring the fact that the Norwegian was a very versatile player.

In 1970, Garbarek spent almost two months in New York and steeped himself in the black avant-garde. He had always admired **Ornette Coleman** and, at one time, could play most of his compositions. *Blow Away Zone* >**2** showed that he was no stranger to the extrovert aspects of the music, although throughout the seventies his playing tended to avoid extremes.

During this time he worked with various American leaders including George Russell, **Don Cherry** and **Keith Jarrett** and his playing on Jarrett's 1975 orchestral work, *Arbour Zena* >**3**, is an example of how well-controlled romanticism could serve a formal background. In the late seventies, a gentle brush with jazz-rock was handled with good taste and, in the eighties, Garbarek continued to work in his native country. There was also some notable trio work in the company of bassist **Charlie Haden** and guitarist/pianist Egberto Gismonti >**4**.

He gave pure jazz performances in clubs and at European festivals, and there were also recording dates outside the jazz field, with the likes of minimalist Jan Erik Vold and atonal composer Arne Nordheim.

Lineage

Garbarek lists saxophonists **Ornette Coleman**, **John Coltrane**, **Archie Shepp** and **Pharoah Sanders** as his main influences but does not discount the effect had on him by hearing the music of **Miles Davis** and **Johnny Hodges** and of working with **Keith Jarrett**.

Media

Wrote the score for the Norwegian film *Henrettelsen* (1980).

Listening

1 Dis
 Jan Garbarek/Ralph Towner/ECM 1093
2 Afric Pepperbird
 Jan Garbarek/ECM 1007
3 Arbour Zena
 Keith Jarrett/ECM 1070
4 Magico
 Garbarek/Gismonti/Haden/ECM 1151

Herbie Hancock

Born: 12th April 1940/Chicago, Illinois, USA
Instruments: Piano, electric piano, organ, synthesizer, composer
Recording Career: 1961-

A PLAYER who could hardly avoid being successful, Herbert Jeffrey Hancock was playing with the Chicago Symphony Orchestra when only eleven and became something of a house pianist for Blue Note Records in the early sixties. Even as a composer he made an early breakthrough and *Watermelon Man >1*, from his first album as a leader, became a popular hit.

Hancock's contribution to the music of **Miles Davis** was of an altogether greater depth. The outstanding quintet, with tenor Wayne Shorter, bassist Ron Carter and drummer **Tony Williams**, presented an, as yet, unseen side of Davis' art, and Hancock's fleet, bop-inspired piano fitted superbly. Each player had the space to breathe, and Hancock even 'sat out' where appropriate. On *ESP >2* he was as much a master of comping behind the horns as he was of playing open-handed and inventive solos.

His writing skill was also of considerable help in Davis' modal explorations and *Madness >3* presented the trumpeter with an ideal launching pad for his scalar improvisations. Hancock remained in the band for the highly influential *In A Silent Way >4* and concentrated his talents onto the use of the electric piano.

After leaving Davis in 1968, the pianist further developed the electronic idea: he formed his own group with powerful tenor assistance first from Joe Henderson and then from Benny Maupin. The 1971 *Crossings >5* was an outstandingly imaginative use of the form but Hancock had now become a pop music property and albums like *Headhunters >6* exhibited a considerable weakening of content.

In 1976, he began a parallel career with a co-operative group, including trumpeter **Freddie Hubbard**, and ex-Davis colleagues Wayne Shorter, Ron Carter and Tony Williams. Not without

Herbie Hancock (left) with bassist Ron Carter

significance, it was called VSOP: the group was dedicated to a return to more righteous jazz values and, for all concerned, was a respite from their rock concerts and from the serious business of making money. In fact, it made quite an impression on tour, and records like *VSOP/The Quintet >7* enjoyed sales figures that must have made Hancock question the need to compromise. Whatever the commercial considerations, Hancock, composer, rock fusion artist and just plain jazzman has now gained two fan followings. He satisfies both.

Lineage

His style is perhaps a composite of **Bill Evans**, **Horace Silver** and Red Garland, but his associations with **Miles Davis** influenced his attitudes to the instrument's role in the jazz combo. His own influence has been strongest in the world of fusion but he has directed **Chick Corea** (electronically) in the jazz world.

Media

Wrote the score for Antonioni's film *Blow Up* (1966), *The Spook Who Sat Behind The Door* (1973), *Death Wish* (1974), and can be heard on the soundtrack of *Bitch* (1979). Hancock also appears in and scored music for *Round Midnight* (1986). Composed the music for Bill Cosby's American TV show *Hey! It's Fat Albert >8*.

Listening

1 Takin' Off
  Herbie Hancock/Blue Note BST 84109
2 ESP
  Miles Davis/CBS 85559
3 Nefertiti
  Miles Davis/CBS 85551
4 In A Silent Way
  Miles Davis/CBS 63630
5 Crossings
  Herbie Hancock/Warner Bros. K 46164
6 Headhunters
  Herbie Hancock/CBS 32008
7 VSOP/The Quintet
  Herbie Hancock/CBS 88273
8 Fat Albert Rotunda
  Herbie Hancock/Warner Bros. 56293

Right: Keith Jarrett

Keith Jarrett

Born: 8th May 1945/Allentown, Pennsylvania, USA
Instruments: Piano, soprano saxophone, recorder, drums, composer
Recording Career: 1966-

FALLING SOMEWHERE – in musical terms – between the Cool Dude American and the English Sloane Ranger, Keith Jarrett's piano playing is smartly executed, often witty, usually imaginative, but ultimately foppish. He came to the notice of the jazz world as a Jazz Messenger with **Art Blakey**, subsequently playing in the occasionally exciting but often undisciplined 'flower power' group of Charles Lloyd. Jarrett then became one of the pianists seeking direction in the **Miles Davis** band of the early seventies.

As a leader himself, he was highly

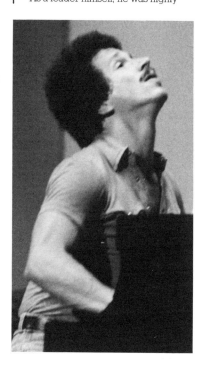

successful. With saxophonist Dewey Redman, bassist **Charlie Haden** and drummer Paul Motian, he produced a great deal of uncompromising jazz. In theory, his 1974 *Death And The Flower* >**1** looked at eternity but, in fact, it was a mundane, if extremely successful, jazz performance. Items such as the 1975 *Flame* >**2** suffered from a slight excess of exoticism, but *The Survivor's Suite* >**3** from 1976 showed how brilliantly the four men could exploit their contrapuntal interplay.

Aesthetically less comfortable was what might be described as Jarrett's Scandinavian quartet, with saxophonist **Jan Garbarek**, bassist Palle Danielsson and drummer Jon Christensen. Working in the late seventies, it rarely equalled the balance achieved by the earlier unit. Jarrett was his normally creative self on titles like *Chant Of The Soil* and *Oasis* >**4**, but the rhythm section failed to sparkle and Garbarek's solos often lost direction after a promising start.

Simultaneously, Jarrett had begun to build for himself a reputation as a solo pianist and a champion of acoustic music. He toured Europe and concerts at Köln (Cologne) >**5** Bremen and Lausanne >**6**, were blueprints of his performing style. *Bremen, July 12th Part Two B* >**6** presented him at his best, playing with enthusiasm on a quality piano. Despite using such a sonorous instrument, he managed to evoke the mood of twenties turpentine-camp pianists in a style full of musical interactions. Delightful musical eddies were allowed to run counter to the general musical flow and to progress without a trace of extravagant chromaticism. It was not a method designed to surprise the listener, but familiarity of phrase was no barrier to Jarrett's creativity.

He had combined head with heart to produce jazz that was exciting even if, visually, his performances were less of a delight. In these, he milked audience reaction with agitated gestures, pre-planned poses and, in his weaker moments, concentrated on presentation more than musical content.

As a composer, Jarrett has written many non-jazz compositions, from a loosely-collated *Brass Quintet* >**7** to a formal *String Quartet* >**7**. He continued to appear as a solo pianist in the eighties, although 1983's *God Bless The*

Child >**8**, with bassist Gary Peacock and drummer Jack DeJohnette reminded us that the discipline of the trio was, for Jarrett, an inspiration, not a restriction.

Lineage
Jarrett has mentioned Hampton Hawes and **Bill Evans** as pianists who have influenced him, but the net could be said to extend much wider. His own course of often inspired eclecticism has denied him personal disciples.

Media
Music from *The Köln Concert* used in *Bad Timing* (1980). Wrote soundtracks for *Mon Coeur Est Rouge* (1976) and *Sorcerer* (1977).

Listening
1 Death And The Flower
  Keith Jarrett/Impulse IMPL 8006
2 Mysteries
  Keith Jarrett/Impulse IMPL 8026
3 The Survivor's Suite
  Keith Jarrett/ECM 1085
4 Nude Ants
  Keith Jarrett/ECM 1171/72
5 The Köln Concert
  Keith Jarrett/ECM 1064/65
6 Solo Concerts
  Keith Jarrett/ECM 1035/37
7 In The Light
  Keith Jarrett/ECM 1033/34
8 Standards Vol 1
  Keith Jarrett/ECM 1-1255

Oliver Lake

Born: 14th September 1942/Marianna, Arkansas, USA
Instruments: Alto, tenor, and soprano saxophones, flute
Recording Career: 1971-

IN AN INTERVIEW with Bill Smith of Coda Magazine, Lake said he would never describe his music as 'free jazz'. Whereas many of the solos he has recorded were freely developed, he suspected that the term itself alienated prospective listeners. More significantly, his work has gradually embraced more organisation and today he places considerable importance on composition.

Lake was raised in St Louis and had early experience in rhythm and blues bands in that town. He formed his own group in 1967 and took as his inspiration the hard bop of altoist **Jackie McLean**. In 1968, as well as gaining a BA in musical education, he helped to found the Black Artists Group and his move toward experimental music had begun. The whole unit shifted to Europe in the early seventies and a 1973 concert *In Paris* >**1** introduced the French to their spare group concept and to Lake's perambulating and well-designed solos. While in Paris, Lake was musician-in-residence at the American Centre For Artists.

When he returned to America, Lake became involved in New York's loft scene. The forward-looking players, denied more legitimate outlets, hired warehouse lofts and turned them into uniquely personal 'clubs'. *Zaki* >**2**, actually recorded at one such place, shows how Lake balanced his playing between melodic freedom and the structural limitations of a theme. His working band at the time, however, contained the strangely incompatible guitar of Michael C. Jackson and it was on records, made away from the group, that his now magnificently mature talents were heard. His stunning duo record with trombonist Joseph Bowie at the Space in Toronto, had alto solos like *After Assistance* >**3** which bristled with creative authority and flute outings like *Orange Butterflies* >**3** that had an almost plaintive gentility. This established the pattern of his style: improvisations built from a strong germ idea but unlikely to return to it of necessity. It was, in fact, the freedom he denied but, as his solos retained their tenuous links with the original theme, they avoided the truly abstract.

In 1977, Lake became a founder member of the World Saxophone Quartet: with saxophonists **David Murray**, Julius Hemphill and **Hamiet Bluiett** he helped distill the group's initial ebullience, heard at the 1977 Moers Festival in *Point Of No Return* >**4**, to the heady brew of controlled, but exciting, music-making best illustrated by the eighties' *Revue* >**5**.

Lake continues to work with other units and also as a solo artist but, for many observers, he is the WSQ's most inventive soloist and the one who has perhaps received less than his critical due.

Lineage

Lake was first influenced by altoist Paul Desmond but, later, 'roughened up' his act with an injection of **Jackie McLean**. His interest in free jazz came through the Black Artists Group and men like Lester Bowie and his brother Joseph.

Listening

1 Black Artists Group In Paris 1973
BAG 324 000
2 Wildflowers Vol 4
New York Loft Sessions/Douglas NBLP 704§
3 Joseph Bowie/Oliver Lake
Sackville 2010
4 Point Of No Return
World Saxophone Quartet/Moers Music 01034
5 Revue
World Saxophone Quartet/Black Saint BSR 0056

John McLaughlin

Born: 4th January 1942/Kirk Sandell, Doncaster, Yorkshire, UK
Instruments: Guitar, piano, synthesizer, composer
Recording Career: 1963-

TO DESCRIBE John McLaughlin as a follower of fashion is not to suggest that he is an empty eclectic but rather that he has adapted his playing to the needs of many different styles. He began with a ragtime unit, before moving over to the flourishing British rhythm and blues scene with the likes of Graham Bond, Herbie Goines and Georgie Fame. He became interested in free jazz, worked with **John Surman** and Dave Holland and then, in 1968, emigrated to the USA.

At first, he worked with drummer **Tony Williams**' Lifetime in a style that reflected his earthy blue-eyed-blues as well as his more sparely delivered free playing >**1**. Through Williams he became involved with **Miles Davis** and

took part in the legendary *In A Silent Way* >**2** and *Bitches Brew* >**3** sessions. In this environment, his idiomatic style had free rein but he was not entirely sure of how he should play. In fact, his intuitive reaction was right and he laid down the ground rules for future guitarists that were featured in Davis' electric bands.

In 1971, McLaughlin formed the Mahavishnu Orchestra with pianist Jan Hammer, violinist Jerry Goodman, bassist Rick Laird and drummer **Billy Cobham** and, with a stage full of hardware, brought jazz and rock into firm contact with Indian music. It was an unlikely marriage of styles but the outcome was well illustrated by *Inner Mounting Flame* >**4**, a virtuoso performance with the appropriately-named *Meeting Of The Spirits* >**4** showing just how easily the disparate inspirational sources could be brought together. Unfortunately, things behind stage were not as smooth and before long ego problems led to a break-up. Predictably, the new Mahavishnu line-up was without 'superstars' and the 1974 *Inner Worlds* >**5** put the spotlight more firmly on to McLaughlin. Exoticism of the more extravagant kind was dropped with McLaughlin's next group Shakti and, although the multiplicity of instruments remained, the mood was more introspective and unquestionably very much quieter. McLaughlin himself soloed impressively and *Shakti* >**6**

presented his calm improvisational flow to full advantage.

Into the eighties he continues to tour prolifically, often in the company of fellow guitarists Al Di Meola and Paco De Lucia. The 1980 *Friday Night In San Francisco* >**7** was typical although, in such music, good taste was a poor substitute for the fire of the original Mahavishnu.

Lineage

Originally inspired by authentic blues men like **Muddy Waters** and Big Bill Broonzy, McLaughlin later listened at great length to **Django Reinhardt** and Barney Kessel. Finally, the influence of **Miles Davis** and the non-musical inspiration of guru Sri Chinmoy affected his entire outlook.

Listening

1 Turn It Over
Anthony Williams/Polydor Super 2425 019
2 In A Silent Way
Miles Davis/CBS 63630
3 Bitches Brew
Miles Davis/CBS 66236
4 Inner Mounting Flame
Mahavishnu Orchestra/CBS 64717
5 Inner Worlds
Mahavishnu Orchestra/CBS 69216
6 Shakti
CBS 81388
7 Friday Night In San Francisco
Al Di Meola/John McLaughlin/Paco De Lucia/CBS 84962

Wynton Marsalis

Born: 18th October 1961/New Orleans, Louisiana, USA
Instrument: Trumpet, composer
Recording Career: 1980-

IF NEW ORLEANS was still awarding 'Kingships' to its trumpet players, Wynton Marsalis would be a prime candidate. Son of pianist Ellis Marsalis, and brother of saxophonist Branford, Marsalis was playing trumpet with the New Orleans Philharmonic while studying at New York's Julliard School of Music. He was still only eighteen when he joined the famous Jazz Messengers of **Art Blakey** in 1980. This was the ideal place for him, following in the footsteps of Donald Byrd, **Lee Morgan** and **Freddie Hubbard** whose tradition Marsalis favoured. His playing was technically brilliant, his tone full and powerful and his creative flow seemed to come quite effortlessly. Untouched by the free-form revolution, he had little time for either straight funk or the rock/jazz fusion but, whatever he played, he projected a warmth and sincerity which communicated with all listeners.

Trumpet features like *Funny Valentine* >**1** exploited the smokey edges of his tone and the conversational logic of his solo style, while Messengers' classics such as *Moanin'* >**1** and *One By One* >**2** placed greater emphasis on his group awareness. Whatever the musical situation, his up-front, melodic statements grew naturally into solo form and his rhetorical asides were delivered with the cunning of an experienced thespian.

Inevitably, his growing popularity made him ambitious and, in 1982, he left to form his own band with brother Branford. The 1983 *Think Of One* >**3** documented the group's early progress but also suggested that Marsalis had not distanced himself too far from the 'Messenger Service'. He did, however, continue to progress as an artist, even though a considerable amount of media hype had begun to grow up around him. For a 1984 album >**4** his sextet was augmented by a twenty-four piece orchestra: fine string arrangements by Robert Freedman gave CBS just what they wanted, but the outcome brought into rather stark relief the fact that this excellent jazz musician had arrived at a means of expression that was more than twenty years out of date. For someone as gifted as Marsalis, this hardly seemed to matter, although later recordings with classical material provided a further reminder that this well-considered, young virtuoso had never tested his talents in the uncertain world of avant-garde experiment.

Lineage

Marsalis is in the **Clifford Brown**, **Freddie Hubbard** line and he plays with similar, clean-lined authority.

Listening

1 Recorded Live At Bubba's
Art Blakey/Kingdom Jazz GATE 7003
2 An American Hero
Art Blakey/Kingdom Jazz GATE 7018
3 Think Of One
Wynton Marsalis/CBS 25354
4 Hot House Flowers
Wynton Marsalis/CBS 26145

Pat Metheny

Born: 12th August 1954/Lee's Summit, Kansas City, Missouri, USA
Instrument: Guitar, composer
Recording Career: 1974-

PAT METHENY emerged in 1974 from the testing ground of the **Gary Burton** Quartet. Playing alongside the vibraphonist, with bassist Steven Swallow and fellow guitarist Mick Goodrick, could not have been easy but Metheny matched them for confidence.

Even as a youngster he had been keen on jazz. He was playing bop by the age of fourteen, becoming something of a **Wes Montgomery** clone. At eighteen, he made a conscious effort to break away from that style and, in the following year, joined Burton. His progress in the band was rapid and his last album with them, *Passengers* >**1**, found him at his creative best.

After three years with Burton, Metheny left to form his own band with pianist Lyle Mays, bassist Mark Egan and drummer Danny Gottlieb. With this step, a move away from straight-ahead jazz performances had begun, though his approach was eclectic: for every

album like *Watercolours* >**2** with its ring of background music, there were concerts such as that at the 1978 Camden Festival in London and albums like *80/81* >**3**, with extrovert tenor work from Dewey Redman and Mike Brecker, to balance the equation. Metheny, however, had deserted jazz in the true sense and with 1984's *Falcon And The Snowman* >**4** moved into film music, with nothing less than a full symphony orchestra as well as attendant choir. But, as an answer to his critics, 1985's *Song X* >**5**, with **Ornette Coleman** in brilliant form, is possibly the finest record Metheny has made to date.

Lineage

Metheny began as a thumb-using **Wes Montgomery** copyist, but listened at length to **Miles Davis** and **John Coltrane**.

Media

Wrote music for film *Falcon And The Snowman* (1984).

Listening

1 Passengers
Gary Burton/ECM 1092 ST
2 Watercolours
Pat Metheny/ECM 1097 ST
3 80/81
Pat Metheny/ECM 1180/81 ST
4 Falcon And The Snowman
Pat Metheny/EMI EJ 24 0305 1
5 Song X
Pat Metheny/Ornette Coleman/Geffen 924 096 1

David Murray

Born: 19th February 1955/Berkeley, California, USA
Instruments: Tenor and soprano saxophones, flute, bass clarinet, composer
Recording Career: 1976-

DAVID MURRAY came from a musical family. He first played saxophone in R & B groups in the Bay area of San Francisco and later studied at Pomona College. He returned to the tenor and, through critic Stanley Crouch, met the free musicians on the West Coast. In 1975 he came to New York and rapidly established a name in the then thriving loft movement, where his style suited their prevailing free-wheeling attitudes. He showed himself to be essentially a melodic improviser, giving his solos room to breath as he outlined each statement with a judicious use of space >**1**.

He often recorded solo >**2** and, when alone, assumed a gladiatorial stance that took him from stringent free expressions to sensuously romantic ballad lines with seamless ease. He retained an unforced sense of humour and this trait was also evident in his striking compositions >**3**.

In 1977, Murray became a founder member of the World Saxophone Quartet. Together with **Hamiet Bluiett,**

Julius Hemphill and **Oliver Lake**, he formed a group that combined brilliant solos, strong counterpoint and superbly executed unison passages. As a speciality they even played pieces such as *Slide* >**4** which were totally unimprovised.

Murray premiered his big band in 1978 and with it saluted **Jelly Roll Morton** and Don Redman as easily as he did **Gil Evans**. He recently (1984) stated that such a musical policy was compatible with his desire 'to make his music more universally accessible'.

Lineage

Murray told Stanley Crouch that he 'worked on a study of tenor man Paul Gonsalves' and there is something of the Ellingtonian's sinuous delivery on ballads such as *Home* >**5**. He also acknowledges **Sonny Rollins** and **John Coltrane** amongst his influences but, as *Flowers for Albert* >**6** shows, it is his position as logical successor to the late **Albert Ayler** that establishes his place in jazz chronology. Today he continues to explore the areas of music that Ayler opened up.

Listening

1 **Low Class Conspiracy**
   David Murray/Adelphi Jazz Line AD 5002
2 **Conceptual Saxophone**
   David Murray/Cadillac SGC 1007
3 **Revue**
   WSQ/Black Saint BSR 0056
4 **Interboogieology**
   David Murray/Black Saint BSR 0018
5 **Home**
   David Murray/Black Saint BSR 0055
6 **Flowers For Albert**
   David Murray/India Navigation IN 1026

Evan Parker

Born: 5th April 1944/Bristol, UK
Instruments: Tenor and soprano saxophones, auto-harp
Recording Career: 1967-

FOR THOSE SUSPICIOUS of his unrelenting pursuit of freedom, Evan Parker's music might appear as a total alternative to the jazz tradition that came from **Louis Armstrong** and his contemporaries. In fact, it is a logical extension of that music, although it is now a very powerful and individualistic style.

Meeting members of the **Spontaneous Music Ensemble** in 1966 opened Parker's eyes to the true possibilities of free improvisation and in guitarist **Derek Bailey** he found an especially kindred spirit. In 1968, with Bailey, he formed the Music Improvisation Company >**1**, one of the first jazz units to use live electronics, and one that gave Parker the incentive to move into the abstract field with greater confidence. His 1969 work with Tony Oxley extended that process, although the drummer's specialised style on titles like *The Baptised Traveller* >**2** retained more discernible contact with the American free-music world of **Archie Shepp** and latter-day **John Coltrane**.

Parker's own style, sometimes pitched at the same nerve-shattering intensity as the Americans, was nevertheless, highly individualistic. Avoiding melodic continuity, the disjointed utterances, strategically hesitant starts and brilliantly executed false notes, produced a tapestry of sound that was at once creative and yet superficially disorganised. He did not respond to traditional rules, refused to prepare solos in advance and represented something of a culture shock to the ill-prepared conservative.

In the seventies, Parker worked with two widely contrasting big bands, the Globe Unity Orchestra >**3**, with their strange mixture of ponderous unisons and inspired mayhem, and The Brotherhood Of Breath >**4** which used his controlled intensity as a foil for the dancing 'high life' gait of altoist Dudu Pukwana. Away from these units, the saxophonist continued to work as a solo artist and in small combinations. Duets were particularly rewarding and the 1975 *London Concert* >**5** with Bailey, *The Longest Night* >**6** with drummer John Stevens and *Abracadabra* >**7** with pianist Greg Goodman all proved how sympathetically he could respond to a fellow free improviser without impairing his own creative flow.

It made him an obvious choice to join Bailey's Company, formed in 1976 and

still flourishing in the eighties. In the superb laissez-faire atmosphere of the group, Parker really had room to move artistically and his exhilarating duos with saxophonist **Anthony Braxton** >**8** and his ducking and weaving work in the saxophone quartet >**8**, with Braxton, **Steve Lacy** and Lol Coxhill demonstrate how much he was at home. To further the cause and appreciation of free improvisation, Parker has founded his own record label, Incus.

Lineage
Parker listened originally to the **Modern Jazz Quartet** and Paul Desmond but the more discernible influence of **John Coltrane** and **Pharoah Sanders** showed after his association with the **Spontaneous Music Ensemble**.

Listening
1 Music Improvisation Company 1968-71
Incus 17
2 The Baptised Traveller
Tony Oxley/Realm 52664
3 Intergalactic Blow
Globe Unity Orchestra/JAPO 60039
4 Live At Willisau
Brotherhood Of Breath/Ogun OG 100
5 A Different World
Evan Parker/Derek Bailey/Incus 16
6 The Longest Night Vols 1 & 2
Parker/John Stevens/Ogun 120 & 420
7 Abracadabra
Parker/Greg Goodman/Beak Doctor 2
8 Company – Seven
Incus 30

Courtney Pine

Born: 18th March 1964/Paddington, London, UK
Instruments: Tenor and soprano saxophones, clarinet
Recording Career: 1986-

ALTHOUGH NOT in the vanguard of European jazz development, Courtney Pine is young, and the media coverage he has attracted is good for the music in general. Like the twenty-one piece British group Loose Tubes, much of this

Above: Courtney Pine

interest has been associated with the laudable attempt to sell jazz to a new generation. Pine's stylistic stance falls somewhere between the conversational **Sonny Rollins** and the liberated sixties music of **John Coltrane**. He has a workable technique and, more importantly, has the confidence to present himself in nearly any musical situation.

In his teens, Pine teamed with several Berklee School Of Music graduates to form Dwarf Steps, a hard bop group whose name was adapted from Coltrane's composition *Giant Steps*. He later scraped a living with reggae performers, Clint Eastwood and General Saint, before joining drummer John Stevens in London's Community Music Workshop scheme.

In 1986, **Art Blakey** invited him to join the Jazz Messengers in New York but Pine declined because of artistic inducements in Britain. He had plenty of freelance work with groups such as Rolling Stones drummer Charlie Watts' Big Band, the more forward-looking Jazz Warriors as well as his own quartet. With the latter, he recorded a first album for Island and, on *Peace >1* shows a willingness to pace his solos around his natural breathing patterns. By contrast, his tenor erupts from *When, Where, How And Why >1* to remind us

that he trades just as skilfully in molten excitement. The record made him the first leader for some time to sign for a major company without being required to resort to funk jazz or Latin exotica.

Despite this, Pine has not closed the door on Blakey's offer and as his technique becomes more secure, he threatens to become the player his followers would have the world believe he already is. Potentially, he is an outstanding jazzman and experience should make him a player of greater subtlety and depth.

Lineage
Pine cites **John Coltrane**, **Sonny Rollins** and Wayne Shorter as his early influences but, later, took considerable interest in the **Art Ensemble Of Chicago** and the **Sun Ra** Arkestra.

Listening
1 Journey To The Urge Within
Courtney Pine/Island ILPS 9846

Sam Rivers

Born: 25th September 1930/El Reno, Oklahoma, USA
Instruments: Tenor and soprano saxophones, bass clarinet, flute, piano, viola, composer
Recording Career: 1964-

A MAN who can leave **Miles Davis** because he finds the music restricting is a man to be considered. This is, in fact, what Samuel Carthorne Rivers did in 1964 before joining avant-garde pianist **Cecil Taylor** for a stay that lasted four years.

At seventeen he had studied at the Boston Conservatory and in the forties worked with stylistically liberated men like pianist Jaki Byard, and saxophonists Paul Gonsalves and Serge Chaloff. He actually accompanied **Billie Holiday** for a short time but he grew up, musically, with bebop. By the time he had begun recording, however, he was past that stage. He had listened constructively to the free-form pioneers and his own playing followed logically in their wake. His use of jazz's more chromatic elements was sparing, but dramatically employed, and he always regarded the throaty shout or regurgitory honk as part of the jazz fabric.

In 1965 he made his recording debut as a leader with Blue Note >**1** and, over a muscle-flexing rhythm section that included Byard, bassist Ron Carter and drummer **Tony Williams**, he paraded his burgeoning talents in a mixture of hard-bop drive and pre-free form euphemisms.

In 1970, with his wife Bea, he opened the Studio Rivbea in New York to ensure that there was a venue for the type of music that he loved to play and to hear. In this non-playing sense, it made him the most significant figure of the seventies, as his action unwittingly sired the loft movement that became so important.

Fortunately, Rivers' musical activities continued to blossom away from his home pitch. He had his own groups, Harlem Ensemble and Winds Of Manhattan and he toured extensively. Two typical concert performances, each roughly divided into four sections and each presenting his different instruments, were recorded at Villalago >**2** and Perugia >**3** in Italy

during 1976 demonstrating the way in which he presented many of his concert programmes in the eighties.

In contrast, his 1982 recording *Colours* >**4** featured eleven saxophonists, no rhythm section, and showed that Rivers could produce extremely formal music with no loss in immediacy. He told critic, Lee Jeske: 'I'm not just free. I consider myself to be a pretty rounded musician in all styles'.

Lineage

Strangely enough it was trumpeter **Dizzy Gillespie** who was his earliest inspiration, although Rivers later listened intently to **Lester Young** and his then colleague **Cecil Taylor**. Despite teaching and encouraging young players at Rivbea, his influence has not emerged strongly in any major new musician.

Listening

1 **Fuchsia Swing Song**
   Sam Rivers/Blue Note BST 84184
2 **Black Africa**
   Sam Rivers/Horo HDP 3-4
3 **Black Africa**
   Sam Rivers/Horo HDP 5-6
4 **Colours**
   Winds Of Manhattan/Black Saint BSR0064

Terje Rypdal

Born: 28th August 1947/Oslo, Norway
Instruments: Guitar, electric guitar,
synthesizer, organ, piano, soprano
saxophone, percussion, composer
Recording Career: 1967-

LIKE THE COMPOSER Jean Sibelius,
Rypdal has been pre-judged by his
Scandinavian origin. Comparisons with
arctic coldness offer an easy, critical
option but, in Rypdal's case, are
somewhat justified. His guitar style has
a bleak, tonal quality which takes tone
poems like *Icing* >**1** through
deliberately surrealistic wastelands of
frozen space. Technically he is always
in command, yet the emotional
detachment in his work often distances
him from the listener.

One cannot deny the cold beauty of
his playing, but the 1976 *After The
Rain* >**2**, with its concentration on
atmospherics, took the style to the brink
of affectation. As a performance, it
certainly has a sense of the dramatic but
there was also a feeling that he was
posturing. The outer wrapping seemed
more important than the content and it
was only on albums by other leaders
that he sounded fully committed. His
playing on *Star Flight* >**3** with Edward
Vesalo and throughout most of Barre
Phillips' *Three Day Moon* >**4** showed
him at his best; but even then there was
a feeling that drama was more
important than improvisational logic.

The presence of specialist sidemen
like bassist Miroslav Vitous and
drummer Jack DeJohnette did not free
him from his clinical approach. The
1981 *To Be Continued* >**5** contained
some funky rock guitar but the outcome
still sounded too polite. The same was
true of his playing in the turmoil of
Graham Collier's International Big Band
at London's 1985 Camden Festival. In
the end, formula defeated substance.

Lineage
Rypdal is a genuinely original guitarist
but his influence can be felt mostly in
the work of popular artists like Mike
Oldfield.

Listening
1 What Comes After
Terje Rypdal/ECM 1031 ST
2 After The Rain
Terje Rypdal/ECM 1083 ST
3 Satu
Edward Vesala/ECM 1088 ST
4 Three Day Moon
Barre Phillips/ECM 1123 ST
5 To Be Continued
Rypdal/Vitous/DeJohnette/ECM 1192 ST

Sonny Sharrock

Born: 27th August 1940/Ossining, NY,
USA
Instrument: Guitar, vocals
Recording Career: 1966-

THE MODUS OPERANDI of free jazz
had been established for horn players
by the early sixties. The same could not
be said for guitarists, who found
themselves caught between the all-
pervading influence of **Wes
Montgomery** and the burgeoning
heavy-rock practitioners. Most took a
comfortable middle road and it was left
to **Derek Bailey** in Europe and Sonny
Sharrock in America to provide the first
meaningful alternatives.

Warren Harding Sharrock began as a
rock singer, later studied at Berklee
and then moved to New York in 1965.
There he came to terms with free jazz
and worked with **Pharoah Sanders**,
drummer Sunny Murray and **Don
Cherry**. He also had spells with
establishment figures like Herbie Mann
and **Cannonball Adderley**.

In the early seventies, he toured with
his wife, singer Linda Sharrock, and
demonstrated on *27th Day* >**1** his
success in coming to terms with the
abstract elements of the new music. His
own free style was strongly blues-
based, it favoured terse, angular figures
and its dense clusters added intensity to
the simplest idea. Sharrock applied
distortion rather than true, chromatic
freedom and improvisations like *Broken
Toys* >**2** were exercises in simple
paraphrasing rather than massive
rebuilding jobs.

There were no jazz record dates as a leader from 1975 until the middle eighties but, with his re-emergence, Sharrock showed that his skill was undiminished. In the mid-eighties, he toured with Last Exit, a group with bassist and sound mixer Bill Laswell, tenor Peter Brotzmann and drummer Ronald Shannon Jackson. In this uncompromising group his turbulent mixture of folk naivety, heavy metal extravagance and natural, melodic freedom was given a loose rein and titles such as *Red Light* and *Enemy Within* >**3** were particularly dramatic.

Lineage

Sharrock's influences stretch from Blind Willie Johnson and Little Richard to the jazz majors like **Ornette Coleman**, **John Coltrane** and **Miles Davis**. Surprisingly, his highly accessible style has attracted fewer followers than that of **Derek Bailey**.

Listening

1 Monkey Pockie Boo
  Sonny Sharrock/Affinity AFF 35
2 Guitar
  Sonny Sharrock/Enemy EMY 102
3 Last Exit
  Enemy EMY 101

Henry Threadgill

Born: 15th February 1944/Chicago, Illinois, USA
Instruments: Alto, tenor and baritone saxophones, flute, bass flute, lubkaphone
Recording Career: 1969-

IT WAS INEVITABLE that any musician involved in Chicago's burgeoning jazz scene in the sixties would become a member of the Association For The Advancement Of Creative Musicians. Henry Luther Threadgill was no exception and he frequently worked in the groups led by founder members like pianist **Muhal Richard Abrams** and trumpeter Phillip Cohran as well as with reed majors from the city such as Joseph Jarman and Roscoe Mitchell.

As a soloist Threadgill was not especially inventive but he had a reasonable grasp of free-form principles and *Wise In Time* >**1**, from his 1969 record debut with Abrams, showed that he was no stranger to the blues. This simple fact probably directed his life in the next couple of years as he reversed the chronology of his career. After successfully crossing avant-garde swords with the AACM worthies, he returned to basics. This involved a spell on the road with gospel artist JoJo Morris and having a permanent place in the house band of a South Side blues club.

In 1971, he was commissioned to adapt the compositions of **Scott Joplin** for a play called *The Hotel*. With the aid of bassist Fred Hopkins and drummer Steve McCall, he also played in the performance for the Columbia College Of Chicago. As a result, the three men remained together as a group, adopting the name Air. The deliberately dated jazz from the play did influence the early years of the group's life and it was never totally eradicated from their 'book'.

This fact was not documented because they did not record until 1975 and, by the time records began to appear, they were working through a wide range of styles and had established a very distinctive character. *The Jick Or Mandrill's Cosmic Ass* >**2** confirmed that the shadow of Chicago's South Side was a constant factor, R.B. >**3** recalled the **Albert Ayler** dirges and there were imaginative smatterings of ragtime and **Jelly Roll Morton** compositions. The word 'parody' must be invoked when discussing the trio's treatment of these early jazz pieces: although *Chicago Breakdown* >**4** is treated gently, Threadgill tears apart the parent strain of *King Porter Stomp* >**5** and Hopkins does a similar job on *Buddy Bolden's Blues* >**5**.

Most of the material for the group was written by Threadgill and, despite the gimmickry of the car hub-cap percussion, featured on the band's 1981 tour of Europe, the musical content has been high. In the early eighties they established themselves on the world jazz circuit and it was Threadgill that shouldered the majority of the solo responsibilities.

Lineage

Threadgill was influenced by saxophonists from the AACM and by pianist **Muhal Richard Abrams**.

Media

Wrote score and additional material for the play, *The Hotel* (1971).

Listening

1 Young At Heart, Wise In Time
Muhal Richard Abrams/Delmark DS 423
2 Open Air Suit
Air/Arista Novus AN 3002
3 Air Mail
Air/Black Saint BSR 0049
4 80 Below '82
Air/Antilles AN 1007
5 Aire Lore
Air/Arista Novus AN 3014

McCoy Tyner

**Born: 11th December 1938/
Philadelphia, Pennsylvania, USA
Instrument: Piano, composer
Recording Career: 1960-**

ALFRED McCOY TYNER came to prominence with **John Coltrane**'s innovative quartet in the early sixties. His contribution was considerable and his powerful style, full of lusty chords and high-speed treble improvisations, was forged during his five years in that group.

In 1959 Tyner began his major league training with the Benny Golson/**Art Farmer** Jazztet >**1** but, with Coltrane, made a series of recordings that are rated among the best in jazz history. It was titles like *Favourite Things* >**2** that demonstrated how well he served his leader's tenor and soprano as he took his scalar excursions into the world of modal jazz. In contrast, his fleet adaptation of bop piano is well displayed on *But Not For Me* >**2**.

In 1965 he left Coltrane and in the late sixties did not always work as often as he would have wished. Albums such as *Extensions* >**3** confirmed his progress toward the powerfully exotic, although it was not until his *Sahara* >**4** album

took off in 1972 that he established himself as a really successful combo leader. From then on, he took on a constructive attitude to his own brand of fusion and described his 1976 band, with saxophonists Gary Bartz, Joe Ford and Ron Bridgewater, as the happiest and most integrated he had ever led. *Focal Point* >**5** bore this out and showed that complexity was no barrier to communication.

Tyner's 1978 tour of the Far East, with bassist Ron Carter and drummer **Tony Williams**, produced *Passion Dance* >**6** to confirm his allegiance to the older virtues but there was a tendency for the later records of the seventies to turn the 'jabbing piano and heart-on-sleeve tenor' into a mere formula.

Violinist John Blake joined the group in 1981 and at the Knebworth Festival of that year brought an acceptable quasi-folkishness to the group. The 1983 *Dimensions* >**7** documented this development and the mood of the square-dance created an alternative route into the eighties.

Lineage

The influence of **John Coltrane** was a major factor in Tyner's career but later work with Ike and Tina Turner and **Jimmy Witherspoon** added a bluesy edge to his playing.

Listening

1 Meet The Jazztet
Art Farmer/Argo LP 664
2 My Favourite Things
John Coltrane/Atlantic ATL 5022
3 Extensions
McCoy Tyner/Blue Note GXK 8070 (JAP)
4 Sahara
McCoy Tyner/Milestone M9039
5 Focal Point
McCoy Tyner/Milestone M9072
6 Passion Dance
McCoy Tyner/Milestone M9091
7 Dimensions
McCoy Tyner/Elektra Musician 960-350-1

Right: Weather Report; l-to-r, Jaco Pastorius, Alejandro Acuna, Manolo Badrena, Wayne Shorter and Joe Zawinul

Weather Report

Original Line-up:
Joe Zawinul (keyboards)/Wayne Shorter (saxophone)/Miroslav Vitous (bass)/Alphonze Mouzon (drums)/Airto Moreira (percussion)
Recording Career: 1971-1982

THE IMPACT OF **Miles Davis'** electric groups in the early seventies cannot be overestimated. As his early group broke up, its members formed groups of their own and a distinct Miles Davis rock 'school' grew up: Lifetime, Return To Forever, Weather Report and **John McLaughlin**'s Mahavishnu Orchestra were all examples, but it was Weather Report that proved artistically the most consistent and, with **Chick Corea**'s Return To Forever, the most durable.

The group was built around the talents of pianist Joe Zawinul and saxophonist Wayne Shorter, both former Davis alumni, and came into being in 1971 when the line-up was completed by bassist Miroslav Vitous, drummer Alphonze Mouzon and percussionist Airto Moreira. In retrospect, this fivesome can be seen as the best of all Weather Report ensembles: the internal balance was superb, and there was no ego-projection. The exquisite *Orange Lady* >**1** signposted the collective direction, and the voicings on *Morning Lake* >**1** confirmed that the overall sound was more important than lengthy solo statements.

Shorter and Zawinul soon emerged as the principals and, as the name Weather Report suggested, they were prepared for change. Eric Gravatt and Dom Um Ramao replaced Mouzon and Moreira and 1972's *The Moors* >**2** showed that change was not necessarily for the better. A Far Eastern tour was undertaken, however, and the ferocious *Directions* >**2**, recorded on their return, indicates the work that had been done to rebalance the band.

Personnel shuffling continued, and Gravatt was the next to go, followed rapidly by his replacement Gregg Errico. He in turn was replaced by Ishmael Wilburn and the Weathers were again faced with a period of artist re-entrenchment. The newcomer was a fast drummer who was sometimes content with understatement. Following Gravatt's more thunderous approach, which had taken them nearer to 'heavy rock', this came as quite a relief. In fact, *American Tango* and *Blackthorn Rose* >**3** both examined space, used electronic effects with care and artistry, and overall are classic Weather Report titles.

The departure of the brilliant

Miroslav Vitous in 1973 disrupted the group more than any other change. Zawinul and Shorter took full responsibility but, with drummers continuing to come and go, replacement bassist Alphonso Johnson did not have an easy task. The line-up in 1974/5 stabilised briefly with drummer Nguda (Leon Chancler) and percussionist Alyrio Lima, and the *Tale Spinnin'* >**4** album announced that another stage had been reached. The group feeling was looser and the gifted Shorter given more solo space but, as Zawinul's haunting *Badia* >**4** shows, they had not deserted strong themes or dropped the beloved chime and bell effects. The 1977 album *Heavy Weather* (with yet another formation) started off with the track which for many listeners, has become their introduction to the music of Weather Report, Zawinul's *Birdland* >**5**.

Sidemen continued to come and go and a new line-up with Jaco Pastorius on bass, Peter Erskine on drums and Robert Thomas on percussion showed real potential at the 1981 New York Festival. Even the call-and-response of old jazz days was evoked on *Dara Factor One* >**6**; but in the following year, *Procession* >**7** had the doubtful privilege of being the worst Weather Report album to date. It took them into the hood-down motorway-cruising field and offered little to stimulate the serious listener.

Weather Report ultimately *was* Zawinul and Shorter. Excellent and skilful arrangements, mainly by the pianist, gave the band a positive identity and the deployment of the electronic and acoustic variables was handled adroitly. Shorter's mighty, individual talent was perhaps underplayed, and Zawinul finally assumed too much power, but in the final analysis Weather Report must be judged an important band of the seventies.

Lineage

Weather Report grew from the electronic **Miles Davis**, featured a highly original style, but suprisingly influenced few bands within the jazz field.

Media

Soundtrack for *Watched* (1974).

Listening

1 **Weather Report**
CBS 32024
2 **I Sing The Body Electric**
Weather Report/CBS 32062
3 **Mysterious Traveller**
Weather Report/CBS 80027
4 **Tale Spinnin'**
Weather Report/CBS/Epic 80734
5 **Heavy Weather**
CBS S81775
6 **Weather Report**
CBS 85326
7 **Procession**
Weather Report/CBS 25241

Tony Williams

Born: 12th December 1945/Chicago, Illinois, USA
Instrument: Drums, composer
Recording Career: 1963-

THE POSITION OF Tony Williams in the drum hierarchy has not always been fully acknowledged. Raised in Boston, where he played with **Sam Rivers**, he then moved to New York. Still only seventeen he immediately found a place in altoist **Jackie McLean**'s uncompromising, hard-bop quintet. If anything, he looked even younger than his years and observers were stunned by this prodigy's speed of execution, finely tuned sense of timing and mature use of brushes.

In 1963, at the age of seventeen, he joined **Miles Davis** and, as *Seven Steps To Heaven* >**1** showed, brought a new approach to the drum function. Joachim Berendt (*The Jazz Book*, 1976) saw it as an 'extreme reduction of the jazz beat to a nerve-like vibration and swing', and it ideally suited the trumpeter's evolving room-to-breathe approach on titles like *Eighty One* >**2**. In fact, the pulsating quality in Williams' drumming encouraged quintet colleagues like **Herbie Hancock** and Wayne Shorter to adopt a similar, rhythmic stance and Williams became a very important voice in the 1964-67 band.

It was inevitably a two-way learning

process but Davis became intrigued by the young man's interest in other musical forms. He began to acquaint himself with rock music and with its different aspirations, and turned to Williams to put theory into practice. This he did in no uncertain manner and his contribution to *In A Silent Way* >**3**, with its subtle, rhythmic undertow, demonstrated the intensity created by lagging but complex accent placements.

Leading his own group, Lifetime, was a logical step after leaving Davis, although the rather fixed dynamic level of albums like *Turn It Over* >**4** was a disappointment. Lifetime was a high-decibel group with guitarist **John McLaughlin** and organist Larry Young but the new rock superstar status brought its own problems and the group broke up.

Williams reformed in 1975 with guitarist Allan Holdsworth and repeated the old formula with more concern for sound balance. In 1976, however, he moved back to a more straight-ahead jazz stance with **Freddie Hubbard**, Wayne Shorter and Herbie

Hancock in the group VSOP. All were men taking time off from their rock/jazz fusion ventures but albums like the 1979 *Five Stars* >**5** suggested that the multi-talented Williams was perhaps in his ideal setting in this group and the quintet continued to get together for special concerts and tours into the eighties.

Lineage

Williams, himself influenced by **Max Roach**, did much to re-direct the metronomic rock drums in the early days of rock/jazz fusion.

Listening

1 Seven Steps To Heaven
  Miles Davis/CBS 62170
2 ESP
  Miles Davis/CBS 85559
3 In A Silent Way
  Miles Davis/CBS 63630
4 Turn It Over
  Anthony Williams/Polydor Super 2425 019
5 Five Stars
  Herbie Hancock/CBS/Sony
  (JAP) 25 AP 2190

RECORD LABELS

ATLANTIC Like all great jazz labels, Atlantic documented a vital part of jazz history. Supervisor Nesuhi Ertegun produced **Charles Mingus**' shattering 1956 *Pithecanthropus Erectus* and, through the late fifties, gave the jazz world the cream of **Ornette Coleman** and **John Coltrane**. The label's insurance was provided perhaps by the **Modern Jazz Quartet**, pianist Les McCann and flautist Herbie Mann but its policy through to the middle seventies remained progressive.

BLACK SAINT Together with stablemate Soul Note, the Italian Black Saint label told the world more about eighties New York than any American label. Billy Harper's 1975 session, *Black Saint*, presaged an issue programme that included the World Saxophone Quartet, various **David Murray** groups as well as outstanding albums by **Oliver Lake**, **Billy Bang** and **Don Pullen**.

BLUE NOTE Founded in 1939 by German emigré Alfred Lion, it was a label fashioned by his team: partner Francis Wolff, recording engineer Rudy Van Gelder and talent scout, tenor saxophonist Ike Quebec. It sold pianist **Thelonious Monk** to jazz and later ushered the label into the hard bop era with such musicians as pianist **Horace Silver**, saxophonists **Jackie McLean** and Lou Donaldson and **Art Blakey**'s Jazz Messengers. The label stayed ahead in the sixties and did much to bring **Andrew Hill**, **Don Cherry** and **Cecil Taylor** to a wider audience.

CAPITOL A major company with only a slight interest in the broad jazz field, its position of fame was assured by its 1949 recordings of the **Miles Davis** nonet and the comprehensive coverage of **Stan Kenton**'s work.

CLEF Norman Granz's Clef label was astylistic; it began by recording the Jazz At The Philharmonic concerts and never lost its touch with saxophonists like **Coleman Hawkins**, **Charlie Parker**, Illinois Jacquet and Flip Phillips, trumpeters **Roy Eldridge**, **Buck Clayton** and **Dizzy Gillespie**, pianist **Art Tatum** and singer **Ella Fitzgerald**.

DIAL In 1947, Ross Russell's label captured **Charlie Parker** at the height of his powers. These legendary sessions also included other bop giants like trumpeters **Miles Davis**, **Dizzy Gillespie** and **Howard McGhee**, saxophonists Lucky Thompson and **Wardell Gray** as well as pianists **Erroll Garner**, Dodo Marmarosa and Duke Jordan.

ECM Manfred Eicher's German label, with its exemplary recording quality, dominated European jazz releases in the seventies. Although it was initially associated with the detached, almost ethereal musings of the Scandinavian school of jazz, ECM (Editions of Contemporary Music) fortunately broadened its outlook to embrace shameless experimentalists such as **Derek Bailey** and more extrovert performers like **Chick Corea**, **Keith Jarrett**, Lester Bowie and the **Art Ensemble Of Chicago**.

Gennett

GENNETT With a home in Richmond, Indiana, this was the collector's label. In 1923, it recorded **Jelly Roll Morton**, the **New Orleans Rhythm Kings** and the **King Oliver** Creole Jazz Band and did much to make the world aware of genuine jazz. Today, copies of these singles change hands for large sums of money.

impulse!

IMPULSE ABC-Paramount's Impulse division was the brainchild of record producer Bob Thiele. It followed vital developments in the careers of men like **Ornette Coleman** and **John Coltrane** but was more important still for providing recording opportunities for the second generation of free-form players in the sixties: **Archie Shepp**, **Albert Ayler**, **Pharoah Sanders**, **Gato Barbieri** and **Roswell Rudd** were among those given career boosts by the label.

INCUS A small label run by saxophonist **Evan Parker**, Incus covered the European free improvisation field and issued mainly live recordings by musicians such as **Derek Bailey** and by groups such as Iskra 1903 and the Company Collective.

OKEH Although it released material other than jazz, the Okeh company was well aware of the potential of the 'race' market during the twenties. It released records by all of the finest **Louis Armstrong** groups, and much

by **Clarence Williams** and **Bix Beiderbecke** but had faded by the middle thirties. A brief resurgence came in 1940 with recordings of **Cab Calloway** and Les Brown among others but its time had passed.

Paramount

PARAMOUNT The Paramount label was founded during World War One by the Wisconsin Chair Company of Port Washington, merely to provide records for the phonographs they sold. Acoustically recorded for many years, the sound quality was sometimes appalling but among the label's major stars were singers like **Ma Rainey** and Ida Cox and musicians like Lovie Austin, **Johnny Dodds**, **Meade Lux Lewis**, Will Ezell, as well as others from Chicago's South Side.

RIVERSIDE Part of the Fontana Company, it was established in the fifties thanks to the efforts of jazz enthusiasts Bill Grauer and Orrin Keepnews. Its stable of artists was impressive and included at some stage **Thelonious Monk**, **Wes Montgomery** and saxophonist **Johnny Griffin**.

VANGUARD The master hand of pioneer critic and record producer John Hammond was a vital element in the Vanguard story. As a label, it reminded the jazz world of the swing-era giants caught in the traditional versus modern controversy of the fifties. Although albums by Vic Dickenson, **Buck Clayton** and **Ruby Braff** were outstanding, it did include other branches of the music.

JAZZ BOOKS

IN MANY WAYS, the pioneer jazz writers were working in the dark. They relied on instinct, they interviewed copiously but their, at times, amateurish research provided the foundation for all that followed. Frederic Ramsey and Charles Edward Smith captured the legends in *Jazzmen* and the musicians had their own input in Nat Hentoff and Nat Shapiro's *Hear Me Talkin'*. Sidney Finkelstein emphasized the music's human side in *Jazz, A People's Music* while vital extras came from Rudi Blesh and Harriet Janis' *They All Played Ragtime* and Blesh's *Shining Trumpets*. Men like George T. Simon documented *The Big Bands* and the second generation built on what had gone before. In *Jazz, Its Evolution And Essence*, Andre Hodier took us into deeper analysis, Paul Oliver brought genuine scholarship to *The Story Of The Blues* and Alun Morgan and Raymond Horricks organised our thoughts on *Modern Jazz*, in the course of her fine avant-garde examination, Valerie Wilmer astutely acknowledged the role of those associated with jazz musicians, and in Gunther Schuller's *Early Jazz* we finally had a book that could be taken as an object lesson in intelligent jazz criticism.

AS SERIOUS AS YOUR LIFE – An insight into the mechanics of playing avant-garde jazz for a living. Valerie Wilmer/Allison & Busby/1977.

THE BIG BANDS – Band by band, the story of the swing era. George T. Simon/Macmillan/1967.

BIRD LIVES – The story of bebop told through the life of Charlie Parker. Ross Russell/Quartet/1973.

BLACK MUSIC – A prejudiced, very personal, look at modern jazz. Leroi Jones/William R. Morrow/1969.

BLUES & GOSPEL RECORDS 1902-1943 – (Discography). R.M.W. Dixon and J. Godrich/Storyville/1982.

BLUES RECORDS 1943-1968 – (Discography). Mike Leadbitter and Neil Slaven/Hanover/1968.

EARLY JAZZ – One of the best jazz books ever written. It tells of early jazz as it really was. Gunther Schuller/Oxford University Press/1968.

THE ENCYCLOPEDIA OF JAZZ IN THE SEVENTIES – The scholarly follow-up to Feather's original astylistic triumph. Leonard Feather and Ira Gitler/ Quartet/1978.

FREE JAZZ – A short but learned look at free jazz. Ekkehard Jost/Universal Edition/1974.

HEAR ME TALKIN' TO YA – The musicians tell it as it is. Nat Hentoff and Nat Shapiro/Rinehart/1955.

IMPROVISATION – A musician's book that explains his art to the listener. Derek Bailey/Moorland/1980.

JAZZ – A PEOPLE'S MUSIC – A book that puts early jazz into its proper bracket. Sidney Finkelstein/Citadel/1948.

THE JAZZ BOOK – A well-balanced look at jazz from ragtime to the present day. Joachim Berendt/Hart-Davis MacGibbon/1976.

THE JAZZ CATACLYSM – An examination of the transition from hard bop to free jazz. Barry McRae/J.M. Dent/1967.

JAZZ, ITS EVOLUTION AND ESSENCE – One of the first books to accurately analyse the great mainstream performances. Andre Hodier/Grove/1956.

THE JAZZ LIFE – An insight into jazz at source. Nat Hentoff/Dial Press/1961.

JAZZMEN – A mixture of folk legend and fact, it established the New Orleans myth for all time. Frederic Ramsey Jr and Charles Edward Smith/Harcourt Brace/1939.

JAZZ ON RECORD – Records of all eras reviewed by a panel of genuine experts. Albert McCarthy, Alun Morgan, Paul Oliver and Max Harrison/Hanover/1968.

JAZZ RECORDS 1897-1942 Vols 1&2 – (Discography). Brian Rust/Arlington House/1978.

JAZZ RECORDS 1942-1969 Vols 1-3, 4A-4D, 5-8 – (Discography). Jorgen Grunnet Jepson/Karl Emil Knudsen/1963-1970.

JAZZ: THE TRANSITION YEARS 1940-1960 – Modern jazz before the free-form revolution. John S. Wilson/Appleton-Century-Crofts/1967.

MODERN JAZZ – An excellent introduction to the vagaries of bebop and just beyond. Alun Morgan & Raymond Horricks/Victor Gollancz/1958.

MODERN JAZZ – Bebop, Hard Bop, West Coast Vols 1-5 – (Discography). W. Bruyninckx.*

MODERN JAZZ – The Essential Records 1945-1979 – A more modern version of Jazz On Record. Max Harrison/Alun Morgan/Ronald Atkins/Michael James/Jack Cook/Centurion/1975.

THE NEW ENCYCLOPEDIA OF JAZZ – The original handbook, a mine of information about jazzmen of all musical persuasions. Leonard Feather/Arthur Barker/1961.

PICTORIAL HISTORY OF JAZZ – Just what it says. Orrin Keepnews and Bill Grauer/Crown/1955.

PROGRESSIVE JAZZ, FREE, THIRD STREAM, FUSION Vols 1-3 – (Discography). W. Bruyninckx.*

RIDING ON A BLUE NOTE – One of jazz's best contemporary writers, on his hobby-horse and in full flow. Gary Giddins/Oxford University Press/1981.

SHINING TRUMPETS – The New Orleans legends, flavoured to taste. Rudi Blesh/Alfred A. Knopf/1950.

SIMON SAYS: THE SIGHTS AND SOUNDS OF THE SWING ERA – A mighty look at a swing era that stems from 1935 to 1955. George T. Simon/Arlington House/1972.

THE STORY OF JAZZ – A logical look at jazz up to the fifties. Marshall Stearns/Oxford University Press/1956.

THE STORY OF THE BLUES – The jazz follower's introduction to Oliver's brilliant *Blues Fell This Morning* (1960) and *Conversation With The Blues* (1965). Paul Oliver/Chilton Books/1969.

SUCH SWEET THUNDER – Full of flowing rhetoric that lets you *hear* the music. Whitney Balliett/Macdonald/1968.

THEY ALL PLAYED RAGTIME – For years it was the bible of ragtime. Rudi Blesh & Harriet Janis/Alfred A. Knopf/1950.

WE CALLED IT MUSIC – The most amusing jazz book ever written. Eddie Condon/Henry Holt/1947.

WHO'S WHO OF JAZZ – A masterful work, full of reliable information and presented in a concise manner. John Chilton/ Macmillan/1965.

* These discographies are issued directly by the author. The volumes listed cover only artists from A-S, with those from T-Z in preparation and due to appear during 1987.

GLOSSARY

AACM Founded in Chicago in 1965, The Association For The Advancement Of Creative Musicians promoted jazz in club or concert hall and fostered a feeling for self-help amongst players involved.

AFTERBEAT In a music basically conceived in 4/4 time, the second and fourth beats in each bar.

BARRELHOUSE A small, often primitive, drinking-house in which a pianist or small group play uninhibited and sometimes raucous jazz; such music in any environment.

BEBOP/BOP A name derived onomatopoeically to describe the revolutionary jazz of the forties. The switch from melodic to harmonic values allowed its practitioners to build their own compositions onto existing chord sequences and thereby create completely new tunes.

BOOGIE WOOGIE A blues piano style in which the player produces a steady bass figure, usually eight beats to the bar, then overlays it with right-hand treble improvisations to create a form of counterpoint.

BREAK A brief interlude in which all bar one member of the band stop playing, leaving that individual space for a terse but appropriate musical comment.

CAKEWALK An American dance style from the early part of this century distinguished by a stiff, high-stepping action; from the habit of presenting cakes at such dance competitions.

CHALUMEAU The lowest register of the clarinet, a term taken from an obsolete forerunner of the clarinet.

CHART Common parlance among musicians for a musical arrangement (the basic theme is often described as a 'head').

CHOPS Originally a musician's term for a brass player's outstanding instrumental technique, now an accepted term for ability on all instruments, even manual ones such as piano, bass or drums.

CIRCULAR BREATHING A device used mainly by saxophonists in which the player breathes in through the nose and simultaneously out through the mouth and instrument to produce continuous sound.

COOL SCHOOL The jazz of the early fifties, born of bebop but smoothed down to avoid the angularities of the parent style. Principally based on West Coast of America, its rather passionless emphasis perhaps explains its early demise.

CRESCENT CITY New Orleans, Louisiana, USA.

DIXIELAND Originally jazz from the Southern States of America and, most particularly, from New Orleans. Latterly, the playing of white bands reviving that older style.

GUTBUCKET A bucket used in bars to catch beer drips. It became a colloquialism for an earthy musician, capable of playing with power and swing.

HARD BOP A fifties version of the original bop style with greater emphasis on solos, and with rhythm players (bass and drums) matching their horn partners in terms of solo responsibility.

HARMONICS A series of subsidiary notes produced by vibrations that occur when the fundamental note is played. Jazz saxophonists use this to create what are in effect saxophone chords and to extend their range far above that originally envisaged for the instrument.

JATP Jazz At The Philharmonic. Norman Granz's touring group of musicians, favouring stylistic integration and, to some extent, responsible for spreading the jazz message worldwide.

JCOA Jazz Composers' Orchestra Association. The somewhat elitist attitudes of the 1964 Jazz Composers' Guild brought about its end. The JCOA rose from its ashes, managed to obtain arts grants and promoted individual works and compositional projects as well as concerts.

JIG PIANO Another name for the ragtime piano style in which improvisation was kept to a minimum and strong themes were reproduced religiously.

JIVE TALK A deliberately esoteric nonsense language used by musicians to exclude the outsider.

JUMP MUSIC The adjective 'jump' first appeared in the late thirties as an alternative to 'swing'. Jump music came to mean the boisterous, small group jazz of the era, played with an infectious, bouncing rhythm.

LOFT SCENE Faced in the seventies

with the problem of no bookings, New York's young players hired lofts and converted them into performance areas; the most famous was Sam Rivers' Studio Rivbea.

MAINSTREAM Originally suggested by critic Stanley Dance as a term to cover the main body of jazz development. As such, it excluded the experimental backwaters and traced jazz through its New Orleans, swing, bop, hard bop and free form periods. By popular misuse, it has come to mean swing or latter-day swing revivalism.

MODES Before the arrival of the diatonic scales, there were many scale systems or modes as old as music itself. In the fifties players such as Miles Davis and John Coltrane reclaimed them from the backwaters of folk song and through them released their improvisations from the restrictions of European harmonic discipline.

NEW ORLEANS STYLE Jazz's most perfectly integrated way of playing collectively. The trumpet played the melody lead, the clarinet wove its free counterpoint and the trombone filled out the lower harmonies. Variations included a second trumpet or an extra reed player but these additions tended to complicate what was a brilliantly dovetailed system of playing.

PIANO PROFESSORS New Orleans whorehouse pianists.

RAGTIME An important music in the development of jazz: completely scored piano music syncopated in an upright, somewhat rigid manner.

RIFF A repeated musical phrase. Often a two- or four-bar phrase, used as a background to individual solos or as a climatic tension-builder by the large orchestras.

SCAT A vocal style using wordless syllable patterns. For many instrumentalists it represented a vocal interpretation of their horn-playing.

SPASM BAND/HOKUM BAND The primitive busking bands of pre-jazz history. Their players were young, they used home-made instruments and many early jazz giants claimed to have played in them as children.

STRIDE PIANO A style in which the left hand produced a chord on the weak (second and fourth) beats of each bar and alternated it with a bass note struck on the strong (first and third) beats. This provided its own accompaniment for the player's treble (right hand) improvisations and produced what could be considered as the most comprehensive of all piano styles.

SWING As an adjective, 'swing' was that almost inexplicable ingredient of jazz, the rubato element that defied notation but gave to jazz its unique, rhythmic emphasis. As a noun, 'swing' was the big band music that gained great popularity in the middle thirties (or swing era).

TAILGATE A trombone style devised in New Orleans by the horn men who played over the 'tailgate' of trucks used to advertise bands. Full of fruity slurs and dashing glissandi, it became the backbone of the city's music (see *New Orleans style*).

TERRITORY BAND The second-division big bands of the twenties and thirties. They stayed in and around their home areas in the West, Mid-West and South but sometimes achieved a high quality of performance.

THIRD STREAM A term chosen by french horn specialist and composer Gunther Schuller to describe music that was a fusion of modern jazz and classical chamber music.

TOBA The Theatre Owners' Booking Agency was a body that organised the vaudeville circuit and its performers through large areas of America. Its treatment of its performers earned it the sobriquet, 'Tough On Black Artists'.

TONE CLUSTER The American term for a group of adjacent keyboard notes played at the same time with fingers, fist or even forearm. In Britain it is referred to merely as *cluster*.

WOODSHEDDING Retiring temporarily from the musical scene to practise or experiment with new music.

WORK SONG A song used as a timing device in the performance of arduous jobs. Such music later came to influence early blues singers like Charley Patton and Blind Lemon Jefferson.

JAZZ INFORMATION

This section lists information sources for the further exploration of jazz, principally jazz magazines and major international jazz festivals. The listing is based on the latest information available at time of going to press, but will inevitably be subject to change. Amendments and suggestions for inclusion should be sent to: The Jazz Handbook, Longman Group Limited, Longman House, Burnt Mill, Harlow, Essex CM20 2JE.

UNITED KINGDOM

Magazines

THE CONNECTION
Bi-monthly (free
distribution/subscription:
focus on Scotland and the
North of England)
Platform (Music Societies)
Limited
26 Howe Street
Edinburgh EH3 6TG
031 226 4179

DISCOGRAPHICAL FORUM
Three issues a year
44 Belleville Road
London SW11 6QT
01 228 3193

FOOTNOTE
Bi-monthly
(New Orleans music)
66 High Street
Melbourn
Royston
Herts SG8 6AJ
0763 60823

JAZZ AT RONNIE SCOTT'S
Bi-monthly
(general jazz information)
c/o Ronnie Scott's
47 Frith Street
London W1V 6HT

JAZZ EXPRESS
10 issues a year (free through
entertainment centres in
London, also subscription)
29 Romilly Street
London W1
01 437 6437

JAZZ IN LONDON
Monthly
(free information sheet)
74E Elsham Road
London W14 8HH
01 602 1329

JAZZ JOURNAL
INTERNATIONAL
Monthly
35 Great Russell Street
London WC1B 3PP
01 580 7244/6976

JAZZ NEWSPAPERS
c/o South West Jazz
Exeter and Devon Arts
Centre
Bradninch Place
Gandy Street
Exeter EX4 3LS
0392 218368

are the publishers of:

JAZZ IN THE SOUTH
(0273 672242)
JAZZ IN THE SOUTH-WEST
(0392 218368)
JAZZ IN WALES
(0222 483422)
THE SCENE: JAZZ IN THE
EAST (0223 312203)
JAZZ IN THE MIDLANDS
(from 1987) (021 632 4921)

All quarterly (free
distribution/subscription)

STORYVILLE
Quarterly (early jazz styles)
66 Fairview Drive
Chigwell
Essex IG7 6HS
01 500 6098

VINTAGE JAZZ MART
Five issues a year
4 Hillcrest Gardens
Dollis Hill
London NW2 6HZ
01 452 4861

WIRE MAGAZINE
Monthly
Units G & H
115 Cleveland Street
London W1P 5PN
01 580 7522

Festivals

BATH FESTIVAL OF JAZZ
May/June
Philip Walker
Bath International Festival
1 Pierrepont Place
Bath BA1 1JY
0225 62231/60030

BRACKNELL JAZZ
FESTIVAL
July
Manor Jazz Festivals
42 Old Compton Street
London W1V 6LR
01 437 4967/439 0807

BRECON JAZZ FESTIVAL
August
The Festival Office
Watton Mount
Brecon
Powys LP2 7AW
0874 2631

BRIGHTON JAZZ FESTIVAL
May
Adrian Kendon
Jazz South
70 Grand Parade
Brighton BN2 2JA
0273 672242

CAMDEN JAZZ FESTIVAL –
LONDON
April (at Shaw Theatre, Town
and Country Club)
Serious Productions
42 Old Compton Street
London W1V 6LR
01 437 4967/439 0807

CAPITAL JAZZ PARADE –
LONDON
July
Jan Reed
Capital Radio
01 388 1288

COMPANY WEEK
FESTIVAL OF IMPROVISED
MUSIC
May (at Great Newport Street
Arts Theatre, London)
Derek Bailey
01 986 6904

DARLINGTON JAZZ
FESTIVAL
October
Darlington Arts Centre
Vane Terrace
Darlington DL3 7AX
0325 483168/480454

DUNDEE JAZZ FESTIVAL
June
Platform (Music Societies)
Limited
26 Howe Street
Edinburgh EH3 6TG
031 226 4179

GLASGOW
INTERNATIONAL JAZZ
FESTIVAL
June/July (1987 first year)
Iwan Williams
Scottish Development
Agency
041 248 2700

LEWISHAM JAZZ FESTIVAL
October
Chris Hare
01 690 2317

McEWAN'S JAZZ FESTIVAL
– EDINBURGH
August
Mike Hart
116 Canongate
Edinburgh EH8 8DD
031 557 1642

NEWCASTLE JAZZ
FESTIVAL
May
Alan Hilary
Jazz Festival Manager
City of Newcastle Recreation
Department
7 Saville Place
Newcastle NE1 8DQ
091 232 8520

ROUND MIDNIGHT JAZZ
FESTIVAL – EDINBURGH
August
(during Edinburgh Festival)
Roger Spence
031 668 3456

SOHO JAZZ FESTIVAL
October
Peter Boizot
Kettners Restaurant
29 Romilly Street
London W1
01 437 6437/3056

SUMMERSCOPE JAZZ
FESTIVAL
July/August
South Bank Centre
London SE1 8XX
01 921 0617

WELSH JAZZ FESTIVAL –
CARDIFF
October
Welsh Jazz Society
c/o New Theatre
Park Place
Cardiff CF1 3LN

WIGAN INTERNATIONAL
JAZZ FESTIVAL
July
Department of Leisure
Westgate House
Green Street
Wigan WN3 4HJ
0942 828076

General information

JAZZ SERVICES
5 Dryden Street
London WC2E 9NW
01 240 2430
National touring, education,
jazz information, marketing
and the media. Working with
the regions:

EASTERN JAZZ
Chris Maughan
Unit 3
25 Gwydir Street
Cambridge CB1 2LG
0223 312203

EASTERN JAZZ (LINCS AND
HUMBERSIDE)
Jim Smith
c/o Lincs and Humberside
Leisure Services
County Library
Albion Street
Hull
0482 224040

GREATER LONDON AREA
Peter Luxton
Jazz Development Officer
c/o Greater London Arts
Association
9 White Lion Street
London N1
01 837 8808

JAZZ ACTION (YORKSHIRE
AND THE NORTH)
Adrian Tilbrook
Jazz Development Officer
Darlington Arts Centre
Vane Terrace
Darlington DL3 7AX
0325 480454

JAZZ CENTRAL
Jan Ford/Charmian Kelly
29/30 Guildhall Buildings
Navigation Street
Birmingham B2 4BT
021 632 4921

JAZZ NORTH WEST
Nick Purnell
c/o Merseyside Arts
Bluecoat Chambers
School Lane
Liverpool L1 3BX
051 708 8771

JAZZ SOUTH
Adrian Kendon
70 Grand Parade
Brighton BN2 2JA
0273 672242

PLATFORM (SCOTLAND)
Roger Spence/Pat
Fazakerley
26 Howe Street
Edinburgh EH3 6TG
031 226 4179

SOUTH WEST JAZZ
Nod Knowles
c/o Exeter and Devon Arts
Centre
Bradninch Place
Gandy Street
Exeter EX4 3LS
0392 218368

WELSH JAZZ SOCIETY
Jed Williams
c/o New Theatre
Park Place
Cardiff CF1 3LN
0222 383413

Jazz video/film companies

HENDRING LIMITED
The Garden Suite
21 Tower Street
Covent Garden
London WC2H 9NS
01 379 5526

KAY JAZZ PRODUCTIONS
77 Sidney Road
Borstal
Rochester
Kent MB1 3HG
0634 405698

TCB RELEASING LIMITED
Stone House
Rudge
Frome
Somerset BA11 2QQ
0373 830769

JAZZ INFORMATION

AUSTRALIA

Magazines

JAZZ MAGAZINE
Eric Myers, Publisher
646 Harris Street
Ultimo NSW 2007
02 212 1517

JAZZ ACTION NEWSLETTER
Jazz Action Society (NSW)
Floor 7, Room 5
74 Pitt Street
Sydney NSW 2000
02 232 1419

Festivals

MANLY JAZZ FESTIVAL
October
36 Austral Avenue
North Manly NSW 2095
02 934 070

MOOMBA FESTIVAL –
MELBOURNE
March
191 Collins Street
PO Box 497H
Melbourne, Victoria 3001
03 637 111

RIVER CITY AQUATIC JAZZ
FESTIVAL
January
Address as for Manly Jazz
Festival

General information

Most states have a jazz co-
ordinator:
New South Wales – Eric
Myers, 5th Floor, 645 Harris
Street, Ultimo NSW 2007
02 212 1510
South Australia – Don Porter,
46 Kintore Avenue, Adelaide
SA 5000
08 228 1755/271 0382
Tasmania – Alf Properjohn, 77
Salamanca Place, Hobart,
Tasmania 7000
002 348 749/439 242
Victoria – Paula Langlands,
c/o School of Music, Victorian
College of the Arts, 234 St
Kilda Road, Melbourne,
Victoria 3004
03 616 9446/534 6465
Western Australia – Garry
Lee, c/o Musicians Union, 200
Hay Street, East Perth,
WA 6000
09 272 8705/421 1895

BENELUX

Magazines

JAZZ FREAK
Bi-monthly
Gastakker 200
4817 XG Breda
Netherlands
76 71 05 58

JAZZ NU
Monthly
Admiraal de Ruyterlaan 12A
9726 GS Groningen
Netherlands
50 18 62 95

LE POINT DU JAZZ
Two/three times a year
c/o Claude Bosseray
Cité Modèle
Bloc 2, Appt 16F
1020 Brussels
Belgium

Festivals

BELGA JAZZ FESTIVAL
October/November
(various Belgian cities)
Jean-Michel de Bie
34 rue Africaine
1050 Brussels
Belgium
02 537 8490

GOLDEN RIVER CITY JAZZ
FESTIVAL – KORTRIJK
September
Jean-Jacques Pieters
Sint-Sebastiaanslaan 21
8500 Kortrijk
Belgium
056 223 720

HONKY TONK JAZZ
FESTIVAL –
DENDERMONDE
June
Piet Heuvinck
Noordlaan 28
Dendermonde
Belgium
052 217 383

JAZZ MARATHON –
GRONINGEN
April
De Oosterpoort
Palmslag 10
9724 CS Groningen
Netherlands
50 18 23 33

MEERVAART JAZZ
FESTIVAL – AMSTERDAM
August
Light Music Department
PO Box 10
12 JB Hilversum
Netherlands
35 77 91 11

NORTH SEA JAZZ FESTIVAL
July
PO Box 87840
2508 DE The Hague
Netherlands
70 50 20 34

OLD STYLE JAZZ FESTIVAL
– BREDA
May
c/o PO Box 1812
4801 BV Breda
Netherlands
76 81 03 31

BRAZIL

Magazines

None specific to jazz, but the
JORNAL DO BRASIL,
Caderno B (Part B) carries
listings of jazz in Rio.
The weekly magazine VEJA
has a supplement of what's on
in Sao Paulo.

Festival

RIO/MONTEREY JAZZ
FESTIVAL
August
Theodoro Sampaio 417-1
05405 Sao Paulo
11 881 2719/2474

CANADA

Magazine

CODA MAGAZINE
Bi-monthly
Box 87
Station J
Toronto
Ontario M4J 4X8

(UK subscriptions:
Rae Wittrick
33 Winton Lodge
Imperial Avenue
Westcliff-on-Sea
Essex)

Databank

Festivals

FESTIVAL INTERNATIONAL DE MUSIQUE ACTUELLE – VICTORIAVILLE
October
Plateforme Inc.
7 Olivier
Victoriaville
Quebec G6P 5G6
819 752 7912

JAZZ CITY INTERNATIONAL JAZZ FESTIVAL – EDMONTON
August
Jazz City Festival Society
PO Box 255, Sub Station 11
Edmonton, Alberta T6G 2EO
403 432 7166/458 0404

MONTREAL INTERNATIONAL JAZZ FESTIVAL
June/July
355 rue Ste-Catherine ouest
Porte 301
Montreal, Quebec H3B 1A5
514 871 1881

TORONTO JAZZ FESTIVAL
June/July
4848 Yonge Street
Willowdale
Ontario M2N 5N2
416 225 1151

DENMARK

Festival

COPENHAGEN JAZZ FESTIVAL
July
Nørregade 7A, 2
DK-1112 Copenhagen K
1 117474

General information

Danish Jazz Centre
Borupvej 66B
DK-4683 Rønnede
3 711327/711381

EASTERN EUROPE

Festivals

DEBRECEN JAZZDAYS
July
Hungarian Radio
Brody Sador u 5-7
H-1800 Budapest
Hungary
1 338 330

JAZZ JAMBOREE
October
Tomasz Tluckiewicz
c/o Polish Jazz Society
Mazowiecka 11
PL-00 052 Warsaw
Poland
277 904/272 109

LJUBLJANA INTERNATIONAL JAZZ FESTIVAL
June
Cankarjev dom,
Trg revolucije 2
YU-61000 Ljubljana
Yugoslavia

EIRE

Festivals

CORK JAZZ FESTIVAL
October
Jazz Festival Secretary
Metropole Hotel
Cork
021 508122

DUBLIN JAZZ FESTIVAL
April
The Festival Director
51 Dawson Street
Dublin 2
Dublin 757911 x5836

FINLAND

Magazines

RYTMI
Keskustori 7A
33100 Tampere

Guide to jazz in Finland
published by
FINNISH JAZZ FEDERATION
PO Box 54
00101 Helsinki
90 646 879

Festival

PORI JAZZ FESTIVAL
July
Eteläranta 6
28100 Pori
39 12 124

FRANCE

Magazines

JAZZ HOT
Monthly

50 rue du Faubourg Saint Antoine
75012 Paris
43 45 12 45

JAZZ MAGAZINE
Monthly
63 avenue des Champs-Elysées
75008 Paris
42 56 72 72

Festivals

ANTIBES/JUAN LES PINS
July
Maison du Tourisme
12 place de Gaulle
06600 Antibes
93 33 95 64

FESTIVAL DE JAZZ DE PARIS
October/November
5 rue Bellart
75015 Paris
47 83 33 58

JAZZ A VIENNE
July
24 place Aristide Briand
69560 Ste Colombe-les-Vienne
74 53 02 61

NICE JVC GRANDE PARADE DU JAZZ
July
Simone Ginibre Enterprises
8 ter, rue Traversière
92100 Boulogne
46 21 08 37

NIMES INTERNATIONAL JAZZ FESTIVAL
July
New-Discoop-Jazz Club
21 rue Porte de France
30000 Nimes
66 21 34 02

ITALY

Magazines

MUSICA JAZZ
Monthly
Via Napo Torriani 19
20124 Milano
02 659 6411

IL BLUES
Quarterly
Edizioni Blues e Dintorni Srl
Piazza Grandi 12
20135 Milano

JAZZ INFORMATION

Festivals

CLUSONE JAZZ
July
Turismo Pro Clusone
0346 21113

PESCARA JAZZ
July
Azienda di soggiorno
Corso Umberto 44
085 22593

PALERMO JAZZ ESTATE
July
The Brass Group
Via di Villa Heloise 21
90143 Palermo
091 294165

RAVENNA JAZZ
July
Via Mariani 2
Ravenna
0544 32577/39903

FESTIVAL JAZZ DI ROMA
July
Christiana Barbieri
06 759 7851

JAZZ IN SARDEGNA –
CAGLIARI
July
Presso Arci
Via Asproni 24
070 664087/668898/651688

UMBRIA JAZZ –
PERUGIA/TERNI
July
Associazione Umbria Jazz
Via Fratti 18
PO Box 228
06100 Perugia
075 62432

JAPAN

Information on jazz in English
can be found in:
Tokyo Journal (monthly)
The Japan Times, The Mai
Nichi Daily News, The Daily
Yomiuri, The Asahi Evening
News

NORWAY

Magazine

JAZZNYTT
Bi-monthly
Toftesgate 69
N-0552 Oslo
02 37 66 34

Festivals

KONGSBERG JAZZ
FESTIVAL
June/July
Postbox 91
N-3601 Kongsberg
03 733166

MOLDE INTERNATIONAL
JAZZ FESTIVAL
July
PO Box 261
N-6401 Molde
072 53779

VOSSA JAZZ
March
Postbox 223
N-5701 Voss
05 51 26 90

General information

NORWEGIAN JAZZ
FEDERATION
Toftesgate 69
N-0552 Oslo
02 37 66 34

SPAIN

Festival

SAN SEBASTIAN JAZZ
FESTIVAL
July
Reina Regente S/N
20003 San Sebastian
43 421002

SWEDEN

Magazine

ORKESTER JOURNALEN
Eleven issues a year
Box 16252
10325 Stockholm
08 10 99 76

Festivals

KRISTIANSTAD
JAZZFESTIVAL
July
PO Box 162
S-291 22 Kristianstad
44 12 14 12

STOCKHOLM JAZZ AND
BLUES FESTIVAL
June/July
Mosebacke Establissement
Mosebacke Torg 1-3
S-11646 Stockholm
08 41 90 20

UMEÅ JAZZ FESTIVAL
October
Vretgatan 12A
S 90231 Umeå
90 11 28 56

SWITZERLAND
Festivals

NEW ORLEANS IN LUGANO
June
Ente Turistico
Riva Albertolli 5
CH-6901 Lugano
984 09 84

MONTREUX JAZZ FESTIVAL
July
Case 97
CH-1820 Montreux
21 63 12 12

WILLISAU
INTERNATIONAL JAZZ
FESTIVAL
August/September
Bahnhofstrasse
CH-6130 Willisau
45 812 731

USA
Magazines

BE-BOP AND BEYOND
Bi-monthly
(LA and West Coast)
Creative Music Collective
PO Box 54337
Los Angeles CA 90054

CADENCE
Monthly
Cadence Building
Redwood NY 13679
315 287 2852

DOWN BEAT
Monthly
222 West Adams Street
Chicago IL 60606
312 346 78 22

JAZZ TIMES
Monthly
8055 13th Street, 301
Silver Springs MD 20910

JAZZIZ
Bi-monthly
PO Box 8309
Gainsville FL 32605
904 375 3705

Databank

Festivals

CHICAGO JAZZ FESTIVAL
August/September
Mayor's Office of Special
Events
121 North LaSalle Street
Room 703
Chicago IL 60602
312 744 3315

MONTEREY JAZZ FESTIVAL
September
PO Box 1770
Monterey CA 93940
408 649 3200

MONTREUX-DETROIT JAZZ
FESTIVAL
August/September
Detroit Renaissance
100 Renaissance Center
Suite 1760
Detroit MI 48243
313 259 5400

NEW YORK JAZZ FESTIVAL
June/July
Festival Productions Inc
PO Box 1169 Ansonia Station
New York NY 10023
212 787 2020

General information

There are a number of City
Jazzlines to phone for
information:

ATLANTA: Jazz Forum
Hotline 404 288 8822
BALTIMORE: Left Bank Jazz
Society Jazzline 301 945 2266
BOSTON: Jazzline 617 262
1300
BUFFALO: Jazz Society
Jazzline 716 875 3397
CHICAGO: Jazz Institute of
Chicago Hotline 312 666 1881
CINCINNATI: WNOP
Jazzline 606 581 673
CLEVELAND: NE OH Jazz
Society Jazzline 216 421 2266
DALLAS: Jazz Society 214 744
2267
ENCINITAS, CA: Jazz Hotline
619 944 6988
HARTFORD, CT: Jazz Society
203 242 6688
KANSAS CITY: Jazz Hotline
816 931 2888
LOS ANGELES: Jazz Guide
213 879 5546
MIAMI: Jazz Hotline 305 382
3938

MINNEAPOLIS/ST PAUL:
Music Dateline 612 546 2022;
Twin Cities Jazz Society 612
292 3222
PHILADELPHIA: Jazz Society
215 876 0761
PHOENIX: Hotline 602 254
4545
PITTSBURGH: Jazz Club Mus-
Line 412 687 5463
RICHMOND, VA: Jazz Society
804 643 1972
SALT LAKE CITY: Jazz
Society 801 571 8020
SAN FRANCISCO: Jazzline
415 769 4818
SEATTLE: Jazz Hotline 206
624 5277
SPRINGFIELD, MA: Jazzline
413 737 9209
TUCSON: Jazz Society Hotline
602 623 2463
WASHINGTON, DC: Trad
Line 202 532 8723

WEST GERMANY

Magazine

JAZZ PODIUM
Monthly
Vogelsangstrasse 32
D-7000 Stuttgart 1
07 11 63 15 30

Festivals

JAZZFEST BERLIN
October/November
Postfach 301648
D-1000 Berlin 30
030 2534 1

MOERS NEW JAZZ
FESTIVAL
May
Kulturamt der Stadt Moers
2 Hdn Frau Gieseck
Postfach 2120
D-4130 Moers
2841 201571/3

General information

JAZZ INFORMATION
CENTRE
Nieder-Ramstädter-
strasse 190
D-6100 Darmstadt
061 51 13 24 16

GENERAL INFORMATION (WORLDWIDE)

INTERNATIONAL JAZZ
FEDERATION
13 Foulser Road
London SW17 8UE
01 767 2213

Magazine

JAZZ FORUM
Magazine of the International
Jazz Federation
Nowogrodzka 49
00-695 Warsaw
Poland
21 94 51/21 77 58

(UK subscriptions:
IJF
13 Foulser Road
London SW17 8UE
01 767 2213)

INDEX

All photographs in this book by David Redfern, except:
William Gottlieb, 22, 24, 26, 29, 33, 35, 51, 54, 56, 60, 64, 66, 69, 74, 76, 80, 81, 84, 86, 89, 90, 98, 100, 102, 111, 113, 119, 122
Suzi Gibbons, 107, 224; Sue Ingle, 185; Andrew Putler, 2, 6, 218, 251; Charles Stewart 148, 174; Valerie Wilmer, 14
Illustrations pages 231, courtesy Atlantic Records; 18, 45, Biograph Records; 155, 197, Blue Note Records; 48, 94, 118, CBS Records; 16, Classical Jazz Masters; 187, Contemporary Music Network; 29, Decca Records; 178, 181, ECM Records; 46, EMI Records; 82, 215, ESP-Disk Actuell Records; 243, Geffen Records; 31, Joker Records; 236, Leo Records; 34, London Records; 44, MCA Records; 17, Music For Pleasure; 25, Parlophone Records; 40, RCA Records; 123, Spotlite Records; 8, 27, 120 Vogue; 38, Yazoo Records.